Designing
Component-
Based
Applications

Mary Kirtland

Microsoft®*Press*

PUBLISHED BY
Microsoft Press
A Division of Microsoft Corporation
One Microsoft Way
Redmond, Washington 98052-6399

Library of Congress Cataloging-in-Publication Data
Kirtland, Mary.
    Designing Component-Based Applications / Mary Kirtland.
        p.   cm.
    Includes index.
    ISBN 0-7356-0523-8
    1. Application software--Development.   2. Electronic data
processing--Distributed processing.   3. Microsoft Windows (Computer
file)   I. Title.
QA76.76.A65K57   1999
005.1--dc21   98-44767
                                                                         CIP

Printed and bound in the United States of America.

1 2 3 4 5 6 7 8 9   MLML   4 3 2 1 0 9

Distributed in Canada by ITP Nelson, a division of Thomson Canada Limited.

A CIP catalogue record for this book is available from the British Library.

Microsoft Press books are available through booksellers and distributors worldwide. For further information about international editions, contact your local Microsoft Corporation office or contact Microsoft Press International directly at fax (425) 936-7329. Visit our Web site at mspress.microsoft.com.

Acquisitions Editor: Eric Stroo
Project Editor: Wendy Zucker
Manuscript Editor: Jennifer Harris
Technical Editor: Jack Beaudry

TABLE OF CONTENTS

PART THREE   Beyond MTS

Acknowledgments

First, I would like to thank my managers at Microsoft for their support while I was writing this book: James Utzschneider, Dave Cameron, and Hugh Teegan. Thanks also to the people who got stuck with my other responsibilities so that I could focus on writing: Jeff Wickman, Cathy Brennan, Marc Levy, and Jocelyn Garner.

I would also like to thank members of the COM team who helped clarify various aspects of COM, MTS, and COM+: in particular, Marc, Jocelyn, Tracey Trewin, Pat Helland, Robert Barnes, Gerald Hinson, Dick Dievendorff, Scott Robinson, and Markus Horstmann. Tracey Trewin and Sharon Chen, of the Visual Studio team, are responsible for the Island Hopper sample application used in this book, and I thank them both for developing the sample and taking the time to explain why certain things were done the way they were. Robert and his team developed the MTS Performance toolkit upon which Chapter 13, "Performance Validation," is based. Bob Beauchemin and Shaun McAravey of STEP Technologies developed the MTS training course that provided the original idea and outline for this book. Gary Voth, Charlie Kindel, Peter Houston, Angela Mills, David Lazar, and Kamaljit Bath wrote the white papers I used to learn about technologies outside my primary area of knowledge.

A number of people waded through early drafts of the book and provided valuable feedback that made it better. They include Jocelyn Garner, Vincent Sacksteder, Mike McKeown, Ralph Squillace, Tim Ewald, Bryan Lamos, Mario Benuzzi, Chris Sells, Govind Kanshi, Paul Stafford, and Mario Raccagni. (If I missed anyone, I apologize. Your comments must have joined the great e-mail inbox in the sky when I accidentally deleted my e-mail archive...) Special thanks to David Chappell, whose words of encouragement arrived on a day when I'd convinced myself everything I'd written was utter garbage.

And, finally, thanks to everyone at Microsoft Press who put up with me and helped turn my ramblings into a real book: Eric Stroo, Wendy Zucker, Jennifer Harris, Jack Beaudry, and all the others whose behind-the-scenes efforts are greatly appreciated.

Mary Kirtland

INTRODUCTION

In the late 1990s, the widespread availability of low-cost computers and access to global connectivity have fueled the demand for a new kind of application: the highly distributed application. Highly distributed applications are used by extremely large numbers of people around the world who are connected to many application and data servers via nonpermanent or slow links. These characteristics create application requirements that strain the capabilities of traditional application architectures.

The Microsoft Windows Distributed interNet Applications (DNA) architecture represents Microsoft's approach to creating highly distributed applications. DNA applications use a logical, three-tier, component-based architecture. Microsoft system services provide the infrastructure needed by this type of application. The key infrastructure services are the Component Object Model (COM), which provides the basic mechanism for component interaction, and Microsoft Transaction Server (MTS), which provides an execution environment for building scalable server applications.

This book is intended to help you succeed in building your first distributed three-tier application based on COM and MTS. It does not attempt to address every issue you will encounter when writing enterprise-wide applications. It does not attempt to define a methodology that will work for every development team. It *does* give you practical advice that will help you design, develop, test, and deploy three-tier applications based on the Microsoft Windows DNA technologies. The primary focus will be on the middle tier, or business logic, where you will use COM and MTS.

The recommendations in this book are based on experience gained from Microsoft's *3-2-1 program*. "3-2-1" stands for *three*-tier application, *two* developers, *one* month—in other words, a project in which two developers work for one month to write a three-tier application. 3-2-1 projects are a way to get started with MTS. For more information, see the Appendix.

Who Should Read This Book?

The primary audience for this book is the full-time professional developer who is familiar with an object-based programming language such as Microsoft C++, Java, or Microsoft Visual Basic. Some familiarity with the Internet and general database concepts, while not required, will be helpful. Several of the topics covered here will be of interest to system administrators as well.

Some portions of the sections of this book assume that you have some experience using Visual Basic or Visual C++. I also assume that you don't need a zillion screen shots to figure out how to install an application or use a development environment and that you understand how to use the documentation that comes with your tools. Pages of screen shots and step-by-step instructions for selecting a menu option bore me; I expect they bore you as well.

Contents Overview

This book is divided into three sections. The first and last sections provide general material about Microsoft technologies that are currently available and that will be available in the future. The middle section describes how to design, implement, test, debug, and deploy a three-tier application based on COM and MTS.

Part One: Technology Overview

This section provides an overview of Windows DNA, the three-tier application architecture, and the technologies used to create solutions based on Windows DNA—COM, data access, MTS, and Active Server Pages (ASP). We'll also take a look at other enabling technologies, such as the COM Transaction Integrator (COMTI) and Microsoft Message Queue Server (MSMQ), which integrate with MTS.

Part Two: Building Applications

This section shows you one way to architect and model three-tier business solutions. It discusses tools, techniques, and thought processes for modeling data, business objects, and various types of clients, and it examines practical issues that must be considered during design, such as security considerations and performance requirements.

The section next looks at how to implement the three-tier application. The emphasis here is on building business objects and data objects. We will also look at writing clients for the Internet and intranets using ActiveX Controls, Distributed COM (DCOM), ASP, and Dynamic Hypertext Markup Language (DHTML).

Finally, this section looks at interactive debugging techniques using the Microsoft Visual Basic and Microsoft Visual Studio debuggers, techniques for checking three-tier solutions against the performance requirements established during application design, and techniques for deploying three-tier solutions.

Part Three: Beyond MTS

This section shows you how to extend your applications to integrate with other platforms using existing technologies such as COM, MSMQ, and COMTI. You'll also get a glimpse of the future direction of COM and MTS, called COM+.

The Tools You Need

To build and deploy an application using the techniques described in this book, you will need to install the following products:

- Microsoft Windows NT 4.0, Workstation or Server. You can use Workstation for testing your applications, but you should use Server for deploying applications in the enterprise.

- Microsoft Windows NT 4.0 Option Pack (located on the companion CD), which includes Microsoft Windows NT 4.0 Service Pack 3, Microsoft Transaction Server 2.0, Microsoft Internet Information Server 4.0, Microsoft Message Queue Server, Microsoft Internet Explorer 4.01, and an evaluation license for Microsoft SQL Server 6.5.

- Microsoft SQL Server 6.5 or Oracle database. These are the two databases supported by Microsoft Transaction Server 2.0 at press time; check the Microsoft COM Web site, *http://www.microsoft.com/com/,* for information about support for other databases. You can use the evaluation copy of SQL Server in the Microsoft Windows NT 4.0 Option Pack for development and test purposes.

- A developer tool that supports the creation of COM objects. Many of the techniques described in this book are described in terms of Microsoft's developer tools; equivalent techniques are possible using other vendors' tools.

To use the distributed debugging and deployment techniques, you will, of course, need to have at least one client machine connected to your Windows NT machine. This machine can be a Windows 95, Windows 98, or Windows NT machine.

If you want to explore interoperability with COM components or resources running on non-Windows platforms, you will need additional software and machines. Microsoft products that directly support interoperability with other platforms or resources include information about the specific products you will need in the product documentation. You can find information about other Microsoft interoperability initiatives, including Microsoft-supported implementations of COM, at *http://www.microsoft.com/com/resource/cominop.htm*.

The Sample Code

Throughout this book, the Island Hopper sample application will be used to illustrate concepts and techniques. Island Hopper was developed by the Microsoft COM and Visual Studio teams to illustrate good design, development, and deployment techniques for three-tier applications. You might find more recent versions of Island Hopper on the Microsoft Web site, but the version of Island Hopper used here is included on the companion CD; instructions for configuring machines to run or build this version of Island Hopper are also provided.

The companion CD includes an electronic version of *Designing Component-Based Applications* as a compiled HTML Help file. This online version of the book offers the power of full-text search and cross-reference hyperlinks throughout so you can locate specific information, such as a procedure or a definition, with only a click of the mouse.

PART

ONE

Technology Overview

In Part One, we'll look at the business problems and technical challenges faced by developers of distributed applications and the Microsoft approach to resolving those problems, Windows Distributed interNet Applications (DNA). We'll look at the three-tier, component-based application architecture recommended in Windows DNA and the technologies used to create DNA solutions—the Component Object Model (COM), universal data access (UDA), Microsoft Transaction Server (MTS), and Active Server Pages (ASP). We'll also look briefly at some enabling technologies for interoperability with non-Windows systems.

1

Windows DNA

Today's business environment is extremely dynamic and competitive. Companies form alliances or merge into new companies. Downsizing and reengineered business processes are used to lower costs and maintain competitive advantages. Regulations and customer needs change continually—and may differ from location to location in a multinational enterprise. Business is fast-paced, ever-changing, and worldwide.

Business Problems, Architectural Solutions

Distributed computer systems play an important role in this active business environment. Every aspect of the modern corporation—marketing, manufacturing, finance, customer support, and almost everything else you can think of—relies on its information technology (IT) assets. IT systems provide support for each organizational function. These systems must work together to provide seamless information access throughout the corporation. In the late 1990s, the scope of these applications is extending outside the enterprise as well. In particular, many companies are providing services to their customers over the Internet. In this environment, great software systems are strategic assets that differentiate companies that can compete effectively from those that will fall by the wayside.

For a company to remain competitive, IT systems must be responsive to changes in business and user requirements. Developers must be able to write applications quickly—and be able to modify them just as quickly. Flexible, incremental development methods that produce libraries of reusable code are key to a company's success.

In addition to time constraints, developers face enormously challenging application requirements. New applications are extremely demanding for a multitude of reasons, some of which are listed here:

■ Applications may be distributed worldwide, via wide area networks (WANs) or the Internet.

■ There are potentially millions of users for these applications. In many cases, these users will be unknown to and outside the control of the company's IT organization.

■ Connections between users and applications might be nonpermanent and low-speed. For example, employees might use portable computers that are connected to the corporate network only part of the time. Customers might connect to the application via the Internet over a low-speed modem.

■ Data required by applications might be stored on multiple machines. These machines might be geographically dispersed and might not be available at all times.

■ Existing hardware and software investments must be leveraged. Users might have different types of machines with differing capabilities. Data might be stored in different types of databases. New applications might need to interact with existing applications running on different platforms.

Put all these together and we think you'll agree that distributed application development is just plain *hard*.

One of the main goals of every system software vendor is to find some way to make writing this type of application easier. And to a surprising extent, vendors agree on the overall approach: build applications from cooperating components, using a three-tier *application architecture*.

Application Architectures

An application architecture is a conceptual view of the structure of an application. All applications contain presentation code, data processing code, and data storage code. Application architectures differ in how this code is packaged.

Many current applications are two-tier, or client/server, applications. In a two-tier architecture, a client process handles the data processing and presentation parts of the application. Data is stored on centrally administered server machines. Clients connect directly to the servers they need, often for the lifetime of the application.

Client/server applications work well in controlled environments in which the number of users can be estimated and managed and resources can be allocated accordingly. However, when the number of users is unknown or very large, the client/server architecture breaks down. Because each client connects to data servers directly, scalability is limited by the number of available data connections. Opportunities for reuse are limited because the clients are bound to the database formats. Each client application contains data processing logic, making the applications relatively large. (This type of client is sometimes called a *fat client*.) If the data processing logic ever needs to change, new applications must be distributed to every client machine.

A slight improvement comes from moving parts of the data processing, or *business logic*, to the data servers—for example, by using Microsoft SQL Server stored procedures. This architecture is sometimes called "two-and-a-half tier." Applications built on this model are somewhat more scalable, but not scalable enough to meet the needs of highly distributed applications. In addition, opportunities for reuse are limited.

Scalability and reuse can be improved significantly by introducing a third tier to the application architecture. In the three-tier model, presentation, business, and data access layers are logically separated, as illustrated in Figure 1-1.

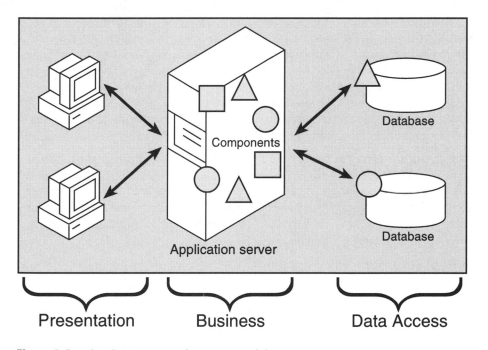

Figure 1-1. *The three-tier application model.*

The presentation layer presents data to the user and optionally lets the user edit data. The two main types of user interfaces for PC-based applications are native and Web-based. Native user interfaces use the services of the underlying operating system. For example, on the Microsoft Windows platform, native user interfaces use the Microsoft Win32 Application Programming Interface (API) and Windows controls. Web-based user interfaces are based on Hypertext Markup Language (HTML), which can be rendered by a browser on any platform.

The business layer is used to enforce business and data rules. The presentation layer uses the services of the business layer. However, the business layer is not tied to any specific client; its services are available to all applications. Business rules can be business algorithms, business policies, legal policies, and so on—for example: "Users get a 10 percent discount for ads placed before Tuesday night" or "8.2 percent sales tax must be collected for all orders delivered to Washington State." Data rules help ensure that stored data is consistent across multiple stores—for example: "An order header must have at least one detail record" or "Money must not be lost or generated during transfers between bank accounts." Business rules are typically implemented in isolated code modules. Each rule is implemented in one place so that it can be easily updated in response to changing business needs. The code modules are usually stored in a centralized location so that multiple applications can use them.

The business layer has no knowledge of how or where the data it works on is stored. Instead, it relies on the data access services, which perform the actual work of retrieving and storing data in a database management system (DBMS) or any other data store. The data access services are also implemented in isolated code modules, encapsulating knowledge of the underlying data store. If the data store moves or changes format, only the data access services need to be updated. Each data access module is responsible for the integrity of a set of data—for example, for a table in a relational database.

It's important to recognize that this is a logical model, not a physical model. The term "three tier" does *not* imply three separate machines. The logical model encompasses a wide range of physical models, depending on where the services are deployed. Applications are constructed as logical networks of consumers and suppliers of services. Services are merely units of application logic that provide well-defined functionality.

This model promotes scalable applications. To create highly scalable applications, resources such as database connections must be shared. Instead of each client application consuming resources to access data servers directly, client applications communicate with business services. One instance of a business service can support many clients, reducing resource consumption and improving scalability, as shown in Figure 1-2. Since business services do not manage data directly, it's easy to replicate these services to support even more clients.

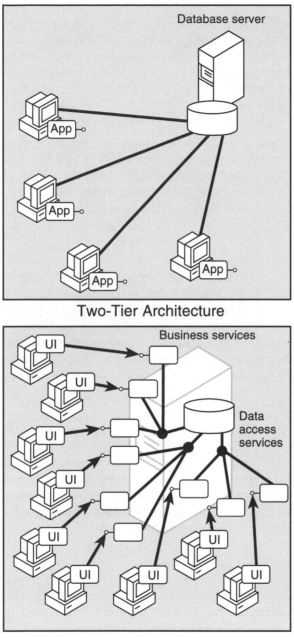

Two-Tier Architecture

Three-Tier Architecture

Figure 1-2. *Resource use in two-tier and three-tier models.*

Services can often be designed and implemented independent of any particular client application, providing flexibility and the potential for reuse in many applications. By encapsulating application logic behind well-defined public interfaces, developers create a body of reusable services that can easily be combined in new ways to create new applications. In addition, common functionality can easily be updated in response to changing business requirements, without impacting the client applications that rely on the functionality. This reduces the management and deployment costs of changing requirements.

The three-tier model can also help developers deal with existing, or legacy, systems. Developers can "wrap" access to existing systems within business logic or data access services. Client applications need to worry only about how to access the business logic, not how to access all the different legacy systems they might rely on. And if the legacy system is modified or replaced, only the wrapper needs to be updated.

Components

The growing consensus in the industry is that future service-based applications will be implemented using components. Traditionally, services have been exposed through APIs. The programming models used by different APIs can vary dramatically, making it difficult for developers to learn and use them effectively. APIs are difficult to version as well. Object-oriented frameworks are another popular way to expose services, but they suffer from many of the same problems as APIs. In addition, frameworks are typically specific to one programming language.

Components provide a standard model for packaging services and exposing them to consumers. Components are "black boxes"—all their data and implementation details are completely hidden. Component services are exposed via public interfaces, and a common programming model is available for discovering and using these interfaces, regardless of the components being used. Unlike language-based object-oriented models, component models provide facilities to enable communication with components regardless of the development language the components are written in or the location of the deployed components.

Three-Tier Enablers

A three-tier, component-based architecture alone does not produce a successful distributed application. High-performance, scalable, reliable server applications require a sophisticated infrastructure, as shown in Figure 1-3. Traditionally, application developers have needed to develop most of the code required to manage server processes, threads, database connections, and other resources, as well as security, administration, and other infrastructure code. The actual business logic is typically a small portion of the total application. Infrastructure code is extremely complex and difficult to implement in a scalable fashion.

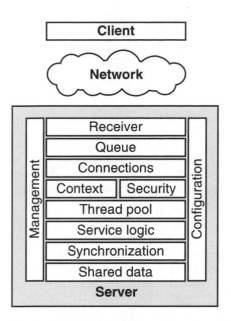

Figure 1-3. *Distributed application infrastructure.*

Middleware is a category of system software that provides infrastructure code to help build distributed applications. Standard middleware is the glue that enables independently developed components to work together to create distributed applications. Middleware masks the underlying system complexity from application developers and is a key enabler for the three-tier component-based application architecture.

Developers will also need to be able to access existing data and applications, regardless of the type of host system. Thus, a second enabler of the application architecture is interoperability services between the selected middleware and existing systems, such as standard interprocess communications protocols or application gateways.

Finally, developers will need access to development tools that facilitate use of the application architecture and middleware services. For example, tools might be able to generate framework code for components automatically, reducing the amount of hand-coding that the developer needs to do. Debugging and trouble-shooting tools are needed to help isolate problems occurring somewhere in the distributed application.

While system software vendors are in general agreement about the application architecture, there is a great deal of disagreement about the middleware, interoperability services, and tools you should use to implement your applications. After all, it's only natural that each vendor will recommend its own middleware, interoperability services, and tools.

Windows DNA Architecture

The Microsoft approach to writing distributed applications is called the Windows Distributed interNet Applications (DNA) architecture. Windows DNA is a framework for building three-tier, component-based applications that can be delivered over any network. The goal of Windows DNA is to unify PC, client/server, and Web-based applications around this common application architecture, which is suitable for applications of any size.

Windows DNA is not a product; it's a strategy—a road map, if you will, to writing applications using Microsoft technologies and products. Microsoft's goal is to provide the platform, component technology, application infrastructure, interoperability services, and tools developers need to write all three tiers of their applications, as shown in Figure 1-4.

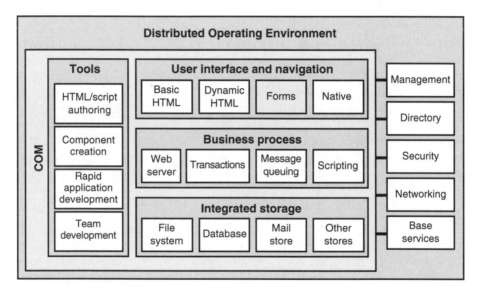

Figure 1-4. *Windows DNA architecture.*

The Component Object Model

The heart of Windows DNA is an integrated programming model based on the Component Object Model (COM) and Internet standards. All services are exposed to applications via published COM interfaces. Windows DNA services also adhere to open protocols such as Hypertext Transfer Protocol (HTTP) and Lightweight Directory Access Protocol (LDAP) to provide interoperability with other systems.

COM is a language-independent, system-level object model that provides a standard way for components and applications to interoperate. Thus, developers can use any language or tool to create applications. Developers create COM components that expose one or more interfaces. Each interface provides a set of methods and properties that can be accessed by other components or applications. Many developer tools provide support for writing and using COM components—for example, Microsoft Visual Studio, PowerBuilder, and Delphi.

Distributed COM (DCOM) extends COM across machine boundaries, providing remote invocation of COM components in a location-transparent manner. Location transparency enables a client application to function consistently, regardless of whether the components it uses are located locally on the client machine or remotely on a separate machine. DCOM supports a variety of network protocols, including Transport Control Protocol/Internet Protocol (TCP/IP), User Datagram Protocol/Internet Protocol (UDP/IP), and Internet Tunneling TCP/IP protocol, and is available on a number of non-Windows platforms to help integrate Windows DNA applications with existing systems.

NOTE   We will examine COM and DCOM in more detail in Chapter 2.

The Presentation Layer

Windows DNA builds a rich, highly integrated application environment on top of Windows operating system services and COM. This environment extends across all three tiers of the distributed application. In the presentation layer, Windows DNA supports a wide variety of client devices, from handheld PCs to high-end workstations. Microsoft products and technologies support a range of user interface types, from vanilla HTML, to Dynamic HTML (DHTML), to native Win32 applications. The key to supporting this diverse set of hardware and user interface styles is a common component model, scripting environment, and other client infrastructure services.

For Web-based clients, Microsoft provides Internet Explorer. Internet Explorer is an integral part of Windows 95 and later and Microsoft Windows NT 4.0 and later, and it is also available for Microsoft Windows 3.1, Macintosh, and UNIX platforms. Internet Explorer supports HTML, DHTML, client-side scripting, Java applets, Netscape plug-ins, and Microsoft ActiveX Controls. These languages and components can be used to create a rich, interactive user interface. Internet Explorer is itself component-based. The browser is actually a thin container for Microsoft's HTML rendering component. This component can easily be used in other applications, giving them access to a wide array of Internet services.

Perhaps one of the most interesting features of Internet Explorer is its support for DHTML. DHTML is an open, language-independent object model for HTML. Using DHTML and client-side scripting, developers can write interactive, platform-independent user interfaces that don't require developing custom components. All Web page elements are exposed as programmable objects. Thus, client-side script can be used to change the style, content, and structure of a Web page without refreshing the page from the server. This capability can have a dramatic impact on application performance by reducing network traffic.

> **NOTE** We will look briefly at designing and coding both Web and native user interface applications, but this book does not discuss the Win32 API, HTML, or DHTML in detail. For more information about these topics, please see the references listed in the bibliography.

The Business Layer

To help developers write scalable component-based business logic, Windows DNA includes a powerful set of integrated application services, or middleware, that takes care of the "plumbing" in a three-tier application. These services are tightly integrated with each other and the underlying operating system and are exposed in a unified way through COM. They include the following:

- Web services, through Microsoft Internet Information Server (IIS)

- Transaction and component services, through Microsoft Transaction Server (MTS)

- Queuing and asynchronous services, through Microsoft Message Queue Server (MSMQ)

- Server-side scripting, via Active Server Pages (ASP) hosted by IIS

- Interoperability services, such as the COM Transaction Integrator (COMTI) for accessing the IBM Customer Information Control System (CICS) and IBM Information Management Systems (IMS)

MTS is a high-performance execution environment for server-side components, as well as a distributed transaction manager. MTS promotes a radically simplified programming model for the middle tier of the three-tier architecture. MTS provides automatic services such as thread pooling, multiuser synchronization, instance management, scaling, fail-over, and database connection management, enabling developers to focus on writing the business logic specific to their applications. Developers can write server-side COM components encapsulating their business logic as if the components will be used by a single user. When these components are run within the MTS execution environment, they automatically scale to support large numbers of concurrent users.

In addition, MTS provides automatic transaction services. Developers can set an attribute on a component to indicate the level of transaction support required. MTS will automatically create transactions, enlist resources, and manage the transactions. Developers need to make only one function call to let MTS know whether their component has successfully completed its work. Transaction management works for a wide array of resources, including Microsoft SQL Server, MSMQ, Oracle, and IBM DB2.

NOTE   We will look at MTS in more detail in Chapter 4.

IIS 4.0 provides key services for server-side Web applications. IIS is integrated with MTS and uses MTS for many run-time services, including transaction management, connection pooling, and process isolation for Web applications.

One of the key features IIS provides for Windows DNA is ASP. ASP provides a server-side scripting environment that makes it easy to create and run dynamic Web applications. Server-side scripts can generate customized HTML pages on the fly. Like client-side scripts, ASP can use COM components to extend the functionality of a Web application. These COM components can run within the MTS environment. ASP can be scripted in any language that has an Active Scripting engine; IIS includes native support for VBScript and JScript. ASP is a powerful bridge between the presentation layer and the business layer for Web-based applications.

NOTE   We will look at ASP in more detail in Chapter 5.

MSMQ provides asynchronous services for distributed applications. MSMQ provides reliable store-and-forward delivery of messages between applications and components over the network. Message queuing guarantees that messages will eventually be delivered even if network links are down, receiving applications are off line, or machines fail. This capability is useful for scenarios in which guaranteed delivery is more critical than immediate delivery. For example, in an order-entry application, it's important that orders get scheduled for shipment eventually. However, it's not critical that the shipment be scheduled while a customer is on the phone with an order-entry operator. MSMQ is interoperable with IBM MQSeries and other message queuing environments through products from Level 8 Systems.

NOTE   We will look at MSMQ in more detail in Chapter 6.

Finally, Microsoft supports a range of interoperability services. Many services are based on open protocols or published interfaces that permit direct interaction with existing mainframe and UNIX systems. In addition, Microsoft provides products such as COMTI.

COMTI enables Windows DNA applications to transparently integrate with code running on IBM mainframes under the control of CICS and IMS. COMTI provides a set of developer tools and run-time services to automate "wrapping" mainframe transactions and business logic as COM components. The COM components run on a Windows NT machine and talk to the mainframe via Microsoft Systems Network Architecture (SNA) Server.

NOTE We will look at COMTI in more detail in Chapter 6.

The Data Access Layer

In addition to the wide array of services for the presentation and business layers, Windows DNA encompasses technologies for accessing data. The Windows DNA approach to data access is called *Universal Data Access* (UDA). UDA is a COM-based framework based on open industry standards.

Rather than requiring all data to be stored in a common data store, UDA provides a common programmatic interface to virtually any type of store, whether for structured or unstructured data. Most applications require access to multiple types of stores; UDA simplifies the development of these applications by reducing the number of APIs developers must learn in order to access their data.

At its core, UDA specifies system-level interfaces called *OLE DB*. Data providers implement OLE DB interfaces to provide access to specific data stores, such as Microsoft SQL Server and Microsoft Exchange. OLE DB service providers build independent services such as query processors and content indexers that work across all data providers. UDA also specifies an application-level programming interface called *ActiveX Data Objects* (ADO) that uses OLE DB to access data but presents a simpler programming model to the developer. ADO is an evolution of earlier Microsoft data object models such as Data Access Objects (DAO) and Remote Data Objects (RDO). Developers can use ADO to easily create data access components for their business components that retrieve and store data across a wide variety of data stores.

NOTE We will look at UDA in more detail in Chapter 3.

SUMMARY

Windows DNA is Microsoft's strategic framework for distributed application development. The Windows DNA framework includes products and services to help developers implement all three tiers of the three-tier, component-based application. The three-tier application architecture is recommended for building scalable distributed applications. Components are recommended as a way to create flexible, maintainable solutions.

The primary technologies and products influencing the Windows DNA programming model are COM, MTS, UDA, ASP, DHTML, MSMQ, and COMTI. We will discuss each of these elements in more detail in the remaining chapters of Part One.

2

The Component Object Model

Let's begin our discussion of Microsoft's technologies for writing distributed applications by looking at the Component Object Model (COM). COM is the foundation of all of the other technologies we will examine in this book. This chapter does not try to cover every detail of COM—many excellent books are available that already do this. Instead, you'll find just those topics you need to understand to successfully write applications using Microsoft Transaction Server (MTS). If you are interested in learning more about COM, several useful resources are listed in the bibliography.

Why COM?

COM is a binary standard for object interaction. But what does this statement mean? What's so important about a binary standard?

The fundamental goal of COM is to enable you to create applications that are assembled from prebuilt parts—that is, components. For example, an order entry application might use a data entry grid component to make entering the ordered items easier. Another component could look up a customer's city and state based on the zip code entered. Yet another component could compute sales tax on the order. To make this type of component-based application a reality, several technical challenges must be met (in addition to overcoming the "not invented here" syndrome and other social challenges).

The first challenge is to provide a standard way to locate components and create objects using those components. Otherwise, the overhead of learning how to use every component and coding the logic to locate the components and create objects presents a barrier to reusing prebuilt code. In conjunction with the standard mechanisms, there must be a way to uniquely identify components that are created independently by different vendors, to prevent scenarios in which an application developer asks for one type of object and gets a completely different type. Component developers must be able to generate unique identifiers for their components and provide those components to others without going through any centralized authority.

The second challenge is to provide a standard way of interacting with objects. Again, if no standards exist, the overhead of learning how to use the objects creates a barrier to reuse. Ideally, this standard mechanism for object interaction would not care where an object was located—in the application's process, in another process on the application's machine, or on another machine altogether. Usually, interprocess and remote communications require a great deal of complex coding in the application. However, if there is a standard way to interact with objects, it should be possible to hide all this complexity from the application developer—and hopefully from the component developer as well.

Third, application developers must not have to worry about what programming language or tool was used to create the components they want to use. Otherwise, the component market becomes fragmented and the cost of identifying and purchasing components that will work in a certain environment is too high. True language independence is a complex challenge for an object model. Everything about the object—memory allocation, method names, parameter types, calling conventions, and so on—must be defined in such a way that the object can be created by code written in one language and used by code written in another.

Finally, it must be possible to create new versions of applications and components. This requirement sounds trivial until you remember that the applications and components may be built at different times and that multiple applications running on a given machine might be using the same component. It must be possible to upgrade a component in such a way that it will continue to work with existing applications. This upgrade might involve fixing problems in existing features of the component or adding new functionality. In either case, existing applications must not break because a component was updated.

The binary standard for object interaction helps COM meet all of these requirements. COM is part specification, part implementation. The specification defines how to call objects in a language-independent and location-independent manner as well as how to locate and identify components and create objects. The implementation provides system services that do the actual work of locating components and loading them into memory, performing interprocess and remote communications, and so on.

The COM Programming Model

The programming model specified by COM is quite simple and powerful. Sometimes it's difficult to see the simplicity and elegance of the basic model underneath all the services built on top of it. So we won't talk about any of those services here; instead, we'll focus on the programming model itself.

COM, OLE, and Microsoft ActiveX

You might be more familiar with the terms "OLE" and "ActiveX" than you are with the term "COM." And you might be confused about what technologies these terms refer to and how they are related. This wouldn't be surprising—Microsoft has changed its definitions of these terms over the past couple of years even though the technologies themselves have not changed. So let's get this tangle straightened out once and for all:

- COM is the fundamental component object model, introduced in 1992. The COM specification is available on the Microsoft Web site (at *http://www.microsoft.com/com/comdocs-f.htm*), and only those items defined in the specification are part of COM proper.

- OLE (Object Linking and Embedding) is built on top of COM and is the mechanism used for compound documents. For example, when you insert a Microsoft Excel spreadsheet into a Microsoft Word document, you are using OLE.

- ActiveX was originally introduced with Microsoft's COM-based Internet technologies in 1996 and was essentially a marketing label used to identify these technologies. Then things got a little crazy, and everything COM-based got grouped under the ActiveX umbrella. That just confused everyone. Today some degree of normalcy has returned and ActiveX is only used in the phrase "ActiveX Controls," which is a specific technology built on top of COM for programmatic controls. When you put a control on a Microsoft Visual Basic form or embed an <OBJECT> tag in an HTML page, you are using ActiveX Controls.

In this book, we talk only about COM. We might use ActiveX Controls in our presentation layer, but we don't need to know how to write these controls ourselves. And we don't discuss OLE at all.

Objects

To start with, let's go over some terminology. "Object" is one of the most over-loaded terms in programming. As in most object-oriented models, objects in COM are run-time instances of some class that represents a real-world entity. We'll come back to exactly what a class is a little later, but conceptually it's a type of object—for example, a *Customer*, an *Order*, or even a *SalesTaxCalculator*. Each *Customer* object represents a specific real-world customer, each *Order* object represents a specific real-world order, and so on.

Objects have *identity*, *state*, and *behavior*. Identity is the unique "name" that distinguishes one object from any other object. State is the data associated with a particular object. Behavior is the set of methods that can be called to query or manipulate an object's state.

To help clarify, let's examine a C++ object. C++ objects are run-time instances of C++ classes. The C++ class defines member variables and methods that apply to objects of that class. When an object is created, a contiguous block of space is allocated for the member variables. The address of that memory is the object's identity. The contents of the memory block are the object's state. The object's behavior is defined by the method implementation code, which is located else-where in memory.

Most language-based object models are similar to the C++ object model, but COM objects are a little different. Recall that two of the challenges faced by COM are language independence and location independence. When you start look-ing at interprocess and remote communications, memory addresses are not sufficient to identify objects. And getting every programming language and tool to agree on a memory layout for object member variables sounds nearly im-possible. Add in the need to update components without breaking existing applications, and you'll realize that locating component method implementa-tions is a challenge too.

So COM takes a different approach than C++. In COM, the notion of an object's public interface and its implementation are completely separate. Applications can interact with objects only through their public interfaces, using something called an interface pointer. COM defines how that happens. Since all interac-tion must go through the interface pointer, COM doesn't need to worry about where an object's state is located or how it is laid out in memory. And since the only thing an application has to reference the object is the interface pointer, the object's identity must somehow be related to that pointer. Clearly, an un-derstanding of interfaces is essential to understanding COM.

Interfaces

A COM interface is a collection of logically related operations that define some behavior. When you define an interface, you are providing only the specification of the set of operations, not any particular implementation. For example, the components for computing sales tax and looking up zip codes in our earlier example might have interfaces with just one method each, as shown in the following code. (Don't worry about the syntax, this is just pseudocode to give you an idea of what's going on.)

```
interface IComputeSalesTax
   Compute([in]long salesAmount, [in]long originatingZipCode,
          [in]long destinationZipCode, [out, retval]long* salesTax)

interface ILookupZipCode
   Lookup([in]long zipcode, [out]String city, [out]String state)
```

A more complex interface might look like this:

```
interface ICustomerMaintenance
   Add([in]String firstName, [in]String lastName,
       [in]String address, ..., [out]String accountNumber)
   UpdateAddress([in]String accountNumber, [in]String address,
                 [in]long zipCode)
   Delete([in]String accountNumber)
```

Interface definitions represent a contract between the caller and implementer: if a component implements a particular interface, the caller can expect the component to obey the interface specification. The specification includes a strict definition of the syntax of the interface methods, as well as a definition of the semantics of the interface.

To be considered a COM interface, an interface must satisfy the following requirements:

- The interface must be identified by a unique identifier.

- The interface must ultimately derive from the special interface *IUnknown*.

- Once published, the interface is immutable (meaning that it can't be changed).

We'll look at these requirements in detail throughout this section.

COM identifiers

Just as unique identifiers are needed to locate components, we also need to provide a unique identifier for each interface. One approach would be to use some type of string identifier, but this raises several problems, the most important being that it's very difficult to guarantee you've picked a truly unique identifier. Even if a naming convention is imposed on these strings—for example, to include a company name—there is always a chance that someone else will use the same name for a different purpose. To guarantee uniqueness, you would need a central authority to hand out prefixes—say, one prefix per company. Each company would in turn need a central registry of names to prevent any duplicates within the company. This method seems much too complicated.

In COM, whenever we need a unique identifier, we use something called a *globally unique identifier* (GUID, pronounced "goo-id" or "gwid"). A GUID is a 128-bit integer. The algorithm used to generate GUIDs is statistically guaranteed to generate unique numbers. Better yet, anyone can create as many GUIDs as he or she wants.

> **NOTE** According to the COM specification, GUIDs can be generated at the rate of 10,000,000 per second per machine for the next 3240 years, without risk of duplication.

GUIDs can be generated using a tool such as GUIDGEN, which comes with the Microsoft Platform Software Development Kit (SDK). GUIDGEN calls the system API function *CoCreateGuid* to generate the GUID and then provides several output options. For example, the following GUID was generated using the *static const* output option and is suitable for inclusion in a C++ source file:

```
// {45D3F4B0-DB76-11d1-AA06-0040052510F1}
static const GUID GUID_Sample = { 0x45d3f4b0, 0xdb76, 0x11d1,
    { 0xaa, 0x6, 0x0, 0x40, 0x5, 0x25, 0x10, 0xf1 } };
```

The first line is a comment showing how the GUID appears in string form. Whenever GUIDs are displayed to a user, they appear in this form. The remaining lines define the GUID as a constant that can be used in C++ code.

> **NOTE** Most development tools automate the process of creating skeleton COM components. These tools also take care of generating the appropriate GUIDs for you in a format that the skeleton code understands.

So, every interface is identified by a GUID. To make it clear that we're talking about interfaces, we call these *interface IDs* (IIDs). Whenever we need to uniquely identify an interface to COM, we use its IID. Every interface also has a string name, because while IIDs are very nice for the computer, they're kind of difficult for us mere mortals to use. (Just imagine asking someone, "Hey, Bob, is that sales tax interface {45D3F4B0-DB76-11d1-AA06-0040052510F1} or {45D3F4B1-DB76-11d1-AA06-0040052510F1}?") By convention, these names usually start with "I"—for example, *IComputeSalesTax*. The string name is what developers use in their source code. String names aren't guaranteed to be unique in the world, but it's unlikely that a developer would need to use two different interfaces with the same string name in one source code file.

Defining interfaces

You might be wondering at this point exactly how interfaces are defined so that component developers know how to implement them and application developers know how to use them. The truth of the matter is that COM doesn't really care how, as long as the caller and the implementer agree on the definition. In practice, however, COM interfaces are usually defined using the *Interface Definition Language* (IDL).

IDL is a C++-like language that lets you describe the exact syntax of your interface. For example, here's an IDL definition of the *IComputeSalesTax* interface:

```
[   object,
    uuid(45D3F4B0-DB76-11d1-AA06-0040052510F1)
]
interface IComputeSalesTax : IUnknown
{
    import "unknwn.idl"
    HRESULT Compute([in]long salesAmount,
                    [in]long originatingZipCode,
                    [in]long destinationZipCode,
                    [out, retval]long* salesTax);
}
```

The interface definition begins with the keyword *interface*. The attributes of the interface are contained in square brackets preceding the *interface* keyword. The *object* attribute indicates that the COM IDL extensions should be used. The *uuid* attribute specifies the IID for this interface.

NOTE   The attribute is named *uuid* because COM IDL is based on the Open Software Foundation's Distributed Computing Environment (DCE) IDL, which uses the term "universally unique identifier" (UUID) instead of GUID.

The *interface* statement itself specifies the human-readable name for the interface, *IComputeSalesTax*, followed by a colon and the name of the base interface, *IUnknown*. This syntax indicates that *IComputeSalesTax* is derived from *IUnknown* and inherits all its methods. (As mentioned, all COM interfaces must ultimately derive from *IUnknown*.)

The next line in this example is an *import* statement, which is used to locate the definition of the *IUnknown* interface. Following the *import* statement is the definition of the interface method *Compute*. The *Compute* method returns an HRESULT value, which is the standard data type used to report success or failure for COM method calls. *Compute* has four parameters: *salesAmount, originatingZipCode, destinationZipCode*, and *salesTax*. COM methods can have any number of parameters, of arbitrarily complex data types. However, not all development languages will support all the data types that can be specified using IDL, so most interfaces use a fairly restricted set of data types. We'll discuss this limitation in more detail in the section "Automation" later in this chapter. In addition to a name and data type, you can specify attributes for each parameter—for example, the *in, out*, and *retval* attributes in the *IComputeSalesTax* interface. These attributes provide clues to development tools about how data should be copied from one place to another. In this example, the attribute *in* specifies that the first three parameters are passed to the *Compute* method and the attributes *out* and *retval* specify that the last parameter is filled in by the method.

IDL is a convenient text format for documenting the interface syntax. Once the IDL code is written, it can be compiled using the Microsoft IDL (MIDL) compiler to generate the following equivalent representations of the interface definition, which are more useful to your development tools:

- **Header file:** Defines the types developers can use to declare interface pointer variables or to derive an implementation class for an interface. The header file can be included in a C or C++ program.

- **Type library:** A binary representation of the IDL code. Developer tools such as Visual Basic read the type library to determine the syntax of the interfaces described in the type library.

- **Source code for a proxy/stub DLL:** Implementation of proxy/stub dynamic link libraries (DLLs) used for interprocess and remote communication. We'll discuss these DLLs in the section "Remote Activation and Marshaling" later in this chapter.

IDL isn't difficult to use, but it's new to many developers, so most development tools offer some assistance. Some, like Visual Basic, completely hide IDL. Developers define interfaces directly in Visual Basic syntax, and Visual Basic generates a type library for the interface. Other tools generate the IDL file for you.

These tools usually provide some sort of wizard to help you define an interface and its methods; they then spit out the correct IDL syntax. We'll see a lot more IDL later in the book, when we start talking about designing and implementing components.

Defining interfaces using IDL is a first step toward language independence, but it doesn't get us all the way there. Given an IDL file, or the equivalent header file or type library, a developer can code an implementation of an interface or a client application that uses the interface in any language that understands the types used in the interface. To ensure that the client and implementation can talk to each other, both sides must agree on what an interface pointer represents and how to make method calls through that pointer.

COM as binary standard

For this reason, COM is called a *binary standard*. COM defines the exact binary representation of an interface. Any programming language or tool that supports COM must create object interfaces that correspond to this standard representation. Figure 2-1 shows what this representation looks like for the *IComputeSalesTax* interface.

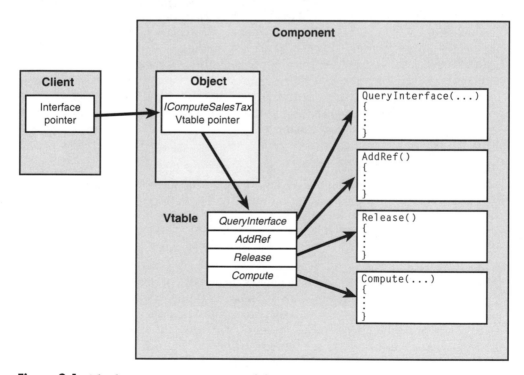

Figure 2-1. *The binary representation of the* IComputeSalesTax *interface.*

The client's interface pointer is actually a pointer to a pointer to a table of more pointers. This table of pointers is called a *vtable*. Each pointer in the vtable points to the binary code for a method in the interface. If you're a C++ programmer, this should sound familiar—it's exactly the same as a C++ virtual function table.

The pointer to the vtable is appropriately called a *vtable pointer*. Each COM object contains a vtable pointer for each interface it supports. When a client asks for an interface pointer to an object, it gets a pointer to the appropriate vtable pointer. Why a pointer to the vtable pointer? Why not the vtable pointer itself? Well, the component needs some way to identify the object it should be working on. When a COM object is created, usually a single block of memory is allocated for both the vtable pointers and any internal data members needed by the object. The component "knows" the relationship between the location of the vtable pointer and the location of the object's entire memory block, and thus the component can identify the appropriate object. COM further specifies that the first parameter passed to each method call is a pointer to the object; this can easily be accomplished by using the interface pointer.

Fortunately, you usually don't have to worry about any of this. Most programming languages and tools that support COM map interface pointers and vtables to equivalent concepts in the language. For example, in C++ interfaces are equivalent to abstract base classes. Developers can implement an interface by deriving a class from the abstract base class. Calling COM methods through an interface pointer is exactly like calling C++ methods through an object pointer. In Visual Basic, interfaces are almost completely hidden within the Visual Basic language. Developers can implement an interface by using the *implements* keyword and implementing the interface's methods. To use a COM object, developers declare an object variable of the interface type, create the object, and make normal function calls.

The binary standard for interfaces, in combination with a common interpretation of interface definitions, gives us language independence. This particular binary standard also puts us well on the way to location independence. Recall that we want a way to make in-process, interprocess, and remote calls look identical to the client. Clearly, within a single process the interface pointer can point directly to the real vtable pointer and we can call methods directly. But this technique probably won't work cross-process or cross-machine. We could, however, redirect the interface pointer to point to a *proxy vtable pointer*. The client-side proxy would understand how to make interprocess or remote calls to an equivalent server-side object, and that object would make in-process calls to the real object. To the client and component, method calls would look the same. In COM, we call the server-side object a *stub*. We'll return to proxies and stubs in the section "Distributed COM" later in this chapter.

The *IUnknown* interface

You might have noticed that the vtable in Figure 2-1 on page 25 contains three methods that don't appear to be part of the *IComputeSalesTax* interface: *QueryInterface*, *AddRef*, and *Release*. These three methods are provided by the *IUnknown* interface. *IUnknown* defines the fundamental behavior for COM interfaces. Because all COM interfaces derive from *IUnknown*, clients can rely on this fundamental behavior. Recall that one of COM's technical challenges is to provide a standard way to interact with objects; the *IUnknown* interface is a big part of the solution. *IUnknown* provides three features: interface navigation, interface versioning, and object lifetime management.

Interface navigation   Interface navigation is provided by the *QueryInterface* method. As we've seen, COM objects can support more than one interface. Now assume that you have one interface pointer to an object and you want a second pointer. What do you do? Simple: you ask the object for the second interface pointer—and the way you ask is with the *QueryInterface* method. Remember that all interfaces derive from *IUnknown*, so every interface supports *QueryInterface*. Convenient, yes?

To use *QueryInterface*, a client passes the IID of the interface it wants to an object. If the object supports that interface, it passes back the interface pointer. If not, it returns an error. *QueryInterface* is an extraordinarily powerful mechanism. It lets clients and components created independently negotiate a common way to communicate. It is also the key to solving the challenge of versioning.

Interface versioning   Because components and applications can be built independently, once an interface has been published, it is immutable—no changes to syntax and no changes to semantics are allowed. Changing a published interface is evil. Imagine what would happen if you had a method definition that looked like this:

```
HRESULT DoSomeWork([in]short inParam1, [out,retval]long* outParam);
```

and you changed it to look like this:

```
HRESULT DoSomeWork([in]short inParam1, [in]short inParam2,
                   [out,retval]long* outParam);
```

An existing client application would think that two parameters needed to be passed to the method, but the component implementing the new version of the method would be expecting three parameters. At best, you would get some recognizably bad value in *inParam2* or *outParam* and could return an error. More likely, your component would crash.

Even changes to the number of methods in an interface could be dangerous. Consider a new client application that thinks an interface has five methods attempting to call an old component that implements only four methods. The results wouldn't be pretty...

COM interfaces are immutable in order to avoid these problems. To "version" an interface, you actually define a new interface. Existing clients don't know anything about the new interface, so they don't care whether components implement the new interface. New clients can implement support for the new interface and access the new features when talking to a new component. If a new client happens to access an older component, it can use *QueryInterface* to safely detect that the component does not support the new interface and avoid using the new features.

Object lifetime management   At this point, you might be wondering how objects are created and how they are destroyed. Let's defer the subject of object creation just a little while longer. But assuming that a client has managed to create an object and holds an interface pointer to it, how does that object get destroyed?

It might seem that the easiest solution would be for the client that created the object to destroy it. Unfortunately, this doesn't work. A single client can use *QueryInterface* to obtain multiple interface pointers to the same object. It might be difficult for the client to keep track of when it had finished using all of the interface pointers so that the object could safely be destroyed. Also, more than one client might use the same object. No single client can tell when all clients have finished using the object. The only element that can tell when all clients have finished using the object is the object itself—with some help from each client.

To address these issues, *IUnknown* provides a third feature: object lifetime management by keeping track of the number of clients using an interface—commonly referred to as *reference counting*. When a new interface pointer to an object is created, the creator is responsible for calling *IUnknown AddRef* to increment the object's reference count. When a client has finished with an interface pointer, it calls *IUnknown Release*, which decrements the object's reference count. When the reference count goes to 0, the object knows that all clients have finished using it and it can destroy itself. This neatly solves both the problem of a single client with multiple interface pointers and the problem of multiple independent clients. From the client's perspective, all it needs to do is create, use, and release—that is, create an object to get an interface pointer, use the interface pointer to make method calls, and release the interface pointer using *IUnknown Release*.

To understand how things work from the component's perspective, we need to move beyond interfaces and talk about interface implementations.

Classes

Remember that all COM objects are instances of COM classes. A COM class is nothing more than a named implementation of one or more COM interfaces. A COM class is named using a *class identifier* (CLSID), which is a type of GUID. Like IIDs, CLSIDs are guaranteed to be unique but are difficult for humans to use. So COM classes can also have a string name, called a *programmatic identifier* (ProgID).

Every COM class has an associated *class object*. A class object knows how to create instances of a single COM class. The COM specification defines a standard API function, *CoGetClassObject*, for creating class objects and a standard interface, *IClassFactory*, for communicating with class objects. (For this reason, class objects are sometimes called *class factories*.) Thus, clients need to learn only one mechanism in order to create any type of COM object. The most important method of *IClassFactory* is *CreateInstance*, which creates an object and returns a specified interface pointer. So a client can create a COM object simply by calling *CoGetClassObject* to get an *IClassFactory* interface pointer, calling *IClassFactory CreateInstance* to get an interface pointer to the object, and then releasing the *IClassFactory* interface pointer. As you might imagine, this sequence happens a lot in COM applications, so COM provides a wrapper function that lets you do it all in one call: *CoCreateInstanceEx*.

Figure 2-2 on the following page shows what happens at run time when an object is created. The client calls *CoGetClassObject*, specifying a CLSID. A portion of the COM run time called the Service Control Manager (SCM, pronounced "scum") looks in its internal data structures to locate the requested class object. If it can't find the class object, it looks in the system registry to locate the code that knows how to create the requested class object and does whatever is necessary to load and execute that code. Once it has a class object, the SCM returns an *IClassFactory* interface pointer to the client. Now the client can call *IClassFactory CreateInstance*, requesting a specific interface pointer. The class object's *CreateInstance* implementation creates the actual object and returns the specified interface pointer.

COM classes are quite different from most language-based classes in the sense that once an object has been created, its class is irrelevant to the client. All interaction with the object occurs through interface pointers. The interface pointers know nothing about the implementation class used to create the object. This rigorous separation of interface and implementation is one of the key features of COM.

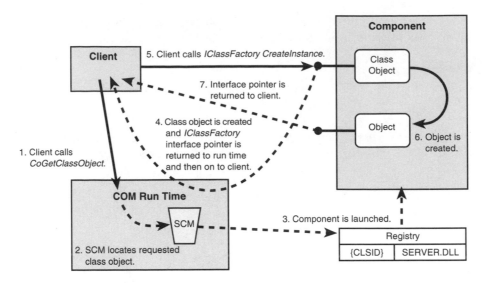

Figure 2-2. *Creating a COM object.*

Components

If COM classes contain interface implementations, what are components? "Component" is another one of those words that means different things to different people. A COM component is a binary unit of software that can be used to create COM objects. For a given CLSID, a component will include the COM class, the code to implement the class object, and usually code to create the appropriate entries in the system registry. Components are also sometimes called *servers*—yet another overloaded term!

On the Microsoft Windows platform, there are three basic ways to package COM components or servers: as Windows services, as executables, or as DLLs. Components are built as Windows services in situations in which the component must always be running, even if no one is logged on to the host machine. Windows executables are often used where the application provides a user interface in addition to serving up COM objects. Microsoft Word is an example of a COM server built as an executable. In most other scenarios, components are packaged as DLLs. In particular, most of the components used to construct three-tier applications, as discussed in Chapter 1, will be packaged as DLLs. The ActiveX Controls used in a presentation layer are DLLs, as are all middle-tier components that run within the MTS environment.

Another way to categorize servers is by where they are located relative to the client, as described here:

- **In-process servers:** Run within the same process as the client. All in-process servers are implemented as DLLs.

- **Local servers:** Run in separate processes on the same machine as the client. A local server can be an executable or a service.

- **Remote servers:** Run on different machines than the client. Remote servers can be executables, services, or even DLLs. To run a DLL server remotely, you use a *surrogate process* on the remote machine. A surrogate process is simply some application you run on the remote machine that knows how to run DLL servers. Both COM and MTS provide standard surrogates for DLL servers. We'll discuss the MTS Surrogate in detail in Chapter 4.

For the remainder of our discussion of COM, we will focus on components implemented as DLLs since these are most prevalent in three-tier applications.

The structure of a DLL server

In addition to the implementations of COM classes and class objects provided by all types of components, DLL servers are expected to implement four well-known entry points:

- *DllGetClassObject* returns an interface pointer to the class object for a specified CLSID implemented by the server.

- *DllCanUnloadNow* indicates whether any objects created by the server are still active. If so, the DLL needs to remain in memory. Otherwise, it can be unloaded, freeing up resources.

- *DllRegisterServer* writes all the registry entries required for all the COM classes implemented in the server, as discussed in the next section.

- *DllUnregisterServer* removes all the registry entries created by *DllRegisterServer*.

DllGetClassObject and *DllCanUnloadNow* are called by the COM run time; your applications should never need to call these functions directly. *DllRegisterServer* and *DllUnregisterServer* are usually called by installation programs and developer tools.

Registry entries

The system registry maintains a mapping between CLSIDs and COM components, so that the SCM can locate the code that knows how to create class objects. Figure 2-3 illustrates the basic entries for a *SalesTaxCalculator* component. The CLSID map is maintained under the predefined registry key HKEY_CLASSES_ROOT, in the CLSID key. For each COM component installed on the machine, there is one CLSID subkey for each COM class in the component. This subkey is named using the text form of the CLSID. The *SalesTaxCalculator* component contains one COM class, with CLSID {45D3F4B1-DB76-11d1-AA06-0040052510F1}. Each COM class key has a subkey indicating where its COM component is located. In this case, the component is implemented as a DLL and will be run in process, so the InprocServer32 subkey is used to specify the DLL name. This COM class also has a ProgID, which is specified using the ProgID subkey.

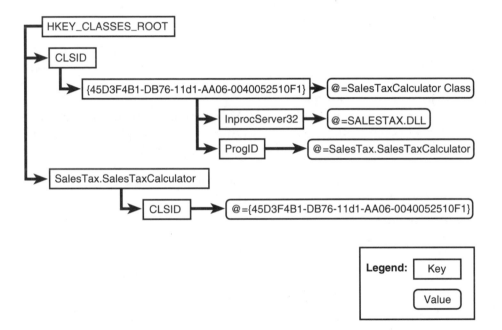

Figure 2-3. *Registry entries for the* SalesTaxCalculator *component.*

The system registry also maintains a ProgID-to-CLSID map under the HKEY_CLASSES_ROOT registry key (also shown in Figure 2-3). Each ProgID gets a named key under HKEY_CLASSES_ROOT. In our example, the ProgID is *SalesTax.SalesTaxCalculator*, so this is the name of the key. The ProgID key has a CLSID subkey whose value specifies the corresponding CLSID.

For the SCM to locate the component for a CLSID, these registry entries must be installed with the component. For DLL servers, this is usually done by running the program REGSVR32, as shown here:

```
regsvr32 salestax.dll
```

REGSVR32 looks in the DLL server for the *DllRegisterServer* entry point. The implementation of *DllRegisterServer* is responsible for writing all the required registry entries for all the COM classes provided by the component. This code is not difficult to write, but it is tedious. Again, we are fortunate to have programming languages and tools that take care of all the dirty work for us, providing standard implementations of *DllRegisterServer* and its partner, *DllUnregisterServer*. Even if you never need to implement registration code yourself, you will find an understanding of COM registry entries useful—poking around in the registry is often part of debugging COM applications.

Threading

COM supports multiple *threading models* for components. A threading model defines what threads a component's objects can run on and how COM will synchronize access to the objects. On the Windows platform, COM components run in a multi-threaded environment. Components must be written to run correctly in this environment.

All COM threading models are based on the notion of *apartments*. An apartment is an execution context for objects. Every object resides in exactly one apartment for its entire lifetime. One or more apartments reside within each process. All threads in the process must be associated with an apartment before making COM calls, by calling *CoInitialize* or *CoInitializeEx*.

All calls to an object are made in the object's apartment. If the calling application is running in a different apartment, COM takes care of synchronizing access to the object's apartment. In addition, cross-apartment calls must be *marshaled*. We'll talk more about marshaling in the section "Remote Activation and Marshaling" later in this chapter; in essence, marshaling means that COM intercepts the call, packages the call stack into some standard format, does some work, and then converts the package back to a method call in the object's apartment. In-process, cross-apartment calls can have a substantial impact on performance. That's why it's important to understand the COM threading models.

In Microsoft Windows 95 and Microsoft Windows NT 4.0, COM supports two types of apartments. A *single-threaded apartment* (STA) is associated with one thread for the lifetime of the apartment. The apartment is created when *CoInitialize* or *CoInitializeEx* is called by the thread. One process can have multiple STAs; the first STA created is called the *main STA*. The threading model based on STAs is called the *apartment model*. Each process can also have one *multi-threaded apartment* (MTA). Multiple threads can be associated with the MTA. The threading model based on MTAs is called the *free-threaded model*. Figure 2-4 illustrates two processes, each with objects created in both an STA and an MTA.

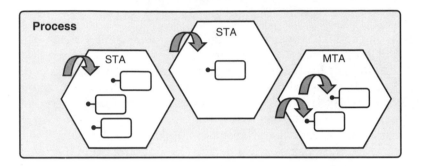

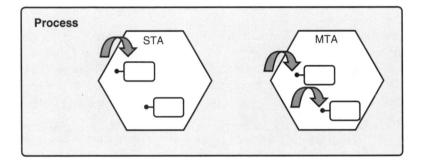

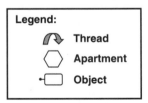

Figure 2-4. *Processes, threads, apartments, and objects.*

Because an STA has a single thread associated with it for its entire lifetime, apartment model objects residing in an STA will never be accessed concurrently and are guaranteed to always run on the same thread. In fact, no matter how many objects are in the apartment, only one method call will be executing concurrently. This helps component developers considerably: they do not need to synchronize access to per-object state, and they can use thread-local storage if necessary. (Developers *do* need to synchronize access to global variables, however.)

Synchronization in the STA is based on Windows messages. Calls are queued as special messages and processed by a hidden window created by COM. This means that threads associated with an STA must have a *message pump*. A message pump is a special program loop that retrieves Windows messages from the current thread's message queue, translates them, and dispatches the messages to other parts of the application. If the thread does not have a message pump, no calls will be processed. The STA synchronization model does not prevent re-entrancy; it just provides thread safety. It is exactly the same model used by window procedures. During method calls to other apartments or processes, COM continues to pump messages, so the STA can process incoming calls and the thread's windows are responsive. Called objects can call back to other objects in the STA without fear of deadlock.

Components obeying the apartment model are easy to write, but the concurrency constraints can create a performance bottleneck that is unacceptable. In this case, the components might need to support the free-threaded model. COM does not synchronize access to objects in the MTA. Threads are dynamically allocated as needed to service all concurrent calls into the MTA. Thus, it is possible for free-threaded objects to be accessed concurrently by multiple threads, which can improve performance.

Writing thread-safe code can be difficult. Developers must protect both global variables and per-object state. They must also worry about whether functions from run-time or statically linked libraries are thread-safe. One of the nice things about COM is that it gives you a choice of threading models when you write your code; it also takes care of any mismatches between the threading models supported by a caller and an object.

This feature is particularly interesting for in-process servers. In-process servers normally use the threads of their client process instead of creating their own threads. And in order for the client process to create a COM object, it must have already called *CoInitialize* or *CoInitializeEx* to establish the apartment associated with the calling thread. But then how does COM ensure that the caller's apartment is compatible with the threading model supported by the created object? When a developer creates a component, he or she specifies the threading model it supports using a named registry value on the InprocServer32 key, as shown here:

```
HKCR\CLSID\{45D3F4B1-DB76-11d1-AA06-0040052510F1}\InprocServer32
   @="salestax.dll"
   ThreadingModel="Apartment"
```

COM uses the *ThreadingModel* value to determine which apartment an object will be created in, as shown in Table 2-1. For example, if the caller's apartment is an STA and the component's *ThreadingModel* is *Apartment*, the object will be created in the caller's STA. All calls from the caller to the object will be direct calls; no marshaling is needed. If the caller's apartment is the MTA and the component's *ThreadingModel* is *Apartment*, however, the object will be created in a new STA. All calls to the object from the caller will be marshaled.

	Caller's Apartment		
ThreadingModel Value	**Main STA**	**STA**	**MTA**
Unspecified	Main STA	Main STA	Main STA
Apartment	Main STA	Calling STA	New STA created
Free	MTA	MTA	MTA
Both	Main STA	Calling STA	MTA

Table 2-1. *In-process server threading model options used to determine where new objects are created.*

Most applications and components available today either support the apartment model or are single-threaded (that is, they use the main STA). Apartment model components offer a nice balance of ease of development and performance. And as we'll see in Chapter 4, MTS provides features to help apartment model components scale to support large numbers of users.

Distributed COM

As we saw in our examination of the COM programming model, servers can be run on remote machines. From the programming model perspective, that's all there is to it. COM's location transparency extends cross-apartment, cross-process, and cross-machine. There are some practical matters to consider when you are communicating across machine boundaries. And we haven't yet looked at how location transparency actually works. So let's spend a little time discussing Distributed COM (DCOM).

> **NOTE** Technically, "DCOM" refers specifically to the wire protocol for making COM calls between two machines. However, you will often see the term used to refer to the whole concept of COM communication across machines. The discussion here focuses on what you need to know to understand at a high level how distributed applications based on COM work. It does not talk about the communication mechanisms or architecture of DCOM in detail. If you want to learn more about DCOM, refer to the bibliography.

Cross-machine COM calls introduce some issues that you normally don't need to consider in the single-machine scenario. First, you might not want everyone in the world to be able to use the components installed on a particular machine. Thus, security becomes an issue. Second, you need some way to tell the people who are allowed to use the components (or more accurately, their computers) where the components are located. You can't rely on the components to register themselves at install time because the components will not be installed on the client machines.

COM Security

The COM security model defines a standard way for COM objects to interact with security services provided by the underlying operating system. The model is independent of the specific security services that might be available.

> **NOTE**   On Windows NT 4.0, the only security service available is NT LAN Manager (NTLM) security. Windows NT 5.0 will provide additional security services, such as Kerberos and Secure Socket Layer (SSL).

COM security addresses the two issues of who is allowed to launch components and how to secure calls through interface pointers by providing *activation security* and *call security*.

Activation security

Activation security is applied by the server machine's SCM whenever it receives a request to activate an object. "Activating an object" means either creating a new object or getting an interface pointer to a "published" object such as a registered class object or an object in the running object table. We won't be looking at published objects in this book; instead, we'll focus on creating new objects.

The SCM uses information in the registry (or obtained dynamically from published objects) to determine whether the activation request should be allowed. First the SCM checks a machinewide setting to determine whether *any* remote activation requests are permitted. If the machinewide check succeeds, the SCM looks for component-specific security settings. We'll talk about these settings in more detail in the section "Registration Revisited" later in this chapter. In essence, however, the registry can contain an access control list (ACL) that indicates which users can activate specific components. The SCM checks the client's identity against the ACL to decide whether the activation request can proceed. If there is no component-specific setting, the SCM looks at a default ACL.

If the access check succeeds, the SCM will launch the component, if necessary, and activate the object. The SCM uses information in the registry to determine what security identity the object should run as. This identity becomes the client identity for any activation requests the object itself might make.

Call security

Once an interface pointer to an object is obtained, a client can make calls to the object. COM also applies security to each method call through an interface pointer. Per-call security has two separate aspects. The first is authentication and authorization of the caller, which is essentially the same as the activation security check just described, except that a different ACL is used and the component and client have some control over how often the check is performed. The other aspect relates to data integrity and privacy—that is, ensuring that the network packets containing the COM method call have not been tampered with and preventing data in the packets from being read during transmission.

As you might imagine, performing security checks on every method call can involve considerable overhead. It might also be overkill for some situations. Thus, COM lets applications configure when and how per-call security will be applied. Both the client and server applications can establish processwide defaults for per-call security by calling the *CoInitializeSecurity* function. The settings include an ACL for authorization checks and an authentication level that determines how often authentication is performed as well as whether data integrity and/or data privacy should be enforced. If an application does not explicitly call *CoInitialize-Security*, the COM run time will call it on the application's behalf before any objects are activated, using information from the registry. As with activation security settings, COM will first look for component-specific settings; if none are found, it uses the default settings.

NOTE   In addition to setting per-call security at a process level, applications and components can tune security settings on individual interfaces and method calls using the standard *IClientSecurity* and *IServerSecurity* interfaces. This is a more advanced technique that we will not cover in this book. For many applications, processwide settings are sufficient. As we'll see in Chapter 4, MTS offers an abstraction on top of the COM security model that makes securing access to components even easier.

Registration Revisited

COM security relies on a number of registry entries. On Windows and Windows NT, these settings are usually configured using the DCOM configuration tool, DCOMCNFG.EXE, shown in Figure 2-5. DCOMCNFG lets you set machinewide and per-application settings without worrying about the actual registry keys involved.

Several key DCOM settings can be configured at the machine level. These settings are stored as values under the registry key HKEY_LOCAL_MACHINE\Software\Microsoft\Ole. Table 2-2 lists the major values, their purpose, and how to set them using DCOMCNFG. The values specified using DCOMCNFG will be used by default if no application-specific values are provided.

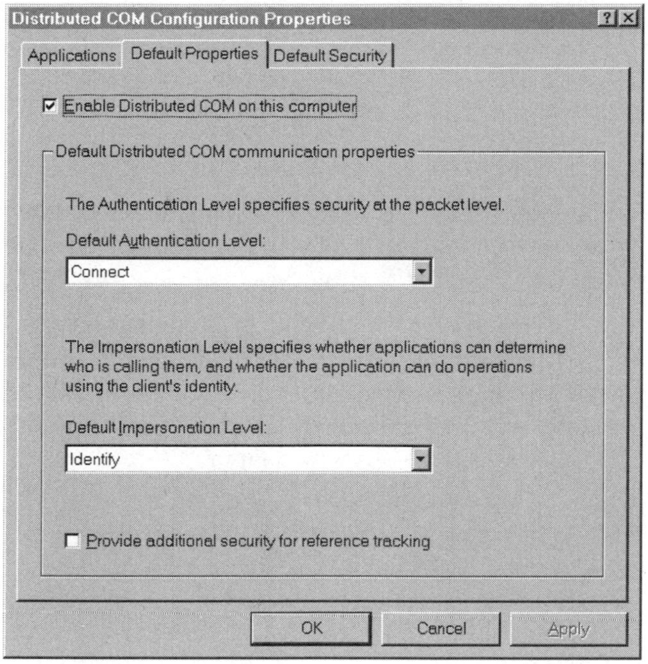

Figure 2-5. *The DCOM Configuration tool used to configure DCOM security.*

Registry Value	Purpose	Configuration
EnableDCOM	Global activation policy for machine	On the Default Properties tab, check the Enable Distributed COM On This Computer check box.
LegacyAuthenticationLevel	Default authentication level applied to network packets	On the Default Properties tab, choose a setting from the Default Authentication Level combo box.
DefaultLaunchPermission	Default ACL for activation security	On the Default Security tab, click the Edit Default button in the Default Launch Permissions group to edit which users have launch permission.

Table 2-2. *Machinewide DCOMCNFG registry entries.*   *(continued)*

Table 2-2. *continued*

Registry Value	Purpose	Configuration
DefaultAccessPermission	Default ACL for per-call security	On the Default Security tab, click the Edit Default button in the Default Access Permissions group to edit which users have access permission.

DCOMCNFG also lets you specify settings for specific applications. In COM today, an application is nothing more than an identified process that hosts one or more components. Applications are identified by (you guessed it) GUIDs, which are called AppIDs.

It should be fairly clear how CLSIDs map to AppIDs for components implemented as executables or services—there is one AppID for each executable or service. Components implemented this way should register an AppID and add AppID values to each CLSID they register, as shown in Figure 2-6.

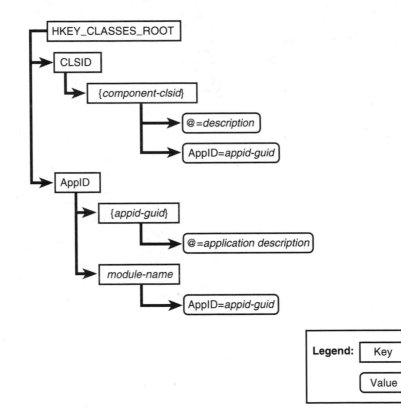

Figure 2-6. *Registering an AppID for an executable.*

Less clear is how CLSIDs map to AppIDs for components implemented as DLLs. If an in-process component is to run remotely, a surrogate process must be defined for the component. First an AppID is defined for the process, as shown in Figure 2-7. For each component that should run in this process, an AppID value should be added to the CLSID key for each class registered by the component. The executable to run when a component is launched is listed under the *DllSurrogate* value on the AppID key. If the *DllSurrogate* value is *NULL* or an empty string, the default system-supplied surrogate is used.

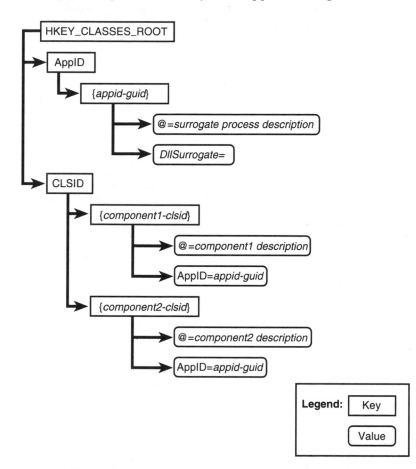

Figure 2-7. *Registering an AppID for a DLL server.*

With the AppID key in place, DCOMCNFG can be used to establish security settings on a per-application basis. These settings will be used if the application does not call *CoInitializeSecurity* explicitly. The per-application settings are stored as named values under the HKEY_CLASSES_ROOT\APPID\{*appid-guid*} registry key for the application on the server machine. Table 2-3 lists the security values, their purpose, and how to set them using DCOMCNFG's Application Properties window. To open the Application Properties window, select an application to configure in the Applications list box on the Applications tab, and then click the Properties button.

Registry Value	Purpose	Configuration
RunAs	Identity used to run the server process	On the Identity tab, select the user account to use to run the application.
LaunchPermission	ACL for activation security	On the Security tab, check Use Default Launch Permissions or check Use Custom Launch Permissions and click the Edit button to select specific user accounts to give launch permission to.
AccessPermission	ACL for per-call security	On the Security tab, check Use Default Access Permissions or check Use Custom Access Permissions and click the Edit button to select user accounts that will have access permission.
AuthenticationLevel	Authentication level applied to network packets (Windows NT 4 Service Pack 4 or later)	On the General tab, select a value from the Authentication Level dropdown listbox to set the per-application Authentication Level.

Table 2-3. *Per-application DCOM security configuration registry entries.*

> **NOTE** It's important to register an AppID for DLL servers that will be used remotely because DCOMCNFG cannot be used to modify settings of servers unless they have an AppID.

In addition to security settings, the registry also contains information about where the component is located. On the server machine, this information is usually written to the registry by the component itself, when it is installed. All that's needed on the server machine is the path to the server, stored under the InprocServer32 or LocalServer32 key for each CLSID. (Services need some additional entries.)

It is also necessary to put information in the registry of remote client machines for those machines to be able to request remote objects, unless client applications are written to specify the server machine name when *CoCreateInstanceEx* is called. In particular, the client machine needs an AppID with a *RemoteServerName* value. The client may also need registry entries for proxy/stub DLLs used to marshal interfaces exposed by the objects. The component can't write the registry information because it isn't installed on the client machine.

There are two common ways to create the client-side registry entries on Windows machines. If no proxy/stub DLLs are required by the component, a .REG file with the registry settings can be distributed to client machines and merged into the local registry. Otherwise, an install program can be distributed that writes the appropriate registry entries and installs any proxy/stub DLLs required for the component to work correctly. In some cases, the install program or .REG file will create the AppID key, but it won't specify where the component is located. If this is the case, DCOMCNFG can be used on the client to set the *RemoteServerName* value of the AppID.

Remote Activation and Marshaling

With the security and server location information in place, objects can be created remotely. Let's look at how this process works.

As we've seen, creating objects is simple: first you get an *IClassFactory* pointer to a class object, and then you call *IClassFactory CreateInstance* to get an interface pointer to the object you've created. The SCM is responsible for locating the class object.

This is still the case for remote objects, but now two SCMs are in play: the client machine SCM needs to detect that a remote object has been requested and contact the SCM on the server machine. The server machine SCM then does its normal work to locate the class object and returns the interface pointer to the client machine SCM (assuming that all security checks pass). This process is illustrated in Figure 2-8 on the following page.

The client machine SCM detects that a remote object has been requested in one of two ways. First, an application can specify a remote server machine name in the call to create an object. Second, when the SCM looks in the registry for information about where a server is located, it might be pointed to a remote machine (typically, by using the *RemoteServerName* value on the AppID). Either way, the client SCM ends up with a machine name. It communicates with the SCM on that machine to retrieve the interface pointer. Once the interface pointer to the object is passed back to the client application, the application makes regular method calls through the interface pointer. As far as the application is concerned, it is calling an in-process object—this is the beauty of location transparency.

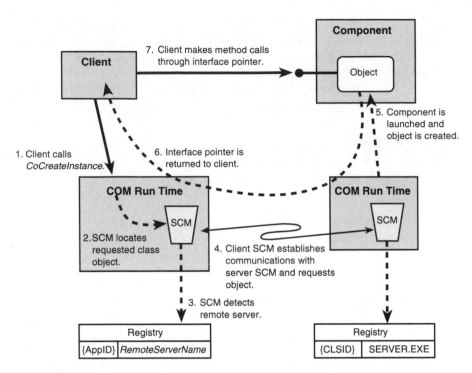

Figure 2-8. *Activation of a remote COM object.*

Behind the scenes, of course, there's a lot going on to create the illusion of an in-process call, as shown in Figure 2-9. Obviously, the actual interface pointer from the remote machine can't be handed to the client application—the memory address in that pointer has no meaning on the client machine. Instead, the client application is handed an interface pointer to a proxy object. This object is really an in-process object. The job of a proxy object is to do whatever is necessary to communicate with a corresponding stub object located in the component server's process.

When the client application makes a method call, it is really calling a method in the proxy. The proxy takes the parameters passed to the method and packages them in a standard format. This process is called marshaling. The proxy sends a request via the appropriate communication mechanism to the server process. The server process hands the request to the stub, which unpackages the parameters and calls the method on the real object. This process is called unmarshaling. After the method completes, any return values are passed back using the same mechanism in reverse.

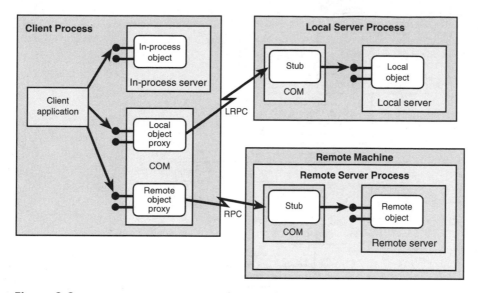

Figure 2-9. *Location transparency using proxies and stubs.*

Recall that one of the goals for COM was to hide all the complexity of cross-machine and cross-process communication from the developer. Proxy and stub objects do exactly that. As we've seen, marshaling occurs not just cross-machine, but also cross-process and cross-apartment. Typically, implementations of proxies and stubs are generated automatically from IDL interface definitions using the MIDL compiler. These DLLs call system functions that encapsulate all the details of marshaling and unmarshaling calls, as well as the details of the actual call request. If a cross-machine call is requested, COM uses a remote procedure call (RPC) to make the call. If a cross-process call is requested, a lighter-weight interprocess communication mechanism called Lightweight (LRPC) is used. If a cross-apartment call is requested, COM switches apartment contexts and synchronizes access appropriately—all without any work on the part of the developer.

Normally, the only thing a developer needs to worry about is making sure that the proxy/stub DLLs are installed and registered on the appropriate machines. For a given interface, the proxy/stub DLL must be registered on all machines that use or implement that interface. The proxy/stub DLLs generated by MIDL can be built to be self-registering, so all you need to do is run REGSVR32 on the DLL and the correct registry entries will be defined, as shown in Figure 2-10 on the following page.

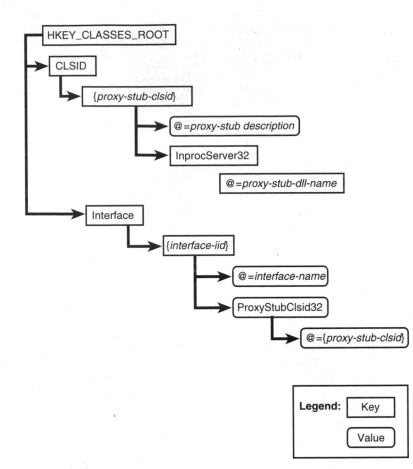

Figure 2-10. *Proxy/stub DLL registration.*

Automation

At this point, we've covered the essentials of COM. A common characteristic of the COM objects and interfaces we've examined is that client applications must understand the interfaces they use when the applications are built. A client application can't create some random COM object and use any interfaces that object might expose; it can only use the interfaces it knows about at build time.

While this works just fine for many applications, there are scenarios in which it would be useful to determine *at run time* what objects to use and how to use their interfaces. This capability is provided by *Automation*, formerly called OLE Automation. Automation was originally developed to provide a way for macro and scripting languages to programmatically control applications. Microsoft Word and Microsoft Excel macros are examples of Automation in action. Today both

Word and Excel use a common macro language, Visual Basic for Applications (VBA). General-purpose scripting languages such as VBA can't have built-in knowledge of every interface that might ever be exposed by an object, so another approach is needed.

The *IDispatch* Interface

The approach Automation takes is to define a standard COM interface for programmatic access to an object. This interface is named *IDispatch*. Components can expose any number of functions to clients by implementing *IDispatch*. Clients access all functionality through a single well-known function, *IDispatch Invoke*, as shown in Figure 2-11.

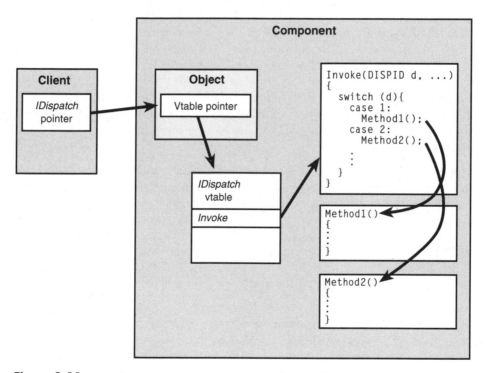

Figure 2-11. *Invoking an Automation method using* IDispatch.

In its simplest form, called *late-binding*, Automation lets clients call objects without any a priori knowledge of the methods exposed by the objects. A client application creates an object in the usual way, asking for the *IDispatch* interface. To access the object's functionality, the client calls the *IDispatch GetIDsOfNames* method with the text name of a function it wants to call. If the function is supported, a number identifying the function, known as a dispatch ID (DISPID), will be returned. The client then packages all the parameters to the function in a standard data structure and calls *IDispatch Invoke*, passing in the DISPID and the parameter data structure.

When the object receives a call to *Invoke*, it uses the DISPID as a key to figure out which internal function to call. It pulls apart the parameter data structure to build the method call to the internal function. If the correct parameters aren't available, the *Invoke* method can return immediately, without risking a component crash due to a poorly formatted method call. After the internal function completes its work, the return value and/or any error information is packaged into standard data structures and returned as *[out]* parameters from the *Invoke* call.

If you're thinking this sounds awfully complicated, you're right—if you have to build all the "plumbing." But it turns out to be enormously useful for interpreted languages. To use Automation-aware objects, an interpreter (sometimes called a script engine) needs to understand only how to create objects, how to call methods through *IDispatch*, how to detect errors, and how to destroy objects. The interpreter doesn't need to worry about how to construct stack frames for different calling conventions, how to interpret interface pointers, or how to figure out just what functions an object exposes. All of this plumbing can be hidden within the interpreter itself, leaving a very simple programming model for the script author.

On the component side, most of the plumbing can be hidden as well. Most COM-aware development tools create Automation-aware components by default. If the language itself is COM-aware, as Visual Basic is, all the details of implementing *IDispatch* can be hidden away so that the developer needs only to implement the exposed functions. If COM support is provided by a framework of some sort, the framework usually provides a standard implementation of *IDispatch* and defines a data-driven mechanism for hooking up DISPIDs to internal methods. Again, all the developer needs to do is implement the actual functions that he or she wants to expose.

The flexibility of late-binding comes at a price. First, all parameters passed to *Invoke* must be of type VARIANT. A VARIANT contains a tag and a value. The tag identifies the type of the value. Automation defines a set of types that can be placed in VARIANTs. If your data is not one of these types, it will need to be converted before you can pass it as a parameter to an Automation method.

> **NOTE** In practice, this limitation is not much of a problem. The set of types supported by Automation is fairly extensive. Windows NT 4.0 Service Pack 4, Windows 98, and Windows NT 5.0 are expected to add user-defined structures to the set of Automation types, eliminating the most obvious omission.

Second, objects can expose only one *IDispatch* interface at a time. While it is possible to expose additional *IDispatch*-based interfaces using different IIDs, in practice no scripting languages can access those interfaces. Thus, you will find that most Automation-aware objects expose a single programmatic interface for clients to use. This can impact your application design, particularly if you have security constraints. We'll return to this issue in Chapter 7.

Finally, considerable overhead is associated with late-binding. Every method call results in *two* calls to the object—one call to *GetIDsOfNames* to find the DISPID, and another call to *Invoke*. Overhead is also associated with packaging and unpackaging the parameters passed into and out of *Invoke*. Generally, this overhead is acceptable in interpreted environments, but it might not be acceptable to all clients.

Type Libraries

Many client applications do not need the absolute run-time flexibility offered by late-binding. These applications are usually compiled. The developers know at development time what objects they want to use and what methods they want to call. So why bother with the overhead of calling *GetIDsOfNames*? Why not just hard-code the DISPID for the method into the application itself?

This form of Automation is called *early-binding* because information about the components being used is bound into the client application at build time. For early-binding to work, development environments must have some way to determine the DISPID of the methods being called. It would also be nice if the development environment could determine whether the correct parameters were being passed to the method, eliminating a huge class of application errors. Essentially, the development tool needs a complete description of the methods exposed by the component. This description is provided by type information, which is usually stored in the form of a type library associated with each component.

Automation defines a set of standard interfaces for creating and browsing type information. Normally, component and application developers don't need to worry about using these interfaces. Component developers define interfaces in some text format and then use a development tool to create a type library. The development tool uses the standard type library interfaces internally. Application development environments provide some way for application developers to indicate that they want to use particular components. The development environment uses the standard interfaces to read the type library and convert source code statements to calls to *IDispatch Invoke*, with the correct DISPID filled in. If the correct parameters are not provided, a compile-time error can be generated so that the developer can correct the source code before the application is deployed.

Dispinterfaces

So how does a component developer define interfaces? As with normal COM interfaces, the developer can use IDL to define Automation interfaces. However, instead of using the *interface* keyword, the *dispinterface* keyword is used. This keyword indicates that the interface will be implemented using *IDispatch* and only Automation types can be used. The methods defined for the dispinterface will not appear in the interface's vtable.

With dispinterfaces, you can explicitly distinguish *properties* from *methods*. A property represents an attribute; a method represents an action. For example, a *Rectangle* dispinterface might have *Height* and *Width* properties and a *Move* method. Each property is implemented as a set of accessor functions, one for reading the property and an optional one for writing the property. Both functions have the same DISPID; a flag is passed to *IDispatch Invoke* to indicate whether a read or write operation is requested. This capability is useful for Automation-aware languages, which can coat properties in syntactical sugar to make the objects easier to use. For example, in VBScript, properties look a lot like variables, as shown here:

```
set rect = CreateObject("Shapes.Rectangle")
rect.Left = 10
rect.Top = 10
rect.Height = 30
rect.Width = rect.Height
```

As mentioned, it is rarely necessary to hand-code interface definitions in IDL. Development environments such as Visual Basic let you define interfaces in standard language syntax and create the type library directly. Other development environments provide wizards to help you define methods and properties on interfaces. The wizards generate correctly formatted IDL, which can be compiled using MIDL to generate a type library.

Dual Interfaces

Early-binding is a substantial improvement over late-binding for compiled clients. However, if a client is written in a development language that supports vtable binding, calling *IDispatch Invoke* seems like a lot of unneeded overhead. To address this concern, Automation supports something called a *dual interface*. A dual interface has characteristics of both vtable-based interfaces and dispinterfaces, as shown in Figure 2-12.

Dual interfaces are defined using the *interface* keyword in IDL. All dual interfaces have the attribute *dual*, which also indicates that parameter types in the interface methods must be Automation types. All dual interfaces are derived from

IDispatch. The methods defined in a dual interface are part of its vtable, so clients that understand vtable binding can make direct calls to the methods. But the interface also provides the *Invoke* method, so clients that understand only early-binding or only late-binding can use the interface too. The implementation of the *Invoke* method still uses the DISPID to decide which method to call. The methods just happen to be part of the vtable interface

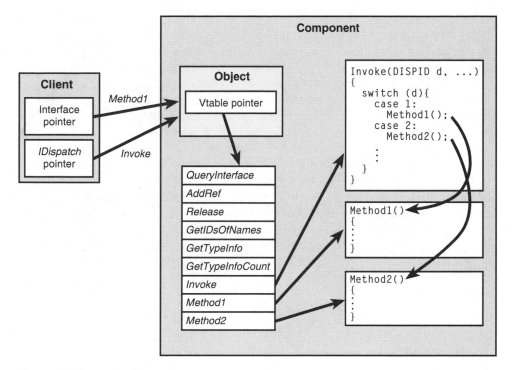

Figure 2-12. *A dual interface.*

For components that expose a programmatic interface, there is very little reason not to define the interface as a dual interface. Today dual interfaces can easily be used by just about every COM-aware development tool, and most tools that let you create COM components generate dual interfaces by default. Client applications that can take advantage of vtable-binding get better performance with essentially no extra work for either the component developer or the application developer. Dual interfaces can also be configured to use the Automation marshaler, eliminating the need to install a custom proxy/stub DLL on client machines for these interfaces.

SUMMARY

COM defines a model for component interaction. The goal of COM is to let developers assemble applications from prebuilt parts, or components, irrespective of where the components are located or what development language was used to implement them. The COM model is defined in such a way that components and applications can evolve independently over time.

The COM programming model is based on objects, interfaces, classes, and components. COM objects are instances of COM classes, which are named implementations of one or more COM interfaces. An interface defines a set of related methods; it represents a contract between the client and the implementer of the interface. All COM interfaces derive from the fundamental interface *IUnknown*. *IUnknown* provides object lifetime management and interface navigation features. COM components are binary units of software that can be used to create COM objects. Components include COM classes, an implementation of a class object used to create instances of each class, and code to create the registry entries needed to locate the classes. Most components available today, including many system services provided by Windows, are Automation-aware components that expose dual interfaces. These components are accessible to almost every development language and programming environment, including scripting languages. COM provides the basic building blocks of the three-tier Windows DNA application.

3

Data Access Fundamentals

With an understanding of COM firmly in place, we can turn our attention to the specific services that are used to build a distributed application. Almost every distributed application produces or accesses stored data, so we'll start by looking at the Microsoft Data Access Components (MDAC).

As with the other chapters in Part One, the intent here is not to give you all the information you need to become a database guru. Instead, this chapter focuses on the concepts you need to understand to successfully write a Microsoft Windows Distributed interNet Applications (DNA) application. If you are interested in learning more about databases and data modeling, please refer to the bibliography.

Why MDAC?

Distributed application developers face two fundamental technical challenges related to data access. First, developers rarely have the opportunity to start from scratch. Most applications need to access existing data. This data can be stored in a variety of formats. Some data might be kept in database management systems (DBMSs); other data might be kept in less structured forms. There are many DBMSs on the market, from mainframe databases such as Information Management Systems (IMS) and DB2, to server databases such as Oracle and Microsoft SQL Server, to desktop databases such as Microsoft Access and Paradox. Even within a single company, multiple DBMSs might be in use. Non-DBMS data can be stored in text files, indexed sequential access method (ISAM) files, spreadsheets, e-mail messages, or any other type of application-specific file. Somehow, the distributed application developer must integrate these disparate data sources into a unified view for the application user.

A second challenge is that by their very nature, distributed applications involve accessing remote data sources. The person who wants to use an application to look at some data is, in most cases, using a different machine than the one(s) on which the data is stored. Thus, it's important to have efficient mechanisms for accessing remote data, to minimize network traffic generated by the application. This requirement becomes increasingly important as applications scale to reach thousands or millions of users, many of whom are connected via expensive wide area network (WAN) connections or slow modem connections.

MDAC addresses both these issues. MDAC is a set of run-time components for accessing structured and unstructured data, based on the Microsoft strategy of universal data access (UDA). These components are described in the following table. One of the primary goals of the run-time components is to provide efficient access to remote data.

Component	Description
ActiveX Data Objects (ADO)	Application-level programming interface to data
Remote Data Service (RDS)	Client-side caching engine; formerly known as Advanced Data Connector (ADC)
Microsoft OLE DB provider for Open Database Connectivity (ODBC)	Access provider for ODBC databases, via OLE DB
ODBC driver manager	The DLL that implements the ODBC API and directs calls to the appropriate ODBC drivers
ODBC drivers	Database drivers for SQL Server, Access, and Oracle

Accessing Data

In this section, we'll address the challenge of accessing a multitude of data sources in a little more detail. Every data store provides a native access method. Each database vendor provides a vendor-specific API to ease database access. Non-DBMS data can be accessed via data-specific APIs, such as the Microsoft Windows NT Directory Service API or the Messaging API (MAPI) for accessing mail data, or via file system APIs. By using the native access method for each data store, a developer can use the full power of each store. However, this technique requires the developer to learn how to use each access method—that is, the developer must understand the API functions as well as how to use them efficiently and how to use diagnostic and configuration tools associated with the data store. The cost of training developers on all the data access methods used within a company can be quite high.

ODBC

Instead of using native data access methods, developers can choose to use a generic, vendor-neutral API such as the Microsoft ODBC interface. ODBC is a C programming language interface for accessing data in a DBMS using Structured Query Language (SQL). An ODBC driver manager provides the programming interface and run-time components you need to locate DBMS-specific drivers. ODBC drivers are typically supplied by the DBMS vendor. These drivers translate generic calls from the ODBC driver manager into calls to the native data access method.

The primary advantage of using ODBC is that developers need to learn only one API to access a wide range of DBMSs. Applications can access data from multiple DBMSs at the same time. In fact, the application developer need not even target a specific DBMS—the exact DBMS to be used can be decided when the application is deployed.

Unfortunately, there are several drawbacks to the ODBC approach. First, there must be an ODBC driver for every data store you want to access. These drivers must support SQL queries, even if the database does not use SQL for its native query language. Second, the ODBC API treats all data as relational tables. Both of these constraints can cause problems for unstructured and nonrelational data stores. Finally, the ODBC API is a standard, controlled by a committee, which means that regardless of the capabilities of the underlying DBMS, the ODBC driver can expose only functionality that is part of the standard. Modifying the API is a complex process. The committee must agree to the proposed change, specify how ODBC drivers should implement the new function(s), and specify how applications or the driver manager can detect whether a given driver supports the new specification. Drivers must be updated, and applications must ensure that the new drivers are installed or that the applications are written defensively against older drivers.

In practice, ODBC is a widely used mechanism for database access and is supported by most major DBMS vendors. For applications that work only with traditional relational databases, ODBC is a fine solution. As applications move beyond the realm of the relational DBMS (RDBMS), however, a more comprehensive solution is needed.

Universal Storage

Another way to attack the problem of disparate data sources is to put all the data into a single data store. This approach is sometimes called the *universal storage* approach because the single data store is supposed to hold any and all kinds of data. Universal storage solves the problem of multiple access methods since there would only be one type of store. However, it presents a huge technical problem: writing a data store that can efficiently store and retrieve *any* type of data. And it presents a huge business problem: what to do about the terabytes of existing data that are stored somewhere else! The cost of converting data to the universal store would be enormous, not to mention the risk associated with the single point of failure represented by the universal store itself.

Realistically, the ODBC approach of a common access method seems more feasible than the universal storage approach. However, the access method cannot be limited to relational database tables and SQL queries. It must encompass all types of data.

Universal Data Access

The Microsoft Universal Data Access (UDA) architecture is designed to provide high-performance access to any type of data—structured or unstructured, relational or nonrelational—stored anywhere in the enterprise. UDA defines a set of COM interfaces that generalize the idea of accessing data, as illustrated in Figure 3-1. UDA is based on OLE DB, a set of COM interfaces for building database components. OLE DB lets data stores expose their native functionality without making nonrelational data look relational. OLE DB also provides a way for generic service components, such as specialized query processors, to augment the features of simpler data providers. Because OLE DB is optimized for efficient data access rather than ease of use, UDA also defines an application-level programming interface, called Microsoft ActiveX Data Objects (ADO). ADO exposes dual interfaces, so it can easily be used with scripting languages as well as with C++, Microsoft Visual Basic, and other developer tools. ADO is discussed further in the section "ActiveX Data Objects," later in this chapter.

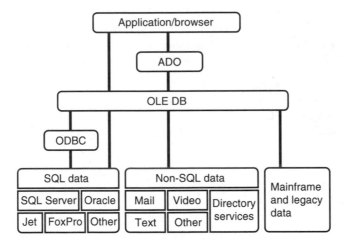

Figure 3-1. *The UDA architecture.*

MDAC provides an implementation of UDA that includes ADO as well as an OLE DB provider for ODBC. This capability means that ADO can be used to access any database that has an ODBC driver—effectively, any major database platform. OLE DB providers are also available for other types of stores, such as the Microsoft Exchange mail store, the Windows NT Directory Services, and the Windows file system itself via Microsoft Index Server. Developers can write applications using ADO as the single data access mechanism, for existing data as well as for new data, structured or unstructured, wherever it is located.

OLE DB

As mentioned, OLE DB is a specification of a set of COM interfaces for data management. The interfaces are defined so that data providers can implement different levels of support, based on the capabilities of the underlying data store. Because OLE DB is COM-based, it can easily be extended: extensions are implemented as new interfaces. Clients can use the standard COM *QueryInterface* method to determine whether specific features are supported on a particular machine or by a particular data store. This capability is a substantial improvement over the function-based API defined by ODBC.

Figure 3-2 on the following page shows the high-level OLE DB architecture. This architecture consists of three major pieces: *data consumers, service components,* and *data providers*. OLE DB providers are COM components responsible for providing data from data stores to the outside world. All data is exposed as virtual tables, known as *rowsets*. Internally, of course, a provider will make calls to the underlying data store using its native data access method or a generic API such as ODBC. Data consumers are COM components that access data using OLE DB providers. OLE DB service providers are COM components that encapsulate a specialized data management function, such as query processing, cursor management, or transaction management. OLE DB is designed so that these service components can be implemented independently from data providers, delivered as stand-alone products, and plugged in as needed. For example, simple data providers might only provide a way to get all the data from a data source, with no ability to query, sort, or filter the data. A service component might implement SQL query processing for any data provider. If a consumer wanted to perform a SQL query on the data from a simple data provider, the service component could then be invoked to execute the query.

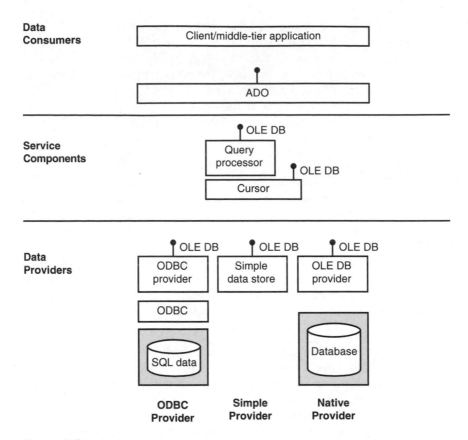

Figure 3-2. *The OLE DB architecture.*

The OLE DB object model consists of seven core components, shown in Figure 3-3. These objects are implemented by data providers or service components and used by data consumers.

In the OLE DB object model, an *Enumerator* object is used to locate a data source. Consumers that aren't customized for a specific data source use an *Enumerator* to retrieve a list of names of available data sources and subordinate *Enumerators*. For example, in a file system, each file might correspond to a data source and each subdirectory might correspond to a subordinate *Enumerator*. The consumer searches the list for a data source to use, moving through the subordinate *Enumerators* as necessary. Once a data source is selected by name, a *Data Source* object can be created.

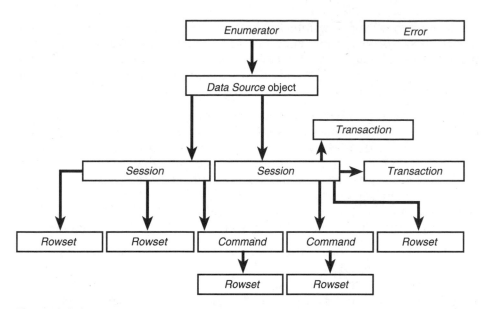

Figure 3-3. *The OLE DB object model.*

A *Data Source* object knows how to connect to a type of data store, such as a file or a DBMS. Each OLE DB provider implements a *Data Source* component class with a unique CLSID. A consumer can either create a specific *Data Source* directly, by calling *CoCreateInstance,* using the *Data Source*'s CLSID, or it can use an *Enumerator* to search for a data source to use. Although each *Data Source* class has a unique CLSID, all the classes are required to expose a certain set of OLE DB interfaces so that a consumer can use any available data source in a standard way. Consumers specify the name of the data source they want to connect to, as well as any authentication information, through the *Data Source* object. Once a *Data Source* object is created, it can be used to reveal the capabilities of the underlying data provider.

Data Sources are factories for *Session* objects—in other words, you create *Session* objects using a *Data Source* object. A *Session* represents a particular connection to a data source. The primary function of a *Session* object is to define transaction boundaries. *Session* objects are also responsible for creating *Command* and *Rowset* objects, which are the primary ways to access data through OLE DB. A *Data Source* object can be associated with multiple *Session* objects.

If an OLE DB provider supports queries, it must implement *Command* objects. *Command* objects are generated by *Session* objects and are responsible for preparing and executing text commands. Multiple *Command* objects can be associated with a single *Session* object. Notice the use of the term "text commands" instead of "SQL commands." OLE DB doesn't care what command language is used. All that matters is whether the *Command* object understands the command and can translate it into calls to the underlying data provider when the command is executed.

Commands that return data create *Rowset* objects. *Rowset* objects can also be created directly by *Session* objects. A *Rowset* simply represents tabular data. *Rowset*s are used extensively by OLE DB. All *Rowset*s are required to implement a core set of OLE DB interfaces. These interfaces allow consumers to sequentially traverse the rows in the *Rowset*, get information about *Rowset* columns, bind *Rowset* columns to data variables, and get information about the *Rowset* as a whole. Additional features, such as updating the *Rowset* or accessing specific rows directly, are supported by implementing additional OLE DB interfaces.

The OLE DB object model also includes an *Error* object. *Error* objects can be created by any other OLE DB object. They contain rich error information that cannot be conveyed through the simple HRESULT returned by COM methods. OLE DB *Error* objects build on a standard error-handling mechanism, *IErrorInfo*, defined by Automation. OLE DB extends this error-handling mechanism to permit multiple error records to be returned by a single call and to permit providers to return provider-specific error messages.

The OLE DB object model provides a powerful, flexible mechanism for consumers to access any type of data in a uniform way. OLE DB does not take a "least common denominator" approach to UDA. Instead, it defines a rich, component-based model that lets data providers implement as much functionality as they are able to support, from sequential access to simple rowsets, to full DBMS functionality. This gives developers the option of writing generic data access components that use only the most basic functionality, or of writing components optimized for a specific DBMS that use a single programming model.

ActiveX Data Objects

The OLE DB object model exposes functionality through COM interfaces that are not Automation compatible, which means that OLE DB cannot be used directly from many programming languages and tools, including Visual Basic and Microsoft Visual J++. Thus, UDA also defines the application-level programming interface ADO. All ADO interfaces are dual interfaces, so they can be used by any COM-aware programming language or tool. ADO is the recommended way to access data stores in Windows DNA applications.

The ADO object model is shown in Figure 3-4. ADO is built on top of OLE DB, so you'll see many similarities to the OLE DB object model. ADO was also designed to be familiar to developers who have used earlier Microsoft data access object models such as Data Access Objects (DAO) and Remote Data Objects (RDO). Unlike DAO and RDO, the ADO object model is not hierarchical. All objects except for *Error* and *Field* objects can be created independently. This feature makes it easy to reuse objects in different contexts. It also means that often there are several ways to accomplish a particular programming task.

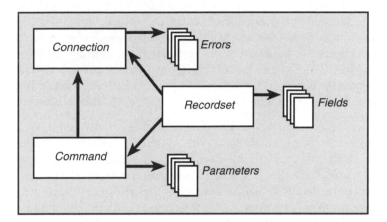

Figure 3-4. *The ADO object model.*

Microsoft has introduced several object models for data access over the years. DAO consists of Automation objects for accessing the Microsoft Jet database engine used by Microsoft Access as well as ISAM and ODBC databases. RDO consists of Automation objects for accessing relational ODBC data sources. These technologies are supported "in-the-box" by Visual Basic 5.0. However, while these technologies will continue to be supported, ADO is where future development efforts will be focused.

The *Connection* object represents a unique session to a data store. *Connection* is essentially a combination of the *Data Source* and *Session* objects in OLE DB. *Connection* objects expose an *Execute* method that lets you perform simple tasks with a minimal amount of effort. Alternatively, *Connection* objects can be attached to *Command* and *Recordset* objects, which also offer methods to access data from the data store.

Command objects in ADO are equivalent to OLE DB *Command* objects—both provide a way to prepare and execute parameterized commands against the data source. Preparing a command lets you save a processed form of the command that can be executed quickly on demand. A *Command* object has a *Parameters* collection, which contains one or more *Parameter* objects, each representing a command-specific parameter. ADO *Command* objects are available only when the underlying OLE DB provider implements OLE DB *Command* objects.

Recordset objects are the heart of ADO. Like OLE DB *Rowset* objects, they represent tabular data from a data source. *Connection* and *Command* methods that return data from the data store return read-only *Recordset* objects that can be accessed sequentially. More flexible *Recordsets* can be created directly by the programmer, connected to *Connection* and optionally *Command* objects, and populated by calling various *Recordset* methods. *Recordsets* support a variety of options for controlling the amount of data retrieved from a data source at a given time. Other available options control the type and duration of locks placed on the underlying data source and specify when updates are applied to the data store.

Recordset objects logically consist of sets of rows and columns. At any given time, a *Recordset* refers to the set of columns associated with a specific row, called the *current row*. Individual columns of the *Recordset* are accessed through its *Fields* collection, with one *Field* object for every column. Associated with every *Recordset* is a *cursor*. In database terms, a cursor is the software that returns rows of data to an application. The cursor in a *Recordset* indicates the current position in the *Recordset* and determines what row will be returned next. ADO supports several cursor types, ranging from simple forward-only cursors, to cursors that let you move to any row, to cursors that let you view changes made by other users as you move through the *Recordset*.

Remote Data Service

Although ADO *Recordsets* offer access to only one row of data at a time, this does not mean that a *Recordset* must access the underlying data store every time the cursor moves. Internally, a *Recordset* can cache multiple rows of data. This caching capability is an important part of building scalable distributed applications.

Consider a scenario in which thousands of users are accessing an online store over the Internet. The catalog of items for sale is probably maintained in a database. If each user maintains a unique connection to the database itself for the entire time he or she browses the store, there is a strict limit on the number of simultaneous shoppers: the number of database connections available on the database server. If, on the other hand, database connections are used only while blocks of data are being read from the database, a single connection can support many users. In addition, if a large block of data can be sent back to the user's machine, the user can browse the catalog with fewer database server accesses. This not only can reduce network traffic, it can also make the online store seem more responsive to the user.

The MDAC technologies that help make this scenario a reality are ADO disconnected *Recordset* and Remote Data Service (RDS). These features were originally introduced under the name Advanced Data Connector (ADC), but they are built into ADO versions 1.5 and later. The RDS architecture is shown in Figure 3-5.

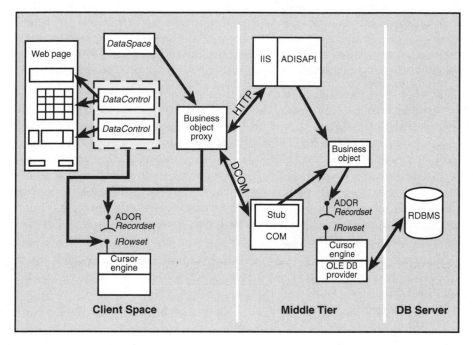

Figure 3-5. *The RDS architecture.*

A disconnected *Recordset* object is simply a *Recordset* object that has been dissociated from its *Connection* object. Disconnected recordsets do not retain locks on the underlying data store. Instead, all the data for all the rows is cached with the *Recordset*. If a *Recordset* is modified and the changes are saved back to the data store, OLE DB checks each modified row for conflicting updates in the data store—in other words, it checks whether someone else has modified the row since the *Recordset* was cached. If so, a conflict is reported to the application so that it can decide what to do.

RDS provides a client-side cursor engine for disconnected recordsets. It also provides a very efficient service for marshaling recordsets between machines, over either the Internet or an intranet. This means that a server application can generate a set of data and copy it to a client application, and the client application can browse the data as if it were connected to the actual data store. RDS also provides a way to bind *Recordset*s to data-bound controls, which can greatly simplify writing this type of client application.

RDS provides three components to help developers write applications: *RDS.Data-Control*, *RDSServer.DataFactory*, and *RDS.DataSpace*. An *RDS.DataControl* object is used to bind data-bound ActiveX controls to *Recordset* objects. Client applications use *RDS.DataControl* to browse or modify a *Recordset*. *RDS-Server.DataFactory* is essentially a generic business object for communicating with data sources. It contains no business rules or other application-specific logic.

The *Recordset* object itself is obtained in one of two ways. First, the *Recordset* can be created implicitly by *RDS.DataControl*. Properties of *RDS.DataControl* are set that identify the data server and query to be used. When the *Refresh* method is called, an *RDSServer.DataFactory* object is used behind the scenes to create the *Recordset*. Second, custom business objects can be defined that return disconnected recordsets. *RDS.DataSpace* objects are used to create client-side proxies to these business objects. The client-side proxy does whatever is necessary to communicate with the business object. Once the proxy has been created, the application can call whatever method returns a *Recordset*; it then sets the *Recordset* property of *RDS.DataControl*.

In this book, we use the second method exclusively. Middle-tier business objects will use data objects to create ADO disconnected recordsets. These *Recordset* objects will be passed back to the presentation layer using RDS. Presentation-layer client applications will use RDS to bind the *Recordset*s to data-bound controls.

In intranet scenarios, DCOM can be used to transfer the *Recordset*s between the client and server machines. In Internet scenarios, however, HTTP will normally be used. In this case, RDS provides services to manage the HTTP communication. An Internet Server API (ISAPI) extension, Advanced Data ISAPI (ADISAPI), is installed on the Web server. ADISAPI does the work required to handle requests for *Recordset*s from client-side business object proxies. It creates server-side objects, calls the methods required to generate the *Recordset*, and converts the data to an efficient form for transmission back to the client. ADISAPI and the business object proxies handle all the details of actually transmitting the data via HTTP.

SUMMARY

UDA is Microsoft's strategy for providing a common data access method for all types of data, regardless of where the data is located. UDA is based on OLE DB, a system-level component architecture for data management. UDA also defines an application-level programming interface for data access, ADO. ADO can be used from any programming language or tool that supports COM.

UDA is implemented by MDAC. MDAC includes ADO, an OLE DB provider for ODBC, as well as several ODBC components. In the ADO programming model, data is manipulated using *Recordset* objects.

A key feature of the ADO model for three-tier distributed applications is the ability to create disconnected *Recordset* objects that can be transmitted between middle-tier business objects and presentation-layer applications using RDS. Disconnected recordsets and RDS can help create the illusion that a user is permanently connected to a data store and can improve the scalability of the application.

We will discuss programming using ADO in more detail in Chapter 8, when we discuss building data objects. We will also look at working with disconnected *Recordset* objects again in Chapters 9 and 11, when we discuss building business objects and presentation-layer applications.

4

Microsoft Transaction Server

With an understanding of COM and universal data access (UDA), developers can easily create the business and data access logic required by distributed applications. However, as we saw in Chapter 1, a great deal of infrastructure is needed to make distributed applications work in a multiuser environment.

In Microsoft Windows NT 4.0, Microsoft Transaction Server (MTS) provides this infrastructure. With the advent of Windows NT 5.0, COM and MTS will merge to form COM+. Although we'll discuss MTS as a separate product, you should really think of it as an extension of COM—"COM-not-quite-+," if you will. MTS is simply a set of COM services for building component-based application servers, the middle tier of the three-tier application architecture.

By the end of this chapter, you should understand the services offered by MTS and how they relate to the basic COM services discussed in Chapter 2 as well as to traditional transaction processing systems. You should also have a good understanding of the application server programming model.

> **NOTE** The ideas presented in this chapter will still apply when COM+ is available. However, some of the details of how things work will change. Chapter 16 provides an overview of COM+ and how it will impact the material covered in this book.

Why MTS?

Distributed applications are all about sharing—sharing data and other resources with all the people who need them. Writing applications that work correctly in a multiuser environment is difficult. Writing applications that both work correctly and perform acceptably is even more difficult. Let's take a quick look at some of the technical issues involved.

First, code must work correctly when it is called concurrently by multiple clients. Access to internal state must be synchronized so that changes aren't lost and all clients see the results they expect. A good example of this is the reference count within a free-threaded COM object. If two concurrent calls are made to *IUnknown AddRef*, the reference count stored in the object must always increase by 2. Otherwise, the object might destroy itself before all the clients have finished using it, and pandemonium would ensue.

Second, access to persistent data must be coordinated so that changes aren't lost and clients don't see partially updated, inconsistent data. This requirement applies both to multiple clients accessing a single data source and to a single client accessing multiple data sources. Regardless of where the data sources are located and who is accessing them, the integrity of the data must be maintained. A classic example here is updating a bank account. Let's say that you have $500 in your checking account and that you use an ATM to make a transfer of $1,000 from a credit card to your account. At the same time, the bank is processing checks drawn on your account for $200. When you finish the credit card transfer and the bank finishes processing the checks, both you and the bank want the balance in your checking account to be $1,300. Not $300 because the record of your $1,000 deposit was lost. Nor $1,500 because the record of the checks was lost. Likewise, you don't want to see a credit card charge for $1,000 without a corresponding deposit to your checking account, and the credit card company doesn't want you to see a deposit without the corresponding charge.

Third, access to code and data must be secure. Businesses want to share information with the people who need it, but they don't want to share it with everyone in the world! Furthermore, different people might need different types of access. For example, you can view the balance of your bank account at an ATM machine, and you can make deposits and withdrawals up to a certain dollar limit. A bank teller, on the other hand, can access information and process transactions for any customer's account. Some transactions can be performed only by a bank manager. Other actions, such as changing your name and address, can be performed by bank employees who cannot access any other account information.

Fourth, distributed applications must be able to scale to meet the needs of large numbers of users. Applications must be able to share limited resources rather than dedicating individual resources to each user. Many different types of limited resources exist in a distributed system, and all must be managed. Processes, threads, memory, database connections, you name it—unless resources are shared, there won't be enough to go around if 10,000 users are accessing your application at the same time.

Finally, the cost of administering and deploying distributed applications must be kept to a minimum. Installing or updating an application should not disrupt normal business operations. Administrative tasks should be as simple as possible to reduce errors. Applications must be reliable so that employees can do their work without waiting for the computer to be "fixed."

The goal of MTS is to make it as easy as possible for component and application developers to meet these technical challenges. It does this by providing a powerful run-time environment that does as much of the difficult work as possible in a generic way that all applications can use. One part of the run time is an execution environment for COM objects. This environment addresses the code concurrency, resource management, and security issues noted earlier. A second part of the run time is a transaction manager. Transactions are the standard technique for coordinating data updates across multiple data stores and multiple users. A simple yet powerful programming model takes advantage of the run time so that developers can focus on writing custom business logic, not application server infrastructure. MTS also provides administrative tools to help simplify deployment and maintenance.

The Many Faces of MTS

At first glance, MTS can be difficult to categorize. It doesn't seem to map neatly to an equivalent product or technology used by existing distributed computing environments. MTS represents a new breed of technology that combines features from traditional distributed object technologies and traditional online transaction processing (OLTP) to provide the following services to applications:

- MTS acts as an Object Request Broker (ORB).

- MTS acts as a surrogate process for COM objects.

- MTS acts as a Transaction Processing Monitor (TP-Monitor).

An ORB is quite simply a broker of objects. When a call comes in to a server requesting an object, the ORB handles the call, checks for availability, and ultimately gives the caller an object. A TP-Monitor is basically an environment that inserts itself between clients and server resources so that it can manage transactions and system resources. A traditional TP-Monitor knows nothing about objects—it only knows how to optimize the use of system resources. An obvious evolutionary path is to combine the features of ORBs and TP-Monitors. This new TP-Monitor is sometimes called an *Object Transaction Monitor* (OTM).

An OTM treats objects as just another kind of server resource that can be managed within a transaction boundary. By itself, an OTM isn't very interesting. Ultimately, the OTM is just a tool that developers can use to build scalable distributed applications. MTS is the world's first publicly available OTM.

MTS as an ORB

MTS provides its object brokering services by intercepting object creation. As we saw in Chapter 2, COM looks in the system registry to determine where a component is located. So to intercept object creation, all MTS needs to do is modify the registry settings to point to code that belongs to MTS.

All components that will use MTS services are required to be in-process components. When a component is registered using the MTS administrative tools, the InprocServer32 registry key for each COM class in the component is replaced by a LocalServer32 key that points to the MTS Surrogate, MTX.EXE, and identifies the component's *package ID*. We will talk about packages in more detail in the section "Packages" later in this chapter. For now, you can think of the package ID as a key that identifies additional configuration information about how the Surrogate should be run and which components should be loaded into the running process.

MTS intercepts object creation so that it can associate an *object context* with every object under its control. The object context keeps track of information about the current *activity,* which is simply a logical thread of execution through a set of objects that starts when a client calls into an MTS process. MTS also creates a *context wrapper* for each object. The context wrapper lets MTS sit between an object and its client(s) and observe all calls to the object. MTS provides its resource management services via the object context and context wrapper.

Figure 4-1 illustrates how object creation works under MTS. A client application, *C*, requests a new object in the usual way—for example, by calling *CoCreateInstance*. The COM run time looks in the registry to determine the location of the required component, *M*. It sees the LocalServer32 key and launches MTX.EXE, passing it a command-line parameter identifying the package ID. When the surrogate process is launched, it loads the MTS Executive, MTXEX.DLL, to initialize MTS services and the specified package. Then COM looks for the class factory for the object. However, the class factory COM gets is actually provided by the MTS Executive, not by the component *M*. When COM calls *IClassFactory CreateInstance* to create the new object, the MTS-provided class factory uses information provided by component *M* to create a context wrapper and passes the wrapper back to COM (and ultimately to the client) as the new object. As far as client *C* is concerned, the context wrapper *is* the new object. The context wrapper exposes all the interfaces exposed by the real object. The MTS-provided class factory also creates an object context, which is associated with the context wrapper.

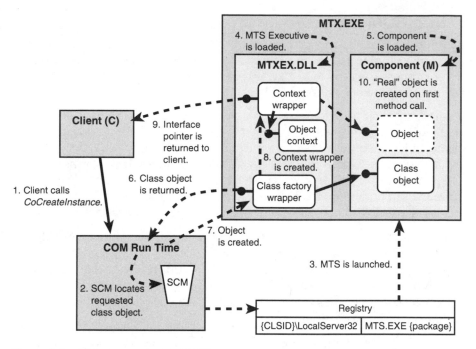

Figure 4-1. *Object creation in MTS.*

Notice that nowhere in this description is anything said about using the component to create the actual object. In fact, it isn't necessary for the real object to be created until a client calls it. MTS uses this fact to manage resource usage by objects in its server processes.

The first time a client makes a method call other than *QueryInterface*, *AddRef*, or *Release*, the context wrapper will create a real object. This process is called *activating* the object. The real object stays in memory until the object itself indicates that it can be *deactivated*. An object indicates that it can be deactivated by calling one of two special methods exposed by the object context, *IObjectContext SetComplete* or *IObjectContext SetAbort*. We'll see why two methods are provided in the section "The Application Server Programming Model" later in this chapter. For now, all we need to know is that both methods simply indicate that the object has finished its work. When an object is deactivated, MTS can choose to reclaim all resources associated with the object—including the memory allocated for the object itself. The next time a client makes a method call on the object, if the real object has been destroyed, the context wrapper creates another real object. This process is known as *Just-In-Time (JIT) activation*.

MTS as a COM Surrogate

As mentioned, all components using MTS services must be in-process components so that all objects can be created within MTS-managed *server processes*. A server process uses the MTS Executive to provide the run-time support required by component-based, scalable application servers.

As a surrogate, MTS provides context management and JIT activation, as described earlier. It manages threads for the process and correctly synchronizes access to objects, so developers do not need to write multi-threaded components. It determines when the process should terminate. It performs security checks on calls into the process to prevent unauthorized clients from using components. In addition, MTS helps manage other resources, such as database connections, using resource pooling so that applications scale and perform well.

MTS also provides transparent access to a distributed transaction manager known as the Microsoft Distributed Transaction Coordinator (MS DTC). Components can be registered with the MTS administrative tools as supporting or requiring transactions. When an object is created, MTS will check whether transaction support is needed. If so, MTS creates a new transaction if necessary and enlists the object in the transaction automatically.

Because MTS is managing all the objects used in its environment, it imposes certain rules on components. In addition to being in-process, each component must provide a class object that exposes the *IClassFactory* interface. Objects running in MTS cannot be aggregated, nor can they create their own threads.

Components in MTS cannot use custom marshaling. MTS cannot create a context wrapper for a custom-marshaled object. Components that expose Automation or dual interfaces must provide a type library. MTS will use the information in the type library to generate the context wrapper. Components that expose interfaces that cannot be marshaled by the Automation marshaler must provide a proxy/stub DLL built in a special way so that MTS can determine what the interface looks like even if no type library is available.

MTS as a TP-Monitor

A TP-Monitor is system software for creating, executing, and managing transaction processing applications. Since transaction processing might be unfamiliar to developers who've worked primarily on PCs, let's do a quick review before we look at how transactions are handled by MTS.

Transaction theory

A transaction is simply a way to coordinate a set of operations on multiple resources. Transactions have the following four properties, known as the ACID properties:

- *Atomicity*

- *Consistency*

- *Isolation*

- *Durability*

Atomicity means that a single transaction has all-or-nothing behavior. In the bank account example mentioned earlier, *Atomicity* is the property that ensures that a transfer from your credit card to your checking account has one of two results. If the transfer succeeds, your credit card is debited and your checking account is credited with the amount of the transfer. If the transfer fails, your credit card is not debited and your checking account is not credited. Debiting the credit card without crediting the checking account is not permitted, nor is crediting the checking account without debiting the credit card. The transfer is all-or-nothing. A transaction that succeeds is said to *commit*. A transaction that fails is said to *abort*.

Consistency ensures that at the end of a transaction, no integrity constraints on the resources it updates are violated. For example, an ATM won't let you withdraw more money than you have in your bank account.

Isolation ensures that concurrent transactions do not interfere with each other. If transactions *T1* and *T2* are concurrent, when both have completed the results will be the same as if *T1* completed before *T2* started or as if *T2* completed before *T1* started. No other results are acceptable. In our bank account example, the *Isolation* property ensures that neither the results of the credit card transfer nor the results of the check processing disappear.

Durability means that changes to resources survive system failures, including process faults, network failures, or even hardware failures. Once a transaction has completed successfully, the results will never be lost.

TP-Monitors ensure that transactions are *Atomic, Isolated,* and *Durable*. TP-Monitors work with transaction processing programs to ensure that transactions are also *Consistent*.

A generic transaction processing model

Let's look now at a generic model for a distributed transaction processing (DTP) system. In this model, applications use a transaction manager to coordinate (create, commit, abort, or monitor) transactions. The transaction manager is responsible for ensuring that all parties in the transaction are notified of the outcome (commit or abort) and coordinating recovery from failures. Each server machine in a distributed system can have a transaction manager. Transaction managers can talk to other transaction managers or to local *resource managers,* as shown in Figure 4-2 on the following page.

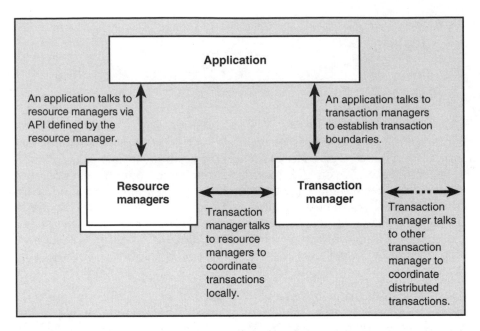

Figure 4-2. *A generic transaction processing model.*

A resource manager guarantees that the ACID properties of a particular resource remain consistent. The resource manager consists of some server code that knows how to commit updates to a resource, roll back changes in the case of an aborted transaction, and recover from system failures. The most common example of a resource manager is a database management system (DBMS), but this is not the only kind of resource manager, as we'll see in the section "Resource managers in MTS" later in this chapter.

> **NOTE**   You might recognize this model as a simple form of the X/Open DTP model. X/Open is part of The Open Group, an international consortium of hardware and software vendors that defines vendor-independent standards for distributed computing. The X/Open DTP model was introduced in 1991 and encompasses the standard features of most TP-Monitors.

Two-phase commit

When all the resources modified in a transaction are owned by a single resource manager, the resource manager itself can perform all the work required to commit the transaction. The resource manager ensures that either all the resource modifications occur or none of them occur, and it notifies the transaction manager of the outcome. For example, if two tables in the same Microsoft SQL Server database are updated, SQL Server, the resource manager, coordinates the updates.

When a transaction updates resources owned by two or more resource managers and perhaps located on different machines, the transaction manager needs to get into the act to ensure the *Atomicity* property of the transaction. This requirement is difficult to meet because machines can fail and recover independently. The solution is a special protocol called *two-phase commit* that is coordinated by the transaction manager. The two-phase commit protocol is illustrated in Figure 4-3. For simplicity, we will look at the single-machine case, with one transaction manager (known as the *coordinator*) coordinating multiple local resource managers (known as the *participants*).

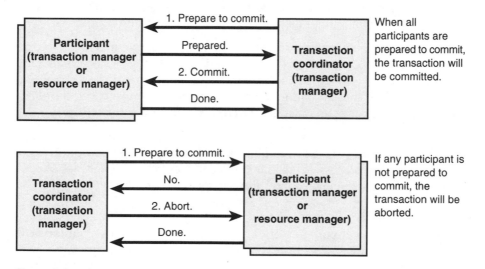

Figure 4-3. *The two-phase commit protocol.*

The protocol consists, appropriately enough, of two phases: prepare and commit. In the first phase, the transaction manager notifies each resource manager enlisted in the transaction to prepare to commit. At this point, each resource manager tries to save its results in durable storage, without actually committing the changes. Because the resource values have not yet been changed, the resource manager is now prepared to either commit the changes or roll back to the previous values. If the resource manager was able to save its results, it sends a message back to the transaction manager voting to commit the transaction. Otherwise, the resource manager sends a message to the transaction manager voting to abort the transaction.

When the transaction manager receives votes from all the resource managers, it proceeds to the second phase. (If a transaction manager does not receive a vote within a reasonable amount of time, it assumes that the resource manager has voted to abort the transaction.) At this point, the transaction manager tallies the votes. If everyone votes to commit, the transaction will be committed. If anyone votes to abort, the transaction will be aborted. The transaction manager sends a second round of messages to all the resource managers, informing them of the transaction outcome. The resource managers are responsible for honoring the decision of the transaction manager. If the transaction is committed, the resource manager commits the changes to its resources. If the transaction is aborted, the resources are rolled back to their prior values. If a resource manager fails before it is notified of the outcome of a transaction, it contacts the transaction manager as part of error recovery, asking for the outcome of its pending transactions. At this point, it can continue with its part of the two-phase commit protocol.

The protocol works in essentially the same way across multiple machines, except that multiple transaction managers are involved, usually one per machine. One transaction manager is selected as the transaction coordinator. The remaining transaction managers act as intermediaries between the transaction coordinator and the local resource managers that are enlisted in the transaction.

> **NOTE** If you are interested in a more comprehensive overview of transaction processing, see Bernstein and Newcomer, "Principles of Transaction Processing," listed in the bibliography.

Transactions in MTS

Now that you have a general idea of transaction processing, let's examine how MTS handles transactions. We've already looked at the MTS Surrogate, MTX.EXE, and the MTS Executive, MTXEX.DLL. These parts of MTS provide the server process that MTS components run in. They also provide the process for auxiliary components such as resource dispensers (more on these in a moment) and in-process COM components that are not controlled by MTS, such as ADO. Multiple server processes can run on a single machine. The MTS Executive is also responsible for creating the context wrappers and object contexts for its objects, so it can monitor calls to the object and manage system resources appropriately.

The MS DTC The transaction manager in an MTS environment is the MS DTC. The MS DTC runs as a Windows NT service and is usually started at system start-up. A copy of the MS DTC runs on each machine that will participate in transactions, but only one copy coordinates a particular transaction.

The MS DTC uses a COM-based protocol, OLE Transactions, to communicate with resource managers. OLE Transactions defines the interfaces that applications, resource managers, and transaction managers use to perform transactions.

Applications use OLE Transactions interfaces to initiate, commit, abort, and inquire about transactions. Resource managers use OLE Transactions interfaces to enlist in transactions, to propagate transactions from process to process or from system to system, and to participate in the two-phase commit protocol.

The X/Open Distributed Transaction Processing group has also defined protocols for communicating with transaction managers. The TX standard defines the API that an application uses to communicate with the transaction manager. Applications use the API to initiate, commit, and abort transactions. The XA standard defines an API for resource managers to communicate with transaction managers. The XA API enables resource managers to enlist in transactions, to perform two-phase commits, and to recover in-doubt transactions following a failure.

The MS DTC uses OLE Transactions instead of the X/Open protocols for several reasons. First, Microsoft's computing model is based on distributed, transaction-protected, object-based components that communicate using COM interfaces. To fit this model, the transaction interfaces needed to be object-based, unlike the X/Open protocols. Second, Microsoft intends to extend the transaction model to support a wide variety of transaction-protected resources beyond the usual database resources. Since OLE Transactions is based on COM, it can easily be extended to provide richer transaction capabilities. Third, OLE Transactions supports multi-threaded programs, whereas XA is oriented toward a single thread of control. Finally, unlike OLE Transactions, the X/Open standard does not support recovery that is initiated by the resource manager; therefore, all recovery must be initiated by the transaction manager.

Resource managers in MTS Resource managers in MTS fulfill the same role as resource managers in the X/Open model—they are services that manage durable state and understand how to participate in the two-phase commit protocol. Resource managers are responsible for logging all changes, so they can handle rollbacks when a transaction aborts or recovers from a system failure. The most commonly used resource managers for MTS are DBMSs such as SQL Server. However, MTS does not impose any constraints on the type of resource, as long as there is a resource manager that meets the criteria defined by OLE Transactions. For example, Microsoft Message Queue Server (MSMQ) provides a resource manager.

Because the X/Open protocols are widely supported by other transaction and resource managers, the MS DTC provides some interoperability with products that comply with the XA standard. OLE Transactions provides a mapping layer to convert XA functions to OLE Transactions functions. OLE Transactions–compliant resource managers can be controlled by XA-based transaction managers, such as Tuxedo or Encina, and XA-based resource managers can be controlled by the MS DTC.

Resource dispensers in MTS   *Resource dispensers* are another part of MTS that can choose to participate in transactions. Resource dispensers manage non-durable state that can be shared—for example, database connections, network connections, and connections to queues as well as threads, objects, and memory blocks. A resource dispenser is implemented as a DLL that exposes two sets of interfaces. One set of interfaces is an API that applications can call to use the resources. The other set is used to connect the resource dispensers with an MTS component called the Resource Dispenser Manager (DispMan). Figure 4-4 illustrates the position of DispMan in the MTS architecture.

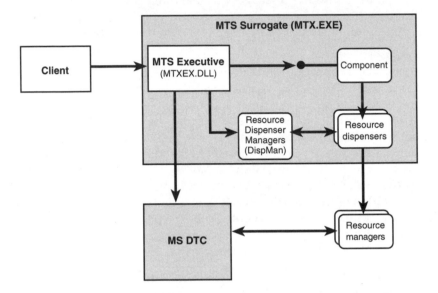

Figure 4-4. *The MTS architecture.*

DispMan provides *resource pooling* for the resource dispensers. Resource pooling improves performance, since applications usually don't need to wait for a new resource to be created from scratch. Instead, they just get an existing resource from the pool. Resource pools can also improve performance by limiting the number of resources that exist at a given time, which can help keep the server from getting bogged down. In MTS, resource pools are managed per-process.

If DispMan is running in an MTS environment, it works with the MTS Executive and the resource dispensers to ensure that resources supplied by the resource dispensers are correctly enlisted in transactions. Resource dispensers are not required to support transactions, but if they do, they must be able to enlist in an OLE Transactions transaction with the MS DTC. The MTS Executive notifies DispMan when a transaction is complete so that DispMan can move resources used by the transaction back into the resource pool. The MTS Executive also notifies DispMan whenever an object is destroyed so that DispMan can reclaim any resources used by the object, eliminating the possibility of resource leaks.

MTS 2.0 supplies two resource dispensers that are visible to developers. The ODBC Driver Manager is a resource dispenser for ODBC database connections. MTS also supplies the *Shared Property Manager* (SPM, pronounced "spam"), which is used to manage shared data. We will look at these resource dispensers in further detail when we discuss building components in Chapters 8 and 9.

In MTS, objects (the real objects, not the context wrappers the client is talking to) can participate in only one transaction at a time. Objects are enlisted in transactions on activation and are recycled when the transaction commits or aborts. Objects call *IObjectContext SetComplete* to indicate that they have finished their work and vote to commit the transaction. Objects call *IObjectContext SetAbort* to indicate that they have finished their work and vote to abort the transaction. Either way, MTS will reclaim an object's resources—including its internal memory—when the transaction ends.

Failfast behavior   MTS-managed processes exhibit a behavior known as *failfast*. Failfast behavior means that if the MTS Executive detects an error in its internal data structures or a problem with one of the objects under its control, it immediately terminates the process. This design decision protects MTS and its components from data corruption. When the MTS process is restarted, MTS does not attempt to re-create the state of objects that might have been running when the process shut down. Instead, MTS relies on the fact that transactions using those objects will time out and then abort. Applications that detect a transaction failure can elect to retry the transaction at a later time, using new objects in the new process.

Nested Transactions or Chained Transactions

Developers familiar with other TP-Monitors often ask whether MTS supports nested or chained transactions. In transaction processing theory, *nested transactions* permit transactions to have subtransactions. The parent transaction does not commit until all subtransactions have committed, and subtransaction results are not made durable until the parent commits. Effectively, objects in a subtransaction would belong to both the parent transaction and the subtransaction. MTS does not support nested transactions. MTS does support starting a new transaction from within an existing transaction, but the transactions succeed or fail independently.

Chained transactions permit a transaction program to commit a transaction and immediately start another, maintaining its internal state across the transaction boundary. MTS does not support chained transactions either. In practice, this usually isn't a problem, but it might require a different way of thinking about transaction boundaries than you have used with other TP-Monitors.

In addition to the MTS run-time components, MTS also provides administrative tools for deploying and monitoring applications. We will examine the administrative tools in detail (well, in as much detail as developers can probably stand) in Part Two, when we talk about packaging, debugging, and testing applications.

The Application Server Programming Model

At this point, you should have a pretty good idea of the services provided by MTS. MTS specifies some rules that components and applications must follow in order to use these services. In addition, the behavior of the services has a definite impact on how application servers should be designed. We'll discuss the general concepts of the programming model here and the specifics in Part Two.

The application server programming model is based on two fundamental ideas:

- The model must be accessible to the typical corporate developer.

- Scalable applications share resources.

Making It Easier

Most developers are not experts at component-based design and database theory and transaction processing theory and multi-threading and networking and everything else that makes up the typical corporate distributed application. A key goal for the application server programming model is to make it possible for a developer to contribute to application server development without expertise in all these areas.

MTS accomplishes this goal by providing the infrastructure services required by all application servers. The programming model strongly encourages developers to follow its rules and let MTS take care of the plumbing. The basic COM programming model offers a lot of options for creating components; the application server programming model specifies which options to use for components that run within the MTS environment. These options correspond to the options best supported by the widest range of COM-aware programming tools, as listed here:

- Components are implemented as in-process COM components.

- Components are written as if they will be used by a single user at a time (that is, supporting the COM apartment threading model).

- Components provide a standard class object (supporting the *IClassFactory* interface).

- Components use standard marshaling for all exposed interfaces, which are usually Automation or dual interfaces.

This correspondence means that a senior developer or application designer can hand a developer on the project team a specification for a component and the developer can use wizards or other assistants provided by his or her programming tools to create the skeleton of the component with very little effort. The developer can then focus on implementing the business logic of the component. For many components, the developer will not need to worry at all about the fact that the component will be used in a distributed, multiuser environment. As developers become more familiar with the distributed application environment, they can take on responsibility for more complex components and design issues.

Scalability Through Sharing

Resources used by application servers are limited: only a finite amount of memory, processing power, network bandwidth, database connections, and so on is available for use. Dedicating resources for individual client use is not very efficient because most of the time the resources are just sitting around waiting for the client to do something. Like get back from lunch...

Application servers achieve scalability by sharing resources. As we've seen, MTS provides the infrastructure support for resource sharing. However, MTS needs some help from the objects it manages to determine when it is safe to discard or recycle resources that are in use. The programming model defines five simple rules for how applications and components should be written to share resources most effectively, listed here:

Rule 1: Objects should call *SetComplete* as often as possible.

Rule 2: Base clients should acquire and hold interface pointers.

Rule 3: Objects should acquire resources late and release them as soon as possible.

Rule 4: Application servers should use role-based declarative security.

Rule 5: Application servers should use transactions when appropriate.

Rule 1: Call *SetComplete*

As mentioned, clients don't really hold interface pointers to objects in the application server process—they hold interface pointers to context wrappers generated by the MTS Executive. MTS uses the context wrapper and its associated object context to perform JIT activation and as-soon-as-possible deactivation of objects running in application server. JIT activation improves scalability by reclaiming resources associated with objects that no one is actively using.

The MTS Executive cannot determine on its own when it's safe to deactivate an object. The object needs to tell MTS when it can be deactivated, and it does this by calling *SetComplete* or *SetAbort*. Calling one of these methods helps ensure that transactions and resources are not held for long periods of time.

SetComplete and *SetAbort* are two methods of the *IObjectContext* interface exposed by the object context, as shown in Figure 4-5. The object context keeps track of information about the object, such as the activity it belongs to, the transaction it belongs to, and its security identity. *IObjectContext* is the primary way objects communicate with the MTS Executive. A component can access an object's object context by calling the aptly named *GetObjectContext* method, which returns an *IObjectContext* interface pointer. Once it has the interface pointer, the component can call either the *SetComplete* method or the *SetAbort* method to indicate that it has finished its work, and the object's state and resources can be reclaimed. *SetComplete* is called if an object wants to indicate that it has completed successfully and votes to commit any transaction it is enlisted in. *SetAbort* is called if the object votes to abort its transaction.

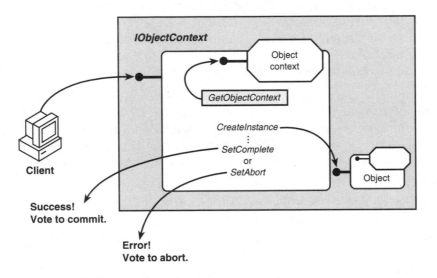

Figure 4-5. *Using the object context.*

You might be wondering what's meant by "call *SetComplete* as often as possible." This notion turns out to be one of the key design points in building application servers. Conceptually, when an object is deactivated everything about that object stored in memory in the application server process disappears. Completely. When an object is reactivated, it must be treated exactly like a newly created object. Clients cannot make any other assumptions about the state of the object. So calling *SetComplete* "as often as possible" means calling it whenever it is safe for the object's in-memory state to disappear.

In the extreme case, *SetComplete* can be called at the end of every method implementation. Objects exist only while being called by a client. Components that are written this way are known as *stateless components* because they retain no per-object state in memory between method calls.

NOTE Many people believe that MTS requires developers to write state-less components. This is not true. MTS provides services to help developers *manage* state effectively. Stateless components are the right approach for many situations, but not for all. The state information needs to be kept *somewhere*, after all. If retrieving the state from wherever it's stored is more expensive than keeping the object in memory between method calls, a stateful component might be more appropriate.

Types of state

When you are deciding what approach is appropriate for a specific component, it's useful to think about the places state can be kept and the cost of accessing the state from an object. The four basic types of state are *client-managed state, per-object state, shared transient state,* and *persistent state.*

Client-managed state   Client-managed state is information kept by the caller. Objects don't really care about any client-managed state, except when it is passed to the object as parameters of a method call.

State that's kept on the client doesn't need to be remembered on the application server, freeing up server resources. However, there are transmission costs associated with moving the state back and forth between the client and the object. Transmission costs depend on how large the state is and the relative locations of the client and object.

In most cases, state that's transmitted to the object as method parameters does not need to be stored in the object at all. The method implementation simply uses the parameters directly.

Per-object state   Per-object state—what developers with an object-oriented background think of simply as "state"—consists of the data members of the object defined by the object class implementation. One of the reasons stateless objects cause so much consternation is that the whole concept of an object without any data members isn't very meaningful in the object-oriented world. Don't panic. You *can* have per-object state in MTS-managed components—you just have to be careful how you use it.

One issue with per-object state is that it is transient. If the system fails, the state is lost. A larger issue, however, is that as long as the state must be maintained, MTS cannot deactivate the object and reclaim its resources. These resources go beyond the memory consumed by the object itself.

For example, the MTS environment provides thread management and concurrency control services to objects. This lets developers write components as if the components will be used by a single client at a time, yet still build scalable application servers. MTS 2.0 maintains a pool of up to 100 STA threads for each MTS-managed server process. When a client calls into the process, MTS picks an unused thread from the pool. The apartment associated with this thread will be used for all objects activated in the process during the current activity. So far, so good. But what happens when all the threads are in use?

As it turns out, MTS 2.0 starts picking from *used* threads once the pool is consumed. Remember that in a single-threaded apartment, access to all objects created in the apartment is synchronized, so at most one object executes concurrently. This is fine for objects in the same activity. By definition, MTS ensures that calls within the activity are serialized anyway. However, if objects from multiple activities are sharing a single apartment, all but one of these activities will be blocked at any given time. This limits performance and scalability of the application server.

What does this have to do with per-object state? Remember too that an apartment threaded object is tied to the thread it was created on for its entire lifetime. If you are maintaining per-object state and your object cannot be deactivated, your object is tying up a thread from the thread pool, increasing the chances that threads will need to be used by multiple concurrent activities.

Using per-object state can also complicate transactions. MTS does not let you maintain per-object state across transaction boundaries. As long as a transactional object does not call *SetComplete*, its transaction cannot commit. The transaction can time out, however, causing the transaction to abort. If you have components that need to participate in transactions, you need to think carefully about using per-object state.

Shared transient state   Shared transient state is state in which process-wide information is stored. It is useful for state that must be shared across transaction boundaries or by multiple clients but that can be lost if the system fails. (Think global variables...)

One difficulty with using shared transient state in a multiuser environment is that the state must be protected from concurrent access. MTS provides the SPM to help manage shared transient state. The SPM ensures that shared state can't be read while it is being updated and that only one activity can update the shared state at a time. We'll look at the SPM in detail in Chapter 9.

The cost of using shared transient state is primarily the memory cost of storing the state. Some overhead also occurs in locating the desired state. Shared state can create a performance bottleneck if state is frequently updated or updates take a long amount of time, since access is serialized.

Persistent state   Unlike other types of state, persistent state survives system failures. Persistent state is stored in durable storage, such as a DBMS, and exists whether or not the client application or application server is executing.

Keeping persistent state consistent in a distributed, multiuser environment is a complex task. As we've seen, transactions are the standard technique for coordinating updates across multiple data stores and multiple users.

Several costs are associated with persistent state. First is the cost of accessing the data store. Second is the cost of any transactions. And last is the cost of copying data into memory. For many applications, any performance costs are more than offset by the benefits of durable storage and transactional updates. Of the four types of state, persistent state is the only type of state that is rolled back on aborted transactions.

Most distributed applications will use all four types of state at some point. The tricky part is figuring out which type to use when. We'll come back to this issue in Chapter 7. For now, the key thing to remember is that calling *SetComplete* as often as possible helps MTS manage application server resources efficiently.

Rule 2: Acquire and Hold Interface Pointers

Let's turn our attention for a moment to the clients calling into application servers. In MTS, any code that calls an MTS-managed object is called a *client*. A client that is not part of an MTS-managed process is known as a *base client*.

If a base client might make many calls to the same type of object, the client should acquire the interface pointers it needs and hold onto them. The reason for this is simple: base clients and application servers normally run on separate machines. Locating the correct server machine, negotiating the network protocol to use for DCOM, establishing a connection, and getting the interface pointer is a relatively expensive process compared to holding onto an established connection. JIT activation on the server ensures that resources aren't tied up unnecessarily if the object isn't being used.

Clients that hold interface pointers *do* need to be aware of how the objects they're calling manage state. Stateless objects aren't a problem. The client will pass any information needed by the object as method parameters. Each time the client uses the object, it acts like a completely new object. Stateful objects can cause trouble, however. The client needs to understand when the object state might be reset, as well as any restrictions on the order in which methods are called. This behavior should be documented as part of the interface definition, and once published it is as immutable as any other part of the interface definition.

Rule 3: Use and Release Resources

Within the application server, the rules are a little different. The goal here is to share resources as much as possible. Most resources need to be shared because they are scarce. For example, a database server might be licensed for a certain number of concurrent connections. Once the connections are gone, incoming requests will fail until a connection is freed up. The less time an object holds onto a resource, the more likely objects will be able to acquire the resource when they want it.

One potential drawback to this approach is the cost of acquiring resources over and over again. Initialization costs can be quite high for things like database connections. The cost can be reduced by pooling resources once they've been initialized. After an object has finished with a resource, the resource can be placed into a pool. The next time an object needs to acquire a resource, it looks in the pool first and creates a new resource only if necessary. For some resources, pools can be populated by background threads while the application server is idle, further reducing the apparent cost of acquiring those resources.

As we've seen, in MTS automatic resource pooling is provided by DispMan and resource dispensers. DispMan works with the MTS Executive to ensure that resources are reclaimed when objects are deactivated or transactions are complete. Thus, at a minimum objects must not try to hold onto resources across transaction boundaries. The sooner an object releases a resource it has been using, the sooner that resource is available for reuse.

Rule 4: Use Role-Based Security

Securing access to components and resources is critical in distributed computing. In Windows NT, access to resources is controlled by access control lists (ACLs). Users are authorized to use a resource if their user ID appears in the ACL with the permissions needed for a particular operation. For example, John might have read-only access to the Employee Records database, whereas Mary has read/write access. As we saw in Chapter 2, COM extends this user/resource model to support components.

It's tempting to argue that this security model does not scale well. Applications consist of many components accessing many resources. As the number of users increases, so does the burden of maintaining all the ACLs. If individual user identities must be used to run components or access resources, objects and resources cannot be shared across users, severely limiting the number of users who can be supported by the application server.

This argument rings false, however. Certainly the COM security model permits applications to be developed and deployed in such a way that resources cannot be shared and maintenance is a nightmare, but it does not force applications to be developed or deployed this way. Windows NT groups can overcome much of the administrative burden of maintaining ACLs for components. In addition, in the three-tier application, users do not directly access resources—components do. Components can be configured to run as specific user identities, and only those identities need access to resources used by the components. If the components are running as a specific identity, objects and resources can be shared.

The real argument against COM security is not that building and maintaining scalable applications is impossible, just that it is harder than it ought to be. The COM security model is very much a *physical* model, closely tied to implementation details. To use it effectively, developers and administrators need to worry too much about plumbing. Developers generally need to write some code to manage call security, and the code is hard to get right without a good understanding of COM security. Developers must also understand how the underlying security providers and remote procedure call (RPC) authentication work, or application development and testing can quickly become a frustrating exercise in trial and error. In addition, system administrators need to understand too much about COM security and RPC authentication in order to use the DCOM Configuration (DCOMCNFG) tool during application deployment.

Enter MTS. MTS defines a new *conceptual* model for security, based on roles and packages. With MTS role-based security, developers and administrators can focus on the big picture—who should be allowed to do what with the system—rather than the plumbing required to secure their applications. Generally, developers do not need to write any security-related code. They simply declare the type of security they want, and the MTS Executive takes care of the details. Thus, role-based security is sometimes called *declarative security* or *automatic security*. Of course, there are some situations in which security decisions rely on information only available at run time, so MTS also provides programmatic access to security information.

Roles

Let's start by looking at authorization security in the MTS model. Authorization security determines whether a client is allowed to use a particular object. MTS performs authorization checks on calls into MTS-managed server processes, as shown in Figure 4-6 on the following page. Authorization checking can be enabled or disabled for the process as a whole. If it's enabled for a process, authorization can be disabled for specific COM classes hosted by the process.

If authorization checking is enabled, MTS must determine whether individual calls to objects should be allowed. This is where *roles* come in. A role is simply a logical group of clients that are permitted to access objects or interfaces. Each role has a human-readable name. Roles usually map directly to real-world concepts, which can be helpful when you try to define security requirements for your customers and then translate those requirements into the application design and implementation. For example, the banking application shown in Figure 4-6 has Teller, Manager, and BankObjects roles. Managers are allowed to call objects created by component A and BankObjects are allowed to call objects created by component B. Developers can define whatever roles are needed to describe each type of client that should have access to their applications.

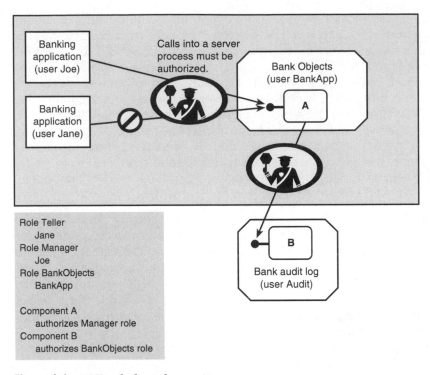

Role Teller
    Jane
Role Manager
    Joe
Role BankObjects
    BankApp

Component A
    authorizes Manager role
Component B
    authorizes BankObjects role

Figure 4-6. *MTS role-based security.*

Before clients can access secured applications, roles must be bound to specific users or groups. Administrators populate roles during application deployment, using the MTS administrative tools. In our example, user Joe is assigned to the Manager role, and Jane is assigned to the Teller role. At run time, the MTS Executive intercepts each call, determines the caller's identity, and figures out which roles the caller is a member of. If the caller is a member of a role that is allowed to access the type of object or interface being called, the call proceeds. Otherwise, the call fails with a security error. Figure 4-6 shows that Joe is allowed to call object A since he is a Manager but that Jane is not allowed to call object A. Likewise, the *Bank Objects* process is allowed to call object B because it is running as the BankApp user, which is a member of the Bank-Objects role.

All this happens automatically, without any custom code in each component, even for relatively sophisticated security requirements like restricting access to specific interfaces exposed by an object. Design and deployment issues are clearly separated. Developers decide what type of security is needed, but they don't need to worry at all about specific user accounts or security providers. Administrators decide which users are allowed to perform roles defined by the application, but they don't need to understand how the plumbing works.

Packages

As mentioned, MTS performs authorization checks on calls into a server process. Think about this for a minute. An MTS server process hosts one or more components. These components share an address space, threads, resource pools, and so on. It seems reasonable that calls from one object to another within the process should not require authorization checks. Only calls coming from outside the process need to be checked.

This raises the question, how does MTS know what components should run in the same process? In the MTS model, components that should run together are collected into *packages*. A package is a set of components that perform related application functions. Packages are the primary unit of administration and trust in MTS. Components are added to packages using the MTS administrative tools. These tools are also used to set MTS-specific options for packages and their components. We'll see how to use the primary administrative tool, MTS Explorer, to manage packages in Chapters 10 and 14.

Most security settings in the role-based model are established at the package level, which greatly simplifies administration of components running under MTS. There are two types of packages: *library packages* and *server packages*. A library package runs in the process of the client that creates it. Library packages are useful for utility components used by multiple applications. A server package runs as a separate MTS-managed process. Only server packages can be secured using MTS.

If authorization checking is required for an application, a developer will create a server package and add the components to the package. The developer enables authorization checking for the package. If some COM classes in the package do not require authorization checks, the developer can disable checks on those classes. The developer then defines roles for the package. Once the roles are defined, the developer can specify which roles are allowed to access each COM class in the package and, optionally, which roles are allowed to access specific interfaces exposed by each class. At deployment time, an administrator will populate the roles defined for the package with actual users and groups.

MTS also lets developers and administrators define other process-wide security settings. The authentication level used for COM calls to each package can be specified to establish how frequently client credentials are authenticated. The package can also be configured to run as a specific user identity. This simplifies administration, since only that identity must be granted access to resources used by the package. It is not necessary to grant all clients of the package access to the resources. Running a package as a specific identity also helps with resource consumption. In general, resources such as database connections cannot be shared by clients running as different identities. This helps ensure that an unauthorized client can't get access to the resource. If a package runs as a specific identity, package-wide resource pools can be used to share resources across components and calling applications.

Programmatic security

With role-based security, authorization checks are performed only on entry to a package and are based solely on who is making the call and what method is being called. In some scenarios, this level of security is not sufficient. For example, bank withdrawals over a certain amount might require manager approval.

MTS provides two methods on the object context, *IsCallerInRole* and *IsSecurityEnabled*, to help developers implement programmatic authorization checks. The *IsCallerInRole* method is used to determine whether the client making a method call is a member of a given role. *IsSecurityEnabled* is used to determine whether authorization checking is enabled. (If security is not enabled, it doesn't make a lot of sense to check whether the client is in a particular role.) These methods are easily used from any language and completely hide the details of the underlying COM and Windows NT security services, as shown in this snippet of Microsoft Visual Basic code:

```
Dim ctxObject As ObjectContext
If (lngAmount > 500 or lngAmount < -500) Then
    Set ctxObject = GetObjectContext()
    If Not ctxObject Is Nothing Then
        If (ctxObject.IsSecurityEnabled and _
           ctxObject.IsCallerInRole("Manager")) Then
            ' Do normal work.
        Else
            ' Report error.
        End If
    End If
End If
```

If more detailed information about the caller is required, MTS also provides an advanced security interface, *ISecurityProperty*, on the object context. This interface is particularly useful for logging security violations. For most other situations, declarative security or simple role-based programmatic security checks are sufficient.

Rule 5: Use Transactions

Last but not least, developers should use transactions as appropriate in their application servers. We've already looked at transactions in general and how they work in MTS. Let's take a quick look at transactions from the programming model perspective.

In the application server programming model, multiple objects work together to provide services to client applications. In general, one object used by a particular client doesn't know anything about the other objects used by that client. For example, let's say you use an online banking application to pay your phone bill. Somewhere in the application are an object that knows how to send payment information to the phone company and an object that knows how to debit your checking account. There's no reason for these objects to know anything about each other. They perform completely independent tasks.

At a higher level, the application might contain a method named *PayPhoneBill* that knows how to use the payment and debit objects to perform the specified task. When all the subordinate objects complete their work successfully, implementing the higher-level behavior is straightforward. Things are considerably more interesting when you start thinking about error handling and recovery. Let's say the *PayPhoneBill* method is implemented something like this:

```
Debit checking account for amount of phone bill.
Credit phone company account for amount of phone bill.
Send payment information to phone company.
```

Now, what should the *PayPhoneBill* method do if sending the payment information fails? One approach would be for the method to carefully code compensating actions to undo the work it has already completed. But these actions are also subject to failure, and even if they were guaranteed to complete successfully, recovering from all the possible combinations of errors is going to add a lot of complexity to the implementation.

A better approach is to use transactions. Transactions ensure that resources are not permanently updated unless all the work done within the transaction completes successfully. For example, if sending payment information fails, the transaction aborts and no money is debited from your checking account or credited to the phone company account.

As with security, MTS provides declarative and programmatic support for transactions. Most developers will find declarative transactions, or automatic transactions, sufficient for their needs. To use automatic transactions, a component developer simply uses the MTS Explorer to specify the transactional attribute for each COM class. The possible attribute values are listed in the table on the following page.

Transaction Attribute	Description
Requires A Transaction	If caller is enlisted in a transaction, object will be enlisted in the same transaction. If caller is not enlisted in a transaction, a new transaction will be created and the object will be enlisted in the new transaction.
Requires A New Transaction	A new transaction will be created and the object will be enlisted in the transaction.
Supports Transactions	If caller is enlisted in a transaction, object will be enlisted in the same transaction. If caller is not enlisted in a transaction, the object will not be enlisted in any transaction.
Does Not Support Transactions	The object will not be enlisted in any transactions.

MTS uses the object context to pass information about transactions from clients to subordinate objects. The object context exposes the *IObjectContext Create-Instance* method for clients to create subordinate objects. This method should be used by components that will run within the MTS environment to create subordinate objects that run within MTS, to ensure that object context values flow correctly to the subordinate objects. Base clients can use normal COM object creation functions.

At run time, the MTS Executive will use the transaction attributes to automatically figure out when new transactions must be created and which transaction to enlist each object in, as shown in Figure 4-7. Developers call *IObjectContext SetComplete* to indicate when a transactional object has completed its work successfully and wants to vote to commit its transaction. When errors occur, developers call *IObjectContext SetAbort* to vote to abort the transaction.

When a new transaction is created, the first object enlisted in the transaction becomes the *root* of the transaction. A transaction exists until the root object signals it has completed its work by calling *SetComplete* or *SetAbort*. At this point, MTS uses the two-phase commit protocol to decide whether to commit or abort the transaction. When the transaction is committed or aborted, MTS deactivates all objects involved in the transaction. This technique helps enforce transaction isolation and consistency, in addition to freeing up resources for use by other transactions.

Note that transactions do not completely eliminate the need for error handling. Transactions simply ensure that persistent state managed by resource managers is updated correctly when multiple objects cooperate to implement some functionality. If a transaction aborts, shared transient state does not get rolled back. Nor does an object's call to *SetAbort* cause an immediate abort—the transaction continues until the root of the transaction has completed its work. So while the transaction is in progress, clients might still want to use errors returned from object method calls to decide whether to continue doing work. For example, in our *PayPhoneBill* method earlier, if crediting the phone company account fails, there's really no point in sending payment information to the phone company. The *Credit* method should call *SetAbort* to vote to abort any containing transaction *and* return a normal COM error. The *PayPhoneBill* method can then detect the COM error and elect to skip the *SendPayment* method.

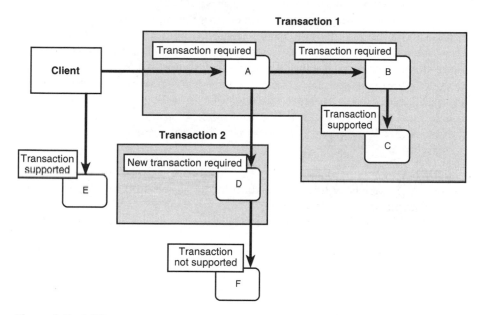

Figure 4-7. *MTS automatic transactions.*

Using automatic transactions ensures that independently developed components can be composed into new functionality without modifying every component. In general, any components that update persistent state should support transactions. Any component that uses two or more subordinate objects to perform a single indivisible task should use transactions to simplify error recovery. If for some reason developers want to control transaction boundaries explicitly, MTS provides a generic transaction context object that can be used to do so. However, many of the benefits of the application server programming model are lost when clients use the transaction context object instead of automatic transactions. We will not discuss using the transaction context object in this book.

SUMMARY

MTS provides the infrastructure to build scalable, distributed applications from COM components in a timely manner. MTS is an OTM, combining the functionality of traditional ORBs and TP-Monitors. It includes a powerful execution environment that handles code concurrency, resource management, and security for components, as well as a transaction manager for coordinating updates across multiple components.

MTS also promotes a powerful, easy-to-use programming model for application server development. The application server programming model is a hybrid of two traditionally distinct models, object-oriented programming and online transaction processing (OLTP). From the client's perspective, everything looks object-oriented: clients create objects and hold object references as long as the references are needed, calling any number of object methods to do work. The reality in the server application more closely resembles traditional OLTP behavior. Objects are instantiated just long enough to do a unit of work. Objects grab resources as late as possible and release them as soon as possible, to promote resource sharing and scalability.

The net effect of this hybrid model is that application and component developers must consider how to manage state in the distributed application. We'll discuss this topic at length in Chapters 7 through 9, as we talk about designing and building distributed applications for MTS.

5

Active Server Pages

The Internet has become an increasingly powerful means of making information available to large numbers of people. Just as with internal corporate applications, an Internet-based application often must generate dynamic displays from one or more data sources. Active Server Pages (ASP) is a technology included with Microsoft Internet Information Server (IIS) that can help developers create Internet applications. With the release of IIS 4.0, ASP is integrated with Microsoft Transaction Server (MTS).

This chapter describes how to use IIS and ASP as an integration and presentation layer for MTS. The focus is on what capabilities ASP provides and how it interacts with MTS, rather than on the specifics of developing pages. For further information about ASP development, refer to the bibliography, which lists several references.

Why ASP?

One of the difficulties in developing Internet applications is the wide variation in client browser capabilities. Different browsers support different versions of the HTML standard. A new standard, called Dynamic HTML (DHTML), is supported by some browsers. Some browsers support Java applets, some support Microsoft ActiveX Controls, and some don't support any type of client-side component. Some browsers support client-side scripting via JavaScript or VBScript; others don't. In addition, browsers might support proprietary extensions to HTML or DHTML. Beyond the various browser capabilities is the wide variation in the screen resolution and color capabilities of user displays. These factors can make it difficult to create Web pages that work well for all users.

Things are complicated enough when Web pages are simply displaying static information. Add the need to generate content dynamically, and things get really complicated. Dynamic content is normally generated from one or more data sources located on the server. In most situations, the application developer will not want clients to connect directly to these data sources. One reason, of course, is that per-client connections don't scale very well. But more important are the security issues involved with giving some random Internet user access to company databases. Therefore, Internet applications are usually structured so that some server-side application is used to generate HTML pages containing the data to be displayed. Whenever the Web client needs more data, a new request is sent to the Web server, and a new page is generated by the server-side application.

With the advent of Java applets, ActiveX Controls, and DHTML, it is now possible to write client-side Web applications that maintain some connection to a server. Instead of forcing a new page to be generated whenever more data is needed, data is transferred directly between client-side components or script code and a server-side application. Internal data sources do not need to be exposed to the outside world because they are accessed only by the server-side applications.

Traditionally, server-side Internet applications have been developed using a gateway interface, such as the Common Gateway Interface (CGI) or the Internet Server Application Programming Interface (ISAPI). One disadvantage of gateway interfaces is that content is essentially embedded within a compiled program. If content authors want to change the format of a page, they need to wade through program source code and locate the statements that generate HTML output. Once changes are made, the program probably needs to be rebuilt. This can make it difficult to maintain server-side applications. CGI programs have an additional disadvantage in that each time a CGI program is called, it runs as a separate process, so these applications might not scale well.

ASP addresses all of these issues. An ASP page mixes server-side scripts and client-side content, as shown in the following code:

```
<%@ LANGUAGE = VBScript %>
<% Option Explicit %>

<HTML>
    <HEAD><TITLE>Sample ASP</TITLE></HEAD>

    <BODY bgcolor="white" topmargin="10" leftmargin="10">

    <!-- Display Header -->
    <font size="4" face="Arial, Helvetica">
    <b>Sample ASP</b></font><br>
    <hr size="1" color="#000000">

    This script uses a component that comes with IIS
    to generate a random number. The random number
    determines what text is displayed on the rest of
    the page.
    <br>
```

```
<% Dim example, aNumber

    ' Instantiate component on the server.
    Set example = Server.CreateObject("MSWC.Tools")
    aNumber = example.Random()
%>
    <P>The random number is <%=aNumber%>.</P>

<%
    ' Use a conditional statement to decide what message to return.
    If (aNumber mod 2 = 0) Then
        Response.Write("<P>This is an even number.</P>")
    Else
        Response.Write("<P>This is an odd number.</P>")
    End If
%>

    </BODY>
</HTML>
```

When an ASP page is accessed, the server-side script is executed on the server. As the script is executed, an HTTP response is generated and sent back to the client. Normally, this response is an HTML page. The server-side script can control which HTML statements coded in the ASP file are included in the response, or it can generate HTML statements on the fly. This technique provides a straightforward way to deal with differing browser capabilities. The ASP developer can determine what features the requesting client supports and adjust the HTTP response accordingly.

Automation Components

Server-side scripts can use Automation objects. ASP provides some standard Automation components to help with common Web tasks, such as determining browser characteristics, parsing parameters and cookies included in a page request, or sharing information between pages in the application. This capability makes it relatively easy to write pages to process HTML forms. In addition, complex operations can be coded one time in custom components and then reused in many server-side applications.

In general, server-side ASP code should defer complex algorithms to COM components. Script code is interpreted at run time. The less interpretation needed, the better your performance. In addition, script code can use only the *IDispatch* interface to access Automation-aware components. Code that simply calls a lot of other COM objects to perform work should be placed in a COM component.

Components are compiled and can usually take advantage of vtable-binding, providing better overall performance. These components can be reused in other applications as well.

The ASP Programming Model

One of the major advantages of ASP is the familiarity of its programming model. Content authors work in a medium familiar to them—HTML—augmented with scripting. Scripts can be written in any language, as long as a scripting engine is available. IIS includes scripting engines for VBScript and Microsoft JScript. Developers who implement complex business logic can encapsulate the logic within COM components written using their favorite development tool, instead of having to learn HTML and scripting.

Because ASP pages are interpreted, it's easy to update an ASP application as necessary—particularly when cosmetic changes to the HTML statements are needed. And since ASP runs on the Web server and controls exactly what gets sent back to the Web client, your intellectual property—data or code—is protected. Client machines will not be able to tell how the HTML was generated or where the data is coming from.

Three-Tier Application Architectures

As we saw in Chapter 1, Internet applications are extremely demanding. Applications must be able to handle large numbers of users connected via slow or intermittent network connections, and the number of users at any particular time is difficult to predict. The three-tier application architecture is promoted by Windows DNA largely to meet the demands of Internet applications.

In an Internet application, a Web browser displays an HTML page–based presentation layer. Requests from the presentation layer are transmitted via HTTP to the Web server. The Web server handles these requests using business services that may in turn talk to data services.

ASP straddles the line between the presentation layer and the business layer. ASP pages are executed on the Web server, in response to requests from the Web browser. In this sense, they are part of the business layer. ASP pages contain server-side script code that uses middle-tier business objects to do much of the work. The business objects call data objects to access data sources, as described by the three-tier architecture. On the other hand, ASP pages are used to generate the presentation layer, HTML pages and the HTML and client-side script code is located within the ASP pages. So ASP pages look a bit like presentation layer code as well.

Integration with MTS

Think of the server-side script in an ASP page as the first layer of business logic. This layer might use several COM objects to satisfy a request. In Chapter 4, we saw how transactions can be used to help ensure that resources are updated correctly when multiple objects are working together to fulfill a request from a client. Thus, it seems reasonable to include the processing of the ASP page itself within a transaction. IIS 4.0 enables this process.

In IIS 4.0, an application is identified by marking a directory or virtual directory as an *application root*. The application includes all files, directories, and virtual directories contained by the root that aren't part of another application.

Any ASP page can be declared to use transactions. When a page is processed, a new transaction will be created. All the objects created within the page are automatically enlisted in the transaction, if appropriate, by MTS. The transaction terminates when the entire file has been interpreted and any server-side scripts have executed. If the transaction aborts, all of the resources in the transaction will roll back to the values they had before page processing began. As you might imagine, this capability is particularly useful for pages that update databases.

IIS also uses MTS to manage server application processes. Each application, denoted by a unique virtual directory, can be configured to run in the main IIS process or in a specific MTS process, which improves overall server reliability. If one application fails, only that application's process is shut down and restarted. The entire Web server does not shut down. Separating applications into individual processes also helps with server maintenance. If an application needs to be updated, only that application process needs to be shut down. The Web server and other server applications can continue to run.

The architectural diagram in Figure 5-1 on the following page illustrates the integration of MTS with IIS and ASP. In IIS, applications are managed by a COM component called the *Web Application Manager* (WAM). The WAM is responsible for loading the ASP run time and other ISAPI DLLs. The WAM communicates with these DLLs whenever an HTTP request is received.

Each application, whether it is running in the IIS process or in a separate process, contains an instance of the WAM object. All application processes are managed by MTS. When you use IIS to configure an application to run in a separate process, MTS administrative objects are called on your behalf to create a new MTS package, generate a new globally unique identifier (GUID), add the WAM to the package using the new GUID, and configure the package to run in a separate process. Applications that are configured to run in the IIS process are registered in the default MTS in-process package.

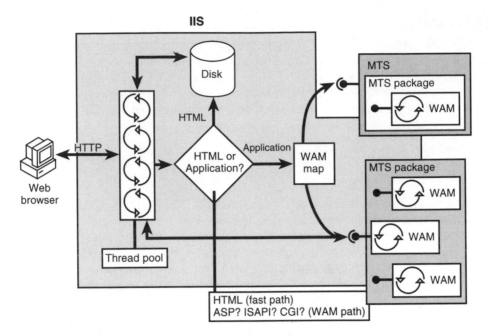

Figure 5-1. *The integration of MTS with IIS and ASP.*

When IIS receives an HTTP request, it determines whether the requested URL is part of an application. If the URL is part of an application, IIS looks in its internal WAM map to locate the correct WAM object. If the application isn't running, its WAM won't exist and will have to be created. IIS creates the WAM object using the application-specific GUID generated at registration time. At this point, MTS starts a new process, if necessary, and begins managing objects and resources for the application.

SUMMARY

ASP is a powerful way to bridge the gap between client-side presentation logic and server-side business logic in the three-tier Internet application. With IIS 4.0, ASP is fully integrated with MTS. MTS provides process, thread, and other resource management services to IIS and ASP applications. Pages in an ASP application can be marked as transactional, giving each page all the benefits of transactions discussed in Chapter 4. We will look at ASP again in Chapter 11 when we discuss building the presentation layer of a distributed application.

6

Extending the Reach of MTS

Using the technologies we've discussed so far, developers can create scalable, component-based, three-tier applications that run on Microsoft Windows NT. Many applications will need to interact with other applications, which might themselves be running on non-Windows platforms. In this chapter, we'll look at the following interoperability mechanisms supported by Microsoft Windows DNA.

- COM implementations for UNIX and other platforms

- Interoperability with XA-based resource managers and transaction managers, using the Microsoft Distributed Transaction Coordinator (MS DTC)

- Interoperability with LU 6.2–based transaction monitors, such as the Customer Information Control System (CICS) and Information Management Systems (IMS), via the COM Transaction Integrator (COMTI)

- Message queuing, via Microsoft Message Queue Server (MSMQ)

COM on UNIX

Some applications simply need to access applications running on other platforms. We'll call these non-Windows applications *legacy applications,* just to distinguish them from the MTS-based applications we've been discussing in this book. (No insult intended.) Rather than implement code that uses a low-level network protocol or proprietary API to communicate between these applications, you might want to use COM as the communication mechanism. COM components can be implemented on the legacy application platform to wrap access to the legacy applications. New applications create objects using the COM wrapper components and communicate with the objects via Distributed COM (DCOM). Internally, the wrapper methods call the native API exposed by the application. The primary reason for using this technique is to provide a consistent programming model for new applications. Developers do not need to learn a new protocol or API to talk to the legacy application, they simply use COM. Writing COM components for other platforms is conceptually no different from writing components on Microsoft Windows, although different programming tools are used. Once a COM wrapper is in place, the legacy application functionality is accessible to rapid application development (RAD) tools such as Microsoft Visual Basic and possibly to scripting languages—for example, to server-side scripts in an ASP page.

Although COM is often thought of as a Windows-only technology, it is available on a number of other platforms. As of April 1998, COM is available for the Solaris platform directly from Microsoft and for Solaris, Linux, and MVS from Software AG. Microsoft plans to release COM for other UNIX platforms later in 1998. Microsoft has also licensed the COM source code to a number of independent software vendors (ISVs) and operating system vendors. These vendors will provide COM implementations directly on platforms such as Silicon Graphics IRIX.

COM implementations on non-Windows platforms include the basic functionality of COM for instantiating and using objects as well as structured storage, monikers, custom marshaling, connectable objects, Automation, and Uniform Data Transfer (UDT). These features are more than sufficient for building components to interoperate with Windows DNA applications.

XA Interoperability

Many applications need to access data stored in databases other than Microsoft SQL Server. In general, these databases are accessed through ODBC drivers that run on a Windows machine. In order to participate in transactions, the ODBC driver must support either the OLE Transactions or XA protocol for communicating between the transaction manager (MS DTC) and the database resource manager.

As we saw in Chapter 4, XA is part of the X/Open transaction processing model. Today most databases—other than SQL Server—support the XA protocol but not OLE Transactions. To provide transaction support for these databases, the ODBC driver must accept OLE Transactions calls and translate them into the message formats and protocols that would result if the corresponding XA function had been called, as shown in Figure 6-1. The resource manager server itself does not need to be changed. The ODBC driver completely hides OLE Transactions from the resource manager.

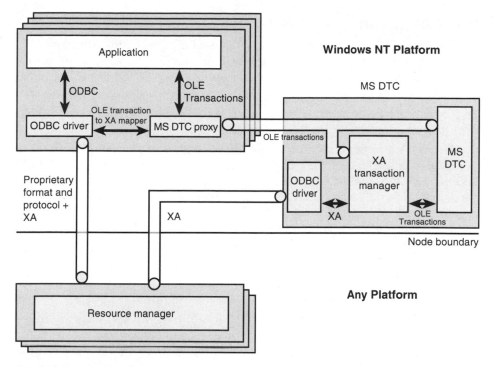

Figure 6-1. *Using the MS DTC to control XA-compliant resource managers.*

NOTE MTS 2.0 included a transaction-aware ODBC driver for Oracle databases. Shortly after MTS 2.0 was released, IBM released an updated ODBC driver for IBM DB2 databases so that they can be used from MTS also. Microsoft is working closely with other database and ODBC driver vendors to make transaction-aware ODBC drivers available for other databases. Check with your database vendor to see whether updated ODBC drivers are available.

In addition, XA-compliant transaction managers can control OLE Transactions–compliant resource managers such as SQL Server and MSMQ. The MS DTC provides a mapping layer to translate XA calls into the corresponding OLE Transactions calls, enabling OLE Transactions resource managers to act as fully XA-compliant resource managers.

COM Transaction Integrator

IBM CICS and IMS are two widely used Transaction Processing Monitors (TP-Monitors) in the enterprise computing world. It's likely that many applications will need to interoperate with CICS or IMS applications. Windows NT applications can interoperate with CICS and IMS applications using the LU 6.2 protocol with the help of COMTI. LU 6.2 is a peer-to-peer transaction protocol supported by CICS and IMS.

COMTI supports sending and receiving information to and from IMS message queues, as well as sending and receiving information to and from CICS. COMTI also enables CICS transaction programs to participate in MTS-coordinated transactions using Sync Point Level 2 LU 6.2 conversations. Using the distributed program link (DPL) emulation provided by COMTI, CICS applications need not even be aware they are participating within a larger distributed transaction.

COMTI effectively encapsulates CICS and IMS applications behind Automation objects, as shown in Figure 6-2. Client applications view the mainframe application as an Automation object. This object is generated by the COMTI run time, which runs within MTS. The run time uses a type library produced by COMTI development tools to generate the Automation object. Method calls are translated into CICS or IMS application invocations. Method parameters are translated into fields in LU 6.2 messages, data entries on IMS queues, or variables in CICS COMMAREAs, to make them available to the CICS or IMS application. Microsoft SNA Server is used to provide LU 6.2 communication with the mainframe.

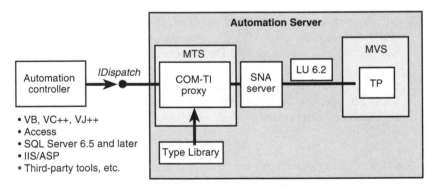

Figure 6-2. *Using COMTI to encapsulate CICS and IMS applications.*

The COMTI Architecture

Internally, COMTI consists of a set of COM components that interact with each other, with MTS, and with the MS DTC. The COMTI architecture is shown in Figure 6-3. The generic COMTI component exposes the appropriate Automation interface to clients. The COMTI state machine sequences the acquisition of input data, marshaling the inputs, sending the inputs, receiving outputs, unmarshaling the outputs, and delivering outputs back through the Automation interface. A *Transport* object isolates the state machine from the specific transport being used, and a *Convert* object isolates it from details of data conversion for the target mainframe. The resource dispenser mechanism in MTS is used to cache instances of the state machine and associated objects to improve performance. The MS DTC coordinates transactions and manages the necessary translation between the transaction identifiers (TRIDs) since MS DTC uses OLE TRIDs and mainframe applications use LU 6.2 logical unit-of-work identifiers (LUWIDs).

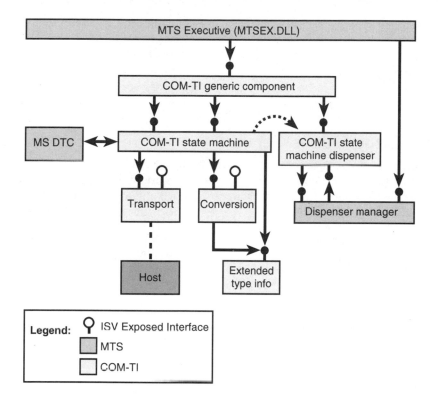

Figure 6-3. *The COMTI architecture.*

The primary advantage of COMTI is that it makes mainframe applications accessible to Windows-based workstations and servers, using standard Windows development tools such as Visual Basic and scripting languages. Developers do not need to learn COBOL, CICS, or IMS programming to take advantage of existing applications.

Creating a COMTI Automation Component

To create the COMTI Automation component, a developer can simply take the data declarations representing the mainframe application's interface and import these definitions into the COMTI Component Builder tool. The Interface Builder is used to create a type library that defines the Automation component's interface. The component is then registered on the host machine. Unlike other components we've seen up to now, COMTI components contain no custom code. The registry entries for the component point to the generic COMTI server and the Component Builder–generated type library. At run time, the generic COMTI server uses the type library information to expose the correct Automation interface for the application.

NOTE	From the system administrator's perspective, COMTI does not require any software on the mainframe or client workstations. COMTI needs to be installed only on machines hosting COMTI Automation components.

Microsoft Message Queue Server

The technologies we have discussed so far are primarily aimed at *time-dependent applications*. In a time-dependent application, the caller and callee must coexist at the time a method is called. If the callee is unavailable for any reason, the method call will fail. To recover, the caller must retry the method call at a later time.

Many distributed applications can be partitioned into time-independent sections. For these applications, it's more important that a method call be processed eventually—without coding retries into the caller—than that it be processed immediately. Some classic examples of applications that have time-independent characteristics are listed in the following table.

Industry	Applications
Banking	Money transfer, foreign exchange
Brokerage	Stock transfer
Manufacturing	Factory floor automation
Railway	Freight management and control
Retail	Ordering, fulfillment, shipping, and billing
Travel	Airline/hotel/car reservations

For instance, consider the case of a company that takes customer orders over the phone. When a customer calls in an order, the person taking the order needs to give the customer an order confirmation number while the customer is still on the phone. This is time-dependent behavior. However, there is no need to keep the customer on the phone until a confirmed ship date is received from the shipping department. All that's needed is to assure the customer that the order will be scheduled for shipment. This is time-independent behavior.

Message Queuing

Message queuing middleware can be used to implement time-independent applications. Communication occurs using one-way messages, which are sent to a queue by the caller for later retrieval by the receiving application, as shown in Figure 6-4. The calling application opens a queue and issues a request by sending a message. The message queuing software does the work required to route the message to its destination. An application at the other end watches the destination queue for incoming messages; when it receives a message, it reads the message, figures out what to do, and does some work. The contents of a message are meaningful only to the sender and the receiver. If the receiver needs to communicate back to the sender, it either sends a message back or updates some common data store that the sender can query. Message queuing is similar to e-mail, except that it is designed for application-to-application communication rather than person-to-person communication.

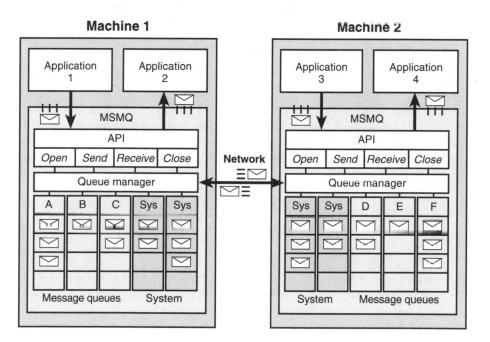

Figure 6-4. *Connecting time-independent applications by using message queuing.*

Message queuing offers some attractive benefits to application developers. Message queuing improves server availability by ensuring that eventually all calls will get through to the server. This capability is particularly useful for disconnected clients or for clients connected via unreliable links. In addition, if a server is temporarily busy, calls are simply placed in a queue instead of timing out. This helps servers deal with peak-time or increasing demands more gracefully. Message queuing improves reliability by ensuring that messages are delivered exactly once, even if the application, communications link, or system fails. Message queuing also provides scheduling convenience. Queues can be configured for optimal throughput. Most queuing software even lets you prioritize messages to ensure that the most important messages are delivered first. Server lifetime is completely independent of the calling application since servers retrieve messages at their convenience.

Using MSMQ

MSMQ, Microsoft's message queuing product, provides the infrastructure for managing queues and routing messages between queues located on different machines. MSMQ also provides an API for creating messaging applications and administrative tools for configuring and monitoring queues. Although messaging is not based on COM, MSMQ provides a set of COM components to help developers write messaging applications. We will see how these components are used in Chapter 15, when we discuss adding messaging support to three-tier distributed applications.

MSMQ provides an OLE Transactions resource manager, so queues can be treated as transactional resources. If a queue is configured to be transactional, the act of sending a message to the queue or receiving a message from the queue can be transacted. Thus, message queuing operations can be composed with operations on MTS objects using MTS automatic transactions. For instance, a business object in our order entry example might take the following actions within the *ConfirmOrder* method:

- Save the order in a database and get a confirmation number in return

- Send a message to the shipping department to schedule shipment of the order

If the business object can't get an order confirmation number because the order isn't saved properly, the *ConfirmOrder* operation should fail and no message should be sent to the shipping department. The *ConfirmOrder* operation should also fail if the message can't be queued for the shipping department. As we saw in Chapter 4, automatic transactions provide a straightforward way to implement this kind of behavior. Failure of either operation causes the transaction to abort, and an error is returned to the client application.

It's important to note that sending messages and receiving messages are parts of two separate transactions, as illustrated in Figure 6-5. Because the sender and receiver aren't necessarily connected and there can be a substantial time delay between sending and receiving a message, a single transaction is not appropriate. Transaction success on the sending side does not imply that the receiver will be able to successfully handle the request in the message. For instance, in our order entry example, the order entry application can accept an order regardless of whether all the ordered items are in stock. When the shipping application receives the shipment request, it won't be able to send the out-of-stock items. In situations like this, applications must provide a *compensating transaction*. A compensating transaction doesn't undo a previously committed transaction, but it can undo the effect of the transaction. For example, the order entry application might compensate for shipments held up by out-of-stock items by sending the customer a postcard notifying her of the delay and giving her an opportunity to change the order.

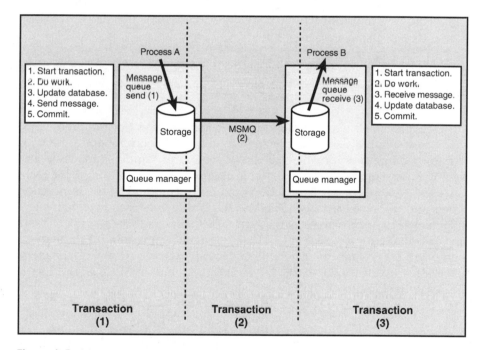

Figure 6-5. *Transactions in a message queuing application.*

Message queuing is a useful interoperability mechanism in addition to providing a way to write time-independent applications. To communicate with another application, you simply send a message to a queue with any information the application needs. The message queue server doesn't care what the contents of the message are—it just passes the message along. If the application already supports message queuing, it will receive the message from the queue and take the appropriate action. If the application does not support messaging, a receiver application can be written that receives messages from the queue and translates them into native calls to whatever API the application exposes. This mechanism can even work for applications that run on different platforms, so long as the message queue servers on the two platforms agree on the general format of a message and on how to move messages from one queue to another. When the message queue servers do not agree, a *bridge* can be used to translate from one message format to another and to move messages between queues.

> **NOTE**   Although MSMQ is available only on Windows platforms, the FalconMQ product from Level-8 Systems provides a client API for UNIX, AS/400, VMS, CICS/MVS, and other platforms that lets developers work with MSMQ queues. FalconMQ also contains a bridge providing interoperability with the very popular IBM MQSeries message queue server.

SUMMARY

Windows DNA provides several ways for three-tier distributed applications based on COM and MTS to interoperate with applications and resources on non-Windows platforms. When transactional interoperability is not required, COM can be used to wrap access to applications within COM components. DCOM is used as the communications mechanism between the Windows machine and the non-Windows machine. If transactional interoperability is required, the technology used depends on the transaction protocols supported by the transaction managers and resource managers. The MS DTC is able to interoperate with many XA-compliant resource managers through ODBC drivers that map OLE Transactions calls into XA calls. The MS DTC also provides a mapping layer that lets XA-compliant transaction managers use OLE Transactions resource managers. Interoperability with LU 6.2–based TP-Monitors such as IBM CICS and IMS is accomplished using the COMTI.

Message queuing is another option for interoperability. In this case, messages are passed from the Windows machine to the non-Windows machine. The messages are interpreted by custom code running on the destination machine. Message queuing can also be used to build time-independent applications.

We will discuss how to develop applications using MSMQ and COMTI in detail in Chapter 15.

Building Applications

In Part Two, you'll learn how to architect and model three-tier business solutions using COM and Microsoft Transaction Server (MTS). We'll examine tools, techniques, and thought processes for modeling data, business objects, and various types of clients. We'll also look at practical issues that must be considered during design, such as security considerations and performance requirements. Next we'll look at how to implement the three-tier application, focusing on how to build business and data objects, but with a brief glimpse at writing clients for the Internet and intranets. And last we'll look at how to debug applications using the Visual Basic and Visual Studio debuggers, how to check our application against performance requirements, and how to deploy the application.

7

Application Definition and Modeling

Components and Microsoft's middleware technologies aren't magic bullets that will solve all your problems. Applications built from bad components are going to be bad applications. Analysis and design are essential to building a successful component based solution.

In this chapter, we'll look at how to plan a distributed application, and we'll go over some of the specific planning issues that differ in a three-tier environment using Microsoft Transaction Server (MTS). You won't find a complete methodology for designing applications here, just some practical field-tested approaches.

NOTE If you're interested in more formal processes and methodologies, additional references are provided in the bibliography.

Creating an Application Definition

Before you start looking at how to implement a solution, you need to be sure you know what the problem is. This is what requirements analysis is all about. The degree of analysis needed depends on how big your project is, how many people will be working on it, and so on. The important thing is to end up with some documentation of what you think the requirements are—this information will be what you test your solution against.

Defining the Business Problem

Start by getting an overview from your customer of the business problem that the application will solve. You should look for the benefits the application will provide (compared to its costs), not just how the customer thinks the problem should be solved. Will the application improve productivity? Improve customer satisfaction? Reduce maintenance and training costs? These are the kinds of questions you need to ask in addition to asking what the application should do.

When you think you understand the problem, write it down in simple language the customer will understand. The following text shows part of the business problem statement for the Island Hopper sample application, which is included on the companion CD:

```
Problem Statement

The "Island Hopper News" would like to automate its classified
advertisement submission and billing process. Customers should
be able to submit classified ads through the "Island Hopper News"
Web site. Customers will be billed later for their ads.

The editor wants to significantly reduce the time spent on
processing paperwork so that the newspaper can run classified
ads every week (instead of bimonthly), thereby generating
more revenue. A joint review by the classified ad and
accounting departments concluded that existing classified
ad processes consume excessive resources without providing
adequate customer service.
```

During requirements analysis, you should try to avoid making assumptions about the technologies used to implement a solution. If the business problem is connecting to existing software or hardware, go ahead and say so. If the business problem is making the application available over the Internet, that's fine too. But try to avoid describing assumptions such as "the application will create a file..." or "using Visual Basic..." at this point. Putting predictions like this in your problem statement can produce tunnel vision during design. Perhaps the application will work better if its results are stored in a database. Perhaps there's really no business reason to save the results at all—it's just the way things have always been done in the past.

Once you've written the problem statement, review it with your customer. The customer should verify that you understand the problem correctly before you continue. This is also an ideal time to discuss the feasibility and desirability of solving the problem. A solution might be technically possible, but the cost or time to market might be too high to justify solving the stated problem. In this case, you might need to narrow the problem scope.

The result of this step is a document describing in plain language the business problem that you and your customer have defined. This document will help keep you focused on solving the identified business problems while you design the rest of the solution.

The entire problem statement for the Island Hopper sample application is contained in the BUSINESSPROBLEM.TXT file, which is located in the \IslandHopper\Requirements directory on the companion CD.

Defining the Functional Specifications

After you have defined the overall business problem, it's time to dig into the specific functional requirements for your application. *Functional specifications* are described in detail within the Microsoft Solution Framework (MSF) and by most analysis methodologies. In essence, a functional specification is a document describing what the application must do from the user's perspective. A good way to generate a functional specification is to enumerate scenarios in which the application will be used. This process is known within MSF as *storyboarding*. Some object-oriented design techniques call this "defining the use case model."

For more information about MSF, contact your local Microsoft consulting services or Microsoft sales office, or e-mail *msf@microsoft.com.*

As you enumerate scenarios, you will begin to see a common usage pattern in most distributed applications. Users interact with applications in an iterative fashion. Some information is presented to the user. The information is analyzed. After a variable number of presentation and analysis steps, the user can elect to update the data. Each user interaction step might take a fairly lengthy and indeterminate period of time.

We'll see how this pattern maps to the three-tier application architecture a little later in this chapter in the section "Designing Classes." For now, just remember that a scenario defines a sequence of steps to complete a user-level task. Start by looking at the normal things the user will do. For example, Figure 7-1 on the following page illustrates the "Place a Classified Ad" scenario for the Island Hopper application, using a Unified Modeling Language (UML) sequence diagram. Once you have defined the normal scenarios, you can look at common error scenarios.

The result of this step is a document containing the functional specification that you and your customer agree to. It's a good idea to label each scenario or specification with a unique number. If you include references to these labels in your design documents or source code, you will be able to trace functionality from requirements clear through to implementation (just in case the requirements change).

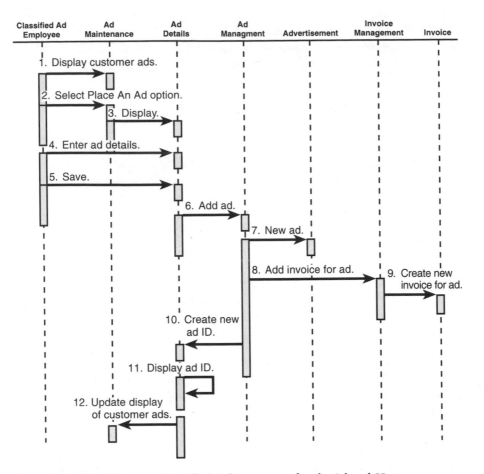

Figure 7-1. *The "Place a Classified Ad" scenario for the Island Hopper application.*

NOTE   The entire functional specification for "Island Hopper" is contained in the FUNCTIONALSPEC.TXT file, which is located in the \IslandHopper\Requirements directory on the companion CD.

Establishing Application Requirements

In addition to functional requirements, you should spend some time up front defining the performance, deployment, and security requirements that must be satisfied by the application. Let's look at a few scenarios from other applications to identify the types of things you need to consider for distributed applications.

Our first scenario involves a customer service call center, as shown in Figure 7-2. A customer calls his local insurance agent at 10 P.M., after the agent has closed the office and gone home for the night. The phone call is forwarded to a customer service center, where an application server looks at the call information, queries a database, and routes the call and insurance agent information to a customer service representative. The representative answers the call using the name of the local insurance agency. This enables the insurance company to deliver 24-hour customer service, even for the customers of small insurance agencies. The representative asks the customer for his name and policy number and starts another database query that pulls up the customer information. The customer and the representative engage in a phone conversation for two minutes. The representative then updates the customer's insurance records as necessary. Changes to the customer's records are securely transacted to a back-end Oracle system.

1. Customer calls local insurance agent after hours.

2. Call is forwarded to a central call center.

3. App server views call information, queries database, and routes call to one of 300 agents.

4. Rep answers call and pulls up customer-specific data.

5. Rep talks to customer for two minutes, and then updates system if necessary.

6. Changes are transacted to back-end Oracle system.

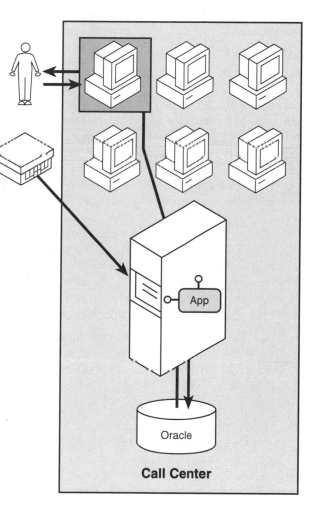

Figure 7-2. *The "Customer Service Call Center" scenario.*

In this scenario, the system must be available whenever local agencies are closed. In addition, quick response time is required. If a customer is trying to reach her insurance agent after hours, she's probably got a problem she wants solved fast—and each service representative can handle only one customer at a time. This response time can be on the order of seconds, however—we don't need milli-second responses.

Another thing to notice about this application is that we can't really predict when customers will call or how many customers will use the service. We know that if a disaster strikes, there will be a surge in calls, but we don't know when the disasters will happen. So the application must be able to handle two types of increased volume: the application must be able to scale as demand on the call center increases, and the application must also be able to handle high-volume periods.

The next scenario we'll look at is banking over the Internet, as illustrated in Figure 7-3. A money center bank (this is a term for huge banks like Citibank or Bank of America) operates a cash management application for corporate customers. The application runs on existing Tandem minicomputers and IBM mainframes. The bank decides to provide better service to its customers by letting them directly access the cash management application via the Internet. Small business customers are provided with a URL to the bank's Web site, along with a Secure Sockets Layer (SSL) account for security. Large corporate customers are provided with a dedicated cash-management computer running on a Microsoft Windows NT workstation. This PC runs value-added applications. Both the Web-based customers and the PC application customers—10,000 customers in all—access the same application server that provides the front-end for the mainframe systems. Multiple firewalls are used to ensure security. Each customer can monitor his or her company's cash position over the Internet throughout the day. Any changes customers make are reliably transacted to the back-end mainframes. Most important, the bank can quickly provide new services to customers by writing new applications on the application server.

As with our first scenario, response time must be good—on the order of seconds at the user level—and the application must scale as more customers access it. We also have the problem of unpredictable load in this scenario. We know that there will be busy periods, but we don't know exactly when the busy periods will be.

In addition, in this scenario security and reliability are vital. Customers don't want their financial information to be visible to anyone else. They also don't want their transactions lost! Data integrity is essential and different levels of service must be made available to different types of users. Finally, the new application must interact with existing mainframe systems.

1. Money center bank extends legacy cash management system.

2. Small customers use browser.

3. Large customers use dedicated PC with enhanced services.

4. All 10,000 customers use the same app server.

5. Multiple firewalls and encryption are used for security.

6. Customers view cash position and post changes.

7. Changes are transacted to back-end legacy system.

8. New services are added easily and quickly.

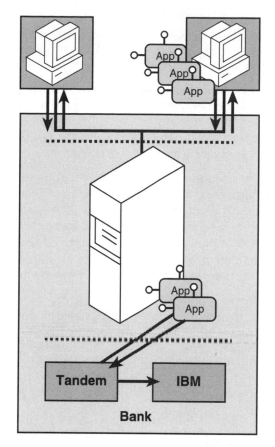

Figure 7-3. *The "Internet Corporate Banking" scenario.*

These two scenarios share the following features, which are common to most distributed applications:

■ Volumes are variable.

■ Spikes in activity occur.

■ The application must be scalable.

■ Application response time is important.

■ In some applications, security and reliability are of utmost importance.

■ Applications might need to interact with legacy systems.

The more specific information you can obtain about how these factors apply to your application, the better.

Performance

Performance can be defined in many ways. The important thing is to come to an agreement with your customers about the required service levels relative to available hardware.

One requirement to consider is availability. What percentage of time does the application need to be available? In the "Customer Service Call Center" scenario, availability might be defined as 99.99 percent between the hours of 6 P.M. and 10 A.M. and 50 percent between the hours of 10 A.M. and 6 P.M., using four replicated application server machines.

Another requirement to consider is the number of concurrent users that must be supported. You might include average and maximum numbers, with corresponding average response times. Another way of stating performance requirements is in terms of the number of transactions that must be processed in a given amount of time. In the "Internet Corporate Banking" scenario, performance might be defined as 50,000 transactions per hour, with a 0.5-second average response time and a 3-second maximum response time.

Whatever requirements are stated, you should define the minimum acceptable performance for a particular hardware configuration. This value will give you a baseline target for testing. Some variables to consider when you are defining hardware configurations are the number of processors, amount of memory, number of server machines, server speed, and network speed. As the application is built, you can test it on the target hardware configuration to determine whether the performance requirements are met. We'll look at performance validation in Chapter 13.

Deployment

Now is a good time to document the existing systems that your application will need to interoperate with. For the most part, integrating into the existing enterprise computing infrastructure and policies will not cause any problems. COM and MTS don't really care where components are located, as long as a communications link can be established between the caller and the component.

Many applications can be designed and implemented without regard to how they will be deployed. In fact, you should try to build your application so that system integrators or administrators have the flexibility to deploy the application in many different ways. This flexibility will help ensure that your application will continue to be useful as machines and network infrastructure change. However, there are situations in which deployment requirements will constrain your design and implementation. Those requirements are the important things to document prior to application modeling and design.

One factor to consider is whether there are existing data or application servers you will need to use. If so, what operating systems do they use? What communications protocols do they support? What API can you use to interact with them? Where are the systems located on the network? Are there restrictions on which machines or user accounts are allowed to connect to the servers? The answers to these questions can impact your application design as well as how you implement and package particular COM classes. For example, consider a corporate policy that dictates all server machines must run within a firewall that permits only HTTP traffic. If you need to support client applications running on machines outside the firewall, you'll need to design your application so that the client application communicates with the server machine only via HTTP.

Another factor to consider is where clients and data sources are located. Are clients geographically dispersed or centrally located? If the clients are dispersed, how are they connected to each other? Is the data centrally located, or is it located near the clients that use it? Are some types of connection more expensive than other types? Are connections intermittent or persistent? Again, the answers to these questions can influence your application design. Consider a scenario in which insurance agents nationwide submit claims, ultimately to a central office. The agents are connected to an office LAN, which in turn is connected to the central office via satellite. In this scenario, it would probably be smart to run as much of the claims applications as possible in each office. For example, agents submit claims to the local office, and the local office then batches all the claims and submits them to the central office. Normal COM calls could be used for all the local traffic, but perhaps Microsoft Message Queue Server (MSMQ) should be used to communicate with the central office.

Security

Finally, you should consider whether there are any security requirements that might impact your application design. A couple of issues are likely to arise. First, you might need to pass sensitive data between applications or components running on different machines. You might need to encrypt the data before transmitting it or perform some type of integrity checking to ensure that the data hasn't been tampered with. For example, in an online shopping application, you would probably want to encrypt the customer's credit card information before sending it across the Internet. If you are going to pass encrypted information as parameters to a COM interface, the mechanism for encrypting and decrypting the parameters must be documented as part of the interface design. If, on the other hand, you are going to use authentication mechanisms provided by the underlying communications and security layer of Windows, you might want to split secure operations into a separate COM class. Otherwise, you could end up paying a performance penalty for operations that don't really need such stringent authentication checking. The important thing at this stage is to identify any special authentication or data protection requirements.

Another issue to consider is whether there are any constraints on who is authorized to perform particular operations. If so, you should first document which operations require authorization. Then document the types of users who can be authorized to perform those operations. These user types will map to roles in the MTS security model. For example, the Island Hopper classified ads application contains some functional specifications that apply to customers, some that apply to the classified ad department employees, and others that apply to the accounting department employees. As we'll see in the section "Grouping Components into Packages and Processes" later in this chapter, these requirements have a big impact on how you package functionality in your application.

This step results in documents containing the performance, deployment, and security requirements that you and your customer agree to. Again, it's a good idea to label each requirement with a unique identifier so that you can trace design and implementation back to specific requirements.

> **NOTE** The performance, deployment, and security requirements for the Island Hopper application are contained in the PERFORMANCE.TXT file located in the \IslandHopper-\Requirements directory on the companion CD.

Modeling the Application

At this point, you and your customer should have a pretty good idea of the problem you're trying to solve. More important, you and your customer should agree what the problem is!

Once the problem is defined, you can turn your attention to the conceptual design of the application. The four key tasks to accomplish during conceptual design are as follows:

- Modeling persistent data
- Modeling the data objects
- Modeling the business objects
- Modeling the presentation layer

We will discuss each of these tasks in detail in the sections that follow.

Modeling Persistent Data

You should begin the conceptual design process by examining the requirements documents for information about persistent data. These documents provide information that will help define the databases the application will use. These could be relational databases or object-oriented databases, but here we'll focus on issues related to relational databases since these are far more prevalent. In some cases, the databases you need to use will already be defined. This certainly simplifies the task, but it doesn't leave us much to talk about, so for the sake of discussion let's assume that you're starting from scratch.

Even if the exact database tables you need don't currently exist, you do need to consider how your data fits in with other data maintained by the organization. You need to consider where the data will reside and who can access it. Will the data be stored on centrally located servers or on individual workstations? Will data need to be replicated to multiple locations in order to meet performance requirements? If so, will the data be partitioned, or do you need to worry about conflicting updates from multiple sites? For the Island Hopper classified ads application, the database is maintained on a single database server. Your application might have more complex requirements.

Selecting entities

One very common way to model persistent data is a technique known as *entity-relationship modeling*. To begin data modeling, look for real-world things, or "entities," in the problem definition. An easy way to start is to look for nouns in the problem definition—these often correspond to entities in the model. An *entity* has a set of *attributes* that describe it. A particular entity has specific values for each attribute. All the entities that share a set of attributes define an *entity type*.

> **NOTE** In object-oriented terms, "entity" = "object," "entity type" = "class," and "attribute" = "property."

When you are using a relational database, entity types are modeled as database tables. Attributes correspond to columns in the database table. A complete definition of the entity type, including the names and meanings of all attributes and any constraints is called a *schema*. One of the main constraints to consider is which attribute(s) can be used to identify each entity. These attributes are used to define *database keys*. A database key is one or more columns in a table used to identify a record; database keys are commonly used as an index for the table.

> **NOTE** This chapter merely scratches the surface of data modeling. For more information, see the sources listed in the bibliography.

After examining the problem definition and functional specification for the Island Hopper classified ads application, you should be able to identify the following three main entity types:

Customer type: Includes name, mailing address, password, and customer ID attributes. The customer ID attribute uniquely identifies a customer. The name and mailing address attributes might need to be divided into separate elements— for example, first name, last name, street, city, state, and zip code.

Advertisement type: Includes category, title, body text, start date, end date, customer, and advertisement ID attributes. The advertisement ID attribute uniquely identifies an advertisement.

Invoice type: Includes customer, list of ads, date, total amount, and invoice ID attributes. The invoice ID uniquely identifies an invoice. The list of ads is a *multivalued attribute*. We'll see how to deal with multivalued attributes in the section "Data object methods" later in this chapter.

Defining relationships

Some implicit relationships exist between these entities. Advertisements and invoices both refer to customers. Invoices refer to a list of advertisements.

Relationship types define associations between entity types. Most relationships are between two entity types. Each entity type plays a particular role in the relationship type. Normally, you don't need to explicitly call out role names when the entity types are distinct, but the names can be very helpful when you are defining relationships between different entities of the same type. (These are called *recursive relationships*.) For example, two *employee* entities might be related by a *supervises* relationship, one entity in the role of *supervisor* and the other in the role of *supervisee*.

To locate the relationship types in your data model, you should look for attributes in your entities that seem to correspond to other entities. For example, both the advertisement and invoice entities mentioned above contain a customer attribute. You should also refer back to the problem definition. Verbs in the problem definition can point out relationships that you haven't recognized yet.

Relationship types usually have a structural constraint associated with them. This constraint defines how many relationship instances an entity can participate in. Usually, the constraint is specified as one-to-one (1:1), one-to-many (1:N), or many-to-many (M:N). For example, if one customer can submit many advertisements, each advertisement is submitted by exactly one customer, and a customer is deleted if no advertisements exist, the relationship between customers and advertisements is 1:N. You can also specify the minimum and maximum number of instances for each entity.

Relationship types can also have attributes associated with them. For 1:1 and 1:N relationships, these attributes can be stored in the entity representing the "1" side of the relationship. However, for M:N relationships, the attributes are a characteristic of the relationship itself.

In the relational database, relationship types can be represented as attributes or tables. For 1:N relationships, the table representing the "N" side of the relationship includes a column corresponding to the key of the other table. (1:1 is just a special case of 1:N.) Attributes for the relationship itself would be stored as columns in the table on the "1" side of the relationship. For example, the Island

Hopper *advertisement* entity should include a customer ID column to represent the 1:N relationship between customers and advertisements. For M:N relationships, a separate table is usually used to represent the relationship. This table includes columns corresponding to keys for each of the tables in the relationship, as well as columns for each attribute of the relationship itself.

Figure 7-4 shows a data model for the Island Hopper classified ads application that includes both entity and relationship types. Notice that some of the attributes have been refined to reflect the relationships between the entities.

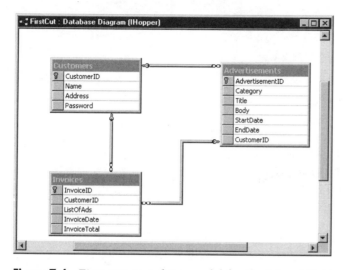

Figure 7-4. *First cut at a data model for the Island Hopper application.*

Normalizing the database

In a relational database, data is usually factored according to the following data normalization rules. These rules help prevent common data problems related to synchronization and consistency of changes.

■ Every attribute must have a single meaning—in other words, you shouldn't need to retrieve part of an attribute.

■ The same fact must not be stored more than once.

■ Entities should not contain repeating groups.

OK, those aren't the formal rules…but you get the idea. (If you really want to know the rules, check out any book on database design.) Your first cut at a data model might not be normalized (unless you've been doing data modeling for a while and these rules are burned into your subconscious). After you've created the basic tables and relationships, normalize the database. But keep in mind that performance requirements might require denormalizing the database.

Figure 7-5 shows the final data model for the Island Hopper classified ads application. A new entity type, *category*, has been defined. This entity type will remove the name of the category from every advertisement, making it easier to maintain a category list. Customer *passwords* have been split into a separate entity to help secure the passwords. The *product* and *payment* entities have been introduced to help with invoicing.

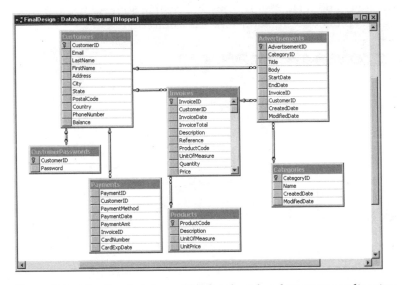

Figure 7-5. *The final data model for the Island Hopper application.*

In addition, the multivalued list of ads attribute in the *invoice* entity type has been converted to a 1:N relationship between invoices and advertisements, with an invoice ID attribute stored in each advertisement. This is how multivalued attributes are normalized in relational databases: the attribute is converted to a separate entity that has a 1:N relationship with the original entity.

You might also have noticed that the *customer* entity includes a *balance* attribute. The customer balance could be computed by querying invoices and payments, but this process would be very slow. So the database is slightly denormalized to include the outstanding balance in the *customer* entity.

Documenting the data model

Many tools are available for documenting a data model. In this book, we use the Microsoft Visual Database Tools to create our data models. With the Visual Database Tools, you can connect to and explore any ODBC-compliant database. The Database Designer tool provides a graphical environment for the following tasks:

- Creating and modifying the structure of Microsoft SQL Server 6.5 databases

- Experimenting with the design of tables, relationships, indexes, and constraints

- Viewing and saving Transact-SQL scripts of changes to a database

Other data tools provide a graphical user interface that lets you add, update, and delete data in the database; design and execute complex queries; and so on.

> **NOTE** The Microsoft Visual Database Tools are included with Microsoft Visual Studio Enterprise Edition, Microsoft Visual InterDev, Microsoft Visual C++ Enterprise Edition, Microsoft Visual Basic 6.0 Enterprise Edition, and as an add-in for Microsoft Visual Basic 5.0 Enterprise Edition.

Designing Classes

Once you have your database schema in place, you can start looking at the COM classes you'll use to implement your application. Remember that the recommended application architecture for MTS applications is a three-tier, component-based architecture. As we've seen, distributed applications follow a common usage pattern. It turns out that this pattern maps quite nicely to the three-tier model, as shown in Figure 7-6 on the following page. Users are presented with data by the presentation layer. The user can request more data through the presentation layer. The presentation layer uses services of the business layer, commonly called *business objects,* to retrieve the data. In addition to viewing the data, the user can update the data through the presentation layer. The presentation layer uses business objects to update the data. The business objects in turn will rely on services of the data access layer, called *data objects,* to interact with persistent data.

As you'll recall from Chapter 1, several reasons exist for introducing a layer of business objects between the presentation and data access layers. A key reason is to reduce the number of database connections required, to improve scalability. When presentation and data access layers are directly connected, each client maintains one or more connections to the database—and database connections are very expensive! A second reason is to isolate the presentation layer from details of the database schema. The presentation layer works with a logical view of the data exposed by the business objects and does not need to worry about where or how the data is actually stored. In general, the presentation layer depends only on the business layer, the business layer depends only on the data access layer, and the data access layer encapsulates knowledge of the physical database structure and data access mechanisms. This separation makes it easier to maintain applications since the presentation, business, and data access layers can evolve independently over time.

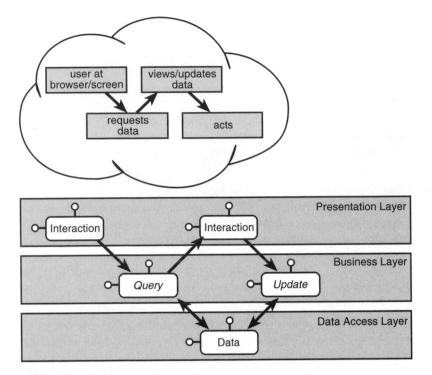

Figure 7-6. *A common usage pattern for MTS applications.*

The following four basic types of objects are found in three-tier applications:

- An *Interaction* object is used in the presentation layer to display data to the user and optionally let him or her update the data. Most Microsoft ActiveX controls fall into this category.

- A *Query* object is a type of business object used to retrieve data, in accordance with business rules.

- An *Update* object is another type of business object used to update data, in accordance with business rules. Sometimes the updated data is given to the object and the object is responsible for validating and saving the data. At other times, the object takes some action to compute updated data itself.

- A data object encapsulates access to the actual persistent data. This persistent data could be a database, a file, a mail message store—anything. Only the data object needs to know.

You might be wondering what the difference is between the query and update objects and a data object. After all, query and update do sound like they have something to do with data access. Business objects (query and update) are defined in terms of real-world business operations and are oblivious to actual data sources. A data object encapsulates access to the actual data. A business object is a client of a data object.

> **NOTE** When most people talk about three-tier, component-based applications, they'll say that applications are implemented from "business objects" and "data objects." However, as we saw in Chapter 2, COM objects are run-time instances of COM classes, which are packaged in COM components. So what we're really talking about here is modeling objects as COM classes. We'll discuss packaging COM classes into COM components in the section "Grouping Classes into Components" later in this chapter.

Documenting the logical classes

Many tools are available that enable you to document your object design. In this book, we use Microsoft Visual Modeler. Visual Modeler is an entry-level design tool based on UML and specifically designed for documenting designs for component-based applications that will be implemented using Visual Basic.

> **NOTE** Visual Modeler is available as an add-on for Visual Basic 5.0 and will be included with Microsoft Visual Studio starting with version 6.0.

Visual Modeler supports a subset of UML. It lets you create *class diagrams, component diagrams,* and *deployment diagrams.* Class diagrams describe the logical structure of your application—the classes, logical packages, and the relationships between them. Component diagrams describe the physical structure of your application—how classes are grouped into physical DLLs and executables. Deployment diagrams show how the application processes will be distributed among machines in your system.

Visual Modeler is a round-trip engineering tool. You can create models and then generate Visual Basic code based on those models. You can also generate models from existing Visual Basic code. This capability is particularly useful for maintenance projects and for documenting the final design of your application.

> **NOTE** For more information about UML, see the references listed in the bibliography.

To begin documenting your design using Visual Modeler, simply start up the application. A blank project window will appear, with a Logical View/Three-Tiered Service Model diagram window. By expanding Logical View in the Browser pane, you can view the different layers of the three-tier model.

You document your data and business objects as classes in this view. To define a class, use the Visual Modeler Class Wizard, shown in Figure 7-7. The wizard lets you specify which tier the class belongs to, as well as its properties and methods.

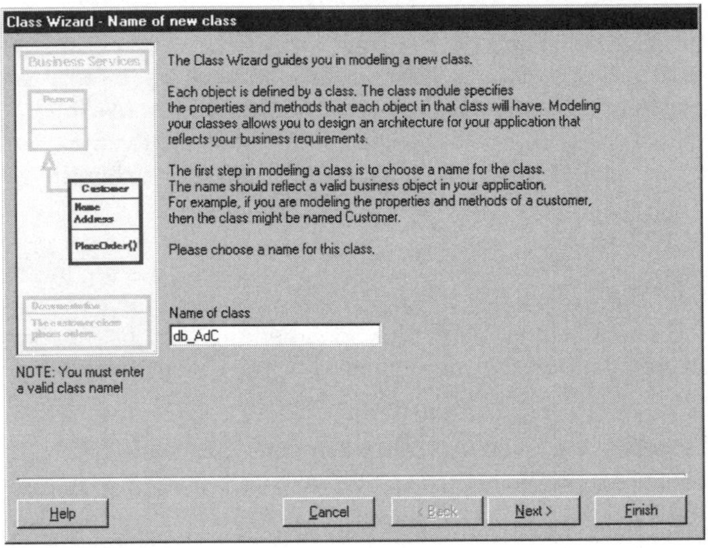

Figure 7-7. *Using the Class Wizard to define a class in Visual Modeler.*

You'll continue to update this diagram and other diagrams in the project as you proceed through the application design process. We'll discuss the component and deployment diagrams in the section "Documenting the Physical Architecture" later in this chapter.

Modeling the Data Objects

A good place to begin your conceptual design is to model the data objects your application will use. Note, however, that design is an iterative process. You don't need to get the data objects exactly right before you move on to business objects or the presentation layer. As you look at the other tiers, you'll probably find an essential piece of data that you just can't get to or a query that you didn't anticipate. Then you can take another look at the data objects and adjust their interfaces appropriately. It's a lot easier to make these adjustments during the design process than after you've started implementation!

Data objects are responsible for pieces of data. The data object is the only thing that should be reading and writing its piece of data to the persistent store. The persistent store can be anything, but it is most commonly a relational database. The unit of data managed by a data object is usually a single table in the database. Data objects are responsible for the accuracy, completeness, and consistency of the data they own. If any invalid data is stored, the data object is at fault. Data objects can rely on services provided by the underlying store to ensure data integrity. For example, if the data is stored in a relational database, the DBMS's referential integrity rules might be used to ensure consistency between tables. The important thing is to keep each rule in one place so that it can easily be modified if necessary.

To begin modeling you first decide which data objects you'll need. For most projects, a good way to start is to define one data object for each database table. Then you can look at the details of each object.

In the traditional object-oriented approach to modeling, you would define a data variable, or property, for each element of the data encapsulated by a data object—for example, one property per column in a database table. Then you would define property accessor methods, as well as methods for the remaining behavior of the object. Things aren't quite this simple when you start working with components that will be used in a distributed environment, particularly those that will be used in MTS.

Recall from Chapter 4 that MTS provides many run-time services to manage object state and resource usage, based on transaction boundaries, as well as services to manage secure object access, based on package, component, and interface boundaries. To get the most benefit from these services, your objects need to be designed with the MTS application server programming model in mind. In particular, you'll need to consider the following object characteristics:

- The object's state—that is, what data it requires and how that data is managed

- The object's behavior—that is, the methods it supports

- The object's resource usage—that is, how it uses locks, database connections, and so on

- The object's transactional behavior

- The object's security requirements—that is, any limitations on who can access the object's methods

- The object's clients

Although we'll look at these items one by one, they can't really be treated independently. How you decide to manage object state will influence the parameter lists of methods you expose. And how you manage state, resources, and transactions will influence which methods you need. Security requirements will influence how those methods are grouped into COM interfaces. The expected clients —in particular, whether there are script-based clients—and how they will use an object influences its state, resource, and transaction management, as well as how methods are grouped into interfaces.

Managing data object state

Let's start by looking at state management. After all, the only reason we have data objects is to encapsulate access to persistent data. State management is a complex topic—no one way is correct for all situations. We'll look at some of the issues here and at an approach that will work for most simple applications. As you gain experience with designing applications for MTS and work on more complex applications, you might decide that a different approach is more appropriate for your application.

One approach would be to read data from the persistent store into a data object and then provide property accessor methods to let clients get to the data. This approach presents a number of potential problems. First is the possibility of an enormous communication overhead if the calling application or component is running in a different process or on a different machine. Each call to an accessor method results in an expensive interprocess or network call to return a small piece of data, limiting performance. Second, if the calling application or component can update the data, resource management becomes very complicated. How long do you need to hold onto database connections and locks? For the duration of each accessor method call? Across calls? To be safe, you probably need to hold onto them for the lifetime of the object—or you'll need to rely on the client to call a special method to indicate that it has finished making updates and that the data should be consistent. This solution can also lead to scalability problems. And it makes writing correct applications harder than necessary.

For a similar reason, this property-based approach might make it difficult to take advantage of the MTS Just-In-Time (JIT) activation feature, object pooling, or automatic transactions. Remember that MTS reclaims object instances at transaction boundaries. Callers cannot rely on the in-memory state of an object across a transaction boundary. If data objects are instantiated only for the lifetime of a business object method call and the business object method call defines the transaction scope, this approach might be perfectly acceptable. In any case, if you design your data objects to retain transient per-object state, you need to be very, very aware of all the issues surrounding the objects' lifetimes.

A more straightforward approach for most data objects is to simply pass all the data through the object back to the client. Objects that use this approach are sometimes called *stateless objects* because they don't keep any state in object data members. With this approach, the issues mentioned above go away. All the data is transferred in a single method call. Resource management is simplified. As far as the object is concerned, when a method call completes, all the resources used by the object are no longer needed. In fact, the object itself isn't needed between method calls—as far as the client is concerned, any object can be used to make a method call because all the required inputs are passed to the object with the call. So stateless objects work extremely well with JIT activation and object pooling.

In general, stateless data objects produce highly scalable solutions. However, you might find situations in which the object state is extremely expensive to compute, or in which you have a priori knowledge of how the object will be used and are willing to take the extra care needed to work with stateful data objects. Consider the trade-offs carefully before you decide how to manage state in your data objects.

> **NOTE** For the remainder of our discussion of data object design, we'll assume that the data objects are stateless—in other words, all data required for a particular action must be passed to an object from the client and all data created by the action will be passed back to the client.

Data object methods

Next let's look at the object behavior. Every data object will expose four basic types of methods: *Add, Update, Delete,* and *Query*. Usually, only one *Add* method and one *Delete* method are present, but a data object might have multiple *Update* and *Query* methods. As mentioned, for each method the client needs to pass in all the information required to complete the action. However, if clients are calling across a slow communications link, you want to be certain that you aren't requiring a lot of extraneous data in each call. For example, if customer address changes are relatively rare and customer password changes are frequent, you wouldn't want to have one customer *Update* method that forced the client to pass in all the information about the customer's address just to update the password. Instead, you should have separate *UpdateAddress* and *UpdatePassword* methods. You'll probably also want a separate *Query* method for each way of retrieving individual records and lists of records.

You can use several techniques to pass information to and from your methods. The simplest approach is to pass each data element as a parameter, but this can become unwieldy if you have a lot of data elements. Another approach is to stuff all the data into a Variant array. The advantage of this approach is that COM automatically handles the marshaling details. But constructing the array and pulling information back out of it can be complicated—especially for clients written in C++. Finally, it is possible to pass an entire object back and forth.

Normally, COM does not marshal objects by value; you just get an interface pointer. So accessing data from the object involves remote calls. However, it is possible to have an entire object marshaled to the client. The ADO disconnected recordsets discussed in Chapter 3 use this technique to pass the entire recordset to the client.

For most data object methods, you can use the following guidelines for method parameter passing:

■ To modify a single record, pass in all data as individual parameters.

■ To modify multiple records, pass in data as a recordset.

■ Return a single value as a function return value (that's a *[retval]*, for the IDL-aware) rather than as an *out* parameter. Return a small number of values as multiple *out* parameters. If you need to return more than a handful of related values, consider using disconnected recordsets.

Other factors

At this point, we have a pretty good first cut at our data objects. Let's look briefly at the remaining characteristics on our list that we should consider when modeling data objects.

With stateless objects, it's possible for MTS to eliminate transient state between method calls. It's also possible to ensure that database connections, locks, and so on are not held open between method calls. Your methods should acquire the resources they need as late as possible, hold them for the shortest possible amount of time, and let MTS know when the resources and object state can be reclaimed. The mechanism you use to let MTS know when resources and object state can be reclaimed is the *ObjectContext SetComplete* method. We'll discuss this method in further detail in Chapter 8, when we discuss implementing data objects.

Another important aspect of data objects is their transactional requirements. Remember from Chapter 4 that transactions are how you ensure that data updates are performed consistently across multiple databases or data objects. In general, at a minimum data objects should be marked as "supports a transaction." When they are marked in this way, data objects will participate in existing MTS transactions. However, if no transaction is currently in progress, MTS will not create a transaction for the data object. As long as the data object method called issues only one database statement, you can usually rely on the underlying database to provide transaction protection. If your data object issues multiple database statements or uses subordinate objects, you should mark the data object as "requires a transaction" to ensure that all actions are rolled back in the event of a failure. If you need your object methods to succeed or fail independent of other object methods, you should mark your data object as "requires a new transaction."

The final two considerations, security and client use, primarily affect how you group methods into COM interfaces. In general, security isn't a major issue during data object design. (It does become important when you deploy the application, as access to the actual data stores must be enabled.) Remember that the only things calling your data objects are business objects. Typically, these will be trusted to perform all operations on the data object. Authorization checking would be performed on calls to the business object rather than on calls to the data object. If for some reason you do need to restrict access to some methods on your data objects, however, you should split those methods out into a separate interface, as this is the smallest authorization unit in MTS.

A potential problem with defining multiple interfaces is that some clients can access only one interface per object—the default *IDispatch*. If your clients are implemented using languages with this restriction (like VBScript), you might need to split the data object into two separate objects, not just two separate interfaces.

Client implementation languages can also affect the data types you can use for method parameters. Most languages support only Automation-compatible data types. Unless you know that all your clients will be implemented in C or C++, you should stick with the Automation-compatible types.

Island Hopper data objects

Enough theory. Let's look at an example. The data model for Island Hopper contains seven tables: *Categories*, *Customers*, *Products*, *CustomerPasswords*, *Invoices*, *Payments*, and *Advertisements*. We'll start by modeling each table as a separate data object, as shown below.

Data Object	Description
db_AdC	Stores information about an advertisement
db_CategoryC	Stores the main descriptive category for advertised items
db_CustomerC	Stores information about a specific customer for billing and contact purposes
db_CustomerPasswordC	Stores customer password
db_InvoiceC	Stores information about a particular invoice
db_PaymentC	Stores information about a payment from a customer
db_ProductC	Stores product/billing codes for invoicing

As a rough start, we can define *Add*, *Delete*, and *Update* methods for each object; the *Add* and *Update* methods will include parameters for each data element provided by the client. We can use the functional requirements to get a pretty good idea of what kind of *Query* methods we'll need too. Island Hopper uses the naming convention *GetBy<X>* to name methods that retrieve a single record using *<X>* as the key and *ListBy<X>* to name methods that retrieve a set of records using *<X>* as the key.

From the functional requirements, we can guess that *CustomerPasswords* will need to retrieve single records by customer ID. We'll also need a way to add, delete, and, update passwords. Thus we'll need a *db_CustomerPasswordC* object with four methods, as shown here:

```
Public Sub Add(ByVal lngCustomerID As Long, _
    ByVal strPassword As String)
Public Sub Delete(ByVal lngCustomerID As Long)
Public Sub Update(ByVal lngCustomerID As Long, _
    ByVal strPassword As String)
Function GetByID(ByVal lngCustomerID As Long) As ADODB.Recordset
```

We can also anticipate that we might need to retrieve single customer records by customer ID or e-mail address or a list of customers by last name, so we'll define three *Query* methods for *db_CustomerC*. And we'll need to be able to update a customer's outstanding balance or contact information, so we'll define two *Update* methods, as shown here:

```
Public Sub Add(ByVal lngCustomerID As Long, _
    ByVal strEmail As String, ByVal strLastName As String, _
    ByVal strFirstName As String, ByVal strAddress As String, _
    ByVal strCity As String, ByVal strState As String, _
    ByVal strPostalCode As String,  ByVal strPhone As String)
Public Sub Delete(ByVal lngCustomerID As Long)
Public Sub Update(ByVal lngCustomerID As Long, _
    ByVal strEmail As String,  ByVal strLastName As String, _
    ByVal strFirstName As String, ByVal strAddress As String, _
    ByVal strCity As String, ByVal strState As String, _
    ByVal strPostalCode As String, ByVal strPhone As String)
Public Sub UpdateBalance(ByVal lngCustomerID As Long, _
    ByVal dblBal As Double)
Public Function GetByID(ByVal lngCustomerID As Long) _
    As ADODB.Recordset
Public Function GetByEmail(ByVal strEmail As String) _
    As ADODB.Recordset
Public Function ListByLastName(ByVal strLastName As String) _
    As ADODB.Recordset
```

We can repeat this process for each of the data tables to produce a first cut at methods for each data object. Now would also be a good time to identify any relationships between the data objects. Does one data object need to use methods of another object to do its work? Is there some common behavior that you want to pull out into a separate interface or base component? At this stage, the answer to both questions is probably no, unless you have a complex data model. But if relationships exist, you should document them. The Island Hopper application has no relationships between its data objects.

> **NOTE** The complete component design for the Island Hopper classified ads application is contained in the CLASSIFIED.MDL file, which is located in the \IslandHopper\Design directory on the companion CD. You can use Microsoft Visual Modeler or Rational Rose to view this model.

Modeling the Business Objects

With the data objects under control, we can turn our attention to the business objects. This is where things really start to get fun!

Business objects encapsulate real-world business operations, independent of how the data they use is actually stored. Your business objects will use the data objects you've already defined. (Of course, if you find something missing from the data objects while you're looking at the business objects, go back and update the data object model.) Business objects usually encapsulate multiple-step operations and can access multiple data objects.

Defining a good set of business objects is hard work. The goal here is to define objects that do all the "thinking" in the application. Business objects control sequencing and enforcement of business rules, as well as the transactional integrity of the operations they perform. They are the heart and soul of your application. Great business objects are important assets that can be reused in many applications.

> **WARNING** The allure of reuse and the desire to define a perfect business object can lead to "analysis paralysis." It's important to design your components around a small number of known clients—one or two immediate uses, perhaps one down the road. Don't try to design components that will be all things to all clients.

As you begin to create a repository of components and work on additional projects, you'll begin to see patterns that can help you refine your components and make them useful to a broader range of clients. The wonderful thing about COM is that you can implement these refinements as new interfaces on existing components, continuing to support existing applications while making the components useful to new clients as well.

Choosing business objects

The six design considerations for data objects mentioned in the section "Modeling the Data Objects" earlier in this chapter apply to business objects as well. But there isn't as obvious a starting point for determining what business objects to apply the considerations to. A reasonable way to choose business objects is to examine the scenarios in your functional specification for real-world objects that are acted on by the application. For example, in the scenario "Place a Classified Ad," the real-world object is the advertisement. Each business object should encapsulate functionality related to one real-world object.

Less well-defined is whether each real-world object should correspond to exactly one business object. For objects with a small number of actions, one object is probably just fine. But for objects with many actions, you might want to split up the actions—not just into separate interfaces, but into separate objects. This helps make your business objects more reusable. Business objects that try to be all things to all people can easily end up as nothing to anyone. These "kitchen-sink" objects can have such a large working set or per-object memory footprint that no one wants to use them. At this point, if you see an obvious split in functionality for different types of clients or in how frequently different functionality will be used, it's probably worth defining a separate business object for special client types or for the more rarely used functionality. Otherwise, just start with one business object per real-world object.

Business object methods

Closely related to the question of what business objects you define is the question of what methods those objects support. The general rule here is that each method should do exactly one unit of work and each unit of work should be implemented in exactly one method. Fine-grained methods that do a single unit of work are easily composed into higher level operations. This is just good old-fashioned structured design…with a twist. Composition across component boundaries introduces some interesting issues that we'll look at in the section "Composition, resource management, and transactions" later in this chapter.

You can start looking for business object methods by examining the scenarios in your functional specification. High-level business object methods typically encapsulate each piece of a scenario between collecting information from the user and returning information to the user. These methods are usually the root of a distributed transaction and use services from several other business and data objects. As you go through the high-level, scenario-driven methods, you'll start to see common behavior. That behavior should be split out into separate methods, to help ensure consistency across your application(s).

Business object methods also encapsulate and enforce business rules. Each rule can be implemented as a separate method or as logic within a larger method. The important thing is to ensure that each rule appears in only one place, just in case that rule changes.

Finally, business object methods can encapsulate and enforce data rules. In particular, business objects encapsulate rules that span multiple data objects. For example, an invoice component in our Island Hopper application could ensure that invoices are generated only when both the header and at least one line-item have been provided.

Managing business object state

State management can be more complicated for business objects than it is for data objects—mainly because you have more choices. Recall the four basic types of state from Chapter 4:

- State maintained by the client and passed to objects as parameters
- Per-object transient state, maintained in object member variables
- Shared transient state, maintained in shared memory
- Persisted state, maintained in a persistent data store and retrieved using a key value passed as a parameter to an object

Now we know that business objects never directly interact with persisted state—they use the data objects. What about the other choices? Let's think about how business objects are used.

First, business objects can be created and used directly by the presentation layer. The presentation layer usually runs on individual user workstations, not on the machines on which the business objects are running. The workstations may be connected to the business object servers by slow links. Minimizing network traffic between the machines is important. In addition, users can take a long time to do things. Holding shared resources or keeping transactions open until the user finishes a task probably isn't feasible. For this type of object, you should not maintain per-object transient state. Each method should stand alone, using the object context to indicate when it has finished with the object's state.

Business objects can also be created and used from other business objects. In this case, the communication overhead might not be a factor and the object might exist only within the scope of a single transaction. For this type of object, you might elect to maintain per-object transient state. This state should only be maintained within a transaction boundary, so that you can take advantage of MTS JIT activation and object pooling.

There will be a few cases in which you need to share information across multiple objects (or across multiple transactions) and the overhead of saving the information in persistent storage is just too high. A good example of this situation is a Web page counter. If the counter is read from storage, incremented, and written back to storage every time a Web page is visited, the system will not be very responsive. Instead, you could cache the counter in shared memory for speedy access and update and periodically write the new value to persistent storage. To share transient state across transaction or object boundaries in MTS, you use the Shared Property Manager (SPM). We'll discuss the details in Chapter 9, when we talk about implementing business objects.

Composition, resource management, and transactions

The way your business objects are used also affects resource management and transactional behavior. You must remember that most business objects will be composed with other components to produce higher-level behavior. Your objects must behave correctly whether they are used directly or in conjunction with other objects.

As with data objects, if your business objects use resources, they should grab the resources as late as possible and release them as quickly as possible. Your objects should use the object context method to tell MTS when object transient state and resources can be reclaimed. Your objects should also use the object context method to create any subordinate objects that are hosted in MTS.

When you use the object context method to create subordinate objects, context information flows from your object to the newly created object. One very important piece of this information is the transaction that the object is a part of. As we saw in Chapter 4, objects that participate in a single transaction all get to vote on the outcome of the transaction. If any object votes to abort the transaction, the transaction is aborted and any managed resources are rolled back. This capability makes error recovery for actions composed from several objects much easier. Thus, it is important to specify the transactional requirements of your business objects correctly.

In general, business objects whose methods use multiple subordinate data objects should be marked as "requires a transaction" to ensure that all actions are correctly rolled back on failures. Business objects that do not access multiple data objects can be marked as "supports transactions," which ensures that if the object is ever composed with a transacted object, it correctly participates in the transaction but does not force transaction overhead if none is needed. If the success or failure of a business object should be independent of the success or failure of its clients, the business object should be marked as "requires a new transaction." Objects that don't access any data objects can be marked as "does not support transactions." If your objects need to retain per-object transient state across method calls, consider the impact of the transaction setting carefully.

Security considerations

Security issues are also more complex for business objects than they are for data objects. Recall from Chapter 4 that MTS role-based security authorizes access to objects only on entry to a package and that authorized roles can be specified for packages, components, and interfaces. Calls from one object to another within the same package are not checked.

You should look at the security requirements defined during requirements analysis to determine whether any methods on your objects require authorization checks or whether any other data protection or authentication requirements apply. If so, group methods with similar requirements into interfaces. If any methods have extremely stringent security requirements, consider splitting off those methods into a completely separate class. You should also split off methods into a separate class if the class will be called via *IDispatch*—for example, from script code in an ASP page. You cannot define roles specific to *IDispatch*. If your classes will be accessed via *IDispatch*, you will need to define roles at the package or component level.

Island Hopper business objects

Let's look at the Island Hopper application again. If we examine the functional specification, a few real-world objects jump out: advertisements, customers, invoices, and payments. We'll start by defining a business object for each real-world object, as shown in the table below.

Business Object	Description
bus_AdC	Places, updates, and deletes advertisements
bus_CustomerC	Validates customer information
bus_InvoiceC	Generates customer invoices for advertisements
bus_PaymentC	Processes payments from customers

Let's look at the *bus_CustomerC* component in more detail. We can use the functional requirements to get a pretty good idea of the kinds of methods we need. We'll need methods to add a new customer, delete an existing customer, and update an existing customer. We'll also need to be able to look up customers by customer ID, customer e-mail name, and customer last name. And we'll need a method to validate customer login information. The necessary methods are shown in the following code:

```
Public Function Add(ByVal strEmail As String, _
    ByVal strLastName As String, ByVal strFirstName As String, _
    ByVal strAddress As String, ByVal strCity As String, _
    ByVal strState As String, ByVal strPostalCode As String, _
    ByVal strCountry As String, ByVal strPhone As String, _
    ByVal strPassword As String) As Long
Public Sub Delete(ByVal lngCustomerID As Long)
Public Sub Update(ByVal lngCustomerID As Long, _
    ByVal strEmail As String, ByVal strLastName As String, _
    ByVal strFirstName As String, ByVal strAddress As String, _
```

(continued)

```
        ByVal strCity As String, ByVal strState As String, _
        ByVal strPostalCode As String, ByVal strCountry As String, _
        ByVal strPhone As String, ByVal strPassword As String)
Public Sub GetByID(ByVal lngCustomerID As Long, _
        rsCustomer As ADODB.Recordset, _
        Optional rsPassword As ADODB.Recordset)
Public Sub GetByEmail(ByVal strEmail As String, _
        rsCustomer As ADODB.Recordset, rsPassword As ADODB.Recordset)
Public Function ListByLastName(strLastName As String) _
        As ADODB.Recordset
Public Function Validate(ByVal strEmail As String, _
        ByVal strPassword As String) As ADODB.Recordset
```

The *bus_CustomerC* object will be used directly by the presentation layer, to maintain customer information. Thus, we will not maintain per-object state. Instead, we will pass all the information required by each function as input parameters and return all information generated by each function as output parameters or return values. The object relies on the *db_CustomerC* object to access the persistent data and is itself used by the *bus_AdC* object, so we'll mark *bus_CustomerC* as "requires a transaction."

From a security perspective, it's reasonable to assume that we might want to restrict access to the *Add*, *Delete*, and *Update* methods. The *GetByID*, *GetBy-Email*, and *ListByLastName* methods also group naturally. These two groups of methods are good candidates for splitting off into separate interfaces. However, we know that one of the client applications for this component is an Internet application that will be implemented using ASP. The Internet application needs to use the *Update* methods and the lookup methods, but scripts in ASP can use *IDispatch* only to access objects. Furthermore, ASP applications usually run as the same identity, regardless of who requested the page. There doesn't appear to be much point in splitting the methods into separate interfaces or separate components after all.

> **NOTE** The complete component design for the Island Hopper classified ads application is contained in the CLASSIFIED.MDL file, which is located in the \IslandHopper\Design directory on the companion CD. You can use Microsoft Visual Modeler or Rational Rose to view this model.

Modeling the Presentation Layer

The final task in application modeling is modeling the presentation layer. Our primary focus in this book is the middle tier of the three-tier architecture, so we won't spend a lot of time on presentation layer modeling. The key task in this phase is documenting what the user interface of your application will look like (roughly) and how the user will work through the various screens.

You should also consider the technology constraints on your presentation layer design. Does the application need to run in a Web browser, or can it be a full-featured Windows application? If it's a Web application, can you assume that the browser supports anything other than pure HTML?

If your client application must be pure HTML, you can't really do anything on the client machine at all. You'll need to call your business objects from server-side scripts. Recall from Chapter 5 that you can use ASP to format HTML pages and run server-side scripts that use your business objects.

On the other hand, if your client application can use objects directly, it might be possible to move some of the work from your server machines to the client machine. You can pass disconnected recordsets all the way to the presentation layer for display and user interaction. You might want to create specialized ActiveX controls or data validation components to run in the presentation layer.

> **NOTE** We'll look at the presentation layer in a little more detail in Chapter 11.

Defining the Physical Architecture

Once the conceptual design is in place, you can start fleshing out the physical architecture of your application. During physical design, you perform the following tasks:

- Group COM classes into components

- Group COM components into MTS packages and processes

- Assign packages and processes to machines

At this stage, you won't fully define the physical architecture. In fact, some decisions about assigning packages and processes to machines can be left to the system administrator who installs your application. However, if there are performance, deployment, or security requirements that will constrain your design and implementation, you should define those now. Also, you will need to determine how COM classes are grouped into components in order to implement the classes.

Grouping Classes into Components

For most classes used in MTS, organizing classes into components is easy. Each externally creatable COM class is implemented in its own in-process component. If you happen to have some COM classes (call them S1, S2, and so on) that are instantiated only via some other class (call it C), you will probably want to include Sn in C's component.

You don't want to include too many classes in a single component for the same reason you don't want to include too many methods in a single interface—if your component carries a lot of unnecessary overhead, people won't want to use it. However, if you have several classes that share implementation code or are generally used together, you might want to put all the classes in one component to simplify deployment and maintenance. For example, independent software vendors (ISVs) that create libraries of COM classes for sale to other developers might want to package those classes into a small number of components to simplify setup, redistribution, and licensing. All the classes defined so far in the Island Hopper application are placed in individual components.

Grouping Components into Packages and Processes

As mentioned, MTS uses packages as units of trust and units of deployment. A package is simply a set of components that perform related application functions. A component can be installed in only one package on a machine. There are two types of packages: *library packages* and *server packages*. A library package runs in the process of the client that created it. A server package runs in a separate process.

We'll discuss grouping components into packages and processes in detail in Chapter 10. For now, all you really need to do is look at your deployment and security requirements to see whether they imply anything about packaging. For example, if you need to authorize calls to a component, the calls must cross a package boundary. Components that must run on separate machines obviously need to go into separate packages. You can also look at the presentation layer to identify processes running outside the scope of MTS. In the Island Hopper application, we can identify two likely packages at this point: one for things controlled by the classified ads department and one for things controlled by the accounting department.

Assigning Packages and Processes to Machines

Most decisions about where packages and processes should run can (and should) be postponed until much later. However, if you have identified particular deployment requirements that apply to certain components, you should document how those requirements apply to the packages and processes you've defined. The Island Hopper application has no special deployment requirements for integrating into an existing enterprise infrastructure. All the components can run on a single machine.

Documenting the Physical Architecture

You can use Visual Modeler to document the physical design of your application as well as the logical design. You use component diagrams to describe how classes are grouped into components and packages. You use deployment diagrams to describe how packages and processes are distributed among machines in your system.

To create a component diagram, open your existing Visual Modeler document and expand the Component View in the Browser pane. You'll see one default component diagram named Main in that view. Double-clicking Main will open its component diagram. You can add an element to the diagram by choosing Create from the Tools menu and then selecting the appropriate element to add. You can add component packages and components to this diagram, as well as create dependencies between them. You can also create additional diagrams and attach them to specific packages in the model.

A component package in Visual Modeler corresponds roughly to an MTS package. A component in Visual Modeler can be a COM component, a separate application, or a utility DLL.

The easiest way to begin your component diagram is to use the Main diagram to list the MTS packages and separate client processes in your application as well as define the dependencies between them. Model each MTS package as a Visual Modeler package. Model each client process as a Visual Modeler component and set its stereotype to Application using the Specification Properties window. Set the name of each package and application using its Specification Properties window—you can access the Specification Properties window by selecting the item and choosing Specification from the Browse menu. If classes in the logical model will be implemented directly in a client application, use the Realizes tab in the Specification Properties window to assign classes to the application.

For each package, create a new component diagram. You can do this by right-clicking on a package name in the Browser pane and choosing New and then Component Diagram from the pop-up menus. Add the COM components assigned to the package to this diagram. Model each COM component as a Visual Modeler component and set its stereotype to DLL using the Specification Properties window. Set the name of the component using its Specification Properties window. Now you can assign classes from the logical model to the component on the Realizes tab. Right-click on a class from the list and choose Assign from the pop-up menu, as shown in Figure 7-8 on the following page.

To create a deployment diagram, open your existing Visual Modeler document and double-click on Deployment View in the Browser pane to open the deployment diagram. You can add an element to the diagram by choosing Create from the Tools menu and then selecting the appropriate element. Machines are represented as nodes in this diagram. Physical connections between machines are represented as connections. You set the name of a node or connection by using its Specification Properties window. You can also use the Specification Properties window to provide additional documentation for each element. You can assign processes to nodes using the Details tab of the Specification Properties window. The processes you enter here are not directly connected to other elements of your model, such as any components or packages you have defined. Nor does Visual Modeler generate any code based on this diagram. However, it is useful for documenting deployment constraints and decisions. A deployment diagram for the Island Hopper application is shown in Figure 7-9.

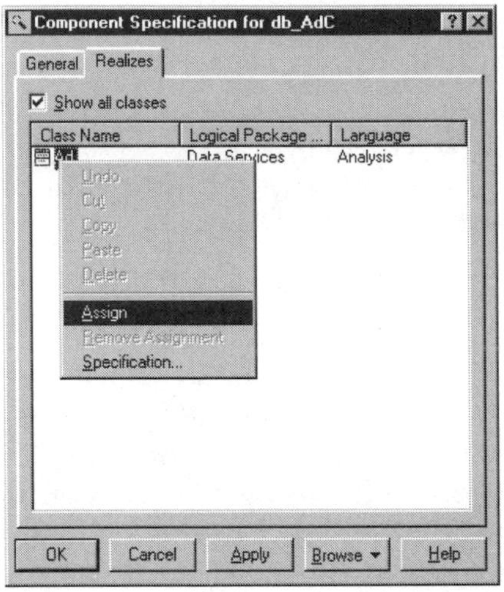

Figure 7-8. *Assigning a class to a component in Visual Modeler.*

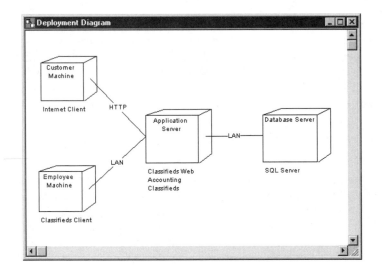

Figure 7-9. *Deployment diagram for the Island Hopper classified ads application.*

You should continue to update the component and deployment diagrams as you make packaging and deployment decisions throughout the application's lifetime.

The complete component and deployment diagrams for the Island Hopper classified ads application are contained in the CLASSIFIED.MDL file, which is located in the \IslandHopper-\Design directory on the companion CD. You can use Microsoft Visual Modeler or Rational Rose to view this model.

SUMMARY

The first step in building a three-tier application is to define the problem you are trying to solve. This is the purpose of application definition. Your completed application definition should include a set of documents defining the business problem, the functional specifications in terms of scenarios, the performance requirements, and the interoperability requirements. You and your customer should sign off on these documents.

Conceptual design follows application definition. During conceptual design, you model the persistent data, the data objects, the business objects, and the presentation layer. The deliverables from conceptual design include a document containing the data model, a design document describing the public interfaces of the data and business objects, and a design document defining the user interface of the application.

When the conceptual design is complete, you can begin looking at the physical architecture of your application. During physical design, you group COM classes into components, group components into MTS packages and processes, and assign packages and processes to machines. The deliverables from physical design include component and deployment diagrams. The physical design does not need to be completely defined at this point; however, you do need to determine how COM classes will be grouped into components prior to implementation.

8

Building Data Objects

In Chapter 7, we looked at designing the overall structure of an application. In this chapter, we'll focus in on the details of implementing the data access tier of the application. We'll start by looking at the general technologies and techniques you can use to implement data objects. Then we'll look at some example data objects from the Island Hopper classified ad application, illustrating how they can be implemented using Microsoft Visual Basic and Microsoft Visual C++.

Moving from Design to Implementation

After completing the application design, your conceptual design documents should contain a pretty good model of the data objects you need. You should also have a rough idea of how these objects should be grouped into components. As you begin figuring out how to implement the objects, keep the following key design points from Chapter 7 in mind:

- Data objects are responsible for the accuracy, completeness, and consistency of the data they own.

- Data objects should work correctly whether the caller is transactional or not.

- Data objects cannot retain state across transaction boundaries. Think carefully about how your data objects will be used and how expensive data access is before you retain state across method calls.

- Data objects should be "network friendly." The fewer network round-trips required to use an object, the better.

Implementing Components for MTS

Let's start by looking at the general concepts behind implementing components that will run within the MTS environment. The four major tasks are as follows:

- Write single-user, in-process COM components.

- Use explicit interfaces to define the public interface of your objects.

- Use the *ObjectContext* methods to tell MTS when object state can be reclaimed.

- Use transactions to manage errors.

All components that run in the MTS environment must be implemented as in-process components. Each component must provide a class factory for each COM class in the component, as well as a type library that describes all of the COM classes and their interfaces.

In addition to these requirements, MTS components should be written as single-user components. The MTS Executive, MTXEX.DLL, provides thread management services, so you don't need to be concerned about multithreading issues in your components. In fact, you should not create threads on your own within your components. You should just write your components as if they will be used by one caller at a time.

Recall from Chapter 2 that every in-process COM component has a *Threading-Model* registry value associated with it that describes how the component's objects will be assigned to threads during execution. If you do not specify a *ThreadingModel* value, the component uses the single-threaded apartment (STA) model and all objects will execute on the main thread of the containing process. COM synchronizes access to all objects on the main thread, so this approach is not very scalable. In addition, single-threaded stateful objects are prone to deadlock. However, if you use nonreentrant libraries within your component, you might need to use the STA model. A better choice for MTS components is to use the apartment threading model. In the apartment threading model, each object is assigned to a single thread for its entire lifetime, but multiple threads can be used to run multiple objects. This approach improves scalability without overly complicating your component implementation. (You do need to protect global variables from concurrent updates.) It's not necessary to implement fully thread-safe components that support the free-threaded model; if you do, you must not create any threads on your own.

Fortunately, every COM programming tool currently available can generate, at the push of a button, skeleton code that meets these requirements. In the section "Implementing Data Objects" later in this chapter, we'll see what buttons to push in Visual Basic and Visual C++.

What About Java?

Java is a great language for implementing COM components. With the COM support provided by the Microsoft Virtual Machine for Java and Microsoft Visual J++, developers can easily create components from Java classes. MTS even provides a package to help developers access its features from Java: *com.ms.mtx.*

We won't discuss implementing components in Java in this book, mainly because the Island Hopper sample application doesn't include any Java code. But if you want to use Java to implement your components, the concepts discussed in this book are still applicable. The details of how you code your components will obviously be a little different. Paul Stafford's article "Writing Microsoft Transaction Server Components in Java" is highly recommended to anyone writing components in Java. This article is available on the Microsoft Developer Network (MSDN) Library.

NOTE The default behavior provided by today's COM programming tools is "good enough" for most components that you will need in a three-tier application. If you use the defaults, you can spend more time focusing on your application-specific logic. You should save hand-coding the basic COM component infrastructure for times when you cannot meet your performance requirements with the default code provided by your tool. Since COM is a binary standard, you can change the implementation of any component without affecting its clients as long as you don't change the public interface—even to the extent of changing implementation languages. In this book, we use the standard COM implementations provided by the Microsoft Visual Studio tools. If you need to hand-tune your components or just want to learn more about how COM works, many books are available that go into the details of writing COM components, especially for C++ developers. Some of these resources are listed in the bibliography.

Once you have the basic in-process component framework in place, you can add the implementations of COM classes to it. Each COM class exposes its behavior through one or more COM interfaces. Some programming tools, such as Visual Basic, let you expose methods and properties directly on the class and internally convert these methods and properties to a COM interface. You should try to avoid this practice and always define your COM interfaces explicitly. Recall from Chapter 2 that COM interfaces represent a contract between caller and callee, and once published they must not be changed. When your interface definition is mixed in with its implementation, it is far too easy for you to make changes without realizing the consequences. Defining interfaces separately is essential if you will have multiple implementations of the interface. Defining interfaces separately also helps when you have multiple developers working on an application. Developers can quickly create test objects that expose the interfaces, so they can verify that client code that relies on those interfaces works correctly. We'll see how to implement separately defined interfaces in COM classes when we walk through the example components in the section "Implementing Data Objects" later in this chapter.

NOTE There might be programming tool features that prevent you from defining interfaces separately. For example, Visual Basic 5.0 always defines a default dispatch-based interface using the methods and properties implemented directly on the class. Scripting languages and other typeless languages that understand only *IDispatch* will be able to access only this default interface. If you are writing objects in Visual Basic that need to be accessed from scripting languages, you'll have to implement the methods and properties directly in the class.

Within each interface method implementation are two things you need to do (in addition to the actual work of the method). First you need to let MTS know when you have finished with the object's state. Second you need to handle errors within your object and let MTS know whether the method was unsuccessful. You do this using the *ObjectContext* associated with each object. The *IObjectContext SetComplete* method indicates that your object has completed its work successfully. The *IObjectContext SetAbort* method indicates the object encountered an error.

When you call *SetAbort*, if the object is participating in a transaction, that transaction will fail and managed resources will be rolled back to their state prior to the transaction. This is an extraordinarily powerful mechanism for handling errors when you have many independently implemented objects working together to perform some higher-level functionality requested by a client. If any one object can't complete its work, the entire request fails.

Since most objects will not retain state across method calls, the basic structure of each method will look something like the following pseudocode:

```
MyMethod(…)
   On Error Goto ErrorHandler

   CtxObject = GetObjectContext()
```

```
    Do work
    If error condition then
       Raise error

    CtxObject.SetComplete
    Return success

ErrorHandler:
    CtxObject.SetAbort
    Return error
```

Note that in addition to calling *SetAbort* when an error occurs, your method should return a normal COM error. Doing so gives clients the information they need to decide whether to continue doing work. *SetAbort* does not have any effect until the containing transaction ends.

These basic ideas apply to both data objects and business objects. With the basic component framework and a skeleton implementation of each class in place, we can turn our attention to the interesting part: implementing the application logic. For data objects, this process consists primarily of retrieving and storing persistent data.

Data Object Technologies

As we saw in Chapter 3, persistent data can be stored in many ways. Each data store typically has a native API for accessing the store. There are also generic APIs such as ODBC for accessing relational databases. There are ODBC drivers available for every major relational database. You can use these APIs to access data within your data objects, but doing so gives rise to one fundamental problem: if you have multiple data stores, especially nonrelational stores, you have to learn multiple APIs to access your data.

The Microsoft technologies that help you deal with any type of persistent data are OLE DB and Microsoft ActiveX Data Objects (ADO). An OLE DB provider implements a specific set of interfaces to provide access to some data store. Clients can use the OLE DB interfaces directly to get data out of the store, but most clients tend to use the more friendly ADO. ADO is the preferred method for accessing persistent data from your data objects.

MTS provides a resource dispenser to handle pools of ODBC database connections. The resource dispenser also automatically enlists connections in transactions, as appropriate. The Microsoft Data Access Components (MDAC) includes an OLE DB provider for ODBC, so ADO can be used to connect to any ODBC data source and we can get the benefits of connection pooling and automatic transactions from MTS (assuming that the data store supports transactions and the ODBC driver meets some minimal requirements).

NOTE At the time this book was written, the only databases with ODBC drivers that fully support both connection pooling and transactions were Microsoft SQL Server, Oracle, and IBM DB2. Microsoft is working with other database vendors to ensure that ODBC drivers are available for those databases as well. For more information about the databases supported by MTS, refer to the MTS Database and Transactions FAQ. A version of this file is located in the $/FAQ directory on the companion CD. The latest version of this file can be obtained from the Microsoft Web site: *http://www.microsoft.com/com/mtsfaq/faq.htm.*

Although the resource dispenser/resource manager model supported by MTS and the data access model supported by OLE DB are completely generic, the most common data source is an ODBC database. For the remainder of this chapter, we'll focus on data stored in ODBC databases—in particular, data stored in SQL Server databases. In Chapter 15, we'll look at some other types of data stores when we discuss extending the application beyond COM and MTS.

Programming with ADO

The ADO object model contains the seven objects listed in Table 8-1.

Object	Description
Connection	Manages a connection to a data source.
Command	Defines a specific command to execute against a data source.
Recordset	Represents a set of records from a data source or the results of an executed command.
Field	Represents a column of data with a common data type. A *Recordset* object has a *Fields* collection, with one *Field* object per column in the *Recordset*.
Parameter	Represents a parameter associated with a *Command* object based on a parameterized query or stored procedure. A *Command* object has a *Parameters* collection, with one *Parameter* object per command parameter.
Property	Represents a dynamic characteristic of an ADO object defined by the OLE DB provider. *Connection, Command, Recordset,* and *Field* objects have *Properties* collections, with one *Property* object per dynamically defined characteristic.
Error	Contains details about data access errors for a single operation. A *Connection* object has an *Errors* collection, with one *Error* object per OLE DB provider error.

Table 8-1. *The objects contained in the ADO object model.*

Connections

You use a *Connection* object to set up a connection with a data source. When the object is used with an ODBC data source, you establish a connection by passing either a data source name (DSN), user ID, and password or a DSN filename to the *Connection* object's *Open* method.

Data objects should generally access data sources using a fixed identity, rather than using the client's identity. This technique greatly simplifies administration and makes it possible to efficiently pool database connections across multiple client requests. If you need to restrict access to a database, you can restrict access to the business objects your clients interact with or you can restrict access to the data objects themselves.

The most straightforward and flexible way to specify parameters for the *Connection* object's *Open* method is to include a DSN filename in your source code and then specify the data source, user ID, and password in the DSN file itself. This technique lets a system administrator modify the data source or account access information without requiring source code changes to your components.

The *Connection* object is used to specify the type of database access you want. You use the *Mode* property to indicate whether you want a read-only, write-only, or read/write connection and what type of sharing you'll permit if other attempts are made to connect to the database. You must set this property before opening the connection.

Typically, you open the connection immediately before accessing the database and close the connection as soon as possible, instead of holding onto a connection for the lifetime of an object. This approach is acceptable, even though creating database connections is an extremely expensive operation, because of the connection pooling services of the ODBC 3.0 driver manager. For each connection request, the driver manager first looks in the pool for an acceptable unused connection. If it finds one, that connection is returned. Otherwise, a new connection is created. Connections are disconnected from the database and removed from the pool if they remain idle for a specified period of time (by default, 60 seconds). Currently, the ODBC connection pool size is limited only by free memory and the number of database connections available. The only way to control the pool size is to set the ODBC pooling time-out value based on your estimated connection rate.

You cannot reuse a connection established using a different user identity. For this reason, you should connect to databases using a fixed identity within your data objects. If you use the client's identity, every unique client will require a unique database connection, eliminating a key scalability benefit of the three-tier architecture and MTS. You also cannot reuse connections across process boundaries. As we'll see in Chapter 9, components that access the same data sources should run within the same process so that connections can be reused.

If you examine the methods of the *Connection* object in the ADO documentation, you'll see the following methods related to transaction processing: *BeginTrans*, *CommitTrans*, and *RollbackTrans*. Components that will be run in the MTS environment should never use these methods. Instead, you should let MTS manage transactions through the *ObjectContext* and use the *ObjectContext SetComplete* and *SetAbort* methods to vote on the transaction outcome.

Accessing data

There are three ways to access data using ADO: the *Connection Execute* method, *Command* objects, and *Recordset* objects. You can use the *Connection Execute* method to execute a specified command against a data source. When used with an ODBC data source, commands can be SQL statements or nonparameterized stored procedures. Any results are returned as a *Recordset* object with a read-only, forward-only cursor. We'll discuss cursors in more detail in the section "Recordset Objects" below.

> **NOTE** Stored procedures can provide a great performance boost, especially for complex data access operations. However, you should use stored procedures only for data access. Business logic should be implemented in business objects, as we'll see in Chapter 9.

You can use *Command* objects to execute parameterized stored procedures and commands or to save a compiled version of a command that will be executed multiple times. You establish a connection to a data source by setting the *Command ActiveConnection* property. You specify the command using the *CommandText* property, and you execute the command using the *Execute* method. Any results are returned as a *Recordset* with a read-only, forward-only cursor. If you have a parameterized command, you specify the parameters in the *Command* object's *Parameters* collection. To compile a command for speedy reuse, you set the *Prepared* property.

Finally, you can manipulate data directly using *Recordset* objects. Creating a *Recordset* object and using its methods directly is the most flexible way to manipulate data.

Recordset objects

When you use ADO, you'll almost always manipulate data exclusively through *Recordset* objects. You get either a *Recordset* as the return value from a *Connection* or *Command Execute* call, or you create your own *Recordset*.

A *Recordset* object consists of a set of rows and columns. At any given time, a *Recordset* refers to the set of columns associated with a specific row, called the current row. The individual columns of the *Recordset* can be accessed through *Fields* collection. You move through the rows of a *Recordset* by using the object's associated cursor.

ADO supports the following cursor types:

- **Dynamic cursor:** Enables you to view additions, changes, and deletions made by other users. All types of movement through the *Recordset* that don't rely on bookmarks are permitted. Bookmarks are supported if the OLE DB provider supports them.

- **Keyset cursor:** Similar to a dynamic cursor, except that you can't see records added by other users and you can't access records deleted by other users. Keyset cursors always support bookmarks.

- **Static cursor:** Provides a static copy of a set of records. You cannot see additions, changes, or deletions made by other users. Static cursors always support bookmarks and thus permit any type of movement through the *Recordset*.

- **Forward-only cursor:** Similar to a static cursor, but allows you only to scroll forward through the *Recordset*.

The *Recordset* features available to you depend on the cursor type specified when the *Recordset* is opened.

> **NOTE** Not every OLE DB provider supports every cursor type. When you're using the OLE DB provider for ODBC, the cursor types available to you depend on the types supported by the underlying ODBC driver for your database. The SQL Server ODBC driver supports all four cursor types.

Recordset objects also support a variety of lock types. Whenever records in a *Recordset* are being updated, a lock must be put on those records. The following *LockType* property values specify what types of locks are placed on records during editing:

- ***adLockOptimistic:*** Optimistic locking applies locks record by record only when the *Update* method is called.

- ***adLockPessimistic:*** Pessimistic locking applies locks record by record at record-read time.

- ***adLockBatchOptimistic:*** Batch optimistic locking applies locks to the entire *Recordset* when the *UpdateBatch* method is called.

- ***adLockReadOnly:*** Read-only locking is the default. When this lock type is specified, you cannot update the data in the *Recordset*.

Not all lock types are supported by all OLE DB providers.

The *Recordset* object provides a set of methods for moving through its rows. The *MoveNext* and *MovePrevious* methods move forward and backward through the *Recordset*, one record at a time. You can use the *BOF* and *EOF* properties to detect when you've reached the beginning or end of a recordset. For a *Recordset* that supports dynamic positioning, *MoveFirst* and *MoveLast* are available. (You can guess what those do…) For a *Recordset* that supports bookmarks, you can use the *Bookmark* property to return a unique identifier for the current record in the *Recordset*. At a later time, you can set the *Bookmark* property to return to that record. *Recordset* objects also provide methods to move to specific records by ordinal number.

The most common way to populate a *Recordset* that you create is to attach the *Recordset* to a *Connection* using the *ActiveConnection* property and then call the *Recordset Open* method. You can also populate a *Recordset* programmatically, if the data does not come from an OLE DB data source.

Recordset objects are tremendously useful for three-tier applications. Remember that we don't want to share state on the server across method calls. We want to connect to the database, get some data, disconnect, and return all the data to the caller. The way to accomplish this in ADO is through *disconnected Recordset objects*. Disconnected *Recordset* objects were originally introduced under the name Advanced Data Connector, but they are now built into ADO 1.5.

Disconnected *Recordset* objects use optimistic locking and are manipulated on the client using a client-side cursor library. (Here, "client" can mean either the presentation layer or the business layer.) Disconnected batch updates are supported through the *UpdateBatch* method. Be careful with this, because during the time records are being modified on the client, another client might have updated some of the records. When the batch update is applied, you will get errors for the conflicting updates. In this case, you need to define as part of your component interface how partial updates will be handled—will they generate transaction failures, or will the client need to handle the error?

To create a disconnected *Recordset*, you set the *CursorLocation* property on either the *Connection* or the *Recordset* to *adUseClient* before opening the connection, you get the data, and then you release the *ActiveConnection*. If you want to allow the client to modify the data, you should create the *Recordset* using batch optimistic locking (*adLockBatchOptimistic*) and either a static (*adOpenStatic*) or a keyset (*adOpenKeyset*) cursor.

Fields

The columns of the current row in a *Recordset* are accessed using the *Fields* collection. You can access a field by its name or by a numeric index. When you are using an ODBC data source, the field name corresponds to its name in a

SQL *SELECT* statement and the numeric index is determined by the field's position in the SQL *SELECT* statement. Once you have a *Field* object, you can get or set information about it using its properties. The most commonly used property is the *Value* property, which can be used to retrieve or set the field's data value.

Two special methods are available on the *Field* object for dealing with long binary or long character data. You use the *GetChunk* method to retrieve a portion of the data. You use the *AppendChunk* method to write a portion of the data. You can determine whether you need to use these methods by examining the *Attributes* property of the *Field*.

Handling errors

Any ADO operation can generate errors, so it's important to handle those errors within your method calls. This error handling consists of two parts: ADO returns error codes for each method call, and it supports the standard COM error reporting mechanism, *IErrorInfo*. Specific OLE DB provider errors, such as native database error codes or ODBC error codes, are stored in the *Errors* collection associated with your *Connection* object. One ADO call can generate multiple errors in the *Errors* collection. You can walk through the *Errors* collection to retrieve rich error information about database failures.

Note that ADO clears the *ErrorInfo* object before it makes a call that could potentially generate errors. However, the *Errors* collection is cleared and repopulated only when the OLE DB provider generates a new error or when the *Clear* method is called. Some methods and properties can generate warning messages in the *Errors* collection without halting program execution. Before calling these methods or properties, you should clear the *Errors* collection so that you can read the *Count* property to determine whether any warnings were generated. Methods that can generate warnings include *Recordset Resync*, *UpdateBatch*, and *CancelBatch*. The *Recordset Filter* property can also generate warnings. A common situation that generates warnings is when conflicting updates are applied to the database.

Implementing Data Objects

For the remainder of this chapter, we will look at the implementation of some of the data objects from the Island Hopper application. We'll start by looking at the *db_CategoryC* component, which is implemented in Visual Basic. This component demonstrates how to use the *Connection Execute* method and *Recordset* objects to access data using ADO. It also shows how default interfaces are implemented in Visual Basic. Next we'll look at the *db_CustomerPasswordC* component. This component is implemented in Visual Basic as well, but it exposes two predefined interfaces rather than using the default interface. The *db_CustomerPasswordC* component also illustrates how to use *Command* objects to access data. We'll take a brief look at the *db_CustomerC* component, implemented in Visual Basic, to see how to call stored procedures. Last we'll look at the *db_PaymentC* component, which is implemented in Visual C++ using the Active Template Library (ATL) and the Visual C++ COM compiler support.

Wondering why all the component names end in "C"? This is because there are multiple versions of the Island Hopper sample application, showing how to move from a client/server design to a three-tier design. "Scenario C" is the three-tier, component-based version. All component names end in "C" to indicate that they are part of "Scenario C."

WARNING If you want to try implementing these components on your own system, you need to take a few extra precautions to ensure that the rest of the Island Hopper application will continue to run. These precautions will be noted in the text prior to each step that might break the application.

Implementing *db_CategoryC* in Visual Basic

Let's start by looking at the *db_CategoryC* component. This component manages access to the Categories table in the Island Hopper classified ads database.

NOTE If you use Microsoft Visual Modeler to design your application, you can use its code generation capabilities to generate the Visual Basic skeleton code.

Creating the skeleton component

The first step is to create a project for the component itself. Remember that an MTS component must be an in-process component. In Visual Basic, you use an ActiveX DLL project to create an in-process component. When you create a new ActiveX DLL project, it will include a single class module. Each class module corresponds to one COM class. The project *Name* property is used as the name of the component's type library. The project *Name* and class *Name* properties together form the programmatic ID (ProgID) for the COM class, *<project name>.<class name>*, so it's important to set these properties before you build your component.

MTS components should also support the apartment threading model and should not produce any graphical output. (The components typically run on an unattended machine.) To ensure that your component meets these requirements, set the *Unattended Execution* and *Threading Model* properties for your project.

That's really all it takes to create a skeleton COM component in Visual Basic. Visual Basic will create the type library and register the component for you when you build it. Visual Basic implements the COM class factory and standard COM interfaces such as *IUnknown* for you as well. Visual Basic completely hides all the COM details from you. You have a completely functional (but really boring) COM component without writing a single line of code.

Step by Step: Creating the Skeleton *db_CategoryC* Component

1. Start Visual Basic, and create a new ActiveX DLL project.

2. Rename the project *db_CategoryC* and the class *Category*. This makes the ProgID for this COM class *db_CategoryC.Category*.

3. From the Project menu, choose the db_CategoryC Properties command. On the General tab of the Project Properties dialog box, check the Unattended Execution check box and verify that the Threading Model option is set to Apartment Threaded.

> **NOTE** If you build the *db_CategoryC* component at this point on a machine that has the Island Hopper application installed, you will break Island Hopper components that use *db_CategoryC*. Wait to build the component until you have implemented the skeleton interface methods.

4. (optional) Build the component by choosing the Make db_CategoryC.dll command from the File menu.

With a class in place, you can turn your attention to implementing the interfaces that class exposes. There are two ways to do this. Most discussions of implementing components using Visual Basic just tell you to implement public methods and properties in your class modules. Behind the scenes, Visual Basic will create an *IDispatch*-based interface for you that exposes those methods and properties. Visual Basic names this interface _<*class name*> and marks it as the default interface. This is a perfectly reasonable approach if you know that you need only one interface or that the interface will be implemented by only one component. It is an absolutely necessary approach if you need to access the object from scripting languages (which can access only the default dispatch-based interface).

However, if you are going to implement multiple interfaces or you think the interface might be implemented by multiple classes, you should explicitly define the interfaces outside the component project. We'll take a look at how to do this from Visual Basic in the section "Implementing *db_CustomerPasswordC* in Visual Basic" later in this chapter.

For now, we will use the default implementation approach. When you use this approach, you need to be very careful about maintaining compatibility with existing versions of your components. Remember, once you publish an interface, it's not supposed to change! To maintain compatibility, select the Binary Compatibility option on the Project Properties' Component tab and verify that the edit control contains the filename of the existing implementation you want to be compatible with.

To decide what properties and methods to implement, look back at your design documentation. For each method you want to expose, you implement a public *Sub* or a public *Function*. For each property you want to expose, you either implement a public data variable or property procedures. The easiest way to do this is by choosing the Add Procedure command on the Tools menu. (Or you could just type in the code by hand.) You'll probably need to add a reference to the ADO 1.5 type library at this point, since probably one or more methods will use an ADO *Recordset*.

Step by Step: Adding Skeleton Interface Methods for *db_CategoryC*

1. If necessary, reopen the *db_CategoryC* project.

2. Choose the Add Procedure command from the Tools menu. In the Add Procedure dialog box, set Name to *Add*, Type to *Function*, and Scope to *Public*, and then click OK to close the dialog box. The following skeleton method will be added to your class module:

```
Public Function Add()

End Function
```

The *Add* method needs some input parameters. You'll need to type these in yourself, as shown here:

```
Public Function Add(ByVal strName As String)
```

3. Add skeleton methods for other methods exposed by this class, as shown here:

```
Public Function Delete(ByVal lngCategoryID As Long)
Public Function Update(ByVal lngCategoryID As Long, _
                       ByVal strName As String)
Public Function GetById(ByVal lngCategoryID As Long) _
    As ADODB.Recordset
Public Function GetByName(ByVal strCategoryName As String) _
    As ADODB.Recordset
Public Function GetBySearchString _
    (ByVal strSearchText As String) As ADODB.Recordset
Public Function ListAll() As ADODB.Recordset
Public Function ListByRange(ByVal intLow As Integer, _
    ByVal intHigh As Integer) As ADODB.Recordset
```

4. Choose the References command from the Project menu. Locate and check the Microsoft ActiveX Data Objects Library in the list of available references. Doing so will ensure that you don't get any errors when you try to build the project, since the *Get* and *List* methods return ADO *Recordset* objects. Also, locate and check the Microsoft Transaction Server Type Library in the list of available references.

> **NOTE** If you want to build the *db_CategoryC* component at this point on a machine that has the Island Hopper application installed, you should select the Binary Compatibility option on the Project Properties Component tab and select IslandHopper\ScenarioC\ Source\Server_Components\CompatibleDLLs\db_CategoryC.dll in your Island Hopper installation. If you don't make this adjustment, Island Hopper components that use *db_CategoryC* will be broken.

5. (optional) Build the component by choosing the Make db_CategoryC.dll command from the File menu. After you build the component, you should select the Binary Compatibility option on the Projects Properties Component tab. If you haven't selected the prebuilt *db_CategoryC* DLL that came with Island Hopper, copy the DLL you just built to a safe place and select the DLL file for version compatibility. This procedure will help prevent incompatible modifications to the *Category* public interface.

Implementing the methods

With the skeleton component in place, we can turn our attention to the interesting part: implementing the data access logic using ADO and using the *ObjectContext* to tell MTS when we have finished with the application state and whether we have completed it successfully.

To start with, you'll need to add references to the Microsoft Transaction Server Type Library and the Microsoft ActiveX Data Objects Library, if you haven't already done so. The MTS type library provides access to the *ObjectContext*.

Next define a couple of global constants, as shown in the following code. The first constant keeps track of the class module name, which comes in handy when you want to report an error. The second constant contains the name of the DSN file you'll use to store information you need to connect to the database. As mentioned, a DSN file helps provide flexibility so that system administrators can change database connection options without requiring changes to your component code.

```
Option Explicit
Const modName = "db_CategoryC.Category"
Const fileDSN = "dbCategoryC.DSN"
```

Each method in a stateless object will have the same basic structure: set up a general error handler, do your work, and call the *ObjectContext SetComplete* method when you have finished. In the error handler, clean up, call the *ObjectContext SetAbort* method, and raise an error to the caller. To get a reference to the current *ObjectContext*, call the *GetObjectContext* function. The code looks something like this:

```
Public Function MyMethod()
On Error GoTo ErrorHandler
    ' Do work.
    :
    GetObjectContext.SetComplete
    Exit Function
ErrorHandler:
    ' Clean up local variables.
    :
    GetObjectContext.SetAbort
```

```
    Err.Raise Err.Number, _
        SetErrSource(modName, "PROCNAME"), _
        Err.Description
End Function
```

SetErrSource is a utility function provided with the Island Hopper application to build error source information that includes the machine, component, and method names. You can find the source for this function in the GLOBAL.BAS file in the \IslandHopper\Source\Server_Components\Globals\ directory on the companion CD. In many cases, bubbling up the error that caused your function to fail is a reasonable choice. You might also choose to raise a component-specific error code.

To perform the database access operation itself, you have three choices. First, you can call the *Execute* method on a *Connection* object, as shown here:

```
Dim conn As New ADODB.Connection
Dim rs As ADODB.Recordset
conn.Open "FILEDSN=" & fileDSN, "", ""
Set rs = conn.Execute strSQL  ' strSQL contains the SQL command.
```

This approach is the easiest to code, but it should be limited to SQL commands that do not return a *Recordset* or to simple queries to return *Recordset* objects that will be scanned only once, because the *Connection Execute* method always returns a read-only, forward-only *Recordset*.

Second, you can create a *Command* object and call its *Execute* method, as shown here:

```
Dim rs As ADODB.Recordset
Dim conn As New ADODB.Connection
Dim cmd As New ADODB.Command
Dim prm As ADODB.Parameter
conn.Open "FILEDSN=" & strFileDSN
Set cmd.ActiveConnection = conn
cmd.CommandText = strSP  ' Assume calling a stored procedure, strSP.
cmd.CommandType = adCmdStoredProc
Set prm = cmd.CreateParameter(strPRM, strPRMType, adParamInput, _
    intPRMLength, strPRMValue)  ' Define a parameter.
cmd.Parameters.Append prm       ' There could be more than one…
Set rs = cmd.Execute
```

This approach is much like the *Connection Execute* option, except that you can specify parameters for your SQL command or stored procedure. It also returns a read-only, forward-only *Recordset*.

Finally, you can create a *Recordset* object and call its *Open* method, shown here:

```
Dim rs As New ADODB.Recordset
Dim conn As New ADODB.Connection
Dim cmd As New ADODB.Command
conn.Open "FILEDSN=" & strFileDSN
Set cmd.ActiveConnection = conn
cmd.CommandText = strSQL    ' strSQL contains the SQL command.
cmd.CommandType = adCmdText
rs.Open cmd
```

This approach is the most flexible—it lets you specify the cursor type and lock type for your *Recordset*. You can specify the cursor type and lock type on the *Recordset Open* call, or you can set the *CursorType* and *LockType* properties on the *Recordset* before you call *Open*.

In the *db_CategoryC* component, the *Connection Execute* approach is used for the *Add*, *Update*, *Delete*, *GetByID*, *GetByName*, and *GetBySearchString* methods. The primary difference is the SQL string passed to the *Execute* call. The source code for these methods is shown in Listing 8-1.

```
Option Explicit
Const modName = "db_CategoryC.Category"
Const fileDSN = "dbCategoryC.DSN"

'********************************************************************
' Add
' Purpose: Adds a new category to the database
' Inputs:  strName -- the name of the new category
'********************************************************************
Public Function Add(ByVal strName As String)

    Dim intID As Integer
    Dim dtmCreated As Date
    Dim strSQL As String
    Dim rs As ADODB.Recordset
    Dim conn As ADODB.Connection

    On Error GoTo ErrorHandler

    ' Open the connection object to the database.
    Set conn = New ADODB.Connection
    conn.Open "FILEDSN=" & fileDSN
```

Listing 8-1. *The* db_CategoryC *source code.*

```
' Get the next category ID number from the database.
strSQL = "SELECT MAX(Id) as NewId, Count(ID) as TheCount " & _
         "FROM Categories"

Set rs = conn.Execute(strSQL)

If CInt(rs("TheCount")) = 0 Then
    intID = 0
Else
    intID = CInt(rs("NewId")) + 1
End If

' Form the SQL INSERT statement, and execute to the database.
dtmCreated = Now()
strSQL = "INSERT INTO Categories " & _
         "(Id, Name, ModifiedDate, CreatedDate) " & _
         "VALUES ( " & _
         intID & ",'" & _
         strName & "','" & _
         dtmCreated & "','" & _
         dtmCreated & "')"

conn.Execute strSQL

' Allow MTS transaction set to proceed.
GetObjectContext.SetComplete

Exit Function

ErrorHandler:
    If Not rs Is Nothing Then
        Set rs = Nothing
    End If
    If Not conn Is Nothing Then
        Set conn = Nothing
    End If

    ' Roll back MTS transaction set.
    GetObjectContext.SetAbort

    Err.Raise Err.Number, SetErrSource(modName, "Add"), Err.Description

End Function
```

(continued)

Listing 8-1. *continued*

```
'**********************************************************************
' Delete
' Purpose: Deletes a category from the database
' Inputs: lngCategoryID -- the unique category ID number
'**********************************************************************
Public Function Delete(ByVal lngCategoryID As Long)

    On Error GoTo ErrorHandler

    Dim strSQL As String
    Dim conn As ADODB.Connection

    ' Open the connection to the database.
    Set conn = New ADODB.Connection
    conn.Open "FILEDSN=" & fileDSN

    ' Form the SQL DELETE statement, and execute to the database.
    strSQL = "DELETE FROM Categories WHERE Id = " & lngCategoryID
    conn.Execute strSQL

    ' Allow MTS transaction set to proceed.
    GetObjectContext.SetComplete

    Exit Function

ErrorHandler:
    If Not conn Is Nothing Then
        Set conn = Nothing
    End If

    ' Roll back MTS transaction set.
    GetObjectContext.SetAbort

    Err.Raise Err.Number, SetErrSource(modName, "Delete"), _
     Err.Description

End Function

'**********************************************************************
' Update
' Purpose: Updates a category with new modified date
' Inputs:  lngCategoryID -- the unique category ID number
'**********************************************************************
Public Function Update(ByVal lngCategoryID As Long, _
                       ByVal strName As String)
```

```
    Dim strSQL As String
    Dim conn As ADODB.Connection

    On Error GoTo ErrorHandler

    ' Open the connection to the database.
    Set conn = New ADODB.Connection
    conn.Open "FILEDSN=" & fileDSN

    ' Form the SQL UPDATE statement, and execute to the database.
    strSQL = "UPDATE Categories " & _
            "SET ModifiedDate = " & "'" & Now() & "'" & _
            " WHERE Id = " & lngCategoryID

    conn.Execute strSQL

    ' Allow MTS transaction set to proceed.
    GetObjectContext.SetComplete

    Exit Function

ErrorHandler:
    If Not conn Is Nothing Then
        Set conn = Nothing
    End If

    ' Roll back MTS transaction set.
    GetObjectContext.SetAbort

    Err.Raise Err.Number, SetErrSource(modName, "Update"), _
    Err.Description

End Function
'**********************************************************************
' ListAll
' Purpose: Lists all the categories in the database
' Returns: A Recordset object containing the category information
'**********************************************************************
Public Function ListAll() As ADODB.Recordset

    Dim strSQL As String
    Dim rs As ADODB.Recordset

    On Error GoTo ErrorHandler
```

(continued)

Listing 8-1. *continued*

```
      ' Form the SQL SELECT statement and execute to the database.
      strSQL = "SELECT CategoryId, Name, ModifiedDate, CreatedDate " & _
               "FROM Categories ORDER BY Name"

      Set rs = New ADODB.Recordset
      rs.CursorLocation = adUseClient

      ' Execute the SQL command to the database
      ' using the Recordset Open method.
      rs.Open strSQL, "FILEDSN=" & fileDSN, adOpenKeyset, _
              adLockReadOnly, adCmdText

      ' Allow MTS transaction set to proceed.
      GetObjectContext.SetComplete

      Set ListAll = rs

      Exit Function

ErrorHandler:
    If Not rs Is Nothing Then
       Set rs = Nothing
    End If

      ' Roll back MTS transaction set.
      GetObjectContext.SetAbort

      Err.Raise Err.Number, SetErrSource(modName, "ListAll"), _
       Err.Description

End Function

'*************************************************************************
' GetByID
' Purpose: Gets the category based on the category ID
' Inputs:  lngCategoryID -- the unique category ID number
' Returns: A Recordset object containing category information
'*************************************************************************
Public Function GetById(ByVal lngCategoryID As Long) As ADODB.Recordset

    Dim strSQL As String
    Dim rs As ADODB.Recordset
    Dim conn As ADODB.Connection
```

```
    On Error GoTo ErrorHandler

    ' Open the connection to the database.
    Set conn = New ADODB.Connection
    conn.Open "FILEDSN=" & fileDSN

    ' Form the SQL SELECT command, and execute to the database.
    strSQL = "SELECT CategoryId, Name, ModifiedDate, CreatedDate " & _
             "FROM Categories WHERE " & _
             "CategoryId = " & lngCategoryID & " ORDER BY Name"

    Set rs = conn.Execute(strSQL)

    ' Allow MTS transaction set to proceed.
    GetObjectContext.SetComplete

    Set GetById = rs

    Exit Function

ErrorHandler:
    If Not conn Is Nothing Then
        Set conn = Nothing
    End If

    ' Roll back MTS transaction set.
    GetObjectContext.SetAbort

    Err.Raise Err.Number, SetErrSource(modName, "GetByID"), _
      Err.Description

End Function

'*********************************************************************
' GetByName
' Purpose: Retrieves category information for this category name
' Inputs:  strCategoryName -- the category name
' Returns: A Recordset object containing category information
'*********************************************************************
Public Function GetByName(ByVal strCategoryName As String) _
    As ADODB.Recordset

    Dim strSQL As String
    Dim rs As ADODB.Recordset
    Dim conn As ADODB.Connection
```

(continued)

Listing 8-1. *continued*

```
    On Error GoTo ErrorHandler

    ' Open the connection object to the database.
    Set conn = New ADODB.Connection
    conn.Open "FILEDSN=" & fileDSN

    ' Form the SQL SELECT statement, and execute to the database.
    strSQL = "SELECT CategoryId, Name, ModifiedDate, CreatedDate " & _
             "FROM Categories WHERE " & _
             "Name = '" & strCategoryName & "'"

    Set rs = conn.Execute(strSQL)

    ' Allow the MTS transaction set to proceed.
    GetObjectContext.SetComplete

    Set GetByName = rs

    Exit Function

ErrorHandler:
    If Not conn Is Nothing Then
        Set conn = Nothing
    End If

    ' Roll back the MTS transaction set.
    GetObjectContext.SetAbort

    Err.Raise Err.Number, SetErrSource(modName, "GetByName"), _
      Err.Description

End Function

'***********************************************************************
' GetBySearchString
' Purpose: Retrieves categories whose name contains the search string
' Inputs:   strSearchText -- the search string
' Returns: A Recordset object containing the category information
'***********************************************************************
Public Function GetBySearchString(ByVal strSearchText As String) _
    As ADODB.Recordset

    Dim strSQL As String
    Dim rs As ADODB.Recordset
    Dim conn As ADODB.Connection
```

```
    On Error GoTo ErrorHandler

    ' Open the connection to the database.
    Set conn = New ADODB.Connection
    conn.Open "FILEDSN=" & fileDSN

    ' Form the SQL SELECT statement, and execute to the database.
    strSQL = "SELECT CategoryId, Name, ModifiedDate, CreatedDate " & _
             "FROM Categories WHERE " & _
             "Name = '" & Left(strSearchText, _
             (InStr(1, strSearchText, "/") - 1)) & "'"

    Set rs = conn.Execute(strSQL)

    ' Allow MTS transaction set to proceed.
    GetObjectContext.SetComplete

    Set GetBySearchString = rs

    Exit Function

ErrorHandler:

    If Not conn Is Nothing Then
       Set conn = Nothing
    End If

    ' Roll back MTS transaction set.
    GetObjectContext.SetAbort

    Err.Raise Err.Number, SetErrSource(modName, "GetBySearchString"), _
    Err.Description

End Function

'*********************************************************************
' ListByRange
' Purpose: Retrieves categories whose ID number falls in the range
'          specified
' Inputs:  intLow  -- lower boundary of the search range
'          intHigh -- upper boundary of the search range
' Returns: A Recordset object containing the category information
'*********************************************************************
```

(continued)

Listing 8-1. *continued*

```
Public Function ListByRange(ByVal intLow As Integer, _
    ByVal intHigh As Integer) As ADODB.Recordset

    Dim strSQL As String
    Dim rs As ADODB.Recordset

    On Error GoTo ErrorHandler

    ' Form the SQL SELECT statement.
    strSQL = "SELECT CategoryID, Name FROM Categories " & _
            "WHERE CategoryID BETWEEN " & intLow & " AND  " & intHigh

    ' Execute SQL command to the database
    ' using the Recordset Open method.
    Set rs = New ADODB.Recordset
    rs.CursorLocation = adUseClient
    rs.Open strSQL, "FILEDSN=" & fileDSN, adOpenKeyset, _
     adLockReadOnly, adCmdText

    ' Allow MTS transaction set to proceed.
    GetObjectContext.SetComplete

    Set ListByRange = rs

    Exit Function

ErrorHandler:

    If Not rs Is Nothing Then
        Set rs = Nothing
    End If

    ' Roll back MTS transaction set.
    GetObjectContext.SetAbort

    Err.Raise Err.Number, SetErrSource(modName, "ListByRange"), _
     Err.Description

End Function
```

Step by Step: Implementing the *db_CategoryC Add*, *Update*, *Delete*, and *Get* Methods

1. If necessary, reopen the *db_CategoryC* project.

2. Add the following lines to the General Declarations section of the Category class module to define constants for the module name used in error reporting and the DSN filename used to connect to the database:

```
Option Explicit
Const modName = "db_CategoryC.Category"
Const fileDSN = "dbCategoryC.DSN"
```

3. Add the GLOBALS.BAS module, located in the \IslandHopper\Source\ Server_Components\Globals directory on the companion CD, to the project by choosing the Add Module command from the Project menu. This step will give you the *SetErrorSource* function used in the method error handlers.

4. Add the following code to the *Add* method to establish the basic framework that calls the *ObjectContext SetComplete* method when all work has been completed successfully or calls the *ObjectContext SetAbort* method and raises an error if one occurs:

```
On Error Goto ErrorHandler
    ' TODO: Do work.
    GetObjectContext.SetComplete
    Exit Function
ErrorHandler:
    ' TODO: Clean up local variables.
    GetObjectContext.SetAbort

    ' Rethrow the error.
    Err.Raise Err.Number, SetErrSource(modName, "Add"), _
    Err.Description
```

5. Replace the line *TODO: Do work* in the *Add* method with the following code, which connects to the database, reads some information, and then creates a new record using the *Connection Execute* technique:

```
Dim intID As Integer
Dim dtmCreated As Date
Dim strSQL As String
Dim rs As ADODB.Recordset
Dim conn As ADODB.Connection
```

(continued)

Implementing the *db_CategoryC Add*, *Update*, *Delete*, and *Get* Methods, *continued*

```
' Open the connection to the database.
Set conn = New ADODB.Connection
conn.Open "FILEDSN=" & fileDSN

' Get the next category ID from the database.
strSQL = "SELECT MAX(Id) as NewId, Count(ID) as TheCount " & _
         "FROM Categories"
Set rs = conn.Execute(strSQL)
If CInt(rs("TheCount")) = 0 Then
    intID = 0
Else
    intID = CInt(rs("NewId")) + 1
End If

' Form the SQL INSERT statement, and execute to the database.
dtmCreated = Now()
strSQL = "INSERT INTO Categories " & _
         "(Id, Name, ModifiedDate, CreatedDate) " & _
         "VALUES ( " & _
         intID & ",'" & _
         strName & "','" & _
         dtmCreated & "','" & _
         dtmCreated & "')"
conn.Execute strSQL
```

6. Replace the line *TODO: Clean up local variables* in the *Add* method with the following code, which ensures that the *Connection* and *Recordset* objects will be cleaned up when an error occurs:

```
If Not rs Is Nothing Then
    Set rs = Nothing
End If
If Not conn Is Nothing Then
    Set conn = Nothing
End If
```

7. Repeat step 4 for the *Update* and *Delete* methods, changing the second *SetErrorSource* parameter from *Add* to *Update* and *Delete*, respectively.

8. Replace the line *TODO: Do work* in the *Delete* method with the following code, which connects to the database and executes a SQL command to delete a record:

```
Dim strSQL As String
Dim conn As ADODB.Connection
```

```
' Open the connection to the database.
Set conn = New ADODB.Connection
conn.Open "FILEDSN=" & fileDSN

' Form the SQL DELETE statement, and execute to the database.
strSQL = "DELETE FROM Categories WHERE Id = " & lngCategoryID
conn.Execute strSQL
```

9. Repeat step 8 for the *Update* method. The only difference is the SQL statement used, as shown here:

```
' Form the SQL UPDATE statement, and execute to the database.
strSQL = "UPDATE Categories " & _
        "SET ModifiedDate = " & "'" & Now() & "'" & _
        " WHERE Id = " & lngCategoryID
```

10. Replace the line *TODO: Clean up local variables* in the *Update* and *Delete* methods with the following code, which ensures that the *Connection* object will be cleaned up if an error occurs:

```
If Not conn Is Nothing Then
    Set conn = Nothing
End If
```

11. (optional) Build the component by choosing the Make db_CategoryC.dll command from the File menu.

12. Add the following code to the *GetById* method to establish the basic framework that calls the *ObjectContext SetComplete* method when all work is completed successfully or that calls the *ObjectContext SetAbort* method and raises an error if one occurs:

```
Dim strSQL As String
Dim rs As ADODB.Recordset
Dim conn As ADODB.Connection

On Error Goto ErrorHandler
    ' TODO: Do work.
    GetObjectContext.SetComplete
    Exit Function
ErrorHandler:
    ' TODO: Clean up local variables.
    GetObjectContext.SetAbort

    ' Rethrow the error.
    Err.Raise Err.Number, SetErrSource(modName, "ListAll"), _
        Err.Description
```

(continued)

Implementing the *db_CategoryC Add*, *Update*, *Delete*, and *Get* Methods, *continued*

13. Replace the line *TODO: Do work* in the *GetById* method with the following code, which connects to the database and executes a SQL query to retrieve a read-only, forward-only *Recordset*:

```
' Open the connection to the database.
Set conn = New ADODB.Connection
conn.Open "FILEDSN=" & fileDSN

' Form the SQL SELECT command, and execute to the database.
strSQL = "SELECT CategoryId, Name, ModifiedDate, " & _
         "CreatedDate FROM Categories WHERE " & _
         "CategoryId = " & lngCategoryID & " ORDER BY Name"

Set rs = conn.Execute(strSQL)
```

14. Following the call to *GetObjectContext.SetComplete* in the *GetById* method, add this line to return the *Recordset* to the caller:

```
Set GetById = rs
```

15. Replace the line *TODO: Clean up local variables* in the *GetById* method with the following code, which ensures that the *Connection* object will be cleaned up if an error occurs:

```
If Not conn Is Nothing Then
    Set conn = Nothing
End If
```

16. Repeat steps 12 through 15 for the *GetByName* and *GetBySearchString* methods, replacing *GetById* with the appropriate method name. The only other difference in these methods is the SQL statement to execute, as shown here:

```
' GetByName SQL query
strSQL = "SELECT CategoryId, Name, ModifiedDate, " & _
         "CreatedDate FROM Categories WHERE " & _
         "Name = '" & strCategoryName & "'"

' GetBySearchString SQL query
strSQL = "SELECT CategoryId, Name, ModifiedDate, " & _
```

```
"CreatedDate FROM Categories WHERE " & "Name = '" & _
Left(strSearchText, _
(InStr(1, strSearchText, "/") - 1)) & "'"
```

17. (optional) Build the component by choosing the Make db_CategoryC.dll command from the File menu.

The remaining two methods in the *db_CategoryC* component are *ListAll* and *ListByRange*. These methods use the *Recordset Open* technique to retrieve a disconnected *Recordset* that is returned to the caller. The code for these methods is shown in Listing 8-1. Note that it does not create an explicit *Connection* object. Instead, it passes a connection string to the *Recordset Open* method. ADO will create a *Connection* object behind the scenes, but it doesn't assign the object to a variable. This technique is useful when you need to connect to the database for only one *Recordset*.

When you are creating a disconnected *Recordset*, keep in mind the following important steps:

- Set the *CursorLocation* property on the *Recordset* or *Connection* object to *adUseClient*.

- If you use an explicit *Connection* object, detach it from the *Recordset* after the *Recordset* has been populated by setting the *Recordset Active-Connection* property to *Nothing*.

For this particular component, we don't need to return a *Recordset* that can be updated since the *Update* method takes individual parameters, not a *Recordset*. If we wanted to create a *Recordset* that could be updated, we would need to set the *LockType* property to *adLockBatchOptimistic* and the *CursorType* to *adOpenStatic* or *adOpenKeyset*.

With that, the *db_CategoryC* component is complete. If you've been following along, your *db_CategoryC* source code should look like that in the \IslandHopper\Source\Server_Components\db_CategoryC directory on the companion CD. We'll see how to set the transactional and security requirements for this component and how to package it for use with MTS in Chapter 10.

Step by Step: Implementing the *db_CategoryC List* Methods

1. If necessary, reopen the *db_CategoryC* project.

2. Add the following code to the *ListAll* method to establish the basic framework:

```
Dim strSQL As String
Dim rs As ADODB.Recordset

On Error GoTo ErrorHandler
    ' TODO: Do work.
    GetObjectContext.SetComplete
    Exit Function
ErrorHandler:
    ' TODO: Clean up local variables.
    GetObjectContext.SetAbort
    Err.Raise Err.Number, _
     SetErrSource(modName, "ListAll"), Err.Description
```

3. Replace the line *TODO: Do work* in the *ListAll* method with the following code, which creates a *Recordset* and retrieves information from the database using the *Recordset Open* method:

```
' Form the SQL SELECT statement, and execute to the database.
strSQL = "SELECT CategoryId, Name, ModifiedDate, CreatedDate " & _
        "FROM Categories ORDER BY Name"
Set rs = New ADODB.Recordset
rs.CursorLocation = adUseClient

' Execute the SQL command to the database
' using the Recordset Open method.
rs.Open strSQL, "FILEDSN=" & fileDSN, _
    adOpenKeyset, adLockReadOnly, adCmdText
```

4. Following the call to *GetObjectContext.SetComplete* in the *ListAll* method, add this line to return the *Recordset* to the caller:

```
Set ListAll = rs
```

5. Replace the line *TODO: Clean up local variables* in the *ListAll* method with the following code, which ensures that the *Recordset* will be cleaned up if an error occurs:

```
    If Not rs Is Nothing Then
       Set rs = Nothing
    End If
```

6. Repeat steps 2 through 5 for the *ListByRange* method, replacing *ListAll* with *ListByRange*. The only other difference in the methods is the SQL statement to execute, as shown here:

```
' ListByRange SQL query
strSQL = "SELECT CategoryID, Name FROM Categories " & _
         "WHERE CategoryID BETWEEN " & intLow & " AND " & intHigh
```

7. (optional) Build the component by choosing the Make db_CategoryC.dll command from the File menu.

Implementing *db_CustomerPasswordC* in Visual Basic

The *db_CustomerPasswordC* component manages access to the Customer-Passwords table in the Island Hopper classified ads database. Unlike the *db_CategoryC* component, *db_CustomerPasswordC* implements externally defined interfaces. It also illustrates how to use ADO *Command* objects to interact with the database.

Defining the interfaces

When a COM class exposes multiple interfaces or you think the interface might be implemented by multiple classes, you should explicitly define the interfaces. There are several ways you can accomplish this. First, you can write an Interface Definition Language (IDL) file to describe the interfaces, as we discussed in Chapter 2. You then compile the IDL file using the Microsoft IDL (MIDL) compiler to generate a C/C++ header file and a type library. Depending on the tools used to implement COM classes exposing your interfaces, developers will either include the header file in their source code or import the type library into their component project. This approach gives you the most control over your interface definitions, but you must understand IDL in order to use it.

A second approach is to use features of a programming tool to define the interfaces without generating an IDL file. For example, Visual Basic lets you define interfaces using Visual Basic syntax. You simply create a new ActiveX DLL or EXE project, create a class module for each interface, and add the desired properties and methods to a class module, without putting any code in the procedures. When you build the project, a type library is generated that describes all the interfaces. This technique is convenient if you know Visual Basic. The downside is that you don't have much control over the definition that gets generated. In addition, there is no straightforward way to generate a C-style header file from the type library. However, if you can live with these constraints, this is an easy way to define interfaces.

A third approach is to use a programming tool to generate the IDL file for you. The Island Hopper application uses this technique. It gives you all the advantages of a separate IDL file for your interface definitions, but it doesn't require quite as much knowledge of the IDL syntax. (Exactly how much IDL you need to understand depends on what programming tool you are using.)

For the *db_CustomerPasswordC* component, Visual C++ was used to generate the interface definitions. Using this approach, you first create an ATL COM AppWizard project. You then use the Insert New Class menu command to define a new ATL class that implements all the interfaces you need, as shown in Figure 8-1. This generates the skeleton IDL file defining the interfaces.

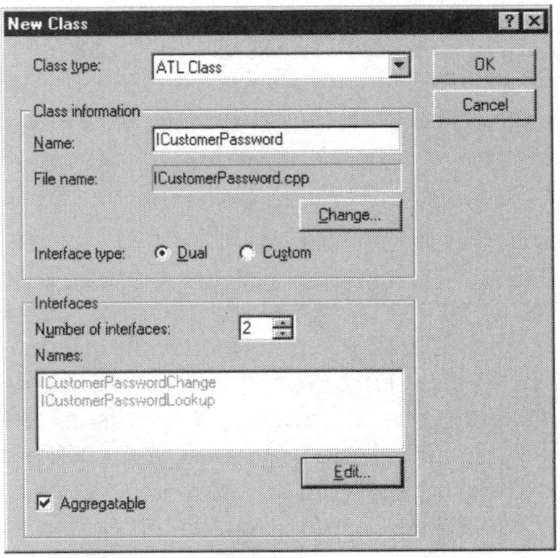

Figure 8-1. *Using the Insert New Class option to define skeleton interfaces.*

Finally, use the Visual C++ Integrated Development Environment (IDE) to add methods and properties to the interfaces, as shown in Figure 8-2. This will add the method and property definitions to the IDL file. Once all the methods and properties are defined, you simply build the project. In addition to building a skeleton component, this technique compiles the IDL file, generating a C/C++ header file and a type library for your interfaces.

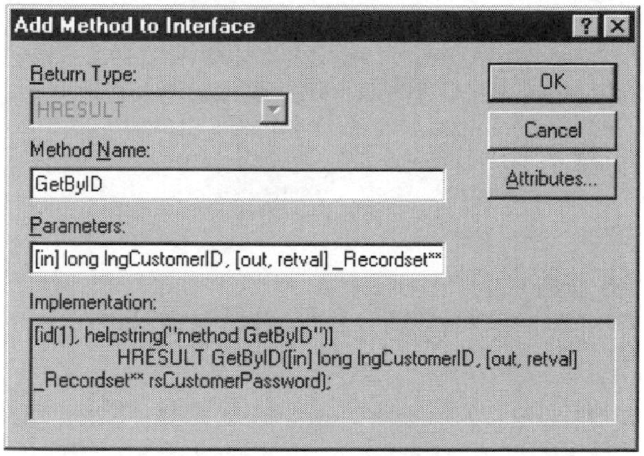

Figure 8-2. *Adding a method definition to an interface using Visual C++.*

Creating the skeleton component

Once the interfaces are defined and you have a type library, you can implement COM classes in Visual Basic that expose these interfaces. The first step is to create an ActiveX DLL project, just as we did for the *db_CategoryC* component. Next you need to set a reference in your component project to the type library with the interface definitions, by choosing the References command from the Project menu, so that Visual Basic knows what methods and properties are exposed by each interface.

To indicate that you want to implement interfaces in your Visual Basic class modules, you use the *Implements* keyword, as shown here:

```
Implements IDBCUSTOMERPASSWORDLib.ICustomerPasswordChange
Implements IDBCUSTOMERPASSWORDLib.ICustomerPasswordLookup
```

Once you have done this, you need to fill in the code for each method. Visual Basic makes it very easy to generate the skeleton code for each method, as shown in Figure 8-3.

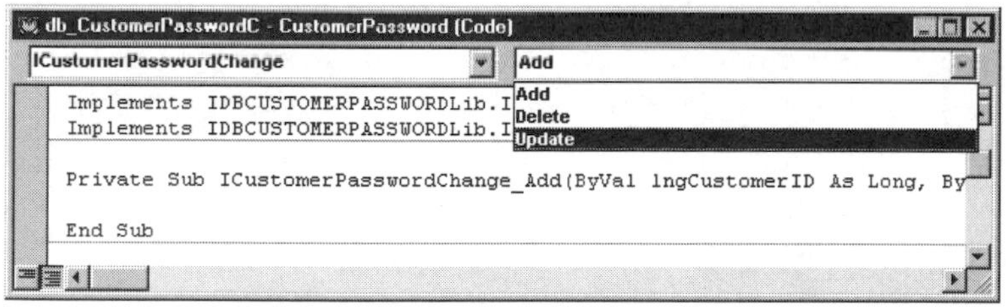

Figure 8-3. *Generating a skeleton method for an interface in Visual Basic.*

With the code window visible for the class, select the interface name in the Object list box. Then select a method name in the Procedure list box. If a skeleton does not already exist for the method, Visual Basic will generate one. In Visual Basic, an implementation of an interface method is a private *Sub* or *Function* with a name in the form *<interface name>_<method name>*. If you implement interfaces correctly, clients will be able to write code similar to this to access the interface methods:

```
Dim x as ICustomerPasswordLookup
Set x = CreateObject("db_CustomerPasswordC.CustomerPassword")
x.Add(lngID, strPassword)
```

Note, however, that if you make the method implementations public, they become part of the default interface, not the interface you are trying to implement. In addition, only the methods on the default interface for the class will be accessible through *IDispatch*.

Step by Step: Implementing the Skeleton *db_CustomerPasswordC* Component

1. Create a skeleton *db_CustomerPasswordC* component, following the instructions for the *db_CategoryC* skeleton component. The project name should be *db_CustomerPasswordC*, and the class name should be *CustomerPassword*.

2. Choose the References command from the Project menu, and check the IdbCustomerPassword 1.0 Type Library check box. If this option does not appear in the list of available type libraries, you might need to build the *IdbCustomerPassword* ATL project located in the Source\Server_Components\Interfaces\IdbCustomerPassword directory in your Island Hopper source installation.

3. Choose the References command from the Project menu again. Locate and check the Microsoft ActiveX Data Objects Library option in the list of available references to ensure that you don't get any errors when you try to implement methods that use ADO *Recordset* objects. Also, locate and check the Microsoft Transaction Server Type Library in the list of available references.

4. Open the source code window for the CustomerPassword class and add the following code to indicate that you want to implement the *ICustomerPasswordLookup* and *ICustomerPasswordChange* interfaces:

```
Implements IDBCUSTOMERPASSWORDLib.ICustomerPasswordLookup
Implements IDBCUSTOMERPASSWORDLib.ICustomerPasswordChange
```

5. For each method of the *ICustomerPasswordLookup* and *ICustomer-PasswordChange* interfaces, generate the skeleton code by selecting the interface name in the Object list box and the method name in the Procedure list box. You should end up with these method definitions:

```
Private Sub ICustomerPasswordChange_Add _
    (ByVal lngCustomerID As Long, ByVal strPassword As String)
Private Sub ICustomerPasswordChange_Delete _
    (ByVal lngCustomerID As Long)
Private Sub ICustomerPasswordChange_Update _
    (ByVal lngCustomerID As Long, ByVal strPassword As String)
Private Function ICustomerPasswordLookup_GetByID _
    (ByVal lngCustomerID As Long) As ADODB.Recordset
```

> **NOTE** If you want to build the *db_CustomerPasswordC* component at this point on a machine that has the Island Hopper application installed, you should select the Binary Compatibility option on the Project Properties Component tab and select the DB_CUSTOMERPASSWORDC.DLL file located in the Source\Server_Components\CompatibleDlls directory in your Island Hopper source installation. If you don't make this adjustment, Island Hopper components that use *db_CustomerPasswordC* will not work correctly.

6. (optional) Build the component by choosing the Make db_CustomerPasswordC.dll command from the File menu. After you build the component, you should select the Binary Compatibility option on the Project Properties Component tab. If you haven't selected the prebuilt *db_CustomerPasswordC* DLL that came with the Island Hopper application, copy the DLL you just built to a safe place and select that. This step will help prevent incompatible changes to the *CustomerPassword* class.

Implementing the methods

With the skeleton code in place, you can start filling in the method implementations. We're going to look at only one method for this component in detail: the *Add* method, which demonstrates how to perform a parameterized query using an ADO *Command* object. The complete source code for all the methods is shown in Listing 8-2 beginning on the following page.

```
Option Explicit
Const modName = "db_CustomerPasswordC.CustomerPassword"
Const fileDSN = "dbCustomerPasswordC.DSN"

Implements IDBCUSTOMERPASSWORDLib.ICustomerPasswordChange
Implements IDBCUSTOMERPASSWORDLib.ICustomerPasswordLookup


'*********************************************************************
' ICustomerPasswordLookup_GetByID
' Purpose: Gets password information from the database for a
'          particular customer ID
' Inputs:  lngCustomerID -- the unique customer ID number
' Returns: A Recordset object containing password information
'*********************************************************************
Private Function ICustomerPasswordLookup_GetByID(ByVal lngCustomerID _
    As Long) As ADODB.Recordset

    Dim strSQL As String
    Dim rs As New ADODB.Recordset

    On Error GoTo ErrorHandler

    ' Form the SQL SELECT statement.
    strSQL = "SELECT Password FROM CustomerPasswords " & _
             "WHERE CustomerID = " & lngCustomerID

    rs.CursorLocation = adUseClient

    ' Execute the SQL command to the database
    ' using the Recordset Open method.
    rs.Open strSQL, "FILEDSN=" & fileDSN, adOpenForwardOnly, adLockReadOnly

    ' Allow MTS transaction set to proceed.
    GetObjectContext.SetComplete

    ' Return the Recordset object containing the password.
    Set ICustomerPasswordLookup_GetByID = rs

    Exit Function

ErrorHandler:
```

Listing 8-2. *The* db_CustomerPasswordC *source code.*

```
        If Not rs Is Nothing Then
            Set rs = Nothing
        End If

        ' Roll back the MTS transaction set.
        GetObjectContext.SetAbort

        Err.Raise Err.Number, SetErrSource(modName, "GetByID"), Err.Description

End Function

'*********************************************************************
' ICustomerPasswordChange_Add
' Purpose: Adds a new customer password record to the database
' Inputs:  lngCustomerID -- the unique customer ID number
'          strPassword   -- the customer password
'*********************************************************************
Private Sub ICustomerPasswordChange_Add(ByVal lngCustomerID As Long, _
    ByVal strPassword As String)

    Dim strSQL As String
    Dim conn As ADODB.Connection
    Dim cmd As ADODB.Command

    On Error GoTo ErrorHandler

    ' Form the SQL INSERT statement. Use the ADODB Command object to make
    ' the SQL command "SQL safe" - that is, correctly handle a password
    ' string that may contain single or double quotes.
    strSQL = "INSERT CustomerPasswords (CustomerID, Password) " & _
             "VALUES ( ?, ? )"

    Set cmd = New ADODB.Command
    cmd.CommandText = strSQL

    cmd.Parameters.Append cmd.CreateParameter(, adInteger, adParamInput, , _
     lngCustomerID)
    cmd.Parameters.Append cmd.CreateParameter(, adVarChar, adParamInput, _
     255, strPassword)
```

(continued)

Listing 8-2. *continued*

```
    ' Open the Connection object
    ' and execute the SQL command to the database.
    Set conn = New ADODB.Connection
    conn.Open "FILEDSN=" & fileDSN
    Set cmd.ActiveConnection = conn
    cmd.Execute

    ' Allow MTS transaction set to proceed.
    GetObjectContext.SetComplete

    Exit Sub

ErrorHandler:

    ' Clean up objects on the way out.
    If Not conn Is Nothing Then
        Set conn = Nothing
    End If

    If Not cmd Is Nothing Then
        Set cmd = Nothing
    End If

    ' Roll back MTS transaction set.
    GetObjectContext.SetAbort

    Err.Raise Err.Number, SetErrSource(modName, "Add"), Err.Description

End Sub

'**********************************************************************
' ICustomerPasswordChange_Delete
' Purpose: Deletes a customer password record from the database
' Inputs:  lngCustomerID -- the unique customer ID number
'**********************************************************************
Private Sub ICustomerPasswordChange_Delete(ByVal lngCustomerID As Long)

    Dim strSQL As String
    Dim conn As ADODB.Connection

    On Error GoTo ErrorHandler

    ' Form the SQL DELETE statement.
    strSQL = "DELETE FROM CustomerPasswords WHERE CustomerID = " & _
     lngCustomerID
```

```
    ' Open the Connection object
    ' and execute the SQL command to the database.
    Set conn = New ADODB.Connection
    conn.Open "FILEDSN=" & fileDSN
    conn.Execute strSQL

    ' Allow MTS transaction set to proceed.
    GetObjectContext.SetComplete

    Exit Sub

ErrorHandler:

    If Not conn Is Nothing Then
        Set conn = Nothing
    End If

    ' Roll back MTS transaction set.
    GetObjectContext.SetAbort

    Err.Raise Err.Number, SetErrSource(modName, "Delete"), Err.Description

End Sub

'***********************************************************************
' ICustomerPasswordChange_Update
' Purpose: Updates the customer password record in the database
' Inputs:   lngCustomerID -- the unique customer ID number
'           strPassword   -- the customer password
'***********************************************************************
Private Sub ICustomerPasswordChange_Update(ByVal lngCustomerID As Long, _
    ByVal strPassword As String)

    Dim strSQL As String
    Dim conn As ADODB.Connection
    Dim cmd As ADODB.Command

    On Error GoTo ErrorHandler

    ' Form the SQL UPDATE statement.
    strSQL = "UPDATE CustomerPasswords SET Password = ? " & _
             "WHERE CustomerID = ?"

    Set cmd = New ADODB.Command
    cmd.CommandText = strSQL
```

(continued)

Listing 8-2. *continued*

```
    cmd.Parameters.Append cmd.CreateParameter(, adVarChar, adParamInput, _
    255, strPassword)
    cmd.Parameters.Append cmd.CreateParameter(, adInteger, adParamInput, _
    , lngCustomerID)

    ' Open the Connection object
    ' and execute the SQL command to the database.
    Set conn = New ADODB.Connection
    conn.Open "FILEDSN=" & fileDSN
    Set cmd.ActiveConnection = conn
    cmd.Execute

    ' Allow MTS transaction set to proceed.
    GetObjectContext.SetComplete

Exit Sub

ErrorHandler:

    ' Clean up objects on the way out.
    If Not conn Is Nothing Then
        Set conn = Nothing
    End If

    If Not cmd Is Nothing Then
        Set cmd = Nothing
    End If

    ' Roll back MTS transaction set.
    GetObjectContext.SetAbort

    Err.Raise Err.Number, SetErrSource(modName, "Update"), Err.Description

End Sub
```

When you use an ADO *Command* object to implement a parameterized query, you need to populate the *Parameters* collection. For each parameter, first call the *Command* object *CreateParameter* method to create a new *Parameter* object. Then call the *Parameters* collection *Append* method to add the *Parameter* object to the collection, as shown here:

```
cmd.Parameters.Append cmd.CreateParameter _
    (, adInteger, adParamInput, , lngCustomerID)
```

Be sure to append the parameters in the order in which they appear in the SQL statement or stored procedure you want to execute. You will get better performance if the parameter types you create match the types expected by the database, since data conversion can be eliminated. Once the *Parameters* collection is populated, you call the *Command* object's Execute method to retrieve a read-only, forward-only *Recordset*. If you need a more flexible *Recordset*, you can create a *Command* object and pass it as the first parameter of the *Recordset Open* method call.

Step by Step: Implementing the *db_CustomerPasswordC Add* Method

1. If necessary, reopen the *db_CustomerPasswordC* project.

2. Add the following lines to the General Declarations section of the CustomerPassword class module to define constants for the module name used in error reporting and the DSN filename that is used to connect to the database:

```
Option Explicit
Const modName = "db_CustomerPasswordC.CustomerPassword"
Const fileDSN = "dbCustomerPasswordC.DSN"
```

3. Add the GLOBALS.BAS module, located in the \IslandHopper\Source\ Server_Components\Globals directory on the companion CD, to the project by choosing the Add Module command from the Project menu. This step will give you the *SetErrorSource* function used in the method error handlers.

4. Add this code to the *Add* method to establish the basic framework:

```
Dim strSQL As String
Dim conn As ADODB.Connection
Dim cmd As ADODB.Command

On Error GoTo ErrorHandler
    ' TODO: Do work.
    GetObjectContext.SetComplete
    Exit Sub

ErrorHandler:
    ' TODO: Clean up local variables.
    GetObjectContext.SetAbort
```

(continued)

Implementing the *db_CustomerPasswordC Add* **Method,** *continued*

```
      Err.Raise Err.Number, SetErrSource(modName, "Add"), _
      Err.Description
```

5. Replace the line *TODO: Do work* in the *Add* method with the following code, which creates a *Command* object, populates the *Parameters* collection, and executes the command:

```
' Form the SQL INSERT statement. Use the ADODB command object to
' make the SQL command "SQL safe"--that is, correctly handle a
' password string that might contain single or double quotes.
strSQL = "INSERT CustomerPasswords (CustomerID, Password) " & _
         "VALUES ( ?, ? )"

Set cmd = New ADODB.Command
cmd.CommandText = strSQL

cmd.Parameters.Append cmd.CreateParameter _
    (, adInteger, adParamInput, , lngCustomerID)
cmd.Parameters.Append cmd.CreateParameter _
    (, adVarChar, adParamInput, 255, strPassword)

' Open the Connection object
' and execute the SQL command to the database.
Set conn = New ADODB.Connection
conn.Open "FILEDSN=" & fileDSN
Set cmd.ActiveConnection = conn
cmd.Execute
```

6. Replace the line *TODO: Clean up local variables* in the *Add* method with the following code, which ensures that the *Connection* and *Command* objects will be cleaned up if an error occurs:

```
If Not conn Is Nothing Then
   Set conn = Nothing
End If

If Not cmd Is Nothing Then
   Set cmd = Nothing
End If
```

7. (optional) Build the component by choosing the Make db_CustomerPasswordC.dll command from the File menu.

A Quick Look at *db_CustomerC*

The *db_CustomerC* component is very similar to the *db_CustomerPasswordC* and *db_CategoryC* components, so we won't look at it in any great detail. Instead, let's just take a quick look at how the *db_CustomerC* query methods are implemented—by using a call to a parameterized stored procedure in the database. This is a common thing to do, so the actual code to call the stored procedure is separated out into a global function, *RunSp*.

The code for the *db_CustomerC* implementation of *ICustomerLookup ListByLastName* method is shown in Listing 8-3.

```
'*******************************************************************
' ICustomerLookup_ListByLastName()
' Purpose: Retrieves customer information from the database
'          for a particular last name
' Inputs:  strLastName -- the customer last name
' Returns: A Recordset object containing customer information
'*******************************************************************
Private Function ICustomerLookup_ListByLastName(ByVal strLastName _
    As String) As ADODB.Recordset

    Dim rs As New ADODB.Recordset

    On Error GoTo ErrorHandler

    ' Execute the stored procedure to the database.
    Set rs = RunSp(fileDSN, "Customer_ListByLastName", 1, _
                Array("@vLastName"), Array(adChar),
                Array(30), Array(strLastName))

    ' Allow MTS transaction set to proceed.
    GetObjectContext.SetComplete

    ' Return a Recordset object containing the customer information.
    Set ICustomerLookup_ListByLastName = rs

    Exit Function

ErrorHandler:

    ' Clean up the object on the way out.
    If Not rs Is Nothing Then
        Set rs = Nothing
    End If
```

Listing 8-3. *The* db_CustomerC *source code for the* ICustomerLookup ListByLastName *method.*

(continued)

Listing 8-3. *continued*

```
    ' Roll back MTS transaction set.
    GetObjectContext.SetAbort

    Err.Raise Err.Number, SetErrSource(modName, _
     "ICustomerLookup_ListByLastName"), Err.Description

End Function
```

Notice that the basic structure is exactly the same as that for every other data object method we've seen: set up a general error handler, do your work, and call the *ObjectContext SetComplete* method when you have finished. In the error handler, you clean up, call the *ObjectContext SetAbort* method, and raise an error to the caller. What's different is the code that does the work, shown here:

```
Set rs = RunSp(fileDSN, "Customer_ListByLastName", 1, _
               Array("@vLastName"), Array(adChar), _
               Array(30), Array(strLastName))
```

RunSp is where all the interesting bits are. The source code for *RunSp* is shown in Listing 8-4.

```
'*********************************************************************
' RunSp()
' Purpose: Calls a stored procedure in the database
' Inputs:
'    strFileDSN    -- the name of the DSN file pointing to the database
'    strSP         -- the name of the stored procedure to run
'    intPRMCount   -- the number of parameters sent to the stored procedure
'    strPRM        -- Variant containing the names of the parameters sent
'    strPRMType    -- Variant containing the types of the parameters sent
'    intPRMLength  -- Variant containing the sizes of the parameters sent
'    strPRMValue   -- Variant containing the values of the parameters sent
' Returns: A Recordset object containing the information returned by the
'          stored procedure
'*********************************************************************

Function RunSp(strFileDSN As String, strSP As String, _
    intPRMCount As Integer, strPRM As Variant, strPRMType As Variant, _
    intPRMLength As Variant, strPRMValue As Variant) As Object
```

Listing 8-4. *The* RunSp *source code, used to execute a parameterized stored procedure.*

```
' Set up Command and Connection objects.
Dim rs As New ADODB.Recordset
Dim conn As New ADODB.Connection
Dim cmd As New ADODB.Command
Dim prm As ADODB.Parameter

' Run the procedure.
conn.Open "FILEDSN=" & strFileDSN
Set cmd.ActiveConnection = conn
cmd.CommandText = strSP
cmd.CommandType = adCmdStoredProc

Dim i As Integer
For i = 0 To intPRMCount - 1
    Set prm = cmd.CreateParameter(strPRM(i), strPRMType(i), _
    adParamInput, intPRMLength(i), strPRMValue(i))  ' PART OF WAY 1
    cmd.Parameters.Append prm
Next i

rs.CursorLocation = adUseClient
rs.Open cmd, , adOpenStatic, adLockBatchOptimistic

Set RunSp = rs

End Function
```

The *RunSp* function creates an updatable, disconnected *Recordset*. It starts by creating a *Connection* object to the database specified in the *strFileDSN* parameter, as shown here:

```
conn.Open "FILEDSN=" & strFileDSN
```

Next it creates a *Command* object, connects it to the *Connection* object, and specifies that the command to execute is the stored procedure passed as the *strSP* parameter, as shown here:

```
Set cmd.ActiveConnection = conn
cmd.CommandText = strSP
cmd.CommandType = adCmdStoredProc
```

Now *RunSp* needs to set up the parameters for the stored procedure. Each parameter for the stored procedure includes four pieces of information: name, data type, size, and value. The *intPRMCount* parameter indicates how many stored procedure parameters need to be set up. The remaining four *RunSp* arguments, *strPRM*, *strPRMType*, *intPRMLength*, and *strPRMValue* are arrays containing the name, type, size, and value of each stored procedure parameter. *RunSp* iterates through these arrays to create *Parameter* objects that are added to the *Command* object, as shown here:

```
Dim i As Integer
For i = 0 To intPRMCount - 1
    Set prm = cmd.CreateParameter(strPRM(i), strPRMType(i), _
     adParamInput, intPRMLength(i), strPRMValue(i))
    cmd.Parameters.Append prm
Next i
```

With the *Command* object initialized, *RunSp* can call *Recordset Open* to retrieve the records, using batch optimistic locking and a static cursor type, as shown here:

```
rs.CursorLocation = adUseClient
rs.Open cmd, , adOpenStatic, adLockBatchOptimistic
Set RunSp = rs
```

The other query methods in *db_CustomerC* are implemented the same way. Note that the call to *RunSp* in *ListByLastName* uses explicit data types, not Variants. Unless you have a true Variant data type, you should use explicit data types in calls to the database and as data variables or parameters within your source code. In addition, you should use the same type for data variables or parameters as you use in the database. Doing so will improve performance by eliminating the need for data conversion.

At this point, you should understand how to implement a data object in Visual Basic. If you are building stateless data objects that own one SQL Server database table each, all your data objects will look a lot like the *db_CategoryC*, *db_CustomerPasswordC*, and *db_CustomerC* components discussed here. If you have lots of data objects, you might want to move the standard functionality into a set of global functions you can reuse, much as we did with the *RunSp* function in the Island Hopper application.

Implementing Data Objects in Visual C++

Visual Basic is a great language for implementing data objects because it provides extensive support for using COM objects such as ADO. However, Visual Basic isn't the right choice for everyone. In the remainder of this chapter, we'll look at writing a data object, *db_PaymentC*, using Visual C++. Conceptually, writing a data object in Visual C++ is exactly like writing one in Visual Basic. You have the same options for using ADO. You make the same method calls. However, the code you end up with looks very, very different.

The easiest way to create data objects in C++ is by using the Active Template Library (ATL). ATL provides template classes to implement small, fast COM components. It includes standard implementations for *IUnknown*, *IClassFactory*, *IDispatch*, dual interfaces, in-process server entry points, and so on. Unlike Visual Basic, however, all the source code for these implementations is visible to you—either within ATL header files or within your component source code. Visual C++ includes wizards that let you generate skeleton components and COM classes very quickly. Starting with version 5.0, Visual C++ also includes native compiler support for COM. This feature can simplify using existing COM objects, such as ADO from C++.

> **NOTE** With the Visual C++ wizards, you can easily write components without understanding very much about ATL. However, when you start debugging your components, you'll probably want to understand what all the code the wizards generated is for. The bibliography provides some pointers to more detailed information about ATL.

Creating the skeleton component

The first step is to create a project for the component. You do this by creating a new ATL COM AppWizard project in the Visual C++ IDE. The IDE launches a one-step wizard that lets you specify that a DLL server should be created, as shown in Figure 8-4.

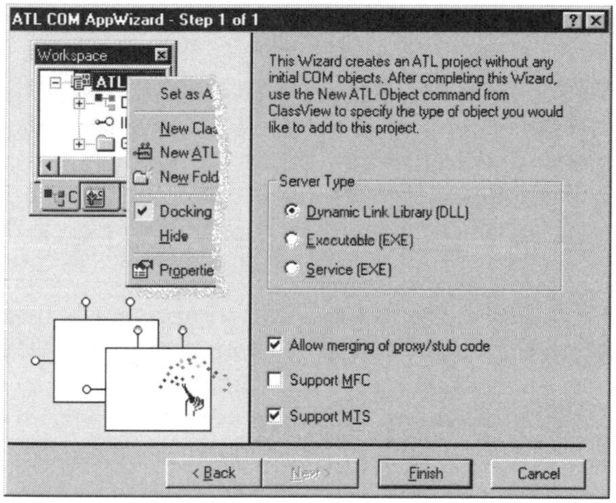

Figure 8-4. *Creating a new ATL component.*

At this point, the component doesn't include any COM classes, just implementations of the entry points required by DLL servers. To create a COM class, you use the ATL Object Wizard, which is accessed by choosing the New ATL Object command from the Insert menu. The Object Wizard lets you choose the type of COM class to create. For data objects and business objects, you should select Objects from the Category list and MS Transaction Server Component from the Objects list. Click Next, and you will be prompted to enter the names of the C++ class, COM coclass, default interface name, and ProgID you want to use. The MTS tab lets you specify MTS-specific options, as shown in Figure 8-5. You will usually want to implement a dual interface and include support for the *IObjectControl* interface.

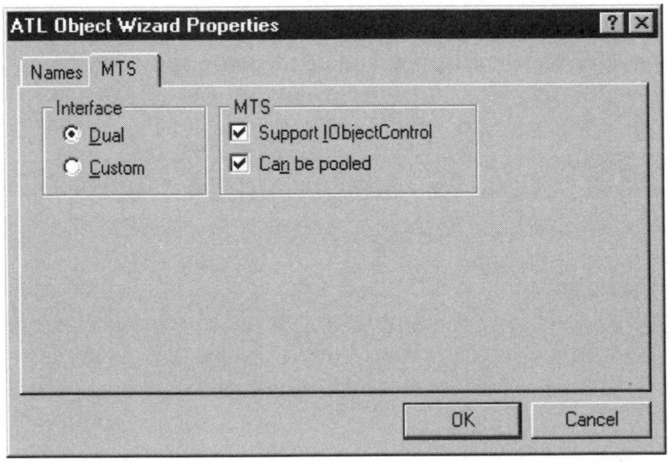

Figure 8-5. *Setting MTS options in the ATL Object Wizard.*

We haven't talked about the *IObjectControl* interface yet. It contains three methods: *Activate*, *Deactivate*, and *CanBePooled*. *Activate* and *Deactivate* give you a chance to do some initialization or cleanup work during JIT activation or deactivation. *CanBePooled* was designed to enable components to indicate whether objects could be placed in an object pool instead of being destroyed upon deactivation. However, this method is not called by MTS 1.0 or MTS 2.0.

The real reason to include *IObjectControl* support in your component is that when you do so, a *smart pointer* to the object context is added to your COM class. A smart pointer is a wrapper for a COM interface pointer that automatically handles calling the *AddRef* and *Release* methods, so you don't need to handle reference counting manually. ATL gets the object context during activation and cleans it up during deactivation, so you always have access to the object context within your COM class.

WARNING The ATL Object Wizard in Visual C++ 5.0 generates incorrect code for the *IObjectControl Deactivate* method. You should change the line

```
m_spObjectContext->Release();
```

to

```
m_spObjectContext.Release();
```

This is no longer a problem in Visual C++ 6.0.

Step by Step: Creating the Skeleton *db_PaymentC* Component

1. Start Visual C++ and create a new ATL COM AppWizard project named *db_PaymentC*. Ensure that the Server Type is set to DLL. If you are using Visual C++ 6.0, check Support MTS so that your project build settings are configured to link to the MTS libraries.

2. Choose the New ATL Object command from the Insert menu to launch the ATL Object Wizard.

3. Select Objects from the Category list and MS Transaction Server Component from the Objects list, and then click the Next button.

4. On the Names tab, enter *db_Payment* as the short name. Change the ProgID to *db_PaymentC.Payment*. You can accept the default values for all other fields on the Names tab.

5. On the MTS tab, click on the Dual Interface radio button and check both Support IObjectControl and Can Be Pooled. (In Visual C++ 5.0, this tab is labeled "MTX" instead of "MTS".)

6. Click the OK button to generate the *Cdb_Payment* class code.

NOTE   If you build the *db_PaymentC* component at this point on a machine that has the Island Hopper application installed, you will break any Island Hopper components that use *db_PaymentC*. Wait to build the component until you have implemented the skeleton interface methods.

7. (optional) Build the component by selecting the Build db_PaymentC.dll command from the Build menu.

That's all there is to creating a skeleton component in ATL. A boring component, to be sure, since the COM class default interface doesn't expose any methods yet. But you do now have a functioning component.

With the class skeleton in place, you can turn your attention to implementing its interfaces. The class generated by the ATL Object Wizard includes one interface. If you want to add additional interfaces to the class, you will need to add the interfaces to the IDL file and your C++ class manually.

The Visual C++ IDE can help you add methods and properties to your interfaces. To do so, open the Workspace window and switch to the class view. You should see an entry for each of your interfaces. Right-click on an interface to display a pop-up menu with options to add methods and properties, as shown in Figure 8-6. Choosing one of these commands opens a dialog box in which you can enter information about the method or property. The syntax you enter in this dialog box is IDL syntax, not C++. The primary advantage of using the dialog box is that it adds the methods and properties to the IDL file, the C++ class header file, and the C++ class implementation at the same time.

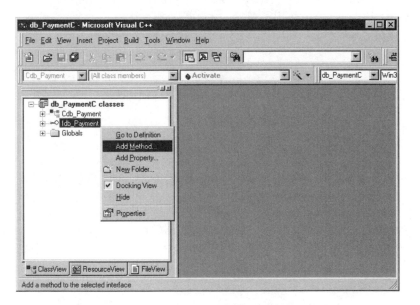

Figure 8-6. *Adding a method to an interface in Visual C++.*

Step by Step: Adding Skeleton Interface Methods for *db_PaymentC*

1. If necessary, reopen the *db_PaymentC* project.

2. From the Workspace window, switch to the class view. Expand the class tree until you see the *Idb_Payment* interface.

3. Right-click on *Idb_Payment* to display the pop-up menu. Choose the Add Method command to open the Add Method To Interface dialog box, and enter these values:

```
Method Name = AddPayment
Parameters = [in] long lngCustomerID,
             [in] long lngPaymentID,
             [in, string] BSTR strPaymentMethod,
             [in] DATE dtmPaymentDate,
             [in] double dblPaymentAmt,
             [in] long lngInvoiceID,
             [in, string] BSTR strCardNumber,
             [in] DATE dtmExpDate
```

4. Click OK to close the dialog box. The method definition will be added to your IDL file and a skeleton method will be added to your C++ class.

5. Repeat steps 3 and 4 for the other method exposed by *Idb_Payment*, *GetByCustID*, as shown here:

```
Method Name = GetByCustID
Parameters = [in] long lngCustID,
             [out, retval] LPDISPATCH *ppRecordset
```

6. (optional) Build the component by selecting the Build db_PaymentC.dll command from the Build menu.

NOTE
You can ignore the MIDL2039 warning that is generated during the build. MIDL is not able to determine that _Recordset is a dual interface and hence an automation compatible type.

Implementing the methods

With the skeleton code in place, you can fill in the data access logic for each interface method. To do this, you need to figure out how to use ADO from C++. This seems like a simple task: create a COM object using *CoCreateInstance* or *CoCreateInstanceEx*, make simple function calls through the interface pointer you get back, and then call *Release* to clean up the interface pointer. However, ADO makes extensive use of two Automation data types that are a little tricky to use from C++: BSTRs and VARIANTs. Both of these types require initialization and cleanup logic to avoid memory leaks. In addition, neither type corresponds directly to a standard C++ type, so data conversion might be necessary before you can operate on the data values. Visual Basic hides all this from the developer; C++ does not.

> **NOTE** ADO 2.0 includes a set of extensions to simplify using ADO from C++. These extensions let you map the fields of a Recordset object to C++ variables. Island Hopper is written to be compatible with both ADO 1.5 and ADO 2.0, so it does not use these extensions. For more information, see the topic "ADO VC++ Extensions" in the Visual Studio 6.0 documentation.

Still, one option you have is to use the ADO interfaces directly. These are defined in the header file ADOINT.H. A second option is to use ATL wrapper classes for BSTR (*CComBSTR*) and VARIANT (*CComVariant*), perhaps in conjunction with ATL smart pointers (*CComPtr* and *CComQIPtr*). The wrapper classes hide the details of initialization and cleanup in their construction and destructor. They also provide useful operator overrides for manipulating data values. Smart pointers wrap interface pointers and automatically call *Release* when the smart pointer is destroyed. Otherwise, using ADO with these helper classes is very much like using the raw interfaces.

The Island Hopper sample application uses a third technique. Starting with version 5.0, Visual C++ includes native compiler support for COM. The compiler can directly read a type library and translate the contents into C++ wrapper classes for each interface. You use the *#import* preprocessor directive to indicate that you want to use a type library, as in the following example:

```
#import "msado15.dll" rename("EOF","ADOEOF") no_namespace
```

This code fragment indicates that you want to use the COM classes and interfaces implemented by MSADO15.DLL. This DLL will contain either ADO 1.5 or ADO 2.0, depending on which version of the DLL is installed on your system. The *rename* attribute is used to change the name of the *Recordset EOF*, to avoid a naming conflict with the C run-time library. The *no_namespace* attribute indicates that the class definitions should not be enclosed in a C++ namespace. This statement will generate two files, MSADO15.TLH and MSADO15.TLI. The .TLH file is a header file containing the class definitions. The .TLI file contains the class implementations. By default, each interface is wrapped by a class with a name in the form *<interface name>Ptr*.

The wrapper classes take advantage of several helper classes provided by Visual C++ to support the VARIANT (*_variant_t*) and BSTR (*_bstr_t*) types, implement smart pointers(*_com_ptr_t*), and encapsulate COM errors (*_com_error*). These helper classes serve the same purpose as the ATL classes, but they promote a slightly different style of coding. The COM wrapper classes include a *CreateInstance* method and convert COM errors to exceptions.

NOTE One disadvantage of this method is that the *#import* statement and other features used by the generated classes are specific to Visual C++. If you are using a different compiler, you might want to use the ATL classes.

As with the Visual Basic methods discussed earlier, each C++ method implementation for a stateless object will have the same basic structure: set up a try/catch exception handler block to handle errors, do your work, and call the *ObjectContext SetComplete* method when you have finished. In the error handler, clean up, call the *ObjectContext SetAbort* method, and raise an error to the caller. If you included *IObjectControl* support in your skeleton component, you can access the *ObjectContext* through the variable *m_spObjectContext* in your C++ class. The code looks something like this:

```
HRESULT CMyInterfaceImpl::MyMethod()
{
    HRESULT hr = S_OK;
    try
    {
        // Do work.
        :

        if (m_spObjectContext)
            m_spObjectContext->SetComplete();
    }
    catch(_com_error &e)
    {
        // Clean up local variables.
        :
```

(continued)

```
        if (m_spObjectContext)
          m_spObjectContext->SetAbort();

        LPVOID lpMsgBuf;
        hr = e.Error();
        FormatMessage(FORMAT_MESSAGE_ALLOCATE_BUFFER |
                      FORMAT_MESSAGE_FROM_SYSTEM, NULL, hr,
                      MAKELANGID(LANG_NEUTRAL, SUBLANG_DEFAULT),
                      (LPTSTR) &lpMsgBuf, 0, NULL);
        AtlReportError(CLSID_MyClass, (LPCOLESTR) lpMsgBuf,
                       IID_IMyInterface, hr);
        LocalFree(lpMsgBuf);
    }
    return hr;
}
```

You should always check whether the *ObjectContext* exists by testing whether *m_spObjectContext* is *NULL* before you make a method call. If you are running your component outside the MTS environment, there won't be an *ObjectContext* and calls will generate faults.

Also, when you catch an error, you'll want to either pass the same error along or generate a component-specific error. The *FormatMessage* call in the preceding code snippet gets a text description of a system error. The *AtlReportError* function is used to initialize the COM *ErrorInfo* object with descriptive information about the error. If you are implementing several components in C++, you'll probably want to wrap this error-handling code in a utility function that all the components can use.

To perform the database access operations themselves, you use one of the three methods discussed earlier: call the *Execute* method on a *Connection* object, create a *Command* object and call its *Execute* method, or create a *Recordset* object and call its *Open* method.

In the *db_PaymentC* component, the *Connection Execute* option is used for both *Idb_Payment* methods. The primary difference is the work required to build the SQL string passed to the *Execute* call. The source code for these methods is shown in Listing 8-5.

```
#include "stdafx.h"

#include "db_PaymentC.h"
#include "db_Payment.h"
```

Listing 8-5. *The* db_PaymentC *source code for the* Idb_Payment *implementation.*

```
#include "comdef.h"
#include "atlconv.h"

#include <sstream>

using namespace std;

///////////////////////////////////////////////////////////////////////
// Cdb_Payment

STDMETHODIMP Cdb_Payment::InterfaceSupportsErrorInfo(REFIID riid)
{
    static const IID* arr[] =
    {
        &IID_Idb_Payment,
    };
    for (int i=0; i < sizeof(arr)/sizeof(arr[0]); i++)
    {
        if (InlineIsEqualGUID(*arr[i],riid))
            return S_OK;
    }
    return S_FALSE;
}

HRESULT Cdb_Payment::Activate()
{
    HRESULT hr = GetObjectContext(&m_spObjectContext);
    if (SUCCEEDED(hr))
        return S_OK;
    return hr;
}

BOOL Cdb_Payment::CanBePooled()
{
    return TRUE;
}

void Cdb_Payment::Deactivate()
{
}

//***********************************************************************
// AddPayment
// Purpose: Adds a payment to the database
```

(continued)

Listing 8-5. *continued*

```
// Inputs:
//    lngCustomerID     -- the unique customer ID number
//    lngPaymentID      -- the unique payment ID number
//    strPaymentMethod  -- the payment method
//                         (e.g., Amex, Visa, Check)
//    dtmPaymentDate    -- the payment date
//    dblPaymentAmt     -- the total amount of the payment
//    lngInvoiceID      -- the ID of the invoice that corresponds to
//                         this payment
//    strCardNumber     -- the credit card number used to make the
//                         payment
//    dtmExpDate        -- expiration date of the credit card
// Returns: N/A
//****************************************************************

STDMETHODIMP Cdb_Payment::AddPayment(long lngCustomerID,
                                     long lngPaymentID,
                                     BSTR strPaymentMethod,
                                     DATE dtmPaymentDate,
                                     double dblPaymentAmt,
                                     long lngInvoiceID,
                                     BSTR strCardNumber,
                                     DATE dtmExpDate)
{
    HRESULT hr = S_OK;

    try
    {

        // Pointer to an ADO connection
        _ConnectionPtr pObjADO_Connection;

        // Create ADO connection.
        pObjADO_Connection.CreateInstance(__uuidof(Connection));

        // DSN file specification
        bstr_t strFileDSN = L"FILEDSN=dbPaymentC.DSN";

        // Open the connection.
        hr = pObjADO_Connection->Open(strFileDSN, (BSTR) NULL,
                                      (BSTR) NULL, -1);

        // String I/O stream to write SQL statement
        basic_stringstream<wchar_t> strSQLStatement;
```

```cpp
        // Use variant_t object to convert dates into strings.
        variant_t vntPaymentDate(dtmPaymentDate, VT_DATE);
        variant_t vntExpDate(dtmExpDate, VT_DATE);

        // Write the SQL statement into a string.
        // Cast variant dates to bstr_t
        // so that they will be converted to a string.
        strSQLStatement << L"INSERT INTO Payments (CustomerID, "
            "PaymentID, PaymentMethod, PaymentDate, PaymentAmt, "
            "InvoiceID, CardNumber, CardExpDate) VALUES ("
            << lngCustomerID << L", " << lngPaymentID << L", '"
            << strPaymentMethod << L"', '"
            << static_cast<wchar_t *>( (bstr_t) vntPaymentDate)
            << L"', " << dblPaymentAmt << L", " << lngInvoiceID
            << L", '" << strCardNumber << L"', '"
            << static_cast<wchar_t *>( (bstr_t) vntExpDate) << L"')"
            << ends;

        // Parameters of Execute statement
        bstr_t strSQLStmt = strSQLStatement.str().c_str();
        variant_t vntRecordsAffected;

        // Execute the SQL statement to create a payment record.
        pObjADO_Connection >Execute(strSQLStmt, &vntRecordsAffected,
                                    adCmdText);

        if (m_spObjectContext)
            m_spObjectContext->SetComplete();
}
catch(_com_error &e)
{
    LPVOID lpMsgBuf;

    hr = e.Error();

    FormatMessage(FORMAT_MESSAGE_ALLOCATE_BUFFER |
                    FORMAT_MESSAGE_FROM_SYSTEM, NULL, hr,
                  MAKELANGID(LANG_NEUTRAL, SUBLANG_DEFAULT),
                  (LPTSTR) &lpMsgBuf, 0, NULL);

    AtlReportError(CLSID_db_Payment, (LPCOLESTR) lpMsgBuf,
                    IID_Idb_Payment, hr);

    LocalFree(lpMsgBuf);
```

(continued)

Listing 8-5. *continued*

```
        if (m_spObjectContext)
            m_spObjectContext->SetAbort();
    }

    return hr;
}

//*********************************************************************
// GetByCustID
// Purpose: Gets a payment from the database by customer ID
// Inputs:  lngCustomerID  -- the unique customer ID number
// Returns: An ADO Recordset object of payments
//*********************************************************************

STDMETHODIMP Cdb_Payment::GetByCustID(long lngCustID,
                                      LPDISPATCH  *ppRecordset)
{
    HRESULT hr = S_OK;

    try
    {

        // Pointer to an ADO connection
        _ConnectionPtr pObjADO_Connection;

        // Create ADO connection.
        pObjADO_Connection.CreateInstance(__uuidof(Connection));

        // DSN file specification
        bstr_t strFileDSN = L"FILEDSN=dbPaymentC.DSN";

        // Open the connection.
        hr = pObjADO_Connection->Open(strFileDSN, (BSTR) NULL,
                                      (BSTR) NULL, -1);

        // String I/O stream to write SQL statement
        basic_stringstream<wchar_t> strSQLStatement;

        // Write the SQL statement into a string.
        strSQLStatement << L"SELECT  CustomerID, PaymentID, "
            "PaymentMethod, PaymentDate, PaymentAmt, InvoiceID, "
            "CardNumber, CardExpDate FROM Payments WHERE CustomerID = "
            << lngCustID << L" ORDER BY PaymentDate DESC" <<ends;
```

```
        // Parameters of Execute statement
        bstr_t strSQLStmt = strSQLStatement.str().c_str();
        variant_t vntRecordsAffected;
        _RecordsetPtr pObjADO_Recordset;

        // Execute the SQL statement to retrieve records from the
        // Payments table that contain a matching customer ID.
        pObjADO_Recordset = pObjADO_Connection->Execute(strSQLStmt,
            &vntRecordsAffected, adCmdText);

        // Return IDispatch interface pointer.
        // (QueryInterface will call AddRef on the interface pointer.)
        pObjADO_Recordset->QueryInterface(IID_IDispatch,
                                          (void**) ppRecordset);
    }
    catch(_com_error &e)
    {
        LPVOID lpMsgBuf;

        hr = e.Error();

        FormatMessage(FORMAT_MESSAGE_ALLOCATE_BUFFER |
                    FORMAT_MESSAGE_FROM_SYSTEM, NULL, hr,
                    MAKELANGID(LANG_NEUTRAL, SUBLANG_DEFAULT),
                    (LPTSTR) &lpMsgBuf, 0, NULL );

        AtlReportError(CLSID_db_Payment, (LPCOLESTR) lpMsgBuf,
                    IID_Idb_Payment, hr);

        LocalFree(lpMsgBuf);

    }
    return hr;
}
```

Once the *Idb_Payment* methods have been implemented, the *db_PaymentC* component is complete. As you can see, the code used to implement data objects in Visual C++ isn't quite as clean as Visual Basic code. However, with ATL and the Visual C++ COM compiler support, you can develop data objects in C++ fairly easily.

Step by Step: Implementing the *db_PaymentC* and *Idb_Payment* Methods

1. If necessary, reopen the *db_PaymentC* project.

2. Add the following statements to the STDAFX.H file, right above the line *//{{AFX_INSERT_LOCATION}}*:

```
#import "msado15.dll" rename("EOF", "ADOEOF")
using namespace ADODB;
```

These statements will create the COM compiler support wrapper classes for ADO. If the compiler is not able to locate MSADO15.DLL when you build the project, you should either specify the complete path to the DLL in the *#import* statement or add its location to your include path.

3. Add these statements to the top of the DB_PAYMENT.CPP file:

```
#include "comdef.h"
#include "atlconv.h"
#include <sstream>
using namespace std;
```

COMDEF.H defines the COM compiler support classes. ATLCONV.H defines macros for converting between ANSI, Unicode, and OLE strings. SSTREAM is a C++ standard library file that defines a standard string type.

4. Replace the skeleton implementation of the *AddPayment* and *GetBy-CustID* methods with the following code to establish the basic framework that calls the *ObjectContext SetComplete* method when all work has been completed successfully or calls the *ObjectContext SetAbort* method and raises an error if one occurs:

```
HRESULT hr = S_OK;
try
{
   // TODO: Do work.
   :
   if (m_spObjectContext)
      m_spObjectContext->SetComplete();
}
catch(_com_error &e)
{
   if (m_spObjectContext)
      m_spObjectContext->SetAbort();
   LPVOID lpMsgBuf;
   hr = e.Error();
```

```
FormatMessage(FORMAT_MESSAGE_ALLOCATE_BUFFER |
              FORMAT_MESSAGE_FROM_SYSTEM, NULL, hr,
              MAKELANGID(LANG_NEUTRAL, SUBLANG_DEFAULT),
              (LPTSTR) &lpMsgBuf, 0, NULL);

    AtlReportError(CLSID_db_Payment, (LPCOLESTR) lpMsgBuf,
                   IID_Idb_Payment, hr);
    LocalFree(lpMsgBuf);
}
return hr;
```

5. Replace the line *TODO: Do work* in the *AddPayment* method with this code, which connects to the database and issues a SQL command:

```
// Pointer to an ADO connection
_ConnectionPtr pObjADO_Connection;
// Create ADO connection.
pObjADO_Connection.CreateInstance(__uuidof(Connection));

// DSN file specification
bstr_t strFileDSN = L"FILEDSN=dbPaymentC.DSN";

// Open the connection.
hr = pObjADO_Connection->Open(strFileDSN, (BSTR) NULL,
                              (BSTR) NULL, -1);

// String I/O stream to write SQL statement
basic_stringstream<wchar_t> strSQLStatement;
// TODO: Initialize SQL statement.

// Parameters of Execute statement
bstr_t strSQLStmt = strSQLStatement.str().c_str();
variant_t vntRecordsAffected;

// Execute the SQL statement to create a payment record.
pObjADO_Connection->Execute(strSQLStmt, &vntRecordsAffected,
                            adCmdText);
```

The Visual C++ keyword *__uuidof* is used to obtain the globally unique identifier (GUID) associated with a class or interface. The data types *bstr_t* and *variant_t* are *#defined* as synonyms for *_bstr_t* and *_variant_t*.

(continued)

Implementing the *db_PaymentC* and *Idb_Payment* Methods, *continued*

6. Replace the line *TODO: Initialize SQL statement* in the *AddPayment* method with the following code:

```
// Use variant_t object to convert dates to strings.
variant_t vntPaymentDate(dtmPaymentDate, VT_DATE);
variant_t vntExpDate(dtmExpDate, VT_DATE);

// Write the SQL statement into a string.
// Cast VARIANT dates to bstr_t
// so that they will be converted to a string.
strSQLStatement << L"INSERT INTO Payments (CustomerID, "
    L"PaymentID, PaymentMethod, PaymentDate, PaymentAmt, "
    L"InvoiceID, CardNumber, CardExpDate) VALUES ("
    << lngCustomerID << L", " << lngPaymentID << L", '"
    << strPaymentMethod << L"', '"
    << static_cast<wchar_t *>((bstr_t) vntPaymentDate) << L"', "
    << dblPaymentAmt << L", " << lngInvoiceID << L", '"
    << strCardNumber << L"', '"
    << static_cast<wchar_t *>((bstr_t) vntExpDate) << L"')"
    << ends;
```

7. Replace the line *TODO: Do work* in the *GetByCustID* method with the following code, which connects to the database, issues a SQL command, and returns an *IDispatch* pointer to the resulting *Recordset*:

```
// Pointer to an ADO connection
_ConnectionPtr pObjADO_Connection;
// Create ADO connection.
pObjADO_Connection.CreateInstance(__uuidof(Connection));

// DSN file specification
bstr_t strFileDSN = L"FILEDSN=dbPaymentC.DSN";

// Open the connection.
hr = pObjADO_Connection->Open(strFileDSN, (BSTR) NULL, (
                             BSTR) NULL, -1);

// String I/O stream to write SQL statement
basic_stringstream<wchar_t> strSQLStatement;
// TODO: Initialize SQL statement.
```

```
// Parameters of Execute statement
bstr_t strSQLStmt = strSQLStatement.str().c_str();
variant_t vntRecordsAffected;
_RecordsetPtr pObjADO_Recordset;

// Execute the SQL statement to retrieve records from the
// Payments table that contain a matching customer ID.

pObjADO_Recordset = pObjADO_Connection->Execute(strSQLStmt,
    &vntRecordsAffected, adCmdText);
// Return IDispatch interface pointer.
// (QueryInterface will call AddRef on the interface pointer.)
pObjADO_Recordset->QueryInterface(IID_IDispatch,
                        (void**) ppRecordset);
```

Notice that *Idb_Payment* could have been defined to return a *_Recordset* interface pointer, but instead it has been defined to return a straight *IDispatch* pointer. When returning interface pointers, you must be careful to return the actual interface pointer, appropriately *AddRef*'d, not a pointer to the C++ wrapper class object.

8. Replace the line *TODO: Initialize SQL statement* in the *GetByCustID* method with the following code:

```
// Write the SQL statement into a string.
strSQLStatement << L"SELECT  CustomerID, PaymentID, "
    L"PaymentMethod, PaymentDate, PaymentAmt, InvoiceID, "
    L"CardNumber, CardExpDate FROM Payments WHERE CustomerID = "
    << lngCustID << L" ORDER BY PaymentDate DESC" <<ends;
```

9. Modify the compiler settings to include exception handling by first choosing the Settings command from the Project menu and then selecting All Configurations in the Settings For drop-down listbox in the Project Settings dialog box. Select the C++ tab, and then select C++ Language in the Category drop-down listbox. Check Enable exception handling, and then click OK.

10. (optional) Build the component by choosing the Build db_PaymentC.dll command from the Build menu.

SUMMARY

Data objects represent the data access tier of your application. They are responsible for the accuracy, completeness, and consistency of the data they own. They should work correctly whether or not their clients are transactional. Data objects for MTS are in-process COM components, preferably supporting the apartment threading model. They should call the *ObjectContext*, *SetComplete*, and *SetAbort* methods as often as possible to help MTS reclaim server resources when the objects are not actively used. Data objects should connect to data sources using a fixed identify so that they can take advantage of connection pooling provided by MTS.

Most COM programming tools can create skeleton implementations of data objects automatically, thereby letting developers focus on implementing their interface methods. The preferred method for data access within data objects is using ADO. The three most commonly used techniques for accessing data through ADO are the *Connection Execute* method, *Command* objects, and *Recordset* objects. The *Connection Execute* method should be reserved for simple, nonparameterized queries since it returns a read-only, forward-only *Recordset*. *Command* objects can be used for simple parameterized queries. The most flexibility is offered by using *Recordset*. Disconnected *Recordset* objects let you pass data back to clients without maintaining a connection to the underlying data source.

9

Building Business Objects

With the data objects in place, we can turn our attention to the substance of the application: the business objects. As you're reading this chapter, you might think that it doesn't really seem to be about business objects. In one sense, this observation is true. Business objects encapsulate your company's business rules and application-specific operations. Once you have designed your components, implementing the methods should be a fairly mechanical coding exercise.

On the other hand, there are some specific issues you should be aware of to ensure that your business objects work well in the MTS environment. Some of these issues, such as using the object context to manage state and using explicitly defined interfaces when possible, have already been discussed in Chapter 8. Others, such as composing functionality, maintaining state across transactions boundaries, propagating errors, and programmatically controlling security are more common to business objects than to data objects—these issues are the focus of this chapter. As we did for data objects, we'll start by looking at the issues and general techniques for handling them. Then we'll look at some example business objects from the Island Hopper classified ads application, demonstrating how these objects can be implemented using Microsoft Visual Basic and Microsoft Visual C++.

Moving from Design to Implementation

At this point, your design documents should include a good first cut at the business objects you need and how these objects should be grouped into components. You also have the data objects your business objects will rely on. As you look at implementing the business objects, keep in mind these key design points from Chapter 7:

- Business objects encapsulate real-world business operations, independent of how the data they use is actually stored.

- Business objects control sequencing and enforcement of business rules, as well as the transactional integrity of the operations they perform.

- Business object methods should do exactly one unit of work, and each unit of work should be implemented in exactly one method. Higher-level operations are composed by calling methods on other business objects and data objects.

- Business objects should work correctly whether or not the caller is transactional.

- Business objects that are called from the presentation layer should not retain per-object state across method calls. Business objects called within the presentation layer can retain per-object state within a transaction boundary.

- Business objects should be "network friendly." Minimizing the network traffic between remote presentation layers and business objects is important.

- Business objects are the "gatekeepers" that control access to your data. Role-based security should be used to restrict access to business objects.

- Transactions provide a straightforward model for handling errors generated within business object methods.

Business object implementations based on these design points are likely to be considered important company assets that will find use in many applications.

Implementing Components for MTS

Chapter 8 covered the basics of implementing components that would run in the MTS environment. These fundamentals, which are the same for both data objects and business objects, are repeated here:

- Write single-user, in-process COM components.

- Use explicit interfaces to define the public interface of your objects.

- Use the object context to tell MTS when object state can be reclaimed.

- Use transactions to manage errors.

By now, you understand how to create a new component, add COM classes representing the business objects in that component, and create skeleton interface implementations. In this section, we'll look at some implementation details that commonly arise in conjunction with business objects: composing functionality from other components, providing complex state management, handling errors, and providing programmatic security.

Composing Functionality

Business objects encapsulate real-world business operations. Typically, you'll have some high-level business objects that expose methods corresponding to business tasks. For example, the Island Hopper application contains a *bus_AdC* component that exposes methods such as *PlaceAd*. These high-level business objects use the services of other business objects and data objects. This process is known as *composing functionality*.

When you compose functionality from multiple components, state management and error handling become critical issues. Components are developed individually, possibly without the knowledge of the other components they are working with. When an error occurs in one component, the actions already performed by other components might need to be undone—particularly those actions that modify persistent state.

As we've seen, MTS uses transactions to help manage state and handle errors, and the easiest transactions to use are automatic transactions. Developers declare how their components should participate in transactions. MTS uses this information to automatically enlist objects in the appropriate transactions.

The object context is the key to automatic transactions. The object context contains MTS-managed state information that MTS uses to provide services to your objects, such as the caller's identity, the activity, and the transaction identifier. We've already discussed using the *SetComplete* and *SetAbort* methods of the *IObjectContext* interface to vote on the transaction outcome. Another important feature of *IObjectContext* is the *CreateInstance* method. This method is used to instantiate new MTS-managed objects that inherit aspects of the caller's context. Components that run within the MTS environment should always use *IObjectContext CreateInstance* to create new MTS objects, to ensure that context information flows properly to those objects. Recall that you get a pointer to *IObjectContext* by calling the *GetObjectContext* API function. In Visual Basic, your code will look something like this:

```
Dim ctxObject As ObjectContext
Dim subObject As IMyInterface
Set ctxObject = GetObjectContext()
Set subObject = ctxObject.CreateInstance("MyComponentProgID")
```

If you don't use the object context to create subordinate objects, those objects might not participate in the appropriate transaction. Each subordinate object that requires a transaction will become the root of a new transaction, which probably isn't what you want to happen. When the object context is used, subordinate objects that require or support transactions will be enlisted in the caller's transaction, if one exists. If the subordinate objects require a new transaction, or if they require a transaction and the caller is not enlisted in a transaction, MTS will automatically create a new transaction. Of course, each component should call *SetComplete* or *SetAbort* to vote on the transaction outcome and to let MTS know that resources can be reclaimed from the object.

Let's walk through an example to see how transaction boundaries are determined when functionality is composed from multiple components. The following pseudo-code shows several simple components:

```
ComponentA (Transaction Required)
    public sub MethodA()
        Dim objB as ComponentB
        Dim objD as ComponentD
    on Error goto ErrorHandler
        Set objB = GetObjectContext.CreateInstance("ComponentB")
        objB.MethodB
        Set objD = GetObjectContext.CreateInstance("ComponentD")
        objD.MethodD
        DoSomeWork()
        GetObjectContext.SetComplete
        exit sub
    ErrorHandler:
        GetObjectContext.SetAbort
    end sub

    private sub DoSomeWork()
        ' Do local work for ComponentA.
        ' If unsuccessful, raise an error.
    end sub

ComponentB (Transaction Required)
    public sub MethodB()
        Dim objC as ComponentC
    on Error goto ErrorHandler
        Set objC = GetObjectContext.CreateInstance("ComponentC")
        objC.MethodC
        GetObjectContext.SetComplete
        exit sub
    ErrorHandler:
        GetObjectContext.SetAbort
    end sub

ComponentC (Supports Transactions)
    public sub MethodC()
    on Error goto ErrorHandler
        GetObjectContext.SetComplete
        exit sub
```

```
     ErrorHandler:
        GetObjectContext.SetAbort
     end sub

ComponentD (New Transaction Required)
     public sub MethodD()
        Dim objF as ComponentF
     on Error goto ErrorHandler
        Set objF = GetObjectContext.CreateInstance("ComponentF")
        objF.MethodF
        GetObjectContext.SetComplete
        exit sub
     ErrorHandler:
        GetObjectContext.SetAbort
     end sub

ComponentE (Supports Transactions)
     public sub MethodE()
     on Error goto ErrorHandler
        GetObjectContext.SetComplete
        exit sub
     ErrorHandler:
        GetObjectContext.SetAbort
     end sub

ComponentF (Does Not Support Transactions)
     public sub MethodF()
     end sub
```

You are encouraged to map out the transaction boundaries and instantiated objects as you read along. Figure 9-1 on the following page illustrates what the transaction boundaries should look like.

Let's start by looking at what happens when a base client creates an instance of *ComponentA* and calls *MethodA*. *ComponentA* is marked as "requires a transaction." Because no transaction exists when *MethodA* is called, a new transaction is created and the object, *A*, is enlisted in the transaction as the transaction root. *MethodA* creates an instance of *ComponentB*, *B*, which is marked as "requires a transaction." Since *A* used the object context to create the new object and *A* is already in a transaction, *B* is enlisted in the same transaction.

Now *A* calls *MethodB*. *MethodB* creates an instance of *ComponentC*, *C*, which is marked as "supports transactions." Since *B* used the object context to create *C* and *B* is already in a transaction, *C* is enlisted in the same transaction as *B* and *A*. *B* calls *MethodC*, which completes its work and calls *SetComplete*. At this point, the resources for object *C* can be reclaimed (including object *C* itself). The transaction is not yet committed, however; *C* has only placed its vote to commit. When *MethodB* completes its work, it also calls *SetComplete*. Now the resources for object *B* can be reclaimed. Again, the transaction doesn't commit yet, but we have another vote to commit.

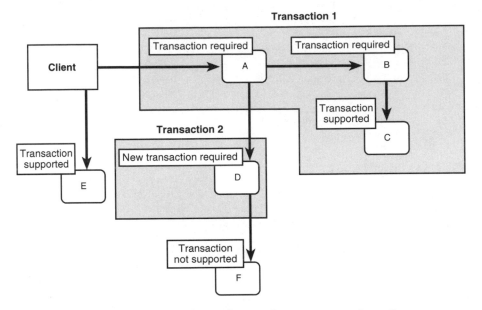

Figure 9-1. *Transaction boundaries for simple components in action.*

Next *MethodA* creates an instance of *ComponentD*, *D*, which is marked as "requires a new transaction." Even though *A* used the object context to create the new object and *A* is already in a transaction, MTS creates a new transaction and enlists *D* as the root of the new transaction. Now *A* calls *MethodD*. *MethodD* creates an instance of *ComponentF*, *F*, which is marked as "does not support transactions." Since *F* doesn't support transactions, it isn't enlisted in a transaction. *D* calls *MethodF*, which completes its work and returns. When *MethodD* completes its work, it calls *SetComplete*. Now the resources for object *D* can be reclaimed. Since *D* is the root of the second transaction, MTS starts the two-phase commit protocol to commit this transaction. At this point, any updates to managed resources such as databases are committed.

Note that committing the second transaction has no direct impact on whether the first transaction commits or aborts. However, because *MethodD* completed successfully, *MethodA* doesn't have any reason to vote to abort the first transaction at this point.

Next *MethodA* calls a local function, *DoSomeWork*. Let's say this function raises an error. This error will be caught by the error handler in *MethodA*. The error handler then calls *SetAbort*. Because *A* is the root of the first transaction, the call to *SetAbort* causes MTS to start the two-phase commit protocol. Since *A* votes to abort the transaction, the transaction will be aborted.

How does aborting the first transaction impact the other objects? Object *B* has already completed its work and been deactivated, but since the transaction aborted, any changes object *B* made to managed resources will be rolled back. Likewise, object *C* has already completed its work and been deactivated. Any changes it made to managed resources will be rolled back as well, since *C* was enlisted in the first transaction. On the other hand, changes made by object *D* are not impacted by the failure of the first transaction. Object *D*'s transaction has already committed.

Let's take a quick look at another example. Suppose our base client creates an instance of *ComponentE*, *E*, and calls *MethodE*. *ComponentE* is marked as "supports transactions." However, the base client is not part of a transaction when it calls *MethodE*. Since *ComponentE* supports transactions but does not require them, MTS will not create a new transaction and object *E* will not be enlisted in any transaction.

As you can see, automatic transactions and composing functionality can create fairly complex behavior without requiring the component developer to write a lot of code. This capability is one of the key benefits of the application server programming model promoted by MTS.

Managing State

In Chapter 8, we assumed that our data objects were stateless. Every method call ended with a call to *SetComplete* or *SetAbort* so that MTS could reclaim object resources. Any state information needed during a method call was either passed in as method parameters by the client or retrieved from a persistent data store.

It's likely that you will encounter situations in your application servers in which these simple assumptions cannot provide the behavior or performance you require. Let's turn our attention to some techniques you can use to fine-tune state management in your components.

Temporarily disabling the commit

You might encounter situations in which an object has done some work but isn't ready to have its transaction commit. The object can exert some control over the transaction by calling the *DisableCommit* method of the *IObjectContext* interface. *DisableCommit* announces that a particular object isn't ready for the transaction to commit. The object will retain its per-object state across method calls. Any attempt to commit the transaction will cause the transaction to abort.

When the object is ready to have its transaction commit, it calls the *EnableCommit* method or the *SetComplete* method of *IObjectContext*. If *EnableCommit* is called, the object will continue to retain its per-object state across method calls. However, it will not prevent the transaction from committing. (Remember, when the root of the transaction calls *SetComplete* or *SetAbort*, MTS will complete the transaction, regardless of whether all the objects in the transaction have cast their vote by calling *SetComplete* or *SetAbort*.) If the object calls *SetComplete*, the object can of course be deactivated by MTS and callers should not rely on its internal state.

In general, this technique should be reserved for scenarios in which a business rule defines some constraint that cannot be easily coded into a single interface method and the business object is not used directly by the presentation layer. For example, in the Island Hopper application, we require every invoice to have a header and at least one detail record. (There's not much point in sending an invoice if an ad has not been placed.) Defining separate *AddHeader* and *AddDetail* methods creates an interface that is much simpler to use than attempting to define a *CreateInvoiceWithArbitraryNumberOfItems* method. (Just imagine what the parameter list would look like!) This technique works for Island Hopper because the invoice is created by another business object when an advertisement is placed—all within the scope of a single transaction on the application server.

The technique doesn't work as well when the client is the presentation layer, particularly if the client must wait for user input between method calls. At best, a transaction will be held open for a relatively long period of time—with all the corresponding database locks, held connections, and so on—while your object is waiting to be called by the remote presentation layer. More likely, the transaction will time out while waiting for the object to reenable the commit, and the entire operation will need to be retried.

The *IObjectControl* interface

In other situations, you might need to perform some context-specific initialization or cleanup for your objects, and this is the purpose of the *IObjectControl* interface. You can optionally implement *IObjectControl* in your components. The interface has three methods: *Activate*, *Deactivate*, and *CanBePooled*.

MTS will call *IObjectControl Activate* each time an object is activated, before any of its other methods are called. You can use this method to perform context-specific initialization. Normally, you would initialize your objects when they are created, either in the constructor of the implementation class or in the class factory *CreateInstance* method. However, you cannot access the object context from your class constructor or your class factory *CreateInstance* method—it isn't hooked up yet. Thus, if you need access to the object context in order to initialize your object, the *Activate* method is the first chance you'll have to do so. MTS calls *IObjectControl Deactivate* each time an object is deactivated. You typically use this method to clean up any per-client state you might be holding in the object.

The *IObjectControl* interface was also designed to handle pooled objects. If you had an object that could be reused from an object pool, you would return *TRUE* from your implementation of *CanBePooled*. When an object was pulled from the object pool, *IObjectControl Activate* would be called. When the object was returned to the pool, *IObjectControl Deactivate* would be called.

Unfortunately, neither MTS 1.0 or MTS 2.0 support this form of object pooling. In the absence of object pooling, implementing *IObjectControl* becomes less compelling. Most cleanup can be performed in your implementation class destructor. If your objects are stateless, you need to initialize them on each method call anyway. However, if you have some common initialization work that needs to be done for every method in a stateless object, *IObjectControl Activate* is a reasonable place to do it. For example, you might get a pointer to the object context and save it for later use.

IObjectControl Activate is also a useful place to initialize context-specific state in stateful objects, if you don't define a specific initialization method in your interface. Note, however, that *Activate* takes no parameters, so you are restricted to initialization based on values you can retrieve from the object context—for example, the client's user identity or a cookie passed in Internet Information Server (IIS) intrinsic objects. Unless the fact that client-specific state is present is completely hidden from your clients, an explicit initialization will probably make your interface easier to use.

The Shared Property Manager
Finally, remember that one type of state is shared transient state. Shared transient state is state information kept in memory that does not survive system failures but that can be shared by multiple objects across transaction boundaries.

In MTS, shared transient state is managed by using the Shared Property Manager (SPM). The SPM is a resource dispenser that stores state on a process-wide basis and manages concurrency for you. Values stored in the SPM are a lot like global variables except that they are outside the scope of any of your components. Thus, the values can be easily shared by different types of objects. Values stored in the SPM are known as *shared properties*.

Keep in mind that shared properties can be accessed only by objects running in the same process, which means that the COM classes must be installed as part of the same server package. It is possible for system administrators to move COM classes from one package to another after your application packages have been deployed. If you rely on two COM classes sharing properties through the SPM, you should clearly document that they must be installed in the same package. Also, the SPM should be used only from MTS components, not from base clients. If shared properties are created from a base client, they will be located in the base client process, which probably isn't what you want.

The object model for the SPM is shown in Figure 9-2. To help prevent naming collisions among properties created by different components, the SPM defines the notion of a *shared property group*. A shared property group establishes a namespace for a set of shared properties. Each property has a name, value, and position within the group. Either the name or the position can be used to retrieve the property value. You access and create shared property groups through the shared property group manager.

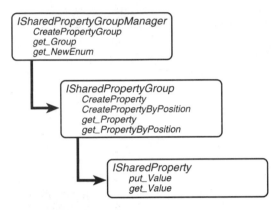

Figure 9-2. *The Shared Property Manager object model.*

When you create a group, you can specify how the SPM should manage concurrent access to the group's properties. If the isolation mode is set to *LockSetGet*, the SPM locks access to a property while the value is read or written. This setting ensures that two clients can't read or write the same property at the same time, but it doesn't prevent clients from concurrently accessing different properties in the same group. If the isolation mode is set to *LockMethod*, all the properties in a group are locked for exclusive use by the client during the current method call. This setting is useful when there are interdependencies among properties in the group or when a client needs to ensure that a read/write operation occurs without interruption. To set the isolation mode to *LockMethod*, the SPM must have access to the calling object's object context.

You can also specify when properties in a group will be destroyed at the time the group is created. If the release mode is set to *Standard*, a property is destroyed as soon as all clients have released their references to the property. If the release mode is set to *Process*, properties are not destroyed until the process terminates.

To use the SPM, you must first create an instance of the shared property group manager. In Visual Basic, you do this by setting a reference to the Shared Property Manager Type Library, MTXSPM.DLL, and creating a new *SharedProperty-GroupManager* object, as shown here:

```
Dim spmMgr As New SharedPropertyGroupManager
```

In C++, you need to include the header file MTXSPM.H to access the interface definitions and you must link to MTXGUID.LIB to access variable definitions for the SPM class identifiers (CLSIDs) and interface identifiers (IIDs). You can create a new shared property group manager by calling *CoCreateInstance* or the object context *CreateInstance* method, as shown here:

```
ISharedPropertyGroupManager* pspmMgr = NULL;
HRESULT hr = m_spObjectContext.CreateInstance(
            CLSID_SharedPropertyGroupManager,
            IID_ISharedPropertyGroupManager,
            (void**)&pspmMgr);
```

Once you have access to the group manager, you can call its *CreateProperty-Group* method to create a new shared property group with a given name. If a group with that name already exists, you get back a reference to the existing group. If you know that the group exists, you use the group manager's *Group* property to obtain a reference to the group. If you need to find out what groups are available, you can use the group manager's *NewEnum* property to retrieve a standard enumerator.

With a reference to the property group in hand, you can create shared properties in the group. The property group lets you create shared properties by name, using the *CreateProperty* method, or by position in the group, using the *CreatePropertyByPosition* method. If the shared property already exists, both methods return a reference to the existing shared property. If you know that the shared property already exists, you can use the group's *Property* or *Property-ByPosition* property to retrieve a reference.

Once you have a reference to a shared property, you use its *Value* property to get or set the data value. *Value* is a VARIANT property, so you can store any of the standard Automation types into your shared properties. However, this capability complicates using the SPM from C++, since C++ does not provide native support for VARIANTs like Visual Basic does. Of course, the BSTR and VARIANT wrapper classes provided by Visual C++ or the Active Template Library (ATL) can help.

When you have finished using the SPM, be sure to release any references you hold to the group manager, groups, or properties. Otherwise, the SPM will not be able to clean up properly.

NOTE By default, MTS will shut down a process after three minutes of no activity. If you are using the SPM, you might want to increase the time-out period for your server packages, to reduce the number of times the SPM must be reinitialized.

The SPM is particularly useful for storing values that are frequently accessed or updated within a process. For example, the Island Hopper application uses the SPM to generate new identifiers for customers, invoices, and so on. If the set of available identifiers was stored in a persistent database, reading the database to retrieve the next identifier would become a serious performance bottleneck. The SPM might also be used to cache static data tables that are frequently accessed. Since the SPM stores information in memory, accessing the information is generally faster than accessing the information from a persistent data store. However, this performance gain must be weighed against the fact that state stored in the SPM can be lost if the process terminates unexpectedly.

Handling Errors

Let's switch gears now and discuss another important topic: error handling. We've talked quite a bit about using transactions to handle errors, but this is actually only one part of the error handling story. Transactions impact only state managed by resource managers. In addition, transactions do not immediately abort when an enlisted resource or object calls *SetAbort*. The transaction does not complete until the root decides to call *SetComplete* or *SetAbort*. Thus, you still need to return error codes from your interface methods and check those error codes within your client code so that the client code can decide whether to continue with any remaining work.

At the most basic level, every COM interface method should return an HRESULT value. HRESULTs are used by the COM run time to report any errors in making the method call—for example, communications or security errors. HRESULTs are also used by MTS to tell a client when a transaction has aborted. When the root object completes its work, if the object returns a success code but the transaction aborts, MTS will change the HRESULT returned by the method call to *CONTEXT_E_ABORTED*. Otherwise, MTS just passes back the HRESULT reported by the object.

An HRESULT is a 32-bit unsigned integer of which specific bits have special meanings, as shown in Figure 9-3. The high-order bit, S, in the HRESULT indicates whether the return value represents success (0) or failure (1). The next four bits, labeled R, C, N, and r, are reserved. The next 11 bits comprise the *facility field*, which indicates the system service responsible for the error. Only Microsoft can define facility fields. Most user-defined error codes use FACILITY_ITF, which indicates an interface-specific error. The lower word of the HRESULT is the *code field*, which defines the specific warning or error within the facility or interface.

As you might imagine, HRESULTs can provide only limited information about an error. In particular, HRESULTs don't tell you anything about where the error occurred. All you know is that somewhere within the implementation of a particular method, the error occurred. Determining what text message to display to an end user can also be complicated. In some instances, the client can call the Windows *FormatMessage* API function to determine the text message for the error. In other cases, the client will probably make up its own message text.

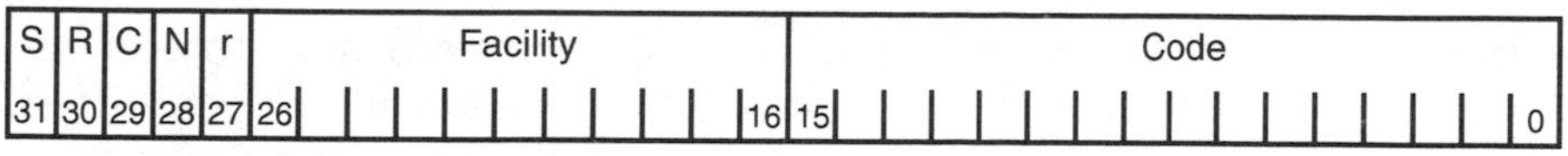

Figure 9-3. *Structure of COM HRESULTs.*

For these reasons, Automation has defined mechanisms to supplement the information returned in the HRESULT. The *IDispatch Invoke* method can return an EXCEPINFO structure. For vtable-binding, Automation defines a standard error object named *ErrorInfo* and three interfaces for managing the object. A component that uses this mechanism for error reporting implements the *ISupportErrorInfo* interface. The component uses the *ICreateErrorInfo* interface to initialize the error object when an error occurs. Clients use the *IErrorInfo* interface to retrieve information from the error object. Both the EXCEPINFO structure and the *ErrorInfo* object can hold rich descriptive information about an error, including a text description, pointers to an entry in a help file, and the source of the error.

You might be thinking that this is starting to sound awfully complicated. Fortunately, most developer tools that support COM provide some assistance to make error reporting and/or handling more straightforward. For example, in Visual Basic all COM errors are exposed through the *Err* object. You use the *Err Raise* function to set an error and the *On Error* statement to catch errors. If you are using the Visual C++ COM compiler support, you can use the *_com_raise_error* class to set an error and the *_com_error* class to retrieve information about an error. ATL provides the *AtlReportError* API function for setting error information.

In general, then, you should return an HRESULT for all methods in all your component interfaces. You should initialize the *ErrorInfo* object for any errors that occur, using whatever mechanism is supported by your development tool. Business objects will generally need to report some interface-specific errors—for example, to indicate that a specific business rule has been broken. These errors should be in the FACILITY_ITF range of errors. In Visual Basic, errors would be defined as an offset from *vbObjectError*, as shown here:

```
Public Const ERROR_NUMBER = vbObjectError + 10
```

In C++, errors can be defined by using the MAKE_HRESULT macro, as shown here:

```
const HRESULT ERROR_NUMBER =
          MAKE_HRESULT(SEVERITY_ERROR, FACILITY_ITF, 10);
```

Alternatively, you can simply figure out the numeric value yourself and hard-code it into a constant definition. Clients should test the return codes to determine whether methods have succeeded before continuing with their work.

That said, HRESULTs and *ErrorInfo* objects can report information on only one error at a time. And the information provided by the *ErrorInfo* object is fixed. You can't add another type of information to the *ErrorInfo* object. If you have additional error information to report, you will need to define a private mechanism for reporting this information. One technique is to fill in a method parameter with information the client will recognize as an error condition. For example, a method might return a Boolean value indicating success or failure. Another method is to provide a method or property on your interface to return a pointer to a custom error object. For example, Microsoft ActiveX Data Objects (ADO) provides the *Errors* collection on its *Connection* object so that multiple errors can be reported for a single method call.

You might need to maintain an audit trail for some types of errors or store trouble-shooting information when unusual errors occur. On Microsoft Windows NT, you can use the system event log to store this kind of information. The Island Hopper application includes a utility component, *util_EventViewer*, that you can use to write information to the event log. Island Hopper also includes a higher-level component, *ErrPlus*, that the Classifieds client application uses to log application specific errors. *ErrPlus* makes use of the *util_EventViewer* component.

> **NOTE** The source code for the util_EventViewer component is located in the \Source\VBClient\Util_EventViewer directory in your Island Hopper installation.

Another approach to logging errors or troubleshooting information is to write the information to a private data store or file. To do this, you create a component that can write generic log messages to your data store or file. This component should either not support transactions or require a new transaction so that logging failures do not cause a "real" transaction to abort. A disadvantage of this approach is that you'll probably need to write a log viewer program too. When the system event log is used, you can use the system event viewer to view and manage log entries. This approach will not work on Microsoft Windows 95 and later, however. If you want to create log entries consistently on all Windows platforms, you can't use the event log.

Securing Access to Your Components

When you create an audit trail for application errors, you generally want to know who was trying to use the application. To determine who is using an application, you must use the programmatic security services provided by MTS. These services also enable you to perform more sophisticated security checks in your components than a simple check of role membership. Let's take a quick look at these services.

Most security needs—even programmatic security—can be met by using role-based security. For example, in a banking application you might have a business rule specifying that a teller can authorize withdrawals of up to $500 from a user's account, but larger withdrawals must be authorized by a manager. In this case, the implementation of the *Withdraw* method needs to take different actions depending on the caller's role. The object context methods *IsSecurity-Enabled* and *IsCallerInRole* can be used to handle this scenario, as we saw in Chapter 4.

In those rare instances in which role-based security is insufficient, MTS provides the *ISecurityProperty* interface, which you can use to access Windows NT user identities. You query the object context to obtain an *ISecurityProperty* interface pointer. Once you have the pointer, you call one of the following four methods to obtain a security identifier (SID):

- *GetDirectCallerSID* returns the SID of the external process that called the currently executing method.

- *GetDirectCreatorSID* returns the SID of the external process that created the currently executing object.

- *GetOriginalCallerSID* returns the SID of the base client process that initiated the sequence of calls from which the call to the current object originated.

- *GetOriginalCreatorSID* returns the SID of the base client process that initiated the current activity.

A SID is a Windows structure containing information about a user and any groups the user belongs to. You must use the Windows API to parse a SID. You can use the information in the SID to restrict access to your components or to obtain information for auditing and logging. After you have finished with a SID obtained from the *ISecurityProperty* interface, you must call *ReleaseSID* to release the SID.

SIDs are not easily accessible from Visual Basic, so MTS also provides a *SecurityProperty* object. The *SecurityProperty* object is defined in the MTS type library. You get a reference to the object using the *Security* property of the object context, as shown here:

```
Dim secProperty as SecurityProperty
Set secProperty = GetObjectContext.Security
```

The *SecurityProperty* object gives you access to the user name only, not to the entire SID. Fortunately, the user name is all you generally need for auditing or logging.

Building Business Objects

For the remainder of this chapter, we'll look at the implementation of three business objects from the Island Hopper application. We'll start by looking at the *bus_PaymentC* component, which is implemented in Visual Basic. This component uses several other components to implement its functionality and illustrates the use of the object context *CreateInstance* method. Next we'll look at the *bus_InvoiceC* component, which is implemented in Visual C++ using ATL and the COM compiler support. This component uses the object context *DisableCommit* method to implement a business rule. It also illustrates how to use the object context *CreateInstance* method from C++. Last we'll look at the *util_TakeANumber* component, which is implemented in Visual Basic and uses the SPM.

> **WARNING** Remember that if you are trying to implement these components on your own system, you need to take a few extra precautions to ensure that the rest of the Island Hopper application will continue to run without being rebuilt. These precautions will be noted prior to each step that might break the application.

Implementing *bus_PaymentC* in Visual Basic

Let's start by looking at the *bus_PaymentC* component, which processes payments for classified ads from customers. The *bus_PaymentC* component has the following two methods:

- *AddPayment* records a payment from a customer in a database and updates the customer's account balance.

- *GetByCustID* retrieves a list of payments for a given customer from the database.

The simplicity of the component's business rules lets us focus in on the mechanics of composing functionality.

As with any MTS component, the first step is to create a skeleton component, just as we did in Chapter 8. For *bus_PaymentC*, the methods can be implemented on the default interface defined by Visual Basic. To create skeleton methods, you simply define a public function in the class module for each method, as shown here:

```
Public Function AddPayment(ByVal lngCustomerID As Long, _
                           ByVal strMethod As String, _
                           ByVal datPaymentDate As Date, _
                           ByVal dblPaymentAmt As Double, _
                           ByVal lngInvoiceID As Long, _
                           ByVal strCardNumber As String, _
                           ByVal datCardExpDate As Date) As Long
Public Function GetByCustID(ByVal lngCustomerID As Long) _
    As ADODB.Recordset
```

This component does not need to retain per-object state across method calls, so the basic structure of each method, shown here, is the same as for our data objects:

```
Public Function MyMethod
On Error GoTo ErrorHandler
    ' Do work.
    :
    GetObjectContext.SetComplete
    Exit Function
ErrorHandler:
    ' Clean up local variables.
    :
    GetObjectContext.SetAbort
    Err.Raise Err.Number, _
        SetErrSource(modName, "PROCNAME"), Err.Description
End Function
```

Where things get interesting is in how *AddPayment* does its work. The business logic looks something like this, in pseudocode:

```
1. Get a payment ID.
2. Add a payment record to the classified ads database.
3. Update the customer record in the classified ads database
   with the new account balance.
```

Naturally, we don't want the customer's account balance to be updated unless the payment is recorded in the database, or vice versa. Thus, the *bus_PaymentC* component should be marked as "requires a transaction" and the object context should be used to create any subordinate objects needed to implement the method's functionality. In this way, if any of the steps fail, the transaction can be aborted and no changes will be made to the database.

In the three-tier model, business objects do not directly access database tables. Instead, they use the services of data objects. Clearly steps 2 and 3 in the preceding pseudocode should be handled by data objects. Fortunately, Island Hopper has just the data objects we need, *db_PaymentC* and *db_CustomerC*.

To accomplish step 1, we'll use the *util_TakeANumber* component, which we'll look at in detail in the section "Implementing *util_TakeANumber* Using the SPM" later in this chapter.

In Visual Basic, the first step to using these components is to add references to their type libraries to the project. Then use the object context to create an instance of each component that's needed, as shown in the following example:

```
Dim objTakeANumber As util_TakeANumber.TakeANumber
Set objTakeANumber =
    GetObjectContext.CreateInstance("util_TakeANumber.TakeANumber")
```

That's all there is to it! The call to *CreateInstance* will ensure that information about the current context, such as its transaction identifier, flows to the new object. Once you have a reference to the object, you make method calls just as you would for any other object. The only time you really need to distinguish MTS objects from other COM objects is if you want to pass a reference to another object or client application. To do that, you must use the *SafeRef* function to create the reference. This technique ensures that the context wrapper reference, not the reference to the "real" object, is passed around.

The complete code for the *bus_PaymentC* Payment class is shown in Listing 9-1. Note that if an error occurs in any of the subordinate objects used by the *Add-Payment* method, the error will be caught by the method's error handler. *AddPayment* calls *SetAbort* to abort the containing transaction if any errors occur in its subordinate objects. Also, *AddPayment* simply reraises the original error, identifying itself as the source of the error. A more sophisticated object might permit a transaction to commit even if some of the subordinate objects reported errors, or it might raise component-specific errors rather than passing on the lower-level error codes.

```
Option Explicit
Const modName = "bus_PaymentC.Payment"

'*****************************************************************
' AddPayment
' Purpose: Adds a payment to the database
' Inputs:    lngCustomerID    -- the unique customer ID number
'            strMethod        -- the payment method
'            datPaymentDate   -- the payment date
'            dblPaymentAmt    -- the payment amount
'            lngInvoiceID     -- the invoice ID for this payment
'            strCardNumber    -- the card or check number used for this payment
```

Listing 9-1. *The* bus_PaymentC Payment *class source code.*

```
'           datCardExpDate -- the credit card expiration date, if needed
' Returns: The new payment ID number
'**********************************************************************
Public Function AddPayment(ByVal lngCustomerID As Long, _
    ByVal strMethod As String, ByVal datPaymentDate As Date, _
    ByVal dblPaymentAmt As Double, ByVal lngInvoiceID As Long, _
    ByVal strCardNumber As String, ByVal datCardExpDate As Date) As Long

    Dim objTakeANumber As util_TakeANumber.TakeANumber
    Dim lngPaymentID As Long
    Dim dblTotal As Double
    Dim objPayment As DB_PAYMENTCLib.db_Payment
    Dim objCustomer As db_CustomerC.Customer

    On Error GoTo ErrorHandler

    ' Create an instance of the util_TakeANumber.TakeANumber object to
    ' get the next payment number.
    Set objTakeANumber = _
     GetObjectContext.CreateInstance("util_TakeANumber.TakeANumber")
    lngPaymentID = objTakeANumber.GetANumber("PaymentID")

    ' Create an instance of the db_PaymentC.Payment object
    ' to add a payment to the database.
    Set objPayment = _
     GetObjectContext.CreateInstance("db_PaymentC.Payment.1")
    objPayment.AddPayment lngCustomerID, lngPaymentID, strMethod, _
     datPaymentDate, dblPaymentAmt, lngInvoiceID, strCardNumber, _
     datCardExpDate

    ' Create an instance of the db_CustomerC.Customer object
    ' to update the customer balance.
    Set objCustomer = _
     GetObjectContext.CreateInstance("db_CustomerC.Customer")
    dblTotal = (-1) * dblPaymentAmt
    objCustomer.UpdateBalance lngCustomerID, dblTotal

    ' Allow the MTS transaction set to proceed.
    GetObjectContext.SetComplete

    ' Return the invoice number.
    AddPayment = lngPaymentID

    Exit Function
```

(continued)

Listing 9-1. *continued*

```
ErrorHandler:

    ' Roll back the MTS transaction set.
    GetObjectContext.SetAbort

    Err.Raise Err.Number, SetErrSource(modName, "AddPayment"), _
      Err.Description

End Function

'***********************************************************************
' GetByCustID
' Purpose: Retrieves invoices from the database for a particular
'          customer ID number
' Inputs:  lngCustomerID -- the unique customer ID number
' Returns: A Recordset object containing the invoice information
'***********************************************************************
Public Function GetByCustID(ByVal lngCustomerID As Long) As ADODB.Recordset

    Dim objPayment As DB_PAYMENTCLib.db_Payment

    On Error GoTo ErrorHandler

    ' Create an instance of the db_PaymentC.Payment object
    ' to retrieve payment information from the database.
    Set objPayment = GetObjectContext.CreateInstance("db_PaymentC.Payment")

    Set GetByCustID = objPayment.GetByCustID(lngCustomerID)

    ' Allow the MTS transaction set to proceed.
    GetObjectContext.SetComplete

    Exit Function

ErrorHandler:

    ' Roll back the MTS transaction set.
    GetObjectContext.SetAbort

    Err.Raise Err.Number, SetErrSource(modName, "GetByCustID"), _
      Err.Description

End Function
```

The *GetByCustID* method is even simpler than *AddPayment*. All it needs to do is call the *db_PaymentC* component's *GetByCustID* method, as shown here:

```
Dim objPayment As DB_PAYMENTCLib.db_Payment
Set objPayment = _
    GetObjectContext.CreateInstance("db_PaymentC.Payment")
Set GetByCustID = objPayment.GetByCustID(lngCustomerID)
```

This is a fairly common pattern, and at first it might seem like unnecessary overhead. Why not just call the data object directly? The main issue is protecting your data. Consider a scenario in which a presentation layer application needs to retrieve a list of payments for a customer. This application probably runs on a remote user workstation, using the interactive user's identity. If the application calls the data object directly, you must grant access to the data object to every user who might run the application. Now, by default, the user has access to every method exposed by the data object. Data objects typically expose low-level methods, without consideration for business rules regarding how those methods should be used. Most application-level users should not have direct access to these methods.

By placing business objects between the presentation layer and the data objects, you can restrict the operations that users can perform and still write general purpose data objects. Business objects also give you the option to apply business rules about how data objects should be used. Unless you are absolutely sure that there will never be any rules about how a particular data object should be used, you are probably better off providing a business object.

Step by Step: Creating the *bus_PaymentC* Component

1. Create a skeleton *bus_PaymentC* component, following the instructions from the sidebar "Step by Step: Creating the Skeleton *db_CategoryC* Component" on page 161 in Chapter 8. The project name should be *bus_PaymentC,* and the class name should be *Payment*.

2. Add the following skeleton method declarations:

```
Public Function AddPayment(ByVal lngCustomerID As Long, _
                           ByVal strMethod As String, _
                           ByVal datPaymentDate As Date, _
                           ByVal dblPaymentAmt As Double, _
                           ByVal lngInvoiceID As Long, _
```

(continued)

Creating the *bus_PaymentC* Component, *continued*

```
                              ByVal strCardNumber As String, _
                              ByVal datCardExpDate As Date) As Long
Public Function GetByCustID(ByVal lngCustomerID As Long) _
    As ADODB.Recordset
```

3. Add the following lines to the General Declarations section of the *Payment* class module to define the module name used in error reporting:

```
Option Explicit
Const modName = "bus_PaymentC.Payment"
```

4. Add the GLOBALS.BAS module from the \IslandHopper\Source\ Server_Components\Globals directory on the companion CD to the project, to provide access to Island Hopper's standard error reporting function.

5. Add references to the following type libraries in your project:

```
Microsoft ActiveX Data Objects Library
Microsoft Transaction Server Type Library
db_PaymentC 1.0 Type Library
db_CustomerC
util_TakeANumber
```

If you don't see *db_PaymentC*, *db_CustomerC*, or *util_TakeANumber* in the list of available references, you need to build or install those components.

6. Add the following code to the *AddPayment* and *GetByCustID* methods to establish the basic framework for the methods:

```
On Error GoTo ErrorHandler
    ' TODO: Do work.
    ⋮
    GetObjectContext.SetComplete
    Exit Function
ErrorHandler:
    GetObjectContext.SetAbort
    Err.Raise Err.Number, SetErrSource(modName, "PROCNAME"), _
    Err.Description
```

Replace *PROCNAME* in the preceding code with *AddPayment* or *GetByCustID*, as appropriate.

7. Replace the line *TODO: Do work* in the *AddPayment* method with the following code, which creates the subordinate objects and calls the appropriate methods to complete the *AddPayment* method's functionality:

```
Dim objTakeANumber As util_TakeANumber.TakeANumber
Dim lngPaymentID As Long
Dim dblTotal As Double
Dim objPayment As DB_PAYMENTCLib.db_Payment
Dim objCustomer As db_CustomerC.Customer

' Create an instance of the util_TakeANumber.TakeANumber object
' to get the next payment number.
Set objTakeANumber = _
 GetObjectContext.CreateInstance("util_TakeANumber.TakeANumber")
lngPaymentID = objTakeANumber.GetANumber("PaymentID")

' Create an instance of the db_PaymentC.Payment object
' to add a payment to the database.
Set objPayment = _
 GetObjectContext.CreateInstance("db_PaymentC.Payment.1")
objPayment.AddPayment lngCustomerID, lngPaymentID, strMethod, _
    datPaymentDate, dblPaymentAmt, lngInvoiceID, strCardNumber, _
    datCardExpDate

' Create an instance of the db_CustomerC.Customer object
' to update the customer balance.
Set objCustomer = _
 GetObjectContext.CreateInstance("db_CustomerC.Customer")
dblTotal = (-1) * dblPaymentAmt
objCustomer.UpdateBalance lngCustomerID, dblTotal
```

8. Following the call to *GetObjectContext.SetComplete* in the *AddPayment* method, add this line to return the payment ID to the caller:

```
AddPayment = lngPaymentID
```

9. Replace the line *TODO: Do work* in the *GetByCustID* method with the following code, which creates a *db_PaymentC* object and calls its *GetByCustID* method to retrieve the list of payments:

```
Dim objPayment As DB_PAYMENTCLib.db_Payment
Set objPayment = _
 GetObjectContext.CreateInstance("db_PaymentC.Payment")
Set GetByCustID = objPayment.GetByCustID(lngCustomerID)
```

(continued)

237

Creating the *bus_PaymentC* Component, *continued*

> **NOTE** If you want to build the *bus_PaymentC* component at this point on a machine that has the Island Hopper application installed, you should select the Binary Compatibility option on the Project Properties Component tab and point to the \Source\Server_Components\CompatibleDlls\bus_PaymentC.dll directory in your Island Hopper installation. If you don't make this adjustment, components and applications that use *bus_PaymentC* will not operate correctly.

10. (optional) Build the component. After building the component, you should select the Binary Compatibility option on the Project Properties Component tab. If you haven't already pointed to the prebuilt BUS_PAYMENTC.DLL that came with Island Hopper, copy the DLL you just built to a safe place and point to that. Doing so will help prevent incompatible modifications to the *Payment* public interface.

Implementing *bus_InvoiceC* in C++

Now let's turn our attention to a slightly more complex business object, *bus_InvoiceC*, which generates customer invoices for classified advertisements. This component is written in Visual C++ using ATL and the Visual C++ COM compiler support. It implements the following four business rules:

- It must be possible to create invoices. An invoice is identified by a unique key and consists of a header and one or more detail records.

- When an invoice is created, the customer's account balance must be updated to reflect the invoice amount.

- Clients must be able to retrieve a specific invoice header, given the invoice identifier.

- Clients must be able to retrieve a list of all the invoices associated with a particular customer. (It's not necessary to return the details of each invoice, just the header.)

The last three rules aren't much different from the rules enforced by the *bus_PaymentC* component. The method implementations in *bus_InvoiceC* will use the object context to create subordinate objects that do part of the work required by each method.

The first rule is much more interesting. It says that an invoice cannot be persisted until at least one detail record has been added to the invoice. As we've seen, defining separate *AddHeader* and *AddDetail* methods creates an interface that is much simpler to use than attempting to define a *CreateInvoiceWith-ArbitraryNumberOfItems* method. But this means that the invoice object must not permit any containing transaction to commit until both *AddHeader* and *AddDetail* have been called. Thus, *bus_InvoiceC* is our first stateful MTS component. Note in this case that the state information isn't stored anywhere. The state is implicit in the sequence of method calls made against the object.

Based on the preceding four business rules, we can define these four methods to expose from *bus_InvoiceC*:

- *AddHeader* creates a new invoice with no detail records.

- *AddDetail* adds a detail record to an invoice. *AddDetail* must be called at least once per call to *AddHeader*, within the same transaction.

- *GetByID* retrieves a specific invoice from the database, given an invoice identifier.

- *GetByCustID* retrieves a list of invoices for a given customer from the database.

The first step in implementing the *bus_InvoiceC* component is to create the skeleton component using the ATL COM AppWizard and ATL Object Wizard, as described in the sidebar "Step by Step: Creating the Skeleton *db_PaymentC* Component" on page 199 in Chapter 8. The Visual C++ IDE can be used to define skeletons for each method, as shown here:

```
HRESULT AddHeader([in] long lngCustomerID,
                  [in, string] BSTR strDescription,
                  [in] double dblTotal,
                  [in] long lngReference,
                  [out, rctval] long *lngInvoiceID);
HRESULT AddDetail([in] long lngInvoiceID,
                  [in, string] BSTR strProduct,
                  [in, string] BSTR strDescription,
                  [in] long lngQty,
                  [in] double dblAmount);
HRESULT GetByID([in] long lngInvoiceID,
                [out, retval] _Recordset **pInvoice);
HRESULT GetByCustID([in] long lngCustomerID,
                    [out, retval] _Recordset **pInvoice);
```

As for our data objects, the COM compiler support can be used to import the ADO type library and generate smart pointers for the ADO objects. In this case, all we need are the definitions for *Recordset* objects, which will be passed back to callers.

GetByID and *GetByCustID* are simple stateless methods that just call through to the equivalent method in the *db_InvoiceC* data object. Thus, we will want smart pointers for the *_Invoice* interface exposed by *db_InvoiceC*. To generate smart pointers, you can use the *#import* preprocessor directive to read in the *db_InvoiceC* type library, as shown in the following code, just as you do to generate smart pointers for ADO objects:

```
#import "..\DLLs\db_InvoiceC.dll" raw_interfaces_only
using namespace db_InvoiceC;
```

Notice the use of the *raw_interfaces_only* attribute on the *#import* statement. This attribute indicates that error handling wrapper functions and property wrappers should not be generated. The lack of property wrappers doesn't really matter, since *db_InvoiceC* doesn't have any properties. However, when error handling wrappers aren't generated, you will need to retrieve and inspect the HRESULT returned by each method call instead of relying on a try/catch block to handle *_com_error* exceptions.

Once you have imported the type library, you can use the object context to create an instance of the *db_InvoiceC* component, as shown in the following example:

```
_InvoicePtr pObjDB_Invoice;
hr = m_spObjectContext->CreateInstance(__uuidof(Invoice),
                                       __uuidof(_Invoice),
                                       (void**)&pObjDB_Invoice);
if (FAILED(hr))
{
    bErrorFlg = true;
    goto errHandler;
}
```

With the interface pointer in hand, you can call whatever methods you want, as shown here:

```
hr = pObjDB_Invoice->GetByCustID(lngCustomerID, pRecordSet);
if (FAILED(hr)) goto errHandler;
```

The complete source for the *GetByID* and *GetByCustID* methods is shown in Listing 9-2.

```
#include "stdafx.h"
#include "comdef.h"

#include "bus_InvoiceC.h"
#include "bus_Invoice.h"
#include <mtx.h>

// Import the VB DLLs.
#import "..\DLLs\util_TakeANumber.dll" raw_interfaces_only
using namespace util_TakeANumber;

#import "..\DLLs\db_CustomerC.dll" raw_interfaces_only
using namespace db_CustomerC;

#import "..\Interfaces\IdbCustomer\IdbCustomer.dll" raw_interfaces_only
using namespace IDBCUSTOMERLib;

#import "..\DLLs\db_InvoiceC.dll" raw_interfaces_only
using namespace db_InvoiceC;

/////////////////////////////////////////////////////////////////////////
// Cbus_Invoice

STDMETHODIMP Cbus_Invoice::InterfaceSupportsErrorInfo(REFIID riid)
{
   static const IID* arr[] =
   {
      &IID_Ibus_Invoice,
   };

   for (int i=0; i <sizeof(arr)/sizeof(arr[0]); i++)
   {
      if (InlineIsEqualGUID(*arr[i],riid))
         return S_OK;
   }
   return S_FALSE;
}

HRESULT Cbus_Invoice::Activate()
{
   HRESULT hr = GetObjectContext(&m_spObjectContext);
   if (SUCCEEDED(hr))
      return S_OK;
   return hr;
}
```

Listing 9-2. *The source code for the* bus_InvoiceC *methods.*   *(continued)*

Listing 9-2. *continued*

```
BOOL Cbus_Invoice::CanBePooled()
{
   return TRUE;
}

void Cbus_Invoice::Deactivate()
{
}

//*********************************************************************
// AddHeader
// Purpose: Adds a header to an invoice
// Inputs:   lngCustomerID  -- the unique customer ID number
//           strDescription -- the header description
//           dblTotal       -- the total amount on the header
//           lngReference   -- the invoice header reference number
// Returns: Invoice number
//*********************************************************************

STDMETHODIMP Cbus_Invoice::AddHeader(long lngCustomerID,
                                     BSTR strDescription,
                                     double dblTotal,
                                     long lngReference,
                                     long * lngInvoiceID)
{
   // Check for an invalid return pointer.
   if (lngInvoiceID == NULL) return E_POINTER;

   HRESULT hr = S_OK;

   // Pointer for util_TakeANumber
   _TakeANumberPtr pObjTakeANumber;

   // Pointer for db_Invoice
   _InvoicePtr pObjDB_Invoice;

   // Pointer for db_Customer
   _CustomerPtr pObjDB_Customer;

   // Invoice ID string
   BSTR bstrTakeANumberType;

   // Error message flag
   bool bErrorFlg = false;
```

```
if (!m_spObjectContext)
{
   AtlReportError(CLSID_bus_Invoice, "No object context",
                 IID_Ibus_Invoice, hr);
   return hr;
}

hr = m_spObjectContext->CreateInstance(__uuidof(TakeANumber),
 __uuidof(_TakeANumber), (void**)&pObjTakeANumber);

if (FAILED(hr))
{
   bErrorFlg = true;
   goto errHandler;
}

// Get the next invoice number.
bstrTakeANumberType = ::SysAllocString(L"InvoiceID");
hr = pObjTakeANumber->GetANumber(&bstrTakeANumberType,lngInvoiceID);
::SysFreeString(bstrTakeANumberType);

if(FAILED(hr)) goto errHandler;

// Add invoice header.

hr = m_spObjectContext->CreateInstance(__uuidof(Invoice),
 __uuidof(_Invoice), (void**)&pObjDB_Invoice);

if (FAILED(hr))
{
   bErrorFlg = true;
   goto errHandler;
}


hr = pObjDB_Invoice->AddHeader(*lngInvoiceID, lngCustomerID,
 strDescription, dblTotal, lngReference, lngInvoiceID);

if(FAILED(hr)) goto errHandler;

// Update customer balance.

hr = m_spObjectContext->CreateInstance(__uuidof(Customer),
 __uuidof(_Customer), (void**)&pObjDB_Customer);
```

(continued)

Listing 9-2. *continued*

```
    if (FAILED(hr))
    {
        bErrorFlg = true;
        goto errHandler;
    }

    hr = pObjDB_Customer->UpdateBalance(lngCustomerID, dblTotal);
    if (FAILED(hr)) goto errHandler;

    // We are finished and happy.
    m_spObjectContext->DisableCommit();

    return hr;

errHandler:

    TCHAR *pErrMsg = NULL;

    // We are finished and unhappy.
    m_spObjectContext->SetAbort();

    if (bErrorFlg)
    {
        FormatMessage(FORMAT_MESSAGE_ALLOCATE_BUFFER |
                    FORMAT_MESSAGE_FROM_SYSTEM, NULL, hr,
                    MAKELANGID(LANG_NEUTRAL, SUBLANG_DEFAULT),
                    (LPTSTR) &pErrMsg, 0, NULL);
        AtlReportError(CLSID_bus_Invoice, pErrMsg, IID_Ibus_Invoice, hr);
        LocalFree(pErrMsg);
    }

    return hr;
}

//*****************************************************************
// AddDetail
// Purpose: Adds a detail record to the invoice
// Inputs:  lngInvoiceID   -- the unique invoice ID number
//          strProduct     -- the name of the product
//          strDescription -- the header description
//          lngQty         -- quantity of items
//          dblAmount      -- the amount on the detail
// Returns: N/A
//*****************************************************************
```

```
STDMETHODIMP Cbus_Invoice::AddDetail(long lngInvoiceID,
                                     BSTR strProduct,
                                     BSTR strDescription,
                                     long lngQty,
                                     double dblAmount)
{
    HRESULT hr = S_OK;

    // Class ID for db_Invoice
    _InvoicePtr pObjDB_Invoice;

    // Error message flag
    bool bErrorFlg = false;


    hr = m_spObjectContext->CreateInstance(__uuidof(Invoice),
     __uuidof(_Invoice), (void**)&pObjDB_Invoice);

    if (FAILED(hr))
    {
        bErrorFlg = true;
        goto errHandler;
    }

    hr = pObjDB_Invoice->AddDetail(lngInvoiceID, strProduct, strDescription,
                                   lngQty, dblAmount);

    if (FAILED(hr)) goto errHandler;

    // We are finished and happy.
    m_spObjectContext->EnableCommit();

    return hr;

errHandler:

    TCHAR *pErrMsg = NULL;

    // We are finished and unhappy.
    m_spObjectContext -> SetAbort();

    if (bErrorFlg)
    {
        FormatMessage(FORMAT_MESSAGE_ALLOCATE_BUFFER |
                      FORMAT_MESSAGE_FROM_SYSTEM, NULL, hr,
```

(continued)

Listing 9-2. *continued*

```
                    MAKELANGID(LANG_NEUTRAL, SUBLANG_DEFAULT),
                    (LPTSTR) &pErrMsg, 0, NULL);
      AtlReportError(CLSID_bus_Invoice, pErrMsg, IID_Ibus_Invoice, hr);
   }
   LocalFree(pErrMsg);

   return hr;
}

//*****************************************************************
// GetByID
// Purpose: Gets an invoice by ID
// Inputs:  lngInvoiceID -- the unique invoice ID number
// Returns: A Recordset object containing invoices
//*****************************************************************

STDMETHODIMP Cbus_Invoice::GetByID(long lngInvoiceID,
                                   _Recordset **pRecordSet)
{
   // Check for invalid return pointer.
   if (pRecordSet == NULL) return E_POINTER;

   HRESULT hr = S_OK;

   // Class ID for db_Invoice
   _InvoicePtr pObjDB_Invoice;

   // Error message flag
   bool bErrorFlg = false;

   hr = m_spObjectContext->CreateInstance(__uuidof(Invoice),
    __uuidof(_Invoice), (void**)&pObjDB_Invoice);

   if (FAILED(hr))
   {
      bErrorFlg = true;
      goto errHandler;
   }

   hr = pObjDB_Invoice->GetByID(lngInvoiceID, pRecordSet);
   if (FAILED(hr)) goto errHandler;

   // We are finished and happy.
   m_spObjectContext->SetComplete();
```

```
      return hr;

errHandler:

   TCHAR *pErrMsg = NULL;

   m_spObjectContext->SetAbort();

   if (bErrorFlg)
   {
      FormatMessage(FORMAT_MESSAGE_ALLOCATE_BUFFER |
                    FORMAT_MESSAGE_FROM_SYSTEM, NULL, hr,
                    MAKELANGID(LANG_NEUTRAL, SUBLANG_DEFAULT),
                    (LPTSTR) &pErrMsg, 0, NULL);
      AtlReportError(CLSID_bus_Invoice, pErrMsg, IID_Ibus_Invoice, hr);
      LocalFree(pErrMsg);
   }

   return hr;
}


//*********************************************************************
// GetByCustID
// Purpose: Adds an invoice customer ID
// Inputs:  lngCustomerID -- the unique customer ID number
// Returns: A Recordset object containing invoices
//*********************************************************************

STDMETHODIMP Cbus_Invoice::GetByCustID(long lngCustomerID,
                                       _Recordset **pRecordSet)
{
   // Check for invalid return pointer.
   if (pRecordSet == NULL) return E_POINTER;

   HRESULT hr = S_OK;

   // Class ID for db_Invoice
   _InvoicePtr pObjDB_Invoice;

   // Error message flag
   bool bErrorFlg = false;

   hr = m_spObjectContext->CreateInstance (__uuidof(Invoice),
    __uuidof(_Invoice), (void**)&pObjDB_Invoice);
```

(continued)

Listing 9-2. *continued*

```
    if (FAILED(hr))
    {
       bErrorFlg = true;
       goto errHandler;
    }

    hr = pObjDB_Invoice->GetByCustID(lngCustomerID, pRecordSet);
    if (FAILED(hr)) goto errHandler;

    // We are finished and happy.
    m_spObjectContext->SetComplete();

    return hr;

errHandler:

    TCHAR *pErrMsg = NULL;

    m_spObjectContext->SetAbort();

    if (bErrorFlg)
    {
       FormatMessage(FORMAT_MESSAGE_ALLOCATE_BUFFER |
                   FORMAT_MESSAGE_FROM_SYSTEM, NULL, hr,
                   MAKELANGID(LANG_NEUTRAL, SUBLANG_DEFAULT),
                   (LPTSTR) &pErrMsg, 0, NULL);
       AtlReportError(CLSID_bus_Invoice, pErrMsg, IID_Ibus_Invoice, hr);
       LocalFree(pErrMsg);
    }

    return hr;
}
```

The *AddHeader* and *AddDetail* methods are somewhat more interesting. The source code for these methods is also shown in Listing 9-2. The basic structure is the same as for the *Get* methods: set up an error handler and then use the object context to create subordinate objects and call their methods. Unlike the methods we've looked at up to now, however, *AddHeader* and *AddDetail* should not call the object context *SetComplete* method when they finish their work successfully.

After *AddHeader* has been called, a new invoice exists without any detail records, which violates one of our business rules. The invoice cannot be persisted until *AddDetail* is called at least once for the invoice. To keep this from happening, you can call the object context *DisableCommit* method. Calling *DisableCommit* ensures that the object's transaction cannot be committed. It can abort, but it can't commit and cause the partial invoice to be persisted.

After *AddDetail* has been called, the business rule requiring at least one detail record for each invoice is satisfied, and the object's transaction can commit. You call the object context *EnableCommit* method to reenable the commit operation. When *EnableCommit* is called, MTS does not reclaim the object's state, which means that you can call *AddDetail* multiple times on the same "real" object. This capability isn't so important for the *bus_InvoiceC* component, since there isn't any per-object state, but it could be very important for a similar component that did maintain per-object state. When the root object calls *SetComplete*, the transaction will commit, the invoice will be persisted, and the *bus_InvoiceC* object will be deactivated.

Step by Step: Implementing the *bus_InvoiceC* Component

1. Create a skeleton *bus_InvoiceC* component, following the instructions from the sidebar "Step by Step: Creating the Skeleton *db_PaymentC* Component" on page 199 in Chapter 8. The project name should be *bus_InvoiceC*. The short name for the object should be *bus_Invoice*, and the ProgID should be *bus_InvoiceC.Invoice*.

2. Add the following skeleton method implementations:

```
HRESULT AddHeader([in] long lngCustomerID,
                  [in, string] BSTR strDescription,
                  [in] double dblTotal,
                  [in] long lngReference,
                  [out, retval] long *lngInvoiceID);
HRESULT AddDetail([in] long lngInvoiceID,
                  [in, string] BSTR strProduct,
                  [in, string] BSTR strDescription,
                  [in] long lngQty,
                  [in] double dblAmount);
HRESULT GetByID([in] long lngInvoiceID,
                [out, retval] _Recordset **pRecordset);
HRESULT GetByCustID([in] long lngCustomerID,
                    [out, retval] _Recordset **pRecordset);
```

3. Add the following statements to the STDAFX.H file, directly above the line *//{{AFX_INSERT_LOCATION}}* to create the COM compiler support wrapper classes for ADO:

```
#import "msado15.dll" rename("EOF", "ADOEOF")
using namespace std;
```

(continued)

Implementing the *bus_InvoiceC* Component, *continued*

If the compiler is not able to locate MSADO15.DLL when you build the project, you should either specify the complete path to the DLL in the *#import* statement or add its location to your include path.

4. Add the following statements at the beginning of the BUS_INVOICE.CPP file to import the type libraries for components used by *bus_InvoiceC*:

```
#import "..\DLLs\util_TakeANumber.dll" raw_interfaces_only
using namespace util_TakeANumber;

#import "..\DLLs\db_CustomerC.dll" raw_interfaces_only
using namespace db_CustomerC;

#import "..\Interfaces\IdbCustomer\IdbCustomer.dll"
    raw_interfaces_only
using namespace IDBCUSTOMERLib;

#import "..\DLLs\db_InvoiceC.dll" raw_interfaces_only
using namespace db_InvoiceC;
```

Note that the type libraries for both *db_CustomerC* and the externally defined interfaces it implements, located in IDBCUSTOMER.DLL, must be imported. The type library for *db_CustomerC* does not contain the actual interface definitions.

5. Add the following code to the *GetByID* and *GetByCustID* methods to establish the basic framework that calls the object context *SetComplete* method when all work has been completed successfully or calls the object context *SetAbort* method and raises an error if one occurs:

```
// Check for invalid return pointer.
if (pRecordSet == NULL) return E_POINTER;

HRESULT hr = S_OK;

// Class ID for db_Invoice
_InvoicePtr pObjDB_Invoice;

// Error message flag
bool bErrorFlg = false;

// TODO: Do work.

// We are finished and happy.
m_spObjectContext->SetComplete();
return hr;
```

```
errHandler:
   TCHAR *pErrMsg = NULL;
   m_spObjectContext->SetAbort();

   if (bErrorFlg)
   {
      FormatMessage(FORMAT_MESSAGE_ALLOCATE_BUFFER |
                    FORMAT_MESSAGE_FROM_SYSTEM, NULL, hr,
                    MAKELANGID(LANG_NEUTRAL, SUBLANG_DEFAULT),
                    (LPTSTR) &pErrMsg, 0, NULL);
      AtlReportError(CLSID_bus_Invoice, pErrMsg,
                     IID_Ibus_Invoice, hr);
      LocalFree(pErrMsg);
   }
   return hr;
```

Notice the use of the variable *bErrorFlg*. This value is *true* when a system error occurs, and *false* otherwise. If *bErrorFlg* is *true*, the method needs to fill in the *ErrorInfo* object. This is what the call to *AtlReportError* does. If *bErrorFlg* is *false*, a subordinate object will have already set the *ErrorInfo* object if an error has occurred, and all the method has to do is return the HRESULT.

6. Replace the line *// TODO: Do work* in the *GetByID* method with the following code, which creates a *db_InvoiceC* object and calls its *GetByID* method:

```
hr = m_spObjectContext->CreateInstance(__uuidof(Invoice),
     __uuidof(_Invoice), (void**)&pObjDB_Invoice);
if (FAILED(hr))
{
   bErrorFlg = true;
   goto errHandler;
}
hr = pObjDB_Invoice->GetByID(lngInvoiceID, pRecordSet);
if (FAILED(hr)) goto errHandler;
```

7. Repeat the preceding step for the *GetByCustID* method, except call the *db_Invoice* object's *GetByCustID* method, as shown here:

```
hr = pObjDB_Invoice->GetByCustID(lngCustomerID, pRecordSet);
```

8. Add the following code to the *AddHeader* and *AddDetail* methods to establish the basic error handling framework:

```
HRESULT hr = S_OK;
```

(continued)

Implementing the *bus_InvoiceC* Component, *continued*

```
         // Error message flag
         bool bErrorFlg = false;

         // TODO: Do work.
         ⋮
         return hr;

     errHandler:
         TCHAR *pErrMsg = NULL;
         m_spObjectContext->SetAbort();

         if (bErrorFlg)
         {
             FormatMessage(FORMAT_MESSAGE_ALLOCATE_BUFFER |
                          FORMAT_MESSAGE_FROM_SYSTEM, NULL, hr,
                          MAKELANGID(LANG_NEUTRAL, SUBLANG_DEFAULT),
                          (LPTSTR) &pErrMsg, 0, NULL);
             AtlReportError(CLSID_bus_Invoice, pErrMsg,
                          IID_Ibus_Invoice, hr);
             LocalFree(pErrMsg);
         }
         return hr;
```

9. At the top of the *AddHeader* method, add this code to ensure that there is a place to write the return value:

```
// Check for invalid return pointer.
if (lngInvoiceID == NULL) return E_POINTER;
```

10. Replace the line *// TODO: Do work* in the *AddHeader* method with the following code, which declares the variables used by *AddHeader* and verifies that the object context exists:

```
// Pointer for util_TakeANumber
_TakeANumberPtr pObjTakeANumber;

// Pointer for db_Invoice
_InvoicePtr pObjDB_Invoice;

// Pointer for db_Customer
_CustomerPtr pObjDB_Customer;

// Invoice ID string
BSTR bstrTakeANumberType;
```

```
if (!m_spObjectContext)
{
   AtlReportError(CLSID_bus_Invoice, "No object context",
                  IID_Ibus_Invoice, hr);
   return hr;
}

// TODO: Continue work.
:
```

Without an object context, there is no way to guarantee that the *Add-Header* call will be followed by at least one call to *AddDetail*. Thus, we return an error if the object context is not available. This error would occur if you tried to use the component outside of the MTS environment.

11. Replace the line *// TODO: Continue work* in the *AddHeader* method with the following code, which creates the subordinate objects, calls their methods to do the work required to create a new invoice, and then calls the object context *DisableCommit* method to ensure that the containing transaction does not commit without any calls to *AddDetail*:

```
hr = m_spObjectContext->CreateInstance(__uuidof(TakeANumber),
   __uuidof(_TakeANumber), (void**)&pObjTakeANumber);
if (FAILED(hr))
{
   bErrorFlg = true;
   goto errHandler;
}

// Get the next invoice number.
bstrTakeANumberType = ::SysAllocString(L"InvoiceID");
hr = pObjTakeANumber->GetANumber(&bstrTakeANumberType,
                                 lngInvoiceID);
::SysFreeString(bstrTakeANumberType);
if(FAILED(hr)) goto errHandler;

// Add invoice header.
hr = m_spObjectContext->CreateInstance(__uuidof(Invoice),
   __uuidof(_Invoice), (void**)&pObjDB_Invoice);
if (FAILED(hr))
{
   bErrorFlg = true;
   goto errHandler;
}
```

(continued)

Implementing the *bus_InvoiceC* Component, *continued*

```
hr = pObjDB_Invoice->AddHeader(*lngInvoiceID, lngCustomerID,
    strDescription, dblTotal, lngReference, lngInvoiceID);
if(FAILED(hr)) goto errHandler;

// Update customer balance.
hr = m_spObjectContext->CreateInstance(__uuidof(Customer),
    __uuidof(_Customer), (void**)&pObjDB_Customer);
if (FAILED(hr))
{
    bErrorFlg = true;
    goto errHandler;
}

hr = pObjDB_Customer->UpdateBalance(lngCustomerID, dblTotal);
if (FAILED(hr)) goto errHandler;

// We are finished and happy.
m_spObjectContext->DisableCommit();
```

12. Replace the line *// TODO: Do work* in the *AddDetail* method with the
    following code, which creates a *db_InvoiceC* component to write the
    detail record to the database and then calls *EnableCommit* to enable
    the containing transaction to commit:

```
// Class ID for db_Invoice
_InvoicePtr pObjDB_Invoice;

hr = m_spObjectContext->CreateInstance(__uuidof(Invoice),
    __uuidof(_Invoice), (void**)&pObjDB_Invoice);
if (FAILED(hr))
{
    bErrorFlg = true;
    goto errHandler;
}

hr = pObjDB_Invoice->AddDetail(lngInvoiceID, strProduct,
    strDescription, lngQty, dblAmount);
if (FAILED(hr)) goto errHandler;

// We are finished and happy.
m_spObjectContext->EnableCommit();
```

13. (optional) Build the component by selecting the Build bus_InvoiceC.dll
    command from the Build menu.

Implementing *util_TakeANumber* Using the SPM

Last let's look at the *util_TakeANumber* component, which is used to generate unique numeric identifiers. The *util_TakeANumber* component contains these two COM classes:

- *TakeANumber*, which retrieves the next available number of a particular type. Number types are implemented as shared property groups in the SPM. Any client of the *TakeANumber* class can define a new number type. *TakeANumber* has a single method, *GetANumber*.

- *TakeANumberUpdate*, which is used by *TakeANumber* to get a block of available numbers of a given type. Information about the last block obtained for each type is persisted to a database table. *TakeANumberUpdate* has a single method, *Update*.

The *util_TakeANumber* component is implemented as two separate classes because the transaction requirements of each class are different. Once *TakeANumberUpdate* returns a block of numbers to *TakeANumber* and that block is placed in the SPM, the fact that the block was allocated absolutely, positively must be persisted. Otherwise, it would be possible for the block of numbers to be allocated twice and there would be no guarantee that the number returned by the *GetANumber* method would be unique. Thus, the *TakeANumberUpdate* class should be marked as "requires a new transaction." On the other hand, *TakeANumber* does not require a transaction to do its work correctly but it should support transactions so that clients can handle an error in *GetANumber* correctly.

The source code for *TakeANumber* is shown in Listing 9-3, and the source code for *TakeANumberUpdate* is shown in Listing 9-4 beginning on page 257.

```
Option Explicit
Const incQty = 100
Const modName = "util_TakeANumber.TakeANumber"


'****************************************************************
' GetANumber
' Purpose: Gets the next available number from the appropriate
'          property group
' Inputs:   strPropGroupIn -- the property group
' Returns: A long value
'****************************************************************
Public Function GetANumber(strPropGroupIn As String) As Long
```

Listing 9-3. *The* TakeANumber *source code.*   *(continued)*

Listing 9-3. *continued*

```
On Error GoTo ErrorHandler

Dim spmMgr As New SharedPropertyGroupManager
Dim spmGroup As SharedPropertyGroup
Dim spmPropMaxNum As SharedProperty
Dim spmPropNextNum As SharedProperty
Dim objTakeUpdate As util_TakeANumber.TakeANumberUpdate
Dim bResult As Boolean
' Attempt to create a new property group. If property group of the
' same name already exists, retrieve a reference to that group.
Set spmGroup = spmMgr.CreatePropertyGroup(strPropGroupIn, _
 LockSetGet, Process, bResult)
' Attempt to create new properties for the above group.
' This will set the individual property values to 0.
' If the group already exists, this will retrieve the
' current value for the properties.
Set spmPropMaxNum = spmGroup.CreateProperty("MaxNumber", bResult)
Set spmPropNextNum = _
 spmGroup.CreateProperty("NextNumber", bResult)

' If the property group did not exist, set the next number to 1.
If Not bResult Then
    spmPropNextNum.Value = 1
End If
' The following If clause creates a new block of ID numbers if the max
' number has been reached. The max number represents the last number in
' a block of ID numbers. The next number represents the current ID number.
' If these values are the same, it's time to issue a new block of numbers.
If spmPropNextNum.Value >= spmPropMaxNum.Value Then
    ' Create an instance of Util_takeANumber.
    Set objTakeUpdate = _
    GetObjectContext.CreateInstance("util_TakeANumber.TakeANumberUpdate")

    ' Set the next number. See TakeANumberUpdate code for specifics.
    spmPropNextNum.Value = objTakeUpdate.Update(incQty, strPropGroupIn)
    'Set the new max number.
    spmPropMaxNum.Value = spmPropNextNum.Value + incQty
End If

' Increase the next number by 1.
spmPropNextNum.Value = spmPropNextNum.Value + 1

' Clean up the object and commit the transaction if one exists.
GetObjectContext.SetComplete
```

```
    ' Return the next number.
    GetANumber = spmPropNextNum.Value

    Exit Function

ErrorHandler:

    ' Clean up object and abort the transaction if one exists.
    GetObjectContext.SetAbort

    Err.Raise Err.Number, SetErrSource(modName, "GetANumber"), _
     Err.Description

End Function
```

```
Option Explicit
Const modName = "util_TakeANumber.TakeANumberUpdate"
Const fileDSN = "dbTakeANumber.DSN"

'*********************************************************************
' Update
' Purpose: Gets the next available ID number for the appropriate table
'          (property group)
' Inputs:  lngInc       -- the increment value
'          strPropGroup -- the property group
' Returns: A long value that is the next number from the table
'*********************************************************************
Public Function Update(lngInc As Long, strPropGroup As String) As Long

    On Error GoTo ErrorHandler

    Dim lngNextNumber As Long
    Dim rs As New ADODB.Recordset
    Dim strSQL As String
    Dim conn As New ADODB.Connection

    ' Get the starting point for the next block of numbers from the database.
    strSQL = "Select NextNumber from TakeANumber " & _
             "where PropertyGroupName = '" & strPropGroup & "'"
    rs.Open strSQL, "FILEDSN=" & fileDSN, adOpenKeyset, _
     adLockBatchOptimistic, -1
```

Listing 9-4. *The* TakeANumberUpdate *source code.*   *(continued)*

Listing 9-4. *continued*

```
    ' Update the starting point for the next block of numbers.
    lngNextNumber = rs!NextNumber
    rs.Close

    strSQL = "UPDATE TakeANumber SET NextNumber = " & (lngNextNumber + _
             lngInc) & " WHERE PropertyGroupName = '" & strPropGroup & "'"
    conn.Open "FILEDSN=" & fileDSN
    conn.Execute strSQL

    ' Return the next number to the caller.
    Update = lngNextNumber

    ' Clean up object and commit the transaction if one exists.
    GetObjectContext.SetComplete

    Exit Function

ErrorHandler:

    If Not rs Is Nothing Then
        Set rs = Nothing
    End If

    GetObjectContext.SetAbort

    Err.Raise Err.Number, SetErrSource(modName, "Update"), Err.Description
End Function
```

The basic structure of the *TakeANumber* and *TakeANumberUpdate* methods should be familiar by now, so we won't walk through the code in detail, but you should be aware of two significant factors. First, note that *TakeANumber-Update* is a typical data access class. It updates a Properties table, which stores the next available number for each property group name. The *Update* method uses a syntax we haven't discussed yet to pull a value from an ADO *Recordset*, as shown here:

```
lngNextNumber = rs!NextNumber
```

This shortcut notation is equivalent to

```
lngNextNumber = rs("NextNumber")
```

in which *NextNumber* is the name of a *Field* in the *Recordset*.

Second, let's look at how to use the SPM. We need to store two values for each property group—the next available number (*NextNumber*) and the last number that has been allocated (*MaxNumber*). Whenever *NextNumber* reaches *MaxNumber*, *TakeANumberUpdate* should be called to get a new block of numbers.

To use the SPM, you must first create an instance of the shared property group manager. To do so, set a reference to the Shared Property Manager Type Library in your project. Then you can create a new *SharedPropertyGroupManager* object, as shown here:

```
Dim spmMgr As New SharedPropertyGroupManager
```

Now you can create the shared property group for the type of number the client wants. If a group with that name already exists, you get back a reference to the existing group. The code looks like this:

```
Dim spmGroup As SharedPropertyGroup
Dim bResult As Boolean
Set spmGroup = spmMgr.CreatePropertyGroup(strPropGroupIn, _
    LockSetGet, Process, bResult)
```

The value returned in *bResult* is *true* if the group has been created, *false* if the group already existed. You can use this value to determine whether you need to initialize your shared properties.

Once you have a reference to the property group, you can create the shared properties by using the *CreateProperty* method. If the shared property already exists, you just get a reference to the existing property. The *Value* property gives you access to the data stored in the shared property. Here's what the code to create a new property and set its value looks like:

```
Dim spmPropNextNum As SharedProperty
Set spmPropNextNum = spmGroup.CreateProperty("NextNumber", bResult)
If Not bResult Then
    spmPropNextNum.Value = 1
End If
```

As you can see, using the SPM from Visual Basic is very straightforward. Whenever you have data that needs to be shared across transaction boundaries or across multiple objects and persisting the data is either unnecessary or too slow, consider using the SPM.

Step by Step: Creating the *util_TakeANumber* Component

1. Create a skeleton *util_TakeANumber* component, following the instructions in the sidebar "Step by Step: Creating the Skeleton *db_CategoryC* Component" on page 161 in Chapter 8. The project name should be *util_TakeANumber* and the class name should be *TakeANumber*.

2. Add a new class module, named *TakeANumberUpdate*, to the project. Verify that the class module's *Instancing* property is set to *MultiUse*.

3. Add the following skeleton method implementations. *GetANumber* should be added to the *TakeANumber* class. *Update* should be added to the *TakeANumberUpdate* class.

   ```
   Public Function GetANumber(strPropGroupIn As String) As Long
   Public Function Update(lngInc As Long, strPropGroup As String) _
       As Long
   ```

4. Add these lines to the General Declarations section of the TakeANumber class:

   ```
   Option Explicit
   Const incQty = 100
   Const modName = "util_TakeANumber.TakeANumber"
   ```

   and these lines to the General Declarations section of the TakeANumber-Update class:

   ```
   Const modName = "util_TakeANumber.TakeANumberUpdate"
   Const fileDSN = "dbTakeANumber.DSN"
   ```

   The *incQty* constant holds the number of values to allocate on each call to *Update*.

5. Add the GLOBALS.BAS module from the \IslandHopper\Source\ Server_Components\Globals directory on the companion CD to the project, to get access to Island Hopper's standard error reporting function.

6. Add references to the following type libraries in your project:

   - Microsoft ActiveX Data Objects Library
   - Microsoft Transaction Server Type Library
   - Shared Property Manager Type Library

7. Use the code in Listing 9-3 to fill in the implementation of *TakeA-Number*'s *GetANumber* method.

8. Use the code in Listing 9-4 to fill in the implementation of *Take-ANumberUpdate*'s *Update* method.

> **NOTE**　If you want to build the *util_TakeANumber* component at this point on a machine that has the Island Hopper application installed, you should select the Binary Compatibility option on the Project Properties Component tab and select the UTIL_TAKEANUMBER.DLL file located in the Source\Server_Components\CompatibleDlls directory in your Island Hopper source installation. If you don't make this adjustment, components and applications that use *util_TakeANumber* will not operate properly.

9. (optional) Build the component. After building the component, you should select the Binary Compatibility option on the Project Properties Component tab. If you haven't already pointed to the prebuilt UTIL_TAKEANUMBER.DLL that came with Island Hopper, copy the DLL you just built to a safe place and select it. Doing so will help prevent incompatible modifications to the public interfaces.

SUMMARY

Business objects represent the real-world operations and rules your application must support. Business objects control the sequencing and enforcement of business rules, as well as the transactional integrity of the operations they perform. They are the gatekeepers that control access to your data. Each business object method should perform one unit of work, and each unit of work should be implemented in exactly one place. Higher-level operations are composed from other business and data objects.

MTS provides many services to help you write business objects that work well in a distributed, multiuser environment. The object context can be used to compose the work of multiple objects into a single transaction. Role-based security and the *ISecurityProperty* interface can help you restrict access to components and log audit information about calls to the components. The object context, the *IObjectControl* interface, and the SPM can be used to manage object and application state efficiently and safely in a multiuser environment.

10

Packaging the Components

After you implement your data and business objects, you still have one last task to perform before you can run those objects within MTS: you need to group the components into MTS *packages*. In this chapter, we'll review what packages are and discuss how to decide which components should be grouped together. We'll also look at how to create packages and how to set attributes that are typically established during development, including security and transaction requirements. In Chapter 14, we'll look at the additional steps the system administrator takes to actually deploy the application.

Packages

As you'll recall from our brief glimpse at packages in Chapters 4 and 7, conceptually a package is a set of COM classes that perform related application functions. Packages are the primary administrative units in MTS. They also define process and security boundaries.

Two types of packages are available in MTS: *library packages* and *server packages*. A library package runs in the process of the client that uses its COM classes. A server package runs as a separate MTS-managed process. Each COM class can be installed in only one package on a given machine. A package can be installed on multiple machines to distribute the workload for large numbers of clients.

NOTE It is possible for a component to include multiple COM classes that are installed in different packages. In general, this practice should be avoided. COM classes located in the same component usually have some interdependencies that might work only if their objects run in the same process. In addition, splitting the classes across packages complicates administration and maintenance.

By default, the MTS administrative tools install all COM classes in a component in the same package. The MTS administrative tools also use the term "component" to mean the same thing we mean by "COM class." For consistency with the MTS administrative tools user interface and documentation, in the remainder of our discussion of packaging, we'll assume that all COM classes in a component are installed in the same package and we'll refer to performing administrative tasks on "components" rather than on "COM classes."

In physical terms, a package is a collection of DLLs and MTS *catalog* entries. The MTS catalog stores configuration information for packages, components, interfaces, roles, and so on. This information supplements the registry entries defined by COM. (These registry entries were discussed in Chapter 2.) In MTS 2.0, the catalog is implemented using the Microsoft Windows system registry. When you create a package and add components to it using the MTS administrative tools, you are adding information to the MTS catalog.

To facilitate moving packages from one machine to another, MTS enables you to save all the information about a package to a file. These package files, which have the extension .PAK, are text files containing all the catalog entries for a package and its roles, components, and interfaces, as shown in Figure 10-1. Package files do *not* contain the components' DLLs, but they do contain references to all the DLLs so that the MTS administrative tools can locate and register the DLLs appropriately.

To enable MTS to use packaged components, developers must ensure that each component is implemented as a DLL. The component must implement the *DllRegisterServer* function, registering the component's CLSIDs, ProgIDs, interfaces, type library, and any other registry entries the component requires for proper operation. MTS will call this function to register the component when the package is installed on a server machine. All COM classes and interfaces in the component must be described by a type library. Most programming tools that support COM produce components that meet these requirements.

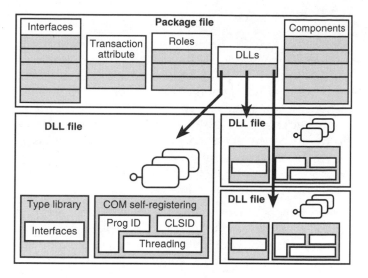

Figure 10-1. *An exported MTS package file.*

Designing Packages

The starting point for package design is the physical design, as discussed in Chapter 7. During the application design phase, the primary goal was to document any constraints imposed by the application requirements, such as requiring authorization checks on calls into particular components or requiring certain components to run on a particular machine. It was not necessary, or even desirable, to have the entire physical design completed before implementing the components.

As you progress through the implementation of your application, you will refine the physical design, placing components into packages and documenting any constraints on how the packages should be deployed. Keep in mind these four main issues when you are deciding how your components should be packaged:

■ Activation

■ Shared resources

■ Fault isolation

■ Security isolation

We'll look at each of these issues in detail in the following sections.

Activation

You can activate your application server's components in one of two ways: in the client's process or in a package-specific MTS-managed process. We've already seen that library packages are used to run the components in the client's process. Note that "client" in this sense is another component or application running on the same machine on which the library package is installed, not an end-user application. Library packages do not support declarative security, nor do they offer the benefits of process isolation. Thus, library packages are typically used for utility components that might be used by multiple applications. Library packages are also useful when the overhead of a separate process is undesirable and authorization checks are not required.

Server packages are used to run components in a separate MTS-managed process. Server packages support declarative security, resource pooling, and so on. Most packages are server packages. You group your application's components into packages based on common resource usage, security requirements, and fault isolation needs.

Deciding how many packages you need in your application is a balancing act. With many packages, system administrators have a lot of flexibility in deploying your application. However, each server process requires a certain amount of overhead to manage resource pools, shared properties, and so on. In addition, interprocess COM calls are much more expensive than in-process COM calls within a single apartment. And too many packages make system management tough. At this point in your application development, create the packages you think you need based on resource usage, security, and fault isolation. During performance testing, you can adjust how components are allocated to packages if you find that process overhead or interprocess calls are a bottleneck.

Shared Resources

Components that use the same resources, such as databases, should be grouped together in a single-server package. Remember from Chapter 4 that MTS manages resource pools on a per-process basis. Each server package gets its own thread pool, database connection pool, Shared Property Manager (SPM), and so on. If two components using the same database are located in separate server packages, they cannot pool database connections. If the components are located in the same server package, they can pool connections. This capability can greatly improve the performance and scalability of your application. Similarly, components located in separate server packages cannot share properties by using the SPM. Components that need to share properties must be located in the same package to ensure correct application operation.

You should also consider the location of resources when you design your packages. In general, components should be deployed as close as possible to the resources they use, particularly data stores, to help reduce network traffic within your application. For example, if two data stores used by your application might be located on different machines, you should consider putting the data objects that use each data store in separate packages. This arrangement gives the system administrator the flexibility to install each package near the data store it uses. Any deployment recommendations or requirements, such as locating a package and a data store on the same machine, should be noted in the physical design documentation distributed with your application.

Fault Isolation

You might also want to consider separating components into different packages to ensure that a fault in one component does not cause other components to fail. Recall from Chapter 4 that MTS will terminate a process whenever it detects internal corruption. Exceptions within a component can also force a server process to terminate. Any transient state maintained in running objects or the SPM will be lost. If your application has components that maintain transient state, you might want to consider placing those components in a separate server package. You might also want to isolate components during quality assurance testing.

Security Isolation

As we saw in Chapter 4, server packages are the units of trust for MTS. Calls into a package can be secured. Calls within the package are trusted. Thus, application security requirements have a big impact on your package design. If calls into a component must be authorized, the clients and the component must be located in different packages. Only components that can safely call each other without requiring an authorization check should be located in the same package.

MTS roles are defined on a per-package basis. If you have multiple components that use the same roles, consider placing them in the same package. Generally, this grouping is a safe thing to do. Since the components can be called by the same set of users, they should be trusted to call each other. Placing components that use the same roles in one package simplifies administration since the system administrator does not need to remember to populate the role in multiple packages.

In addition, a server package runs as a particular identity, and all components in the package run as the package identity. Components that need to run as different user identities should be located in separate packages. Components might need to run as different identities because they should have different access rights to some resource or in order to maintain an audit trail. Although you generally cannot define the exact identity each server package will run as during development, you should document any recommendations along with the permissions required by package components. For example, if a data object in a given package requires read/write access to a particular data store, you should document that the identity used to run that package must have read/write access to the data store.

Island Hopper Package Design

In Chapter 7, we identified two likely packages for the components of the Island Hopper application, one for things controlled by the classified ads department and one for things controlled by the accounting department. Our original high-level component diagram is shown in Figure 10-2.

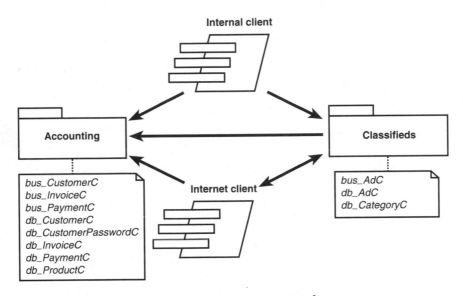

Figure 10-2. *The initial Island Hopper component diagram.*

During our initial design work, we had not yet identified a need for the two utility components, *util_TakeANumber* and *util_WordCount*. These are generally useful components, so they should be put in a separate library package. The remaining components are divided into customer service and billing-related components controlled by the accounting department and advertising-related components controlled by the classified ads department. The primary issue for the Island Hopper application is security isolation for database tables controlled by the different departments. In a more sophisticated example, these tables might be located in separate databases maintained on separate database servers. In this case, separating the components into two packages would give the system administrator some flexibility in how the application was deployed. The final component diagram for the Island Hopper application is shown in Figure 10-3.

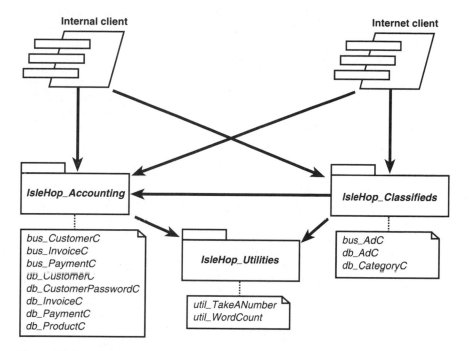

Figure 10-3. *The final Island Hopper component diagram.*

Building Packages

Once you've decided how to divide your components into packages, you need to build the packages themselves. The six key packaging tasks during application development are as follows:

1. Create the package.

2. Add components to the package.

3. Set activation properties.

4. Configure security.

5. Set transaction properties.

6. Export the package.

We'll discuss each of these steps in detail in the sections that follow.

Creating Packages

To create a package, start the MTS Explorer. In the left-hand pane, highlight the name of the computer on which you want to create the package, and then select the computer's Packages Installed folder. From the Action menu, choose New and then Package to start the Package Wizard. The Package Wizard lets you install a prebuilt package or create a new one. In this chapter, we'll focus on creating new packages; in Chapter 14, we'll look at installing prebuilt packages.

Click the Create An Empty Package button then enter the name of the new package. It is generally a good idea to include the name of your company or of the application in the name of the package to reduce the chances of naming collisions between different applications. After you have entered a name, click the Next button and then specify the package identity.

By default, the package identity is set to Interactive User—that is, the user account logged onto the computer on which the package is installed. This default is usually an acceptable setting during application development. However, if your package requires access to resources that are not available to the interactive user, you should set the package identity to a specific user account with the appropriate permissions.

Once you have selected a package identity, click the Finish button to exit the Package Wizard. Your empty package should appear in the Packages Installed folder. If you open the Properties window for your package, you will see the package name and ID displayed on the General tab, as shown in Figure 10-4. This tab includes a Description text box in which you can enter a short description of your package.

Tools for Package Management

The most straightforward way to create and manage MTS packages is by using the MTS Explorer. The MTS Explorer is a SnapIn, an application extension, for the Microsoft Management Console (MMC). You can use the MTS Explorer to administer and monitor MTS servers.

MTS also provides a programmable interface to its administrative services. The MTS 2.0 Programmer's Reference, included in the Microsoft Windows NT 4.0 Option Pack documentation and current versions of the Platform SDK, documents administrative objects that you program using Automation. These objects are scripting-language friendly, so you can use VBScript to write command-line scripts to automate administrative tasks.

In this book, we'll focus on using the MTS Explorer to perform management activities.

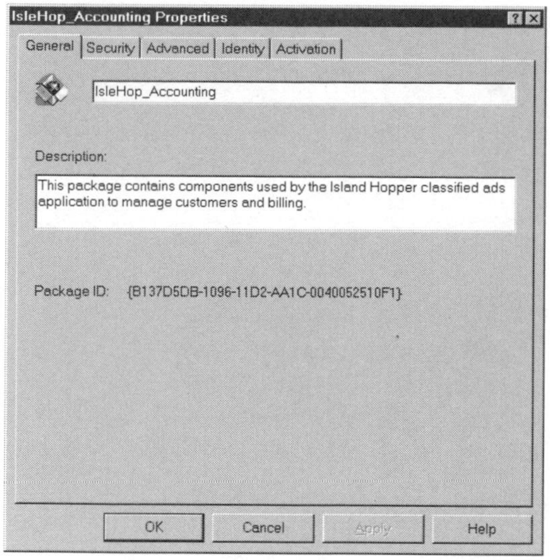

Figure 10-4. *The Properties window for a newly created package.*

Adding Components to a Package

With your package created, you can start adding components to it. In the left-hand pane of the MTS Explorer, highlight your package and then select its Components folder. From the Action menu, choose New and then Component to start the Component Wizard. The Component Wizard lets you install new components or import components that are already registered on your computer. Importing a component does not install the interface or method information required to set interface properties or to configure access to the component from a remote client. Generally, you should install components instead of importing them.

Click the Install New Component(s) button to move on to the Install Components step, shown in Figure 10-5 on the following page, in which you can select the files containing your components. Select the DLL that contains the component you want to install. If the component uses an external type library or a proxy/stub DLL, add those files as well. After you have added your component files, the Install Components wizard step displays information about the files you added and the components they contain. If you check the Details check box, you will see more information about file contents and the components that were found. If MTS cannot find your component's type library, your component will not appear in the list.

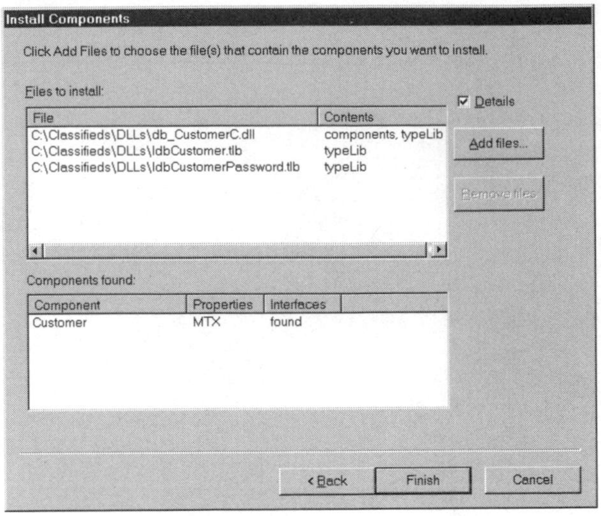

Figure 10-5. *Adding components to a package.*

After you have selected all the files for the components you want in the package, click the Finish button. Your components should now appear in the Components folder for the package.

> **NOTE** Be sure that the Hidden Files option is set to Show All Files in the Windows Explorer. Otherwise, you might not see any DLLs in the Component Wizard Add Files dialog box.
>
> You can also add components to your package by dragging a component DLL from the Windows Explorer and dropping it on the package in the MTS Explorer.

Setting Activation Properties

Once you have created a package, you need to specify whether it is a library package or a server package. By default, all new packages are server packages. To change the activation property, highlight your package in the left-hand pane of the MTS Explorer. From the Action menu, choose the Properties command to display the Properties window for the package. Select the Activation tab, as shown in Figure 10-6, and then select the type of package you want.

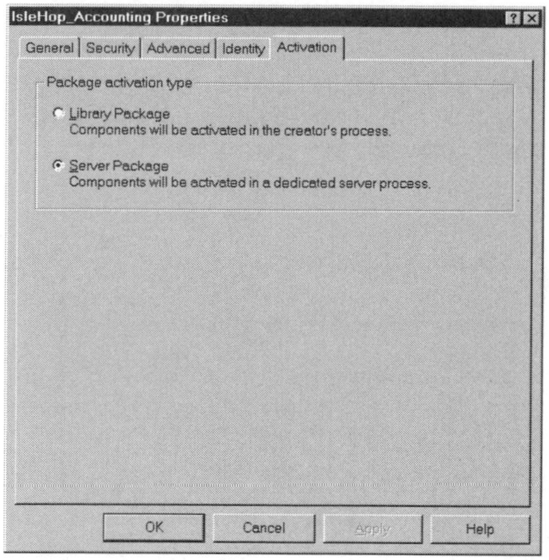

Figure 10-6. *Setting the* Activation *property for a package.*

Configuring Security

If you have identified security requirements for your COM classes, you should also configure the security settings for your packages. To configure these settings, follow these steps:

1. Decide whether any authorization checking is needed for the components in the package.

2. Define the roles used by the package.

3. For each component, decide whether authorization checking is needed.

4. If a component requires authorization checking, assign roles to the component.

5. For each interface exposed by each component, decide whether the interface is accessible to all roles assigned to the component. If it is not accessible, assign roles to the interface.

6. Set the authentication level for the package.

As you go through this process, refer to Figure 10-7 on the following page, which illustrates how MTS performs authorization checks.

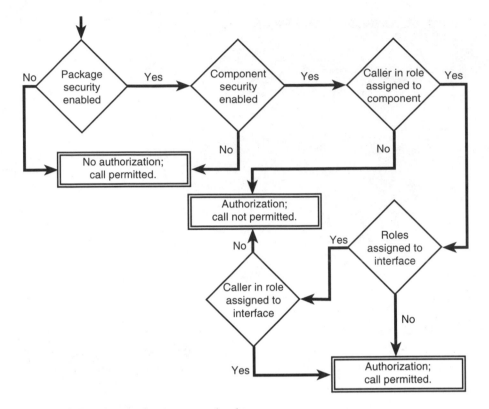

Figure 10-7. *MTS authorization checking.*

Enabling package authorization checks

If any components in your package require authorization checks on incoming calls, you must enable authorization checking for the package as a whole. If you do not require any automatic authorization checks, you can disable authorization checking for the package. As long as the authentication level is not set to *NONE*, programmatic security is available for all server packages, regardless of whether authorization checking is enabled.

To enable or disable authorization checks, highlight your package in the left-hand pane of the MTS Explorer. From the Action menu, choose the Properties command to display the Properties window for the package. Select the Security tab, as shown in Figure 10-8, and then check or uncheck the Enable Authorization Checking check box.

Defining package roles

If you have enabled automatic authorization checks for your package or if you call *IsCallerInRole* to perform programmatic security checks within a component, you should define roles for your package. You must define all the roles used by all the components in a package at the package level.

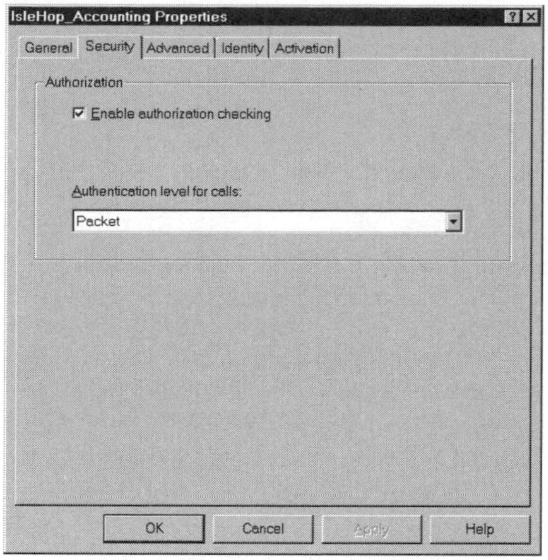

Figure 10-8. *MTS package security settings.*

To define a role, expand your package in the left-hand pane of the MTS Explorer and then highlight its Roles folder. From the Action menu, choose New and then Role, and enter the role name in the dialog box that is displayed. Click OK to close this dialog box, and your role will appear in the Roles folder for the package. If you want to provide some documentation about the role, you can enter a description in the role's Properties window, as shown in Figure 10-9.

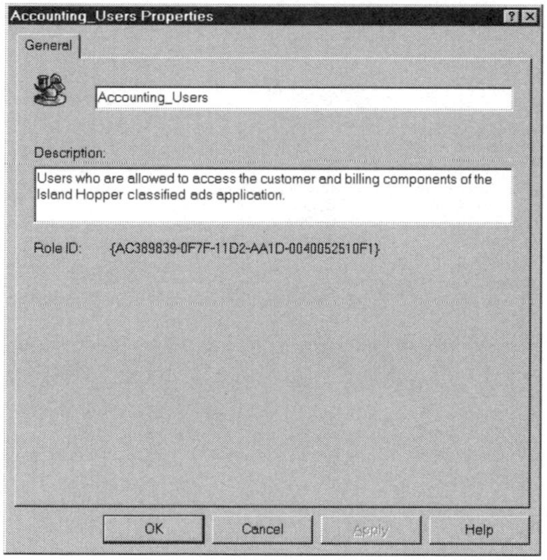

Figure 10-9. *Defining a role in MTS.*

Typically, you will not populate roles with user accounts during development, except for testing. We will look at populating roles in detail in Chapter 14.

Disabling component authorization checks

By default, if you have enabled authorization checking for a package, all the components within the package will have authorization checking enabled. If there are components within the package that do not require authorization checking for calls into the package, you can disable authorization checking for those components. You will still be able to use programmatic security, even if authorization checking is disabled.

To enable or disable authorization checking, highlight your component in the left-hand pane of the MTS Explorer. From the Action menu, choose the Properties command to display the Properties window for the component. Select the Security tab, and then check or uncheck the Enable Authorization Checking check box, as shown in Figure 10-10.

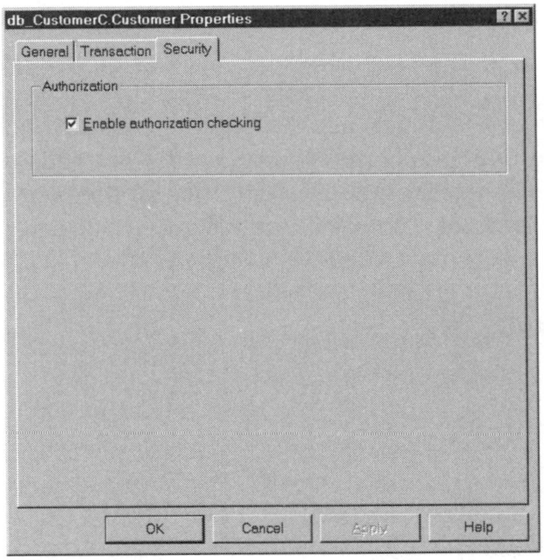

Figure 10-10. *Disabling component authorization checks in MTS.*

Assigning roles to components

If authorization checking is enabled for a component, you must assign roles to that component. Only callers that are members of roles assigned to the component will be permitted to create or access component objects. You must include all the roles that are permitted to access any interface exposed by the component in the roles assigned to the component.

To assign a role to a component, expand the component in the left-hand pane of the MTS Explorer and then highlight the Role Membership folder. From the

Action menu, choose New and then Role to open the Select Roles dialog box, shown in Figure 10-11. This dialog box displays all the available roles in the package and allows you to select the roles permitted to access the component.

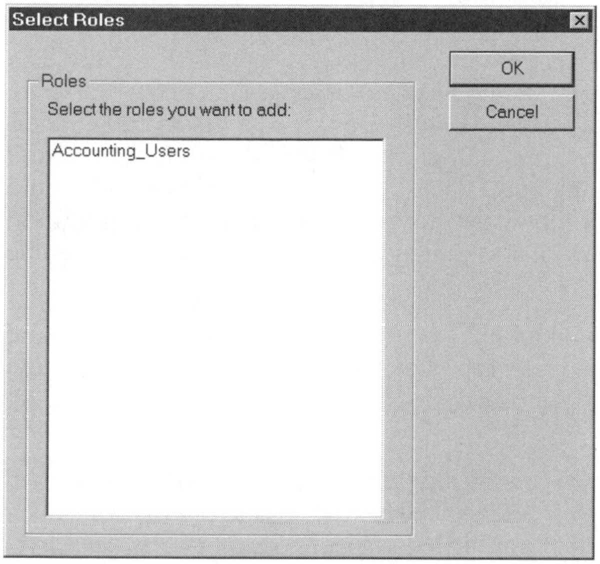

Figure 10-11. *Assigning roles in MTS.*

Assigning roles to interfaces

If you have enabled authorization checking for a component and you need to restrict access to particular interfaces exposed by the component, you can also assign roles to individual interfaces.

To assign a role to an interface, expand the component in the left-hand pane of the MTS Explorer and then expand its Interfaces folder. Next expand the specific interface you want to configure and highlight its Role Membership folder. From the Action menu, choose New and then Role to open the Select Roles dialog box. Select the roles for the interface, and then click the OK button to save your changes.

> **NOTE** The roles you assign to a specific interface must also be assigned to the component as a whole. Otherwise, clients will receive a permission denied error when they attempt to create instances of the component and MTS writes a message to the Windows NT application log identifying the user who was denied access. Also remember that MTS 2.0 does not perform interface-specific authorization checks when the component is accessed via *IDispatch*.

Setting the authentication level

The final step in configuring security for your package is specifying the authentication level used for calls to objects. The authentication level determines how often COM authenticates the caller's identity, as well as whether data packets in the call are secured.

By default, MTS uses packet-level authentication, which means that every data packet transmitted on the network during a COM method call is checked to verify that it comes from the expected caller. However, no checks are made to determine whether the packets have been tampered with, and the packet data is not encrypted. If you require data integrity checks or packet encryption, you should set the authentication level appropriately. Note that these higher authentication levels can impose a severe performance penalty because every packet must be inspected.

To set the authentication level, highlight your package in the left-hand pane of the MTS Explorer and display its Properties window. Select the appropriate authentication level from the drop-down list on the Security tab, shown in Figure 10-8 on page 275.

When the authentication level is set to anything other than *NONE*, MTS will provide security information to server packages. The *ObjectContext IsSecurityEnabled* method will return *TRUE*, and the *IsCallerInRole* and *ISecurityProperty* methods can be used. If you do not need any security information or authorization checks, you can set the authentication level to *NONE*. This setting will completely disable MTS security features for the package.

Security configuration is a shared responsibility between developers and system administrators. System administrators are responsible for enforcing company security policies. To do this, they might need to adjust your security settings to enable authorization checking for additional components, categorize users into different roles, or provide more stringent authentication checks. You should clearly document any assumptions made by your component implementations regarding available roles, authentication levels, and so on. This documentation will help system administrators avoid breaking your components.

Setting Transaction Properties

Component developers are also responsible for setting the transaction properties of every component installed into MTS. You should set the transaction property for your component so that it will update managed resources correctly, regardless of whether the component's clients are transactional.

You can use the MTS Explorer to set the transaction properties of your components. First highlight the component and open its Properties Window. Select the

Transaction tab, as shown in Figure 10-12, and specify the level of transaction support required by your component.

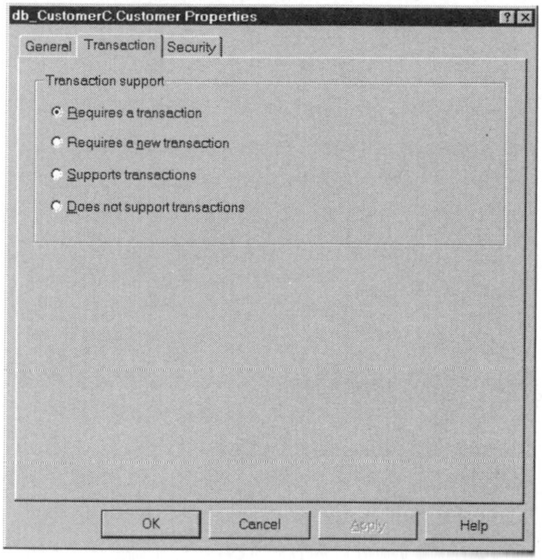

Figure 10-12. *Setting a component's transaction property in MTS.*

You might also be able to set transaction properties for your components using your development tool. MTS defines custom type library attributes that can be used to add the transaction property to a *coclass* in an IDL file. If you have an IDL file you can edit, simply include the MTXATTR.H header file in your IDL file and add the transaction property setting to your *coclass* definition, as shown here:

```
#include <mtxattr.h>
⋮
[
    uuid(74DC33EF-5B52-11D1-99F8-00600840299E),
    helpstring("bus_Invoice Class"),
    TRANSACTION_REQUIRED
]
coclass bus_Invoice
{
    [default] interface Ibus_Invoice;
};
```

NOTE If your development tool manages the IDL file or generates a type library for you, it might provide a way to set the transaction properties as well. Check your tool's documentation for details.

Exporting Packages

Once you have created your packages, you need to make them available for deployment. Remember that a package is simply a collection of catalog entries that contain package settings and reference one or more component files. These catalog entries need to be persisted so that they can be transferred to another machine.

To export a package, highlight the package in the left-hand pane of the MTS Explorer. From the Action menu, choose the Export command to display the Export Package dialog box, as shown in Figure 10-13. Enter the name of the package file you want to create. All the component files will be copied to the same directory as the package file. Creating a unique directory for each package will make it easier to keep track of which files need to be included on distribution disks.

```
┌─────────────────────────────────────────────────────────────┐
│ Export Package                                            [X] │
│                                                               │
│  Export the 'IsleHop_Accounting' package:                     │
│                                                               │
│  Enter the full path for the package file to be created.  Component files will be copied │
│  into the directory you specify for the package file.         │
│                                                               │
│  ┌────────────────────────────────────────┐   ┌──────────┐   │
│  │C:\Classifieds\Packages\Accounting        │   │ Browse...│   │
│  └────────────────────────────────────────┘   └──────────┘   │
│                                                               │
│  ┌─Options──────────────────────────────────────────────┐    │
│  │                                                        │    │
│  │   □ Save Windows NT user ids associated with roles     │    │
│  │                                                        │    │
│  │                                                        │    │
│  └────────────────────────────────────────────────────────┘   │
│                                                               │
│                          ┌──────────┐    ┌──────────┐         │
│                          │  Export  │    │  Cancel  │         │
│                          └──────────┘    └──────────┘         │
└─────────────────────────────────────────────────────────────┘
```

Figure 10-13. *Exporting an MTS package.*

If you have populated package roles with the user accounts that will be used in deployments, check the Save Windows NT User Ids Associated With Roles check box. Normally, developers will not use this option. It is primarily intended for system administrators who need to move or copy deployed packages to new machines.

When the package export settings are to your liking, click the Export button to export the package. A package file will be created in the location you've specified, and all the component files will be copied to that location. The export utility will also create a client install program, which is written to the Clients subdirectory of your package location. When executed from a client computer, the client install program copies the necessary proxy/stub DLLs and type libraries to that computer and updates the client's system registry with information required by DCOM, including the name of the server machine.

To minimize the size of your client install programs and eliminate unnecessary registry entries, you might want to export two versions of your package. The first version, which we'll call the *full package*, includes all the package components. During deployment, this package will be installed on server machines. You can delete the Clients subdirectory for the full package since it won't be used. Then remove the components that aren't accessed directly by clients from your package. Export the package again to a different location. We'll call this package the *client package*. During deployment, the client package will be temporarily installed to generate client install packages that point clients to the deployed server machines. You can delete the Clients subdirectory for the client package if it does not point to a server machine you want clients to use.

By default, client install programs will point clients to the machine from which the package was exported. If you do not want your development machine name to appear in client install programs, highlight My Computer in the left-hand pane of the MTS Explorer. From the Action menu, choose the Properties command to display the Properties window. Select the Options tab, shown in Figure 10-14, and enter a dummy name as the Remote Server Name value. All client install programs you generate will now point clients to this dummy machine name. During deployment, system administrators can re-export the client package to point to the correct server machine.

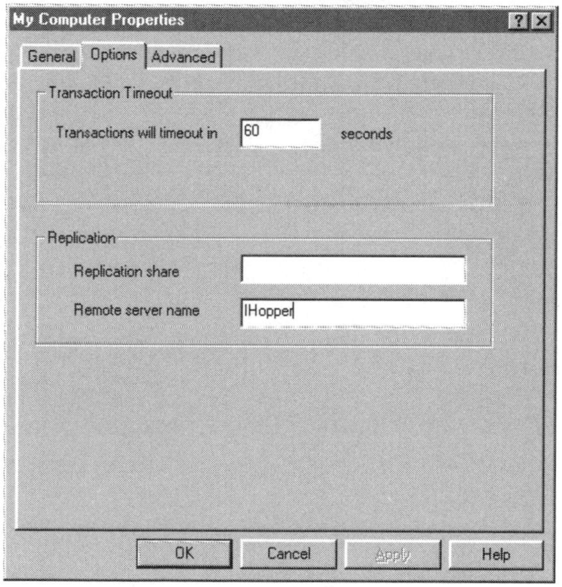

Figure 10-14. *Entering a Remote Server Name.*

For in-house deployment, simply sharing the exported package directories might be sufficient. If not, you will need to create distribution disks and a setup program. If this step is necessary, be sure that you keep all the files for each package, including the package file, in the same directory so that the MTS Explorer import utility can install your packages.

SUMMARY

Packages are collections of components that perform related application functions. They are the primary unit of administration and trust in MTS. Packages straddle the line between application development and application deployment. Certain decisions about packages should be defined by developers; others should be deferred until deployment.

Developers should decide which components should be packaged together, based on application requirements and implementation constraints. The four primary factors influencing package design are activation, shared resources, fault isolation, and security isolation. Developers should also define roles, set the authentication level, and define transaction requirements for their components.

In general, developers should avoid decisions that would unduly constrain application deployment. Packages should be designed to give a system administrator the flexibility to tune deployment for best overall system performance. Decisions about role membership and which user identities to run packages as should be deferred until deployment.

Developers should produce exported packages, suitable for server installation. The physical design documentation should be updated to reflect the actual package design as well as any recommendations for or constraints on deployment. We will return to packages and application deployment in Chapter 14.

11

Building the Presentation Layer

Now that we've examined the data access and business layers of the three-tier distributed application, let's turn our attention to the remaining tier: the presentation layer. We'll start by looking at the different types of presentation layer applications and how your application requirements and design affect your implementation choices. Then we'll look at some of the techniques you can use in your implementations. Finally, we'll look at some examples from the Island Hopper sample application.

> **NOTE** Although the vast majority of code in a presentation layer application deals with displaying the user interface, our focus here will be on the code that communicates with the business layer, not the display code. For more information about writing user interfaces, please consult the references listed in the bibliography.

Moving from Design to Implementation

In Chapter 7, we looked briefly at modeling the presentation layer. The primary task during modeling was to document roughly what the user interface of your application should look like and how the user is expected to work through the various screens. You might also have noted some design constraints on your implementation—for example, the presentation layer application might need to run on both Microsoft Windows and Apple Macintosh platforms or the application might need to run over the Internet and use a Web browser interface. These constraints dramatically affect which technologies you use to implement your application.

Types of Presentation Layer Applications

As we saw in Chapter 1, the Windows DNA architecture supports a wide range of presentation layer types. The two basic categories of presentation layer are *native user interfaces* and *Web-based user interfaces*. Native user interfaces rely on user interface services provided by the underlying operating system. On Windows, native user interfaces use the Microsoft Win32 API. Web-based user interfaces are typically based on HTML, which can be rendered on any operating system by a Web browser.

Of course, there are many points between the extremes of pure Win32 applications and pure HTML applications. Win32 applications can host a Web browser Microsoft ActiveX control to gain access to the Internet or to use the Web browser's HTML rendering capabilities. Most Web browsers today support scripting languages so that you can include code within an HTML page that will execute when the page is rendered. Some browsers, such as Microsoft Internet Explorer, let you include ActiveX controls and other COM objects on an HTML page and control the objects using scripting code. Microsoft Internet Explorer 4 and later support the newly emerging Dynamic HTML (DHTML) standard, which lets you dynamically change the contents of a page from scripting code on the client, as well as data-binding, which lets you manipulate persistent data directly on the client.

The presentation layer itself can be distributed. Server-side applications can generate the client-side user interface, which is downloaded to each user's machine at run time. Distributed presentation layers are common for dynamic Web-based applications. For example, ASP uses server-side components and script code to generate Web pages that can be returned to the user machine via HTTP. The Web pages can contain HTML, client-side script code, DHTML, and references to ActiveX controls or other components, just like static Web pages. Since the page is generated at run time, it can be tuned to the capabilities of the user's Web browser. And, of course, the information displayed on the page can be computed by the server-side code.

In the Windows DNA architecture, the entire range of presentation layer types has some common characteristics. The business logic of the application is encapsulated in business layer (middle-tier) components, rather than coded within the presentation layer application. This arrangement makes the business logic easier to reuse if your presentation layer needs to be changed. The presentation layer communicates with the business logic using COM method calls. The presentation layer might also use COM-based ActiveX controls to display the user interface. The same ActiveX controls can be used in native Win32 applications and in Web-based applications running on Windows, so it might even be possible to reuse user interface code between different types of presentation layer applications.

Selecting a Presentation Layer Architecture

You should consider several factors when choosing the architecture for your presentation layer applications, as listed here:

- Are there application requirements that specify the type of user interface?

- Are there firewalls or other security issues that might impact communication between user workstations and server-side machines?

- What operating systems must be supported on user workstations?

- What Web browsers must be supported?

- Can COM components be installed and run on user workstations?

- Can remote COM components be accessed from user workstations?

Let's look at how each of the factors listed above affects your presentation layer architecture.

Application requirements

It is entirely possible that the major decision—native or Web-based—has already been made for you. If one of your application's requirements is that the application must be made available to users over the Internet, a Web-based architecture will almost always be the correct choice. Although you can write native applications that communicate with server-side code over the Internet, when a requirement states that users must be able to access the application over the Internet, most likely the intent is that users must be able to access the application through their Web browsers.

You might also have corporate policies regarding user interfaces for new applications. Many companies are standardizing on Web-based applications because it is easier to teach employees how to access Web pages than how to run multiple native applications. Other companies might have a standard user interface style based on native code applications. This standardization is done to reduce costs. Development costs are reduced by reusing existing code and developer skills. Training costs are reduced because it is easier to teach employees how to use the application. The cost of maintaining the application over time will likely be lowered as well. Thus, if your company has a standard user interface policy, you'll probably know up front whether you need a native or Web-based application.

Firewall and security issues

Firewalls and security policies that might impact communications between user workstations and server-side machines also impact your architecture choices. These issues primarily affect Web-based applications in which users access the application over the Internet. However, the same issues may apply to applications running on a wide area network (WAN).

Server-side machines might be located behind firewalls that permit only certain communications protocols to penetrate the firewalls. User workstations might need to use proxy servers to access remote machines. In these situations, it might be difficult to use DCOM to communicate between the presentation layer and the business layer. Although it is possible to get DCOM to work through a firewall, doing so normally involves modifying the firewall to permit DCOM traffic to pass through. Access through proxy servers presents an additional challenge, since most proxy servers hide user workstation IP addresses. The usual DCOM network protocols need the workstation IP addresses to establish proper communication between the workstation and server machines.

To deal with firewalls and proxy servers, you have four options. First, you can configure the firewall to permit DCOM traffic and the proxy servers to not hide user workstation IP addresses. Normally, this is not a practical solution, since the proxy servers are not likely to be under your control and corporate policy might not permit modifications to the firewall.

Second, you can use the *Internet Tunneling TCP/IP protocol* for DCOM. This protocol tunnels all DCOM traffic over TCP/IP port 80, which is the TCP/IP port used by HTTP. Most firewalls permit HTTP traffic through the firewall, so the Internet Tunneling TCP/IP protocol avoids the firewall issue. To get through proxy servers, however, the proxy servers must be configured to permit tunneling on port 80. Again, this might not be a practical solution, since the proxy servers are not likely to be under your control.

> **NOTE** The Internet Tunneling TCP/IP protocol is included with Microsoft Windows NT 4.0 Service Pack 4 and Microsoft Windows NT 5.0. (Client-side support is also available for Windows 95 and Windows 98.)

Third, you can use the Remote Data Service (RDS). As we saw in Chapter 3, RDS can be used to marshal ADO *Recordset* objects over DCOM or over HTTP. More generally, RDS can be used to marshal calls over HTTP from client-side code to any server-side business object that exposes an *IDispatch* interface. This option lets you use the COM programming model but avoids firewall and proxy server issues. You can use this technique from either native or Web-based applications. We'll discuss using RDS to access remote business objects in the section "Using RDS to Access Remote Objects" later in this chapter.

Fourth, you can structure the application so that it doesn't need to make COM calls through a proxy server or firewall. This option normally implies a Web-based application, typically implemented using ASP. The user accesses the application through a Web browser. ASP pages use server-side scripting to create and use business objects and then generate Web pages to return via HTTP to the user's machine. These pages might contain client-side scripts and components, but they would never reference remote COM objects through a firewall. We'll look at how to access business objects from ASP pages in the section "Using ASP" later in this chapter.

In addition to firewall issues, you might have to address security issues. Usually, COM and MTS applications are secured. The caller must be authorized to use a particular component, and each call might need to be authenticated. In Windows NT 4.0, authorization and authentication can be performed only if the caller can provide security credentials from a trusted Windows NT domain. But in Internet scenarios, most users will probably not be part of a trusted Windows NT domain. Essentially, the users are anonymous. If you want to make COM calls from the user workstation to business objects on the server, you will need to configure the server to permit these anonymous users to access your business objects. If this is not acceptable, a distributed presentation layer application that buffers access to your secure business objects through unsecured business objects or ASP pages should be used.

Operating system constraints

It's important to determine early on which operating systems must be supported by client-side code. If the presentation layer needs to run on Win32 operating systems only, the full range of technologies discussed in this chapter are available to you. If the presentation layer must run on other platforms, you face significant constraints.

First, COM might not be available on one of your target platforms. If it is not available, you can neither use client-side COM objects nor communicate with remote COM objects. Even if COM is available, DCOM might not be available on one of your target platforms. For example, DCOM is not available on Windows 3.1 or Macintosh platforms. On Windows 95, you must install DCOM95 on client machines in order to use DCOM. If DCOM is not available, you will not be able to communicate with remote COM objects. In this case, a distributed presentation layer that uses ASP on the server to generate Web pages for the client will probably be the most suitable architecture.

Second, COM components are normally distributed as platform-specific binary executables. If you want to use client-side COM objects, you need to ensure that the components are available for each of your target platforms. Otherwise, you will need to create special versions of your presentation layer application that don't use those components.

Finally, the user interface or Web browsing services supported on each platform might vary. To work around platform differences for native applications, you can use a platform-neutral user interface framework. To work around platform differences for Web-based applications, you might need to use a restricted subset of HTML and scripting languages. Otherwise, you will need to write platform-specific presentation layer applications.

Web browser constraints

Even if you need to support only a single operating system, you might be required to support multiple Web browsers. If you are writing a Web-based application, it's important to determine early on what HTML tags, scripting languages, object models, components, and so on are supported by the browsers you need to target. As noted earlier, you'll need to either find a common subset of features supported by all the browsers or write browser-specific presentation layer applications.

The Browser Capabilities component provided with ASP lets you dynamically generate Web pages that use the highest level of functionality the browser is capable of. Using this object, you can find out which browser requested your ASP page and what features the browser supports. Because the Browser Capabilities component determines supported features using an .INI file indexed by the browser's HTTP User Agent string, you can easily customize the .INI file to provide information about any browser features you want.

In general, if you are using client-side scripting, you'll want to use JavaScript for browser-neutral applications. You'll still need to watch out for incompatibilities between browser object models that might break your script code, however. Server-side scripts can be written in any scripting language supported by the Web server, since those scripts are never sent to the browser.

If you need to support only Internet Explorer 4.0 or later, all the technologies discussed in this chapter are available to you. If you need to support Internet Explorer 3.0, you cannot use DHTML, but you can use RDS if the necessary ADO components are installed on the users' machines. If you need to support other Web browsers, you might not be able to use either client-side or remote COM objects from within Web pages.

Client-side COM components

If your presentation layer application is a native Win32 application, installing and running COM components on user workstations probably isn't an issue. You'll need to install the Win32 application, of course, but the COM components are just treated as part of the application.

Things are a bit more complicated for Web-based applications. If the browser supports client-side COM components, the components are usually downloaded the first time a user accesses a page that uses the components and are automatically installed on the user's machine. Some users (or the companies they work for) might have concerns about the safety of automatically downloading and installing executable code that will run on client machines. Some users might not allow any components to be downloaded to their machine. If your Web-based application must support this type of user, you probably cannot use any client-side COM components (including ActiveX controls) unless you can guarantee that the components are already installed on the user's machine. Other users will decide on a case-by-case basis whether they want to download and install particular components. In this case, you might choose to use client-side COM components. We'll look at how to make client-side COM components available to user machines in the section "Using Client-Side Components" later in this chapter.

Client-side access to remote components

You also need to consider whether user machines will be able to access remote components. We've already looked at some of the issues related to accessing remote components. First, there must be a way for the user machine to make remote COM calls, either using DCOM or using RDS. Second, if you are writing a Web-based application, the browser must support creating and scripting COM objects.

In addition, accessing remote components usually requires installing some code or registry entries on users' machines. If your application uses vtable-binding or early-binding to access COM components, the proxy/stub DLLs or type libraries must be installed on the users' machines. Most applications will also rely on registry information to locate the remote server machine name. Thus, you might face some of the same issues for remote components that you do for client-side components: users might not feel safe using these components. We'll look at how to make remote components available to user machines in the section "Using Business Objects" later in this chapter.

After considering these six factors, you should have a pretty good idea of the overall architecture of your presentation layer application. You should be able to start coding prototype applications to verify the functionality of the user interface, using hard-coded data. You should also verify that the business objects and data objects you have meet the needs of the presentation layer application. If you are missing functionality, modify the components—hopefully before they are deployed so that you don't have to worry about versioning issues. If you are writing a Web-based application, verify that the functionality you need is exposed via the *IDispatch* interface. Most scripting languages supported by Web browsers support late-binding only through *IDispatch*. If the functionality you need is exposed on another interface, you'll probably need to modify your components.

Implementing Presentation Layers

Let's turn our attention now to some specific techniques you can use to implement your presentation layer applications. This is by no means a comprehensive discussion of all the techniques you will use to implement your applications. It does, however, cover the primary techniques you use to work with business objects.

Using Business Objects

First let's look at how you use business objects from applications running on user machines. We'll assume that the user machine can communicate with servers via DCOM and that the user machine is properly configured so that COM can locate the server machine on which a component is located.

Using business objects from Win32 applications

For native Win32 applications, the mechanics of accessing remote business objects really aren't much different from those for using any other COM component. You simply call *CoCreateInstance*, *CoCreateInstanceEx*, or the equivalent object creation mechanism provided by your development language. Once you've created an object, you make method calls as usual.

Note that you do *not* use the object context's *CreateInstance* method to create remote business objects from applications running on user machines. These applications are base clients, running outside the MTS environment. You need to use the object context's *CreateInstance* method only when you create MTS-hosted objects from within the MTS environment.

Recall from Chapter 4 that base client applications should acquire and hold pointers to MTS objects rather than re-creating the objects each time they are needed. One of the reasons for doing this is to avoid the expensive process of locating the remote server and establishing the communication session between the machines. Typically, an application will create objects during application initialization or when a specific portion of the application is first accessed. The interface pointers returned from object creation should be stored in application variables for future use. The pointers don't need to be released until the application shuts down, unless the application receives a communications error during a method call. A communication error might indicate that the remote server machine is unavailable. By releasing and reacquiring the interface pointer, you will be able to take advantage of MTS fail-over support on the server.

Using business objects from Web pages

From a Web page, you have two ways to create COM objects: by using the HTML <OBJECT> tag or by using client-side script code. The <OBJECT> tag is used to create objects as the page is rendered. This technique is normally used for visual objects, such as ActiveX controls. With script code, the objects are created only when the script is executed. These mechanisms work for both client-side and remote COM objects. In order to call methods on objects, regardless of how the objects were created, you'll need to write client-side script code. From the script code, you have access to methods and properties exposed by the *IDispatch* interfaces of your objects.

To use the <OBJECT> tag, you need to specify the CLSID of the business object and give it an ID so that you can access the object from your client-side script code. The following <OBJECT> tag could be used to create an instance of the Island Hopper *bus_CustomerC.Customer* component:

```
<OBJECT ID="objCustomer"
   CLASSID="clsid:6FED8869-EAC5-11D1-80F4-00C04FD61196">
</OBJECT>
```

The exact script code you use to create objects depends on the scripting language you are using. In VBScript, you use the *CreateObject* function, as shown here:

```
<SCRIPT LANGUAGE="VBScript">
   Dim objCustomer
   Set objCustomer = CreateObject("bus_CustomerC.Customer")
   ⋮
   Set objCustomer = Nothing
</SCRIPT>
```

In Microsoft JScript, you use the *ActiveXObject* object, as shown here:

```
<SCRIPT LANGUAGE="JScript">
   var objCustomer;
   objCustomer = new ActiveXObject("bus_CustomerC.Customer");
   ⋮
   objCustomer = "";
</SCRIPT>
```

Once the object is created, you can access its methods through script code, using the object ID as the variable name, as shown in the following example:

```
<SCRIPT LANGUAGE="VBScript">
   Dim rsCustomer
   Set rsCustomer = objCustomer.GetByEmail("someone@microsoft.com")
   ⋮
</SCRIPT>
```

Making business objects available to client machines

So far, we've assumed that the components were properly configured simply so that object creation would work. But what exactly is involved in configuring components for access from client machines?

To start with, you must either provide a CLSID and the remote server name in a call to *CoCreateInstanceEx* to create the object or install some information in the client machine's registry. To access components from Microsoft Visual Basic and most scripting languages, this information would include the ProgID, CLSID, and RemoteServerName registry entries. For business objects running in MTS environments, the easiest way to provide this information is to run the client install program discussed in Chapter 10 on each client machine. The client install program will also take care of installing and registering any type libraries or proxy/stub DLLs required in order to use vtable-binding or late-binding to access your components.

You can use the <OBJECT> tag on a Web page to download the client install program automatically using the Internet Component Download service. You use the CODEBASE parameter of the <OBJECT> tag to point the browser to a location where it can find the client install program. If you want to use Internet Component Download to automatically install the required registry entries for your remote component from a Web page, you must use the <OBJECT> tag to create the object; you cannot download and install component information from script code.

In addition to the normal registration, you will also need to consider code safety issues if your business objects will be used from Web pages. If you are using Internet Component Download, you will want to be sure that your install programs are signed with a digital signature. Depending on the user's browser settings, the browser might prevent unsigned install programs from being downloaded. The digital signature lets browsers determine the origin of the install program and detect whether it has been tampered with.

> **NOTE** The Platform SDK contains information about and tools for creating signed packages for download. Some development tools, such as Visual Basic, also provide packaging and deployment tools that can be used to sign packages.

You should also mark your components as safe for scripting and initialization. This is usually a safe thing to do because your objects are not running on the client's machine. When you say a component is *safe for scripting*, you are telling users that client-side scripts can't use your component to harm their computers or obtain unauthorized information. When you say a component is *safe for initialization*, you are telling users that Web pages can't harm their computers by passing the component invalid data on initialization. The easiest way to mark your controls as safe for scripting and initialization is to add the following subkeys to the registry under your component's CLSID:

```
Implemented Categories\{7DD95801-9882-11CF-9FA9-00AA006C42C4}
Implemented Categories\{7DD95802-9882-11CF-9FA9-00AA006C42C4}
```

If you don't mark your components as safe for scripting and initialization, the browser might elect not to create objects or make method calls to the objects, depending on the user's browser settings.

Using RDS to Access Remote Objects

Another option for accessing remote objects from client machines is by using RDS. RDS gives you the option of calling the objects via DCOM or via HTTP, which can be very helpful if you are accessing the remote objects from a Web page. One disadvantage of RDS is that it can be used to access methods only on the *IDispatch* interface exposed by your components. However, this limitation already applies to most scripting languages that you would use on a Web page.

To use your business objects with RDS over HTTP, you must add their ProgIDs to the ADCLaunch registry key on the server machine, HKEY_LOCAL-_MACHINE\SYSTEM\CurrentControlSet\Services\W3SVC\Parameters-\ADCLaunch. To use the business objects with RDS over DCOM, you must mark them as safe for scripting and initialization, as described earlier. The client machine only needs a registry entry mapping the component's ProgID to its CLSID.

The *RDS.Dataspace* object is used to invoke your business objects. The following code fragment shows how a Web page could create an Island Hopper *bus_CustomerC.Customer* object and call its *GetByEmail* method, using RDS over HTTP:

```
<SCRIPT LANGUAGE="VBScript">
   Dim rdsds, objCustomer, rsCustomer
   Set rdsds = CreateObject("RDS.Dataspace")
   Set objCustomer = rdsds.CreateObject("bus_CustomerC.Customer", _
                             "http://IHopper")
   Set rsCustomer = objCustomer.GetByEmail("someone@microsoft.com")
   ⋮
</SCRIPT>
```

The *DataSpace CreateObject* method is used to generate a client-side proxy that understands how to call methods on the object using *IDispatch*, either over DCOM or over HTTP. The first parameter specifies the ProgID of the object to create. The second parameter specifies the name of the server machine on which the object is located. This parameter controls whether the object is called over DCOM or over HTTP. If the machine name is specified using the form

machineName, DCOM is used. If the machine name is specified using the form *http://machineName*, HTTP is used. HTTP Secure (HTTPS) is also supported.

NOTE For more information about using RDS, including sample code, refer to the Microsoft Data Access SDK documentation included in the Platform SDK. The white paper "Remote Data Service in MDAC 2.0" by Kamaljit Bath is another excellent source of information; this white paper is available from the MSDN Web site, *http://msdn.microsoft.com/developer/news/feature/datajul98-/remdata.htm*.

Using Data-Binding

We saw in Chapter 3 that RDS can also be used to return disconnected ADO *Recordset* objects to client machines. In Internet Explorer 4 and later, DHTML data-binding can be used to connect these *Recordset* objects to HTML elements on your Web pages. Using data-binding and client-side scripting, you can let users browse through the *Recordset* objects without accessing the Web server.

The data-binding support in Internet Explorer 4 is not specific to any particular type of data. Internet Explorer 4 will bind to any type of data for which there is a data source object (DSO). The DSO is responsible for transporting data between client and server machines, manipulating the data, and providing an object model for script access. The DHTML attributes *DATASRC*, *DATAFLD*, *DATAFORMATAS*, and *DATAPAGESIZE* are used to determine where the data comes from, what fields of the data are bound to which HTML elements, whether the data should be treated as text or some other data type, and how many records should be displayed on a page.

The *RDS.DataControl* object is a DSO for OLE DB *Rowset* objects and ADO *Recordset* objects. This component supports both two-tier and three-tier models for data access. In the two-tier model, information about the data source is embedded in the Web page and each client gets its own connection to the data source. In the three-tier model, business objects are used to return a disconnected *Recordset* to the client, which is then attached to a *DataControl* object. The following code shows how you could bind the *Recordset* returned from an Island Hopper business object to a *DataControl*:

```
<!-- The RDS DataControl object -->
<OBJECT classid="clsid:BD96C556-65A3-11D0-983A-00C04FC29E33"
        ID=dsoCustomer HEIGHT=0 WIDTH=0>
</OBJECT>
```

```
<SCRIPT LANGUAGE="VBSCRIPT">
    Dim objCustomer
    Set objCustomer = CreateObject("bus_CustomerC.Customer")
    Set dsoCustomer.SourceRecordset = _
        objCustomer.GetByEmail("someone@microsoft.com")
    ⋮
</SCRIPT>
```

Microsoft Visual Studio 6.0 also supports data-binding to ADO *Recordset* objects. You can use the ADO *Data Control* object to establish a connection between data-bound controls and a *Recordset* object. First you create an ADO *Data Control* object, and then you set its *Recordset* property to the *Recordset* object returned from your business objects. For each data-bound control on a form or in a dialog box, set its *DataSource* property to the ADO *Data Control* object. You can also attach the *Recordset* object directly to each data-bound control using the *DataSource* property.

Using ASP

The techniques we have discussed so far work only if you can use COM objects from your client-side presentation layer applications. If you can't use COM objects on the client side, you can use ASP to call your business objects from the server and return Web pages to the client.

In Chapter 5, we looked briefly at how ASP and MTS are integrated with Microsoft Internet Information Server (IIS) 4. However, we did not discuss how to use your business objects from ASP pages. The mechanics are really quite simple. ASP pages contain a combination of directives, script, and text. Directives and script are delimited using the characters "<%" and "%>". You can also use the <SCRIPT> tag to mark a block of server-side script. Anything that is not directives or server-side script is copied as is into the Web page returned to the client.

Remember that ASP page scripts are executed when a request for a page is received from the client. Objects created in the scripts exist only for the duration of page processing, unless they are explicitly saved in *Session* or *Application* variables. Saving objects in *Session* or *Application* variables might limit scalability or affect dynamic load balancing, so you should carefully consider the implications before saving objects. Just to be clear: you cannot create an object during ASP page processing and pass it back to the client machine.

Within the scope of a page, you can create whatever objects you need to perform the work of the page. In general, you should try to encapsulate as much business logic as possible in components rather than using script code to do the work. Your server-side script should focus mainly on calling business objects and creating the Web page to be returned to the client.

With IIS 4.0, ASP pages can be marked as transactional. The page processing defines the transaction boundary for all objects created by the page. If any object aborts the transaction, you can return an error page instead of the normal page that was requested. To mark a page as transactional, you use the *TRANSACTION* directive on the first line of the page, as shown here:

```
<%@ LANGUAGE="VBSCRIPT" TRANSACTION=REQUIRED %>
```

You can use the *OnTransactionCommit* and *OnTransactionAbort* events to return different information to the client depending on whether the transaction committed or aborted, as shown here:

```
<%' Display this page if the transaction succeeds.
   Sub OnTransactionCommit()
      Response.Write "<HTML>"
      Response.Write "<BODY>"
      :
      Response.Write "</BODY>"
      Response.Write "</HTML>"
      Response.Flush()
   End Sub
%>
<%' Display this page if the transaction fails.
   Sub OnTransactionAbort()
      Response.Clear()
      Response.Write "<HTML>"
      Response.Write "<BODY>"
      Response.Write "We are unable to complete your transaction."
      Response.Write "</BODY>"
      Response.Write "</HTML>"
      Response.Flush()
   End Sub
%>
```

Within a page, you use the *Server CreateObject* method to create objects. This ensures that your objects are created within the proper transaction context and that you have access to the ASP intrinsic objects, such as *Response* and *Request*. For example, the following code could be used to create an Island Hopper *bus_CustomerC.Customer* object and call its *GetByEmail* method:

```
<%
   Dim objCustomer, rsCustomer
   Set objCustomer = Server.CreateObject("bus_CustomerC.Customer")
   Set rsCustomer = objCustomer.GetByEmail("someone@microsoft.com")
   :
%>
```

If you need to abort a transaction from within server-side script, you can call the *ObjectContext SetAbort* method, as shown here:

```
<%
   Dim objCustomer, rsCustomer
   Set objCustomer = Server.CreateObject("bus_CustomerC.Customer")
   ' Verify that object was created.
   If Err.Number <> 0 Then
      strErrorMessage = strErrorMessage & _
         ERROR_CREATING_BUS_CUST & "<BR>"
      GetObjectContext.SetAbort
      Err.Clear
   End If
   ⋮
%>
```

Using Client-Side Components

Finally, just a few words about client-side components. Using client-side components is no different than using remote business objects. However, if you are developing components to be used from client-side applications, you need to pay special attention to the code safety and download issues described earlier.

If you want to let client-side applications use Internet Component Download to download and install your components, you should package your components in a self-installing executable or .CAB file, according to the guidelines in the Microsoft Internet Component Download documentation in the Platform SDK. The downloadable file should be code-signed so that users can verify that the file comes from a trusted source and has not been tampered with. You should include or reference *all* the DLLs your component relies on in the download package. For example, you will need to ensure that the correct versions of any language run-time DLLs are properly installed. Your development tool documentation should explain what DLLs are required by components generated by the tool and might explain how to package those components for download.

Regardless of whether the components are downloaded, you should verify that your components are safe for scripting and initialization. As mentioned, some browser configurations might not let unsafe components be created or scripted. You can use the registry entries discussed earlier in the section titled, "Making Business Objects Available to Client Machines," to mark your components as safe for scripting and initialization, or you can implement the *IObjectSafety* interface which is explained in the Platform SDK.

Implementing the Island Hopper Application Presentation Layer

For the remainder of this chapter, we'll look at the implementation of parts of the Island Hopper application. We'll focus on the code that uses the business objects to manage customers and classified ads.

Design Decisions

During the modeling phase, discussed in Chapter 7, we noted two primary groups of users for the Island Hopper application: employees and customers. Employees of the *Island Hopper News* must be able to manage classified ads, invoices, and payments. External customers must be able to browse ads and place ads over the Internet. This suggests two presentation layer applications are needed: a Web-based application for external customers and a second application for employees. The employees' application could be either a native application or a Web-based application. For Island Hopper, we have chosen to make the employees' application a native application.

For the native application used by employees, we'll assume that all users have a Win32-based operating system with DCOM enabled. Thus, the Win32 client application can make remote COM calls directly to the business objects on the server. The application, named Classifieds, has been written using Visual Basic. Because the application is written so that it can be built using either Visual Basic 5.0 or Visual Basic 6.0, it does not use ADO data-binding. Instead, the forms contain code to populate controls from ADO *Recordset* objects returned by business objects and to retrieve user input from controls to pass to business objects.

For the Island Hopper Web-based application, we'll assume that all users have Web browsers that support DHTML but that neither client-side COM components nor remote COM calls can be used. Thus, the Island Hopper Web-based application uses ASP pages to access the business objects on the server and generate DHTML pages that are returned to the client via HTTP. Users enter data via standard HTML forms. When these forms are submitted, the ASP pages parse the form parameters and use server-side script to call the necessary business objects. Client-side scripting will be used to perform simple validation of data before submitting the form.

Implementing the Classifieds Application

The Classifieds application is a fairly standard forms-based Visual Basic application. The Ad Maintenance form for this application is shown in Figure 11-1. Most of the code is devoted to displaying the correct form, based on user selections, and enabling or disabling controls on the forms so that users know which values must be filled in or can be modified.

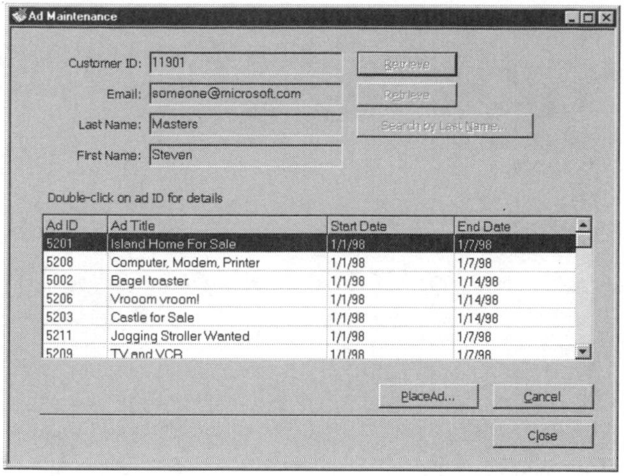

Figure 11-1. *The Classifieds application Ad Maintenance form.*

The code that interests us handles three tasks: creating business objects, calling business objects, and handling errors. Listing 11-1 contains most of the business object–related code from the Ad Maintenance form. (The code to retrieve customer information by ID is not shown.)

```
Option Explicit
Private objErrPlus As New ErrPlus.Logger
Private epRV As ErrPlus.LogRetCodes
Private objCustomer As bus_CustomerC.Customer
Private iCustomerLookup As IBUSCUSTOMERLib.IbusCustomerLookup
Private iCustomerChange As IBUSCUSTOMERLib.IbusCustomerChange
Private Const Modname As String = "frmAdC"
    ⋮
Private Sub Form_Load()
    Set objCustomer = CreateObject("bus_CustomerC.Customer")
    ⋮
End Sub
    ⋮
Private Sub cmdRetrieveEmail_Click()
    Dim rsCustomer As ADODB.Recordset
    Dim rsPassword As ADODB.Recordset

    On Error GoTo ErrorHandler

    Me.MousePointer = vbArrowHourglass
```

Listing 11-1. FrmAdC *form source code fragments.*   *(continued)*

Listing 11-1. *continued*

```
        ' Use variable objCustomer, which is an instance of a
        ' bus_CustomerC.Customer object and global to this form,
        ' to retrieve information about this customer.
        Set iCustomerLookup = objCustomer
        iCustomerLookup.GetByEmail txtField(frmAdC_Email).Text, _
                rsCustomer, rsPassword

        If rsCustomer.EOF And rsCustomer.BOF Then    ' No records in set
            ' Customer was not found.
            MsgBox LoadResString(CUSTOMER_NOT_FOUND)
            cmdCancel_Click
        Else
            ' Customer was found. Fill the text fields with information.
            FillFields rsCustomer

            ' Prevent the user from searching again until the Cancel
            ' button is clicked, and disable the user from editing the
            ' text fields.
            cmdRetrieveEmail.Enabled = False
            DisableText
        End If
        Me.MousePointer = vbDefault

        ' Clean up Recordset objects on the way out.
        Set rsCustomer = Nothing
        Set rsPassword = Nothing
        Set iCustomerLookup = Nothing

        Exit Sub

ErrorHandler:
    epRV = objErrPlus.Log(Err.Number, Err.Description, _
            App.Title, Err.Source, "RetrieveByEmail", _
            Modname, logToEventViewer, elShowUserYes)
    Me.MousePointer = vbDefault
End Sub

    ⋮


'******************************************************************
' FillAdList
' Purpose: Lists the ads for this customer ID in the flex grid
'******************************************************************
```

```
Public Sub FillAdList()
    On Error GoTo ErrorHandler
    Dim rsAd As ADODB.Recordset
    Dim objAd As bus_AdC.Ad
    Dim i As Integer

    ' Create an instance of the bus_AdC.Ad object to retrieve ads
    ' from the database for this customer.
    Set objAd = CreateObject("bus_AdC.Ad")
    Set rsAd = objAd.ListByCustID _
            (CLng(txtField(frmAdC_CustomerID).Text))
    If rsAd.EOF And rsAd.BOF Then ' No ads were found.
        MsgBox LoadResString(NO_ADS_FOUND)
    Else
        ' Ads were found. Loop through Recordset, filling the flex
        ' grid with ad information, until Recordset EOF is reached.
        i = 1
        Do Until rsAd.EOF
        With flxAdList
            .Rows = .Rows + 1
            .TextMatrix(i, 0) = rsAd!AdvertisementID
            .TextMatrix(i, 1) = rsAd!Title
            .TextMatrix(i, 2) = rsAd!StartDate
            .TextMatrix(i, 3) = rsAd!EndDate
            End With
            i = i + 1
            rsAd.MoveNext
        Loop
        With flxAdList
            .ForeColorSel = &H8000000E
            .BackColorSel = &H8000000D
            .ColSel = 3
            .SetFocus
        End With
    End If

    ' Clean up the Recordset object on the way out.
    Set rsAd = Nothing

    Exit Sub

ErrorHandler:
    epRV = objErrPlus.Log(Err.Number, Err.Description, _
        App.Title, Err.Source, "FillAdList", Modname, _
        logToEventViewer, elShowUserYes)
```

(continued)

Listing 11-1. *continued*

```
End Sub

      ⋮

'******************************************************************
' FillFields
' Purpose: Fills in the customer information text fields
'******************************************************************
Private Sub FillFields(rsCustomer As ADODB.Recordset)
    ' Fill text fields with customer information.
    txtField(frmAdC_CustomerID).Text = rsCustomer!CustomerID
    txtField(frmAdC_Email).Text = rsCustomer!Email
    txtField(frmAdC_LastName).Text = rsCustomer!LastName
    txtField(frmAdC_FirstName).Text = rsCustomer!FirstName

    ' Disable the Retrieve and Search buttons until the user clicks
    ' the Cancel button.
    cmdRetrieveID.Enabled = False
    cmdRetrieveEmail.Enabled = False
    cmdSearchCustomer.Enabled = False
    cmdPlaceAd.Enabled = True

    ' Fill the flex grid with ad information.
    FillAdList
End Sub

      ⋮
```

For the most part, this code is no different from code you would write to use client-side COM objects. However, a few interesting points warrant review. First, as noted earlier, base client applications should acquire and hold pointers to MTS objects rather than re-creating the objects each time they are needed. In the Classifieds application, the MTS objects needed by each form are usually created when the form is loaded and the object references are held in variables global to the form. For example, on the Ad Maintenance form, a *Customer* object is created in the *Form_Load* function, with the reference stored in the form's global variable *objCustomer*. When the form is unloaded, Visual Basic will automatically release the object reference. Objects that are used for only one specific operation are normally created within a specific function. For example, the Ad Maintenance form creates an *Ad* object in *FillAdList*, since this is the only function that needs to use the *Ad* object.

Notice that nothing in the call to *CreateObject* indicates that the object should be created remotely. In Visual Basic 5.0, *CreateObject* has no way to specify the remote server location. Instead, it relies on information in the system registry on the client machine to determine where the object should be created. In Visual Basic 6.0, *CreateObject* takes an optional argument to specify the remote server name. However, you will still need to have information in the system registry to map the ProgID specified in the *CreateObject* call into a CLSID. This information is written by the client install programs generated when you export an MTS package.

Second, recall that some of the Island Hopper application business objects expose more than one interface. The *bus_CustomerC.Customer* class exposes the *IbusCustomerLookup* and *IbusCustomerChange* interfaces, as well as the default *_Customer* interface. When *Form_Load* creates the *Customer* object, it obtains a reference to the default *_Customer* interface. To look up customer information, however, the Classifieds application needs a reference to the *IbusCustomerLookup* interface. In Microsoft Visual C++, you would use *IUnknown QueryInterface* to get a reference to another interface on the same object. In Visual Basic, all you need to write is a *Set* statement, as shown here:

```
Private iCustomerLookup As IBUSCUSTOMERLib.IbusCustomerLookup
Set iCustomerLookup = objCustomer
```

This statement has the same effect as calling *QueryInterface*. If you want to release a reference to an object, you set the variable to *Nothing*, as shown here:

```
Set iCustomerLookup = Nothing
```

Third, remember that we elected not to use ADO data-binding to connect user interface controls to ADO *Recordset* objects returned by the business objects. Instead, each form includes code to populate controls with data retrieved from the business objects and to take new data from the controls before calling the business objects to create or update records. On the Ad Maintenance form, the code to populate controls with data retrieved from a *Recordset* is contained in the functions *FillFields* and *FillAdList*. *FillFields* simply pulls individual field values out of the *Recordset* for the current record and places the values in form controls, as shown here:

```
txtField(frmAdC_CustomerID).Text = rsCustomer!CustomerID
txtField(frmAdC_Email).Text = rsCustomer!Email
txtField(frmAdC_LastName).Text = rsCustomer!LastName
txtField(frmAdC_FirstName).Text = rsCustomer!FirstName
```

FillAdList is a little more complicated because it is filling a grid control with a set of records. Thus, it uses ADO to iterate through the *Recordset* object, pulling information from the current record and putting it into a new row in the grid. The following code from the Ad Details form, *FrmAdDetailC*, shows how data is retrieved from controls and passed to business object methods:

```
'****************************************************************
' UpdateAd
' Purpose: Updates an ad in the database
'****************************************************************
Private Sub UpdateAd()
    Dim datEndDate As Date
    Dim objAd As bus_AdC.Ad
    Dim rsCustomer As ADODB.Recordset
    Dim lngAdID As Long

    On Error GoTo ErrorHandler

    ' Check whether information in text boxes is valid.
    If ValidateFields Then
        ' Use variable objCustomer, which is an instance of
        ' a bus_CustomerC.Customer object and global to this
        ' form, to retrieve information about this customer.
        objCustomer.GetByID lngCustomerID, rsCustomer

        ' Determine end date by adding the selected duration
        ' to the start date.
        datEndDate = CDate(txtField(frmAdDetailC_StartDate).Text) _
                    + (cboDuration.ListIndex + 1) * 7 - 1

        ' Create an instance of the bus_AdC.Ad object to update
        ' ad and customer information in the database.
        Set objAd = CreateObject("bus_AdC.Ad")
        objAd.UpdateAd CLng(txtField(frmAdDetailC_AdID)), _
                    txtField(frmAdDetailC_Title), _
                    txtField(frmAdDetailC_Body), _
                    txtField(frmAdDetailC_StartDate), _
                    CStr(datEndDate), _
                    cboCategory.ItemData(cboCategory.ListIndex), _
                    lngCustomerID, _
                    rsCustomer!Email, _
                    rsCustomer!LastName, _
                    rsCustomer!FirstName, _
                    rsCustomer!Address, _
                    rsCustomer!City, _
```

```
                        rsCustomer!State, _
                        rsCustomer!PostalCode, _
                        rsCustomer!Country, _
                        rsCustomer!PhoneNumber
        MsgBox LoadResString(UPDATE_AD_CONFIRM)
    End If

    ' Clean up Recordset object on the way out.
    Set rsCustomer = Nothing

    Exit Sub

ErrorHandler:
    epRV = objErrPlus.Log(Err.Number, Err.Description, _
        App.Title, Err.Source, "InsertAd", Modname, _
        logToEventViewer, elShowUserYes)
End Sub
```

Finally, note that errors generated by the business objects (and other run-time errors) are handled in a consistent manner throughout the code. The Classifieds application uses a COM object, *ErrPlus.Logger*, to handle error logging, as shown here:

```
Private Sub MyFunction()
    On Error GoTo ErrorHandler
       ⋮
    Exit Sub
ErrorHandler:
    epRV = objErrPlus.Log(Err.Number, Err.Description, _
        App.Title, Err.Source, "MyFunction", Modname, _
        logToEventViewer, elShowUserYes)
End Sub
```

The error logging component optionally displays errors to the user, and the errors are also written to the Windows NT Event Log. This redundancy helps system administrators or help desk technicians troubleshoot errors encountered by application users, who might not understand what a message displayed on the screen means or who might not record the message before asking for help.

The other forms in the Classifieds application use the same techniques as the Ad Maintenance and Ad Details forms for communicating with the Island Hopper business objects. Figure 11-2 on the following page illustrates the relationships between the various forms in the Classifieds application.

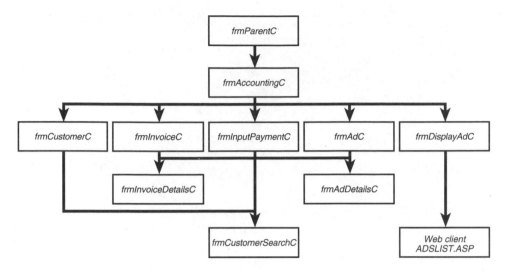

Figure 11-2. *The Classifieds application architecture.*

Implementing the Internet Client

Let's switch gears now and look at the Web-based application. The Ad Entry page from the Internet client is shown in Figure 11-3. This application uses DHTML and JavaScript on the client. ASP and VBScript are used on the server to generate the DHTML pages returned to the client. Only the ASP pages communicate with the Island Hopper business objects; all data is embedded within the DHTML pages returned to the client.

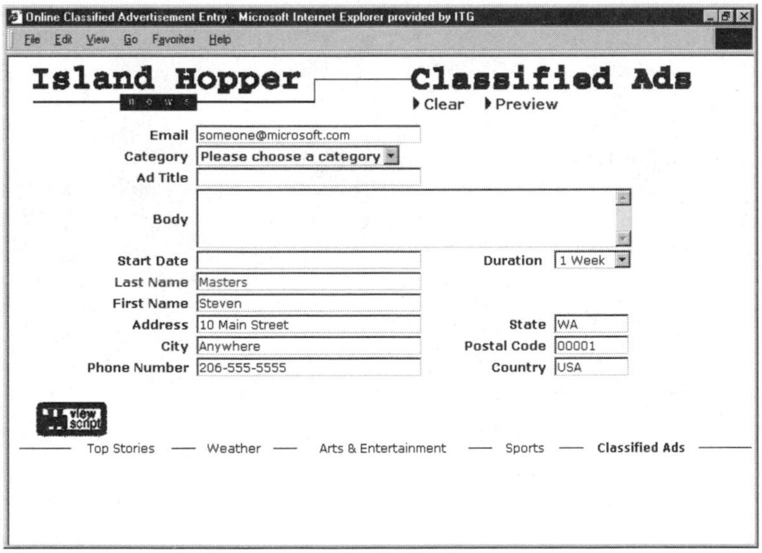

Figure 11-3. *The Island Hopper application's Internet client Ad Entry page.*

As with the native Win32 application, most of the code—in particular, all the client-side JavaScript code—is devoted to the user interface. The interesting code is contained in the server-side scripts and ASP directives in the ASP pages. Listing 11-2 contains the relevant portions of the Ad Entry page.

```
<%@ LANGUAGE="VBSCRIPT" TRANSACTION=REQUIRED %>
<% Option Explicit %>
<%
    ' File: ADENTRY.ASP
    ' Overview: Uses COM objects to perform the following tasks:
    '           Verify user's e-mail and password
    '           Enter user information on the page
    '           Generate list of categories
    '           Get unit price of an ad
%>
<!--#INCLUDE FILE = "strFile.vbs"-->
<%
    ' ASP Variables
    ' Module-level variables used throughout the page
    Dim m_strEmail, m_strLastName, m_strFirstName, m_strAddress, _
        m_strCity, m_strState, m_strPostalCode, m_strPhoneNumber, _
        m_strCountry, m_arrCategory(), m_unitPrice(), _
        m_intNavBarLeft, m_intNavBarTop, m_intCounter, m_strPassword


    VerifyUserByEmail
    AdUnitPrice
%>
<!--#INCLUDE FILE = "BROWSERCHECK.VBS"-->
<HTML>
<HEAD>
<META NAME="GENERATOR" CONTENT="Microsoft Developer Studio">
<META HTTP-EQUIV="Content-Type" CONTENT="text/html; charset=iso-8859-1">
<TITLE>Online Classified Advertisement Entry </TITLE>
<LINK REL=STYLESHEET HREF="SIYLES.CSS" TYPE="text/css">

<SCRIPT LANGUAGE="JavaScript">
⋮
</SCRIPT>
</HEAD>
<BODY CLASS=body>
⋮
<FORM METHOD=POST NAME="frmAd" ACTION="ADCONFIRM.ASP">
<INPUT type="hidden" value="<% =m_strPassword %>" name="Password">
<!-- This is the Ad Entry form. -->
```

Listing 11-2. *ADENTRY.ASP page source code.*   *(continued)*

Listing 11-2. *continued*

```
⋮
<TABLE BORDER=0 CELLPADDING=0 CELLSPACING=0
   STYLE="position:absolute; top:30; left:83">
   <TR>
      <TD CLASS=label ALIGN=right>Email  </TD>
      <TD COLSPAN=3>
         <INPUT CLASS=text ID=strEmail readOnly NAME=strEmail
            TYPE=TEXT SIZE=36 VALUE="<%= m_strEmail %>"></INPUT>
      </TD>
   </TR>
   <TR>
      <TD CLASS=label ALIGN=right>Category  </TD>
      <TD COLSPAN=3>
         <SELECT CLASS=label ID=lngCategoryId NAME=lngCategoryID>
            <OPTION ID=lngCategoryIdColl VALUE="" SELECTED>
               Please choose a category.
            <% ListCategories %>
         </SELECT>
      </TD>
   </TR>
   <TR>
      <TD CLASS=label ALIGN=right>Ad Title  </TD>
      <TD COLSPAN=3>
         <INPUT CLASS=text SIZE=36 ID=strTitle NAME=strTitle
            TYPE=TEXT MAXLENGTH=30 VALUE=""></INPUT>
      </TD>
   </TR>
   <TR>
      <TD CLASS=label ALIGN=right>Body  </TD>
      <TD COLSPAN=3>
         <TEXTAREA CLASS=text WRAP=physical rows=4 cols=72
            ID=strBody NAME=strBody SIZE=200 VALUE=""></TEXTAREA>
      </TD>
   </TR>
   <TR>
      <TD CLASS=label ALIGN=right>Start Date  </TD>
      <TD>
         <INPUT SIZE=36 CLASS=text NAME=varStartDateTime
            TYPE=TEXT SIZE=10 VALUE=""></INPUT>
      </TD>
      <TD CLASS=label ALIGN=right>Duration   </TD>
      <TD COLSPAN=2 ALIGN=left>
         <SELECT CLASS=text ID=varDuration NAME=varDuration>
         <!-- Did not use radio button here because object value
            was inaccessible. -->
```

```
            <OPTION VALUE=1 SELECTED>1 Week
            <OPTION VALUE=2>2 Weeks
         </SELECT>
      </TD>
   </TR>
   <TR>
      <TD CLASS=label ID=last ALIGN=right>Last Name  </TD>
      <TD COLSPAN=3>
         <INPUT SIZE=36 CLASS=text ID=strLastName NAME=strLastName
             MAXLENGTH=40 TYPE=TEXT SIZE=48
             VALUE="<%= m_strLastName %>"></INPUT>
      </TD>
   </TR>
   <TR>
      <TD CLASS=label ALIGN=right SIZE=36>First Name  
      </TD>
      <TD COLSPAN=3>
         <INPUT CLASS=textBox ID=strFirstName NAME=strFirstName
             MAXLENGTH=40 TYPE=TEXT SIZE=36
             VALUE="<%= m_strFirstName %>"></INPUT>
      </TD>
   </TR>
   <TR>
      <TD CLASS=label ALIGN=right>Address  </TD>
      <TD><INPUT SIZE=36 CLASS=text ID=strAddress NAME=strAddress
         MAXLENGTH=40 TYPE=TEXT SIZE=10
         VALUE="<%= m_strAddress %>"></INPUT>
      </TD>
      <TD CLASS=label ALIGN=right>State  </TD>
      <TD ALIGN=left><INPUT CLASS=text ID=strState NAME=strState
         MAXLENGTH=40 TYPE=TEXT SIZE=10
         VALUE="<%= m_strState %>"></INPUT>
      </TD>
   </TR>
   <TR>
      <TD CLASS=label ALIGN=right>City  </TD>
      <TD>
         <INPUT CLASS=text SIZE=36 ID=strCity NAME=strCity
             MAXLENGTH=40 TYPE=TEXT VALUE="<%= m_strCity %>">
         </INPUT>
      </TD>
      <TD ALIGN=right CLASS=label>Postal Code  </TD>
      <TD ALIGN=left>
         <INPUT CLASS=text ID=strPostalCode NAME=strPostalCode
             MAXLENGTH=40 TYPE=TEXT SIZE=10
```

(continued)

Listing 11-2. *continued*

```
                  VALUE="<%= m_strPostalCode %>"></INPUT>
         </TD>
      </TR>
      <TR>
         <TD CLASS=label ALIGN=right>Phone Number  </TD>
         <TD>
            <INPUT SIZE=36 CLASS=text ID=strPhoneNumber
               NAME=strPhoneNumber MAXLENGTH=40 TYPE=TEXT SIZE=10
               VALUE="<%= m_strPhoneNumber %>"></INPUT>
         </TD>
         <TD ALIGN=right CLASS=label>Country  </TD>
         <TD ALIGN=left>
            <INPUT CLASS=text ID=strCountry NAME=strCountry MAXLENGTH=40
               TYPE=TEXT SIZE=10 VALUE="<%= m_strCountry %>"></INPUT>
         </TD>
      </TR>
</TABLE>
⋮
</FORM>

<!--#INCLUDE FILE = "NAVIGATIONBAR.JS" -->

</BODY>
</HTML>

<SCRIPT RUNAT=SERVER LANGUAGE=VBScript>
' ServerSide Helper Functions
' *************************************************************************
' AdUnitPrice
' Purpose: Retrieves cost of an ad from the database, adding scalability
' *************************************************************************
Sub AdUnitPrice()
   Dim objProduct

   On Error Resume Next
   ' Create the unitPrice array.
   Redim m_unitPrice(2)
   ' Create an instance of db_productC object.
   Set objProduct = Server.CreateObject("db_ProductC.Product")
   ' Check for errors in creating the object.
   ' Show error messages if there are any.
   If Err.Number <> 0 Then
      Response.Write(ERROR_GETTING_PRICES)
      Err.Clear
      Exit Sub
```

```
      End If
      ' Find unit prices for 100-word ads and 200-word ads in the
      ' database.
      m_unitPrice(0)= objProduct.GetUnitPrice("AD-100")
      m_unitPrice(1) = objProduct.GetUnitPrice("AD-200")
   End Sub


   ' ********************************************************************
   ' VerifyUserByEmail
   ' Purpose: Validates user's e-mail address and password before
   '          proceeding; fills out form if information is valid
   ' ********************************************************************
   Sub VerifyUserByEmail()
      Dim objCustomer
      Dim rsCustomer
      ' Establish error handling.
      On Error Resume Next
      ' Create an instance of bus_Customer object.
      Set objCustomer = CreateObject("bus_CustomerC.Customer")
      ' Check for errors in creating object.
      If Err.Number <> 0 Then
         Response.Write(ERROR_RETRIEVING_CUST)
         Err.Clear
         Exit Sub
      End If
      ' Check for an e-mail address for the user; send user to
      ' login page if no address exists.
      If len(Request.Form("UserEmail")) = Null Then
         Response.Redirect("Login.asp?FailedAttempt=Yes")
      Else
         ' Validate the password and e-mail address.
         Set rsCustomer =  _
            objCustomer.Validate(Trim(Request.Form("UserEmail")), _
            Trim(Request.Form("Password")))
         ' An error means that password was not validated and
         ' user must be sent to login page.
         If Err.Number <> 0 Then
            Response.Redirect("Login.asp?FailedAttempt=Yes&Email=" _
                             & Trim(Request.Form("UserEmail")))
         End If
      End If
      ' If the preceding code completes without errors, fill in the
      ' Ad Entry form with user information.
      FillOutForm rsCustomer
   End Sub
```

(continued)

Listing 11-2. *continued*

```
' ********************************************************************
' FillOutForm
' Purpose: Enters customer information from database into form
'          variables
' Inputs: rsCustomer--an ADODB Recordset object containing user
'          information
' ********************************************************************
Sub FillOutForm(rsCustomer)
    On Error Resume Next
    ' Insert values from rsCustomer into the module-level
    ' variables on the form.
    m_strEmail = rsCustomer("Email")
    m_strLastName = rsCustomer("LastName")
    m_strFirstName = rsCustomer("FirstName")
    m_strAddress = rsCustomer("Address")
    m_strCity = rsCustomer("City")
    m_strState = rsCustomer("State")
    m_strPostalCode = rsCustomer("PostalCode")
    m_strCountry = rsCustomer("Country")
    m_strPhoneNumber = rsCustomer("PhoneNumber")
    m_strPassword = Trim(Request.Form("Password"))
    If Err.Number <> 0 Then
        ' Display a friendly message.
        Response.Write(ERROR_UPDATING_CUSTOMER)
        Err.Clear
    End If
End Sub


' ********************************************************************
' ListCategories
' Purpose: Writes category names in an option box on the Ad Entry form
' ********************************************************************
Sub ListCategories
    Dim dbCat, rsCat, intID, strName, m_intCounter
    ' Establish error handling.
    On Error Resume Next
    ' Set initial value for counter.
    m_intCounter = 0
    ' Create db_Category object.
    Set dbCat = Server.CreateObject("db_CategoryC.Category")
    ' Make rsCat a Recordset object containing all categories.
    Set rsCat = dbCat.ListAll()
    ' Check for errors.
```

```
   If Err.Number <> 0 Then
      ' Return friendly error message to the user.
      Response.Write(ERROR_GETTING_CATEGORIES)
      Err.Clear
      Exit Sub
   End If
   ' Write the option list from list of categories.
   Do While Not rsCat.EOF
      intID = rsCat("CategoryID")
      strName = rsCat("Name")
      Response.Write("<OPTION ID=lngCategoryId(" _
                     & m_intCounter & ") VALUE=" & _
                     intID & " NAME=" & strName & _
                     ">" & _
                     strName & "</OPTION>" & _
                     vbCrLf)
      rsCat.MoveNext
      m_intCounter = m_intCounter + 1
   Loop
   If Err.Number <> 0 Then
      ' Return friendly error message to the user.
      Response.Write(ERROR_GETTING_CATEGORIES)
      Err.Clear
   End If
End Sub

</SCRIPT>
```

We start by marking the page as transactional using the *TRANSACTION* directive. Because transaction processing does add some overhead, you should mark pages as transactional only if they might need to perform special processing based on the transaction outcome or if they directly modify managed resources, such as databases.

A large portion of the code is devoted to constructing a data entry form. The main point of interest here is that the form is initialized using data retrieved from our business objects. The data is retrieved in pagewide variables by calling the functions *VerifyUserByEmail* and *AdUnitPrice*, as shown here.

```
<%
   ' ASP Variables
   ' Module-level variables used throughout the page
   Dim m_strEmail, m_strLastName, m_strFirstName, m_strAddress, _
      m_strCity, m_strState, m_strPostalCode, m_strPhoneNumber, _
      m_strCountry, m_arrCategory(), m_unitPrice(), _
      m_intNavBarLeft, m_intNavBarTop, m_intCounter, m_strPassword
```

(continued)

```
    VerifyUserByEmail
    AdUnitPrice
%>
```

Once the variables have been initialized, the ASP "=" directive can be used to write the variable value into the Web page returned to the client. For example, the following code initializes the value of a text input field with the current e-mail address of a customer:

```
<INPUT CLASS=text ID=strEmail readOnly NAME=strEmail
    TYPE=TEXT SIZE=36 VALUE="<%= m_strEmail %>"></INPUT>
```

The server-side script functions *VerifyUserByEmail* and *AdUnitPrice* are responsible for creating and calling Island Hopper business objects. The objects are created by calling the *Server CreateObject* method. You might also notice that error handling is a little different in the script code than in the Visual Basic code we've looked at. In VBScript, you cannot jump to an error handler. All you can do is continue with the next line of code and examine the *Err* object for error conditions. When an error occurs, you can write a message into the Web page returned to the user. The following code from *AdUnitPrice* demonstrates this technique:

```
Dim objProduct
On Error Resume Next
' Create the unitPrice array.
Redim m_unitPrice(2)
' Create an instance of db_ProductC object.
Set objProduct = Server.CreateObject("db_ProductC.Product")
' Check for errors in creating the object.
' Display error message if an error occurs.
If Err.Number <> 0 Then
    Response.Write(ERROR_GETTING_PRICES)
    Err.Clear
    Exit Sub
End If
```

The ADENTRY.ASP page is responsible for setting up the data entry form for new advertisements. When the user submits a new ad, the form is processed by the ADCONFIRM.ASP page. The following code from the *InsertAd* method on this page shows how to abort a transaction from script code using the object context's *SetAbort* method if an error occurs:

```
Sub InsertAd
   Dim objAd, objCustomer
   Dim strResultID
   On Error Resume Next
   ' Create bus_Ad component.
   Set objAd = Server.CreateObject("bus_AdC.Ad")
   ' Verify that object was created.
   If Err.Number <> 0 Then
      strErrorMessage = ERROR_CREATING_BUS_AD & "<BR>"
      GetObjectContext.SetAbort
      Err.Clear
   End If
   ⋮
End Sub
```

The ADCONFIRM.ASP page also implements the *OnTransactionCommit* and *OnTransactionAbort* event handlers, to adjust the Web-page contents depending on whether the transaction is successful, as shown here:

```
'*****************************************************************
'Purpose: Verifies successful transaction through MTS
'*****************************************************************
Sub OnTransactionCommit()
    response.write("<DIV CLASS=box-label FONT SIZE=3 " & _
        "STYLE='position:absolute; top:75; left:120'>" & _
        AD_PLACED_SUCCESSFULLY & m_strResultID & "</DIV>")
End Sub


'*****************************************************************
'Purpose: Reports unsuccessful transaction through MTS
'*****************************************************************
Sub OnTransactionAbort()
   response.write ("<DIV CLASS=box-label FONT SIZE=4 " & _
      "STYLE='position:absolute; top:75; left:25'>" & _
      ERROR_INSERTING_AD & "<BR>" & strErrorMessage & "</DIV>")
End Sub
```

The other ASP pages in the Island Hopper application use the same techniques as ADENTRY.ASP and ADCONFIRM.ASP to communicate with business objects and return information to user machines. Figure 11-4 on the following page shows the relationships between the ASP pages in the Island Hopper application.

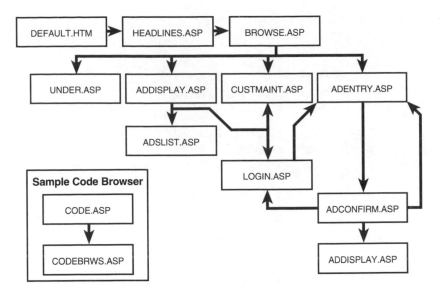

Figure 11-4. *The Island Hopper application architecture.*

SUMMARY

The presentation layer of the three-tier application architecture is responsible for displaying data from your business objects and data objects to users and retrieving data from those users. The Windows DNA architecture supports a wide range of presentation layer architectures, from native Win32 applications to pure HTML Web-based applications. In all cases, the presentation layer applications use COM to access services from business layer components.

Although it is possible that the type of presentation layer application is defined as part of the application requirements, the architecture you select for a presentation layer application depends primarily on how the application will be deployed. Business objects can be accessed from user machines only if the user machines support COM and are configured to allow remote objects to be used. If business objects cannot be accessed directly from user machines, an ASP-based application architecture can be used. If business objects can be used from user machines, you might be able to use RDS, data-binding, or client-side scripting in your presentation layer implementation. The exact combination of technologies available to you will depend on the capabilities of the operating systems and Web browsers you must support.

12

Debugging and Troubleshooting

Building a distributed application requires more than just writing code. You also need to ensure that the code works. Debugging distributed applications is a complex task, mainly because so many pieces need to work together—GUI code, Web pages, components, databases, middleware, network infrastructure, and so on. Divide and conquer is the name of the game when it comes to debugging your distributed application.

In this chapter, we will look at some of the techniques you can use to debug your applications during development and testing. We'll focus primarily on techniques for debugging middle-tier components, but we'll also look at tools you can use for diagnosing errors in other parts of the application.

Component-Level Testing

The first step in testing your application should be to test each component individually, outside the MTS environment—the same kind of unit testing that you do for any other kind of code. The easiest way to test your components is to write a simple test harness that exercises all the functionality exposed by the COM classes. Scripting languages and rapid application development (RAD) tools such as Microsoft VBScript and Microsoft Visual Basic are great ways to build simple test harnesses. You might also want to write a multithreaded test harness to be sure that you don't have any concurrency problems in your component. The goal is to verify that the application logic of your component works correctly, before you put the component into the distributed application environment. Many programming tools provide only limited support for debugging components running within MTS, so the more bugs you can eliminate up front, the better.

NOTE Microsoft Visual J++ 1.1 and Microsoft Visual Basic 5.0 are among the tools with poor debugging support for components running within MTS. The Visual J++ 1.1 debugger cannot debug Java classes that have been converted to COM classes. The Visual Basic 5.0 debugger cannot debug compiled components such as those you would install in MTS. Visual Basic 6.0 provides better debugging support for MTS components in some scenarios.

One potential problem with testing components outside the MTS environment is that your component code typically uses the object context. When your component runs outside the MTS environment, the object context is not available. There are several ways to address this problem.

If the release version of your component might run both within and outside the MTS environment, you should check whether the object context exists at run time before you make any method calls. If your released component always runs within MTS, you probably don't want to add the overhead of checking for the object context before every method call. In this case, conditional compilation is a useful approach if your programming language supports it. This technique is straightforward for calls to *SetComplete* or *SetAbort*—you can just leave the call out, as shown here in C++:

```
#ifndef NO_MTS_CONTEXT
    m_spObjectContext->SetComplete();
#endif
```

However, you can't leave out calls to create subordinate objects. In this case, you need to call a regular object creation function instead of the *ObjectContext CreateInstance* method, as in the following example:

```
IMyInterface* ptr;
#ifdef NO_MTS_CONTEXT
    hr = CoCreateInstance(__uuidof(MyClass), NULL, CLSCTX_SERVER,
            reinterpret_cast<void**>(static_cast<IMyInterface**>&ptr))
#else
    hr = m_spObjectContext->CreateInstance(__uuidof(MyClass),
            reinterpret_cast<void**>(static_cast<IMyInterface**>&ptr))
#endif
```

This code is ugly enough to deserve encapsulation in a macro or inline function! The disadvantage of this approach is that you need to build a special version of your component to run outside MTS. There is a slight risk that your application logic might be correct in this version and incorrect in the version built for MTS, but it is the best approach available for testing components written in C++ or Visual Basic 6 outside MTS.

Another approach can be used with components written using Visual Basic 5.0. MTS provides a debug version of the *ObjectContext*, whose methods provide the behavior described in the following table.

Method	Debug Behavior
CreateInstance	Calls COM *CoCreateInstance* (no context flows, no transactions, and so on)
SetComplete	No effect
SetAbort	No effect
EnableCommit	No effect
DisableCommit	No effect
IsInTransaction	Returns *FALSE*
IsSecurityEnabled	Returns *FALSE*
IsCallerInRole	Returns *TRUE*

This debug version of the *ObjectContext* can be enabled by adding the following registry key in the HKEY_LOCAL_MACHINE hive: Software\Microsoft\Transaction Server\Debug\RunWithoutContext.

This registry key is recognized only by Visual Basic 5.0; Visual Basic 6.0 will ignore the key. In Visual Basic 5.0, the *GetObjectContext* function will return the debug *ObjectContext*. Before testing your components within MTS, you need to remember to disable the debug *ObjectContext* by removing this key. The major advantage of this approach is that you don't need to build a special version of your component—it's the easiest way to test components written in Visual Basic 5.0 outside MTS.

> **WARNING** Be careful when you are testing components that perform multiple database updates outside MTS. Since you do not have automatic transactions outside MTS, it is possible to end up with partial updates and inconsistent data. Use test databases, along with scripts to clean out and repopulate the databases with good data, during development testing and debugging.

Local Testing

Once the basic functionality of your components is working, you should test the components within MTS on a single machine. This testing helps eliminate network errors and reduce security problems as you start to assemble your application. The goal is to get the entire application working on one machine—with correct transactional behavior and security checking—before you try deploying it across multiple machines. Start with individual components with no dependencies, and then test their client components, gradually working your way up to the full application.

Focus initially on ensuring that transactions work as expected. It's important to check error paths as well as the normal code path, to be sure that you are calling *SetAbort*, *SetComplete*, *EnableCommit*, and *DisableCommit* appropriately; returning the correct error codes; and handling errors correctly in your clients. Some error conditions might be difficult to reproduce in your test environment. In this case, one approach is to build special test versions of certain components that expose the same interfaces as the components but that simply generate errors rather than doing real work.

You'll probably want to start with authorization checking disabled and all components running as the interactive user. This setup helps reduce the amount of work you need to do to configure the test environment. Once the application is working, however, you should test that the components work correctly when configured to run as a particular user account other than the currently logged in user. You should also enable authorization checking and verify that any role-based security checks, declarative or programmatic, work as expected.

Debugging MTS Components

If your application isn't working as expected, you might want to run your components in a debugger so that you can step through your code line by line. The mechanics of debugging components that are running within MTS vary greatly from tool to tool. The primary issues are building components with debug information and configuring the debugger so that the MTS surrogate is properly launched. In the following sections, we'll look at three debugging scenarios: using the Microsoft Visual Studio Symbolic Debugger to debug a component written in Microsoft Visual C++, using the Visual Studio Symbolic Debugger to debug a component written in Visual Basic, and using the Visual Basic 6.0 debugger to debug a component written in Visual Basic.

Debugging Visual C++ components

Debugging Visual C++ components is a fairly straightforward process. You simply need to build your components with debug information, set breakpoints, and then start the symbolic debugger. (The symbolic debugger is the usual debugger for Visual C++.) For components installed in a server package, you have two ways to launch the debugger: by using Just-In-Time (JIT) debugging or by starting the debugger from the Visual Studio Integrated Development Environment (IDE). When JIT debugging is enabled and if a program faults while the debugger is not running, the fault is trapped and you are given the option to start debugging the process at the point of the fault.

MTS supports the Visual C++ JIT and OLE/RPC debugging feature. If OLE/RPC debugging is enabled, you start debugging the application by running the client under the debugger. When you step into a method call to an object, the debugger will automatically step into the object's code in the server process (even if the server process is on another machine). Single-stepping past the return statement in the object's code returns to the next statement in the client's code. To enable JIT and OLE/RPC debugging, open the Visual Studio Options dialog box by choosing the Options command from the Tools menu, select the Debug tab, and check the Just-In-Time Debugging and OLE/RPC Debugging check boxes.

If you can't run your client under the debugger, you can prelaunch the server process under the debugger from the Visual Studio IDE. First get the package ID for your component. You can get this information from the package's Properties window in the MTS Explorer, as shown in Figure 12-1.

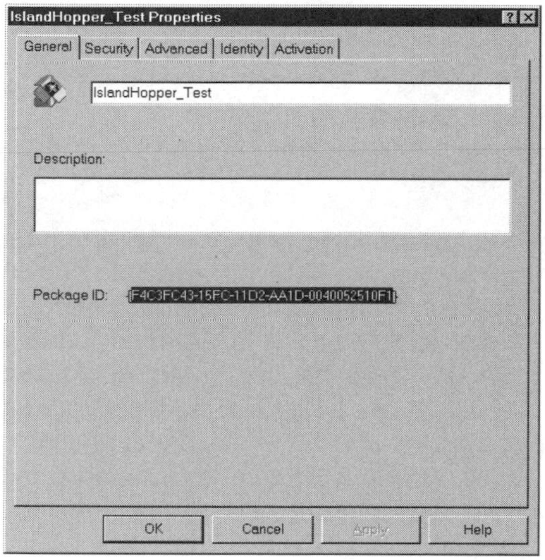

Figure 12-1. *Locating an MTS package's package ID.*

Once you have the package ID, open the Project Settings dialog box for your component in the Visual Studio IDE, as shown in Figure 12-2 on the following page. Be sure that the Microsoft Win32 Debug configuration is selected, click on the Debug tab, and select the General category. Now set the executable for the debug session to the MTS Surrogate, MTX.EXE. You need to enter the complete path to the MTS Surrogate, which is located in your Windows system directory— for example, c:\winnt\system32\mtx.exe. Next set the program arguments to the string */p: {<package ID>}*, where *<package ID>* is the value you read from the package's Properties window. (In MTS 2.0, you can also use the package name—for example, */p: <package-name>*.) To save the project settings and close the dialog box, click the OK button. You can now launch the debugger from the IDE. When clients call into your components, your breakpoints will be hit and you can debug to your heart's content.

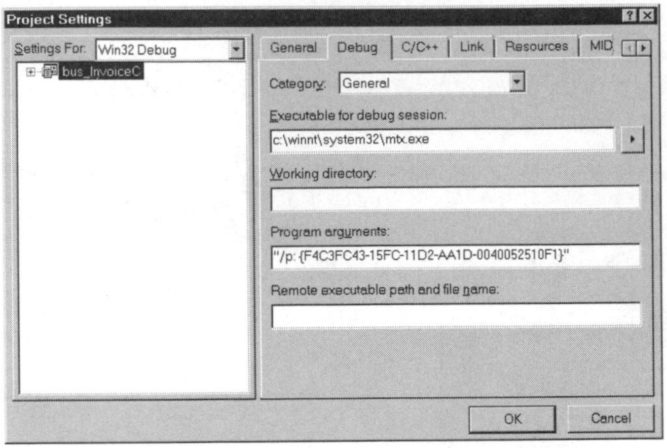

Figure 12-2. *Configuring a Visual C++ project to launch MTS during debugging.*

For components that are installed in a library package, you need to configure settings in the project associated with the client process. For example, if a library package is used by the *bus_DoWork* component, you would need to modify the settings for the *bus_DoWork* project. Select the Win32 Debug configuration in the Project Settings dialog box, click on the Debug tab, and select the Additional DLLs category, as shown in Figure 12-3. In the Modules list, add the component DLLs you want to debug from the library package. After you have entered the DLLs you want to debug, save the project settings and close the dialog box by clicking the OK button.

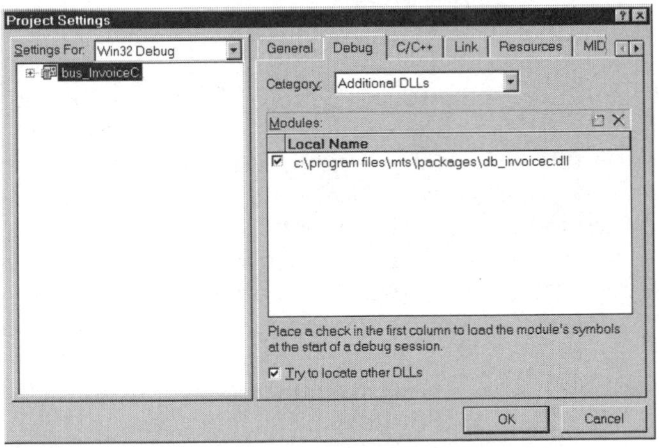

Figure 12-3. *Adding MTS components to a Visual C++ debug session.*

After you halt the debugger, it's a good idea to use the MTS Explorer to shut down any server processes that might be hanging about on your test machine. You do this by highlighting My Computer in the left-hand pane of the MTS Explorer and choosing Shut Down Server Processes from the Action menu. If a server process is left running, you might get an error message the next time you try to build a component whose DLL file cannot be written to because the existing DLL is still loaded in memory.

If you are using transactions, you might also want to increase the transaction time-out, which defaults to 60 seconds. Using the MTS Explorer, change the transaction time-out setting on the Options tab of the My Computer Properties window.

Debugging Visual Basic 5 components

Debugging Visual Basic components within MTS is a little more complicated, at least with Visual Basic 5.0. The Visual Basic 5.0 debugger cannot be used to debug compiled components. Instead, you need to use the Visual Studio Symbolic Debugger.

First you will need to build your component with symbolic debugging information. To do this, open the Project Properties window for your component's project in the Visual Basic IDE, and then click on the Compile tab. Select the Compile To Native Code and No Optimization options and check the Create Symbolic Debug Info check box, as shown in Figure 12-4.

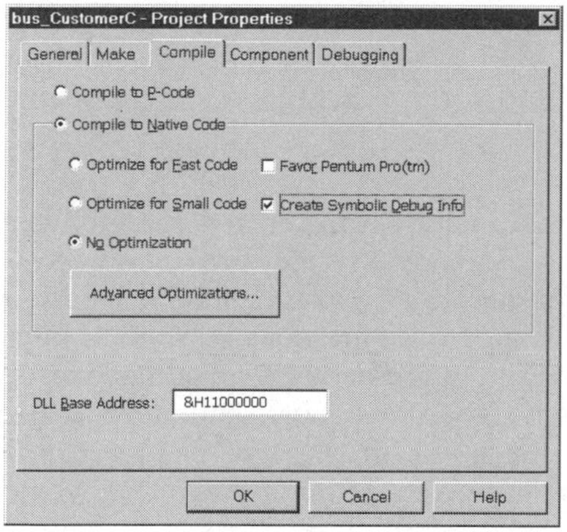

Figure 12-4. *Building a Visual Basic 5.0 component with symbolic debugging information.*

Next you will need to move your component DLL to wherever packages are normally installed in MTS—usually in the c:\program files\mts\packages directory. If you do not move your component DLL to this directory, you will receive an error message when you launch the debugger informing you that symbolic debugging information for the DLL could not be located. If you have trouble getting the debugger to stop at breakpoints in your component, confirm that the DLL is in the standard packages directory, delete the component from its package, and re-add the component.

You also need to set up a project in the Visual Studio IDE for your debugging session. In this project, set up the debug executable and command-line arguments as described earlier for debugging Visual C++ components. Then add the DLLs you want to debug to the list of Additional DLLs on the Debug tab of the Project Settings dialog box. Load the .CLS file for your COM classes, set breakpoints as needed, and you're ready to go.

Debugging Visual Basic 6 components

Visual Basic 6.0 lets you debug components running in MTS for certain scenarios. You can debug only one component from one client at a time. The component always runs as a library package, within the Visual Basic process. This means that you cannot debug security problems, multithreading problems, or problems that involve multiple components using the Visual Basic 6.0 debugger. However, you can use the method described earlier for Visual Basic 5.0 components to debug these problems using the Visual Studio Symbolic Debugger.

If your situation can be handled by the Visual Basic debugger, all you need to do is build the component DLL, set binary compatibility for the project, and install the component into MTS. Set breakpoints in your component code, and start the debugger from the Visual Basic IDE. When a client is run and calls into your component, the breakpoints will be hit and you can debug your component.

Traces and Asserts

In addition to running your components under a debugger, you might find it helpful to have your components output information as they are running. This information is particularly useful for troubleshooting in situations in which a debugger is not available, symbols and source code are not available, or bugs exist that don't happen when the code is run in the debugger. You need to be careful when using this technique, however, because your components might not have access to the interactive user's desktop—in other words, that handy assertion that displays a message box might position the message box where you can't see it—and where you can't click on it to close it.

The three primary places to output trace and assertion information are the desktop display, a debugger, and a file. Information written to the desktop display typically uses the *MessageBox* function. To be sure the message box is visible, use the *MB_SERVICE_NOTIFICATION* flag when you create the message box.

This method is commonly used for assertions. The following code shows how you might implement an *Assert* or *Trace* function in Visual Basic:

```
#If DEBUGGING Then
    'API Functions
    Private Declare Sub OutputDebugStringA _
        Lib "KERNEL32" (ByVal strError As String)
    Private Declare Function MessageBoxA _
        Lib "USER32" (ByVal hwnd As Long, _
                      ByVal lpText As String, _
                      ByVal lpCaption As String, _
                      ByVal uType As Long) As Long
    'API Constants
    Private Const API_NULL              As Long = 0
    Private Const MB_ICONERROR          As Long = &H10
    Private Const MB_SERVICE_NOTIFICATION As Long = &H200000

Public Sub Assert(ByVal bCondition As Bool, _
                  strError As String)
    Dim lngReturn As Long
    If Not bCondition Then
        lngReturn = MessageBoxA(API_NULL, strError, _
                    "Error in Component", _
                    MB_ICONERROR Or MB_SERVICE_NOTIFICATION)
    End If
End Sub

#End If
```

To write information to a debugger, use the *OutputDebugString* function. If you are using MFC, the TRACE macro uses *OutputDebugString* to generate its output in debug builds. You can use the TRACE source code as a template for writing your own C++ macro that would work in nondebug builds as well. The following listing shows how you might implement a *Trace* function in the Visual Basic code above:

```
Public Sub Trace(ByVal strError As String)
    Call OutputDebugStringA(strError)
End Sub
```

If an application is running under a debugger, *OutputDebugString* sends its text argument to the debugger. (In the Visual C++ debugger, *OutputDebugString* messages are displayed in the Output window.) Otherwise, *OutputDebugString* sends its text argument to the system debugger. If the system debugger is not active, the function does nothing. This technique is useful for tracing calls in which you don't have symbols and source code available.

Last you can write trace messages to a log file. This technique involves simply writing a function to open a file, append a text message, and close the file. This process will slow down your application but has the advantage that it can be used when a debugger is not available. A registry setting is a convenient way to enable or disable logging for a particular application or component.

Decoding Error Messages

You should check return values from all COM method calls. COM might be reporting information about system errors, in addition to any application-specific errors your components generate. This information becomes particularly important when you start testing in a distributed or secure environment, because COM might report access violations or communication errors in the method return value.

As we saw in Chapter 9, COM reports errors using 32-bit values called HRESULTs. To figure out what a particular HRESULT means, you can use the Error Lookup utility provided with Visual C++, ERRLOOK.EXE. ERRLOOK is shown in Figure 12-5. You can enter the HRESULT value as either a decimal value or a hexadecimal value.

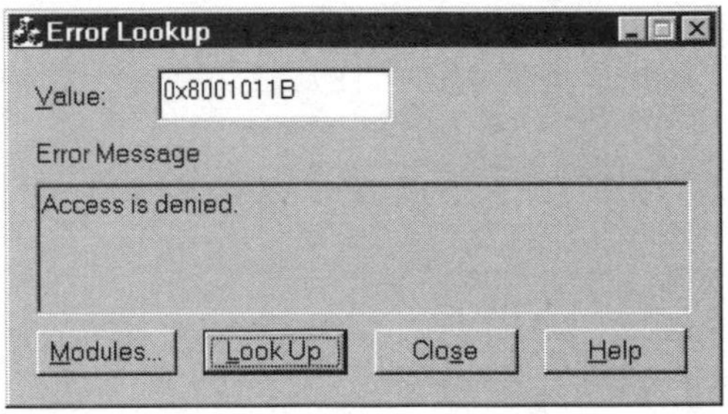

Figure 12-5. *The Error Lookup utility.*

ERRLOOK uses the *FormatMessage* API function to retrieve the message text for system error codes. You can easily call this API function in your own code to retrieve standard message text for system errors.

Troubleshooting Database Problems

If your data access components are not able to access their data sources, you'll need to use your database management system (DBMS) tools and the tools provided by ODBC to track down the problem. If you are using SQL Server, you can use the SQL Enterprise Manager to test connecting to a database, issuing queries, and so on. The SQL Trace program can be used to watch operations against your database. You can also use the Visual Data Tools and SQL debugging features of Microsoft Visual Studio Enterprise Edition.

If you are accessing a data source via ODBC, your data source driver may allow you to use the ODBC driver manager to test accessing the data source using a particular data source name (DSN). Open the ODBC Control Panel applet, select a DSN, and click the Configure button to launch the DSN Setup dialog. Step through the setup dialog boxes until you get to the option to test the DSN.

ODBC also provides a trace facility that you can use to help troubleshoot ODBC errors. Tracing is enabled from the ODBC Control Panel applet. Trace messages are written to a log file. After you run your program, you can examine this log file for details of the ODBC commands that were executed. Remember to turn off tracing once you have a log file that captures the ODBC calls and errors for the scenario you are troubleshooting!

If you are able to access data sources manually but not from your MTS components, verify that you are using data sources that are compatible with MTS. In particular, ensure that the ODBC drivers you are using support MTS. If you can access data sources from within MTS but transactions aren't working correctly, verify that the Microsoft Distributed Transaction Coordinator (MS DTC) is running and properly configured on all machines involved in the transaction.

MTS Tools for Troubleshooting

In addition to trace code you add to your components, you can use two tools provided by MTS to figure out whether your components are being activated and what methods are being called. We'll look at these tools in detail in the following sections.

MTS Explorer as a diagnostic tool

If you are having trouble figuring out whether an object has been created, you can use the MTS Explorer to monitor the status of components in your server packages. You can see whether objects are created by viewing the Components folder for your package. When an object running in a server process is activated, the icon associated with its COM class in the right-hand pane of the MTS Explorer will spin. To see how many objects are activated and how many objects are handling calls, use the Status view for the Components folder, as shown in Figure 12-6 on the following page.

NOTE   If you don't have a client application handy to create an object, you can use the OLE/COM Object Viewer, OLEVIEW.EXE, to conduct a quick and dirty test. This tool is provided with the Platform SDK and Visual C++. Select a COM class in the left-hand pane of the viewer, and then choose the Create Instance command from the Object menu to create an object. Choose the Release Instance command from the Object menu to destroy the object.

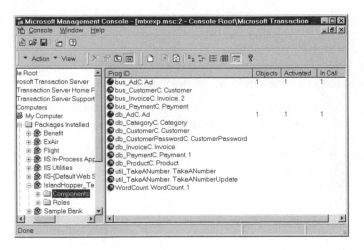

Figure 12-6. *Monitoring package status using the MTS Explorer.*

You can also use the MTS Explorer to monitor transactions. The Trace Message, Transaction Statistics, and Transaction List windows provide information about the status of transactions managed by the MS DTC. To view one of these windows, highlight the computer that is hosting the transactions in the left-hand pane of the MTS Explorer—for local testing, highlight My Computer. Next double-click on the icon for the window you want to view. The Trace Message and Transaction List windows are most useful once you start testing your application in a distributed environment, where MS DTC errors are most likely to occur. The Transaction Statistics window is useful for figuring out whether transactions are being used the way you expect them to be.

MTS Spy

MTS Spy is a debugging aid included as a sample in the MTS SDK. MTS Spy produces a trace of MTS events, including the following:

■ Package shutdown

■ Object creation and release

■ Object references, consistency, activation, and deactivation

■ Method call, return, and exceptions

■ Transaction startup, preparing to commit, and abort

■ Resource dispenser connection, allocation, and recycling

■ Thread allocation and recycling

You can also add code to your components to fire custom events. MTS Spy is especially useful for determining exactly what is going on while your application is running, particularly in multiple-client scenarios.

NOTE The MTS SDK is included in Platform SDK releases after January 1998. You can also download it from ftp://ftp.microsoft.com-/bussys/viper/SDK/.

MTS Spy is built on top of a general event notification system included in MTS. The MTS Executive generates events, which are queued by the MTS Event system, MTSEVENTS.DLL. MTSEVENTS.DLL then broadcasts events to any event sinks listening for particular events. MTSEVENTS.DLL does not guarantee that all events will be delivered to all event sinks. Still, MTS events are a useful diagnostic tool.

Before you can use MTS Spy, you need to build it. MTS Spy is written using Active Template Library (ATL) 2.0 and can be built using Visual C++ 5.0 or later. Once you have installed the MTS SDK, build the MtsSdkPs project, located in the ProxyStub subdirectory, and the Include project, located in the Inc subdirectory, to build and register proxy/stub DLLs, type libraries, and header files used by the SDK samples. Then build the MtsSpyCtl project, located in the MtsSpyCtl subdirectory, and the MtsSpy project, located in the MtsSpy subdirectory.

To start spying on a package, first start the package process or client application. The package must be running before you can start spying on it. Then run MTSSPY.EXE, as shown in Figure 12-7.

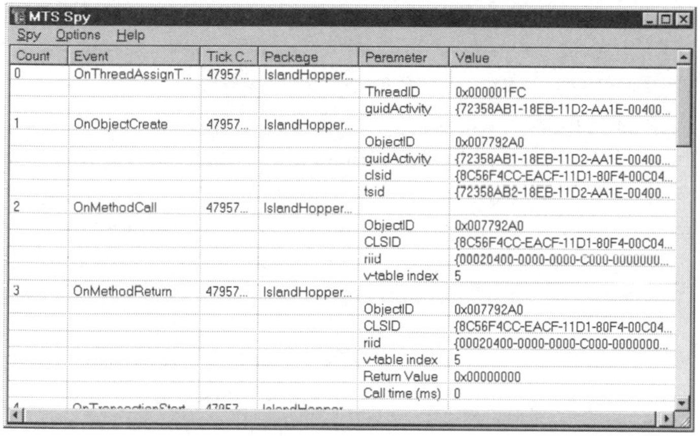

Figure 12-7. *The MTS Spy utility.*

From the Spy menu, choose the Select Packages command to open the Select Events dialog box, as shown in Figure 12-8. Select the package you want to monitor from the Running Packages combo box. Then select the types of events you want to monitor from the Possible Events list box and click the right arrow button to move the events to the Current Events list box. Click OK to close the dialog box. MTS Spy will start capturing the specified events and will display them in the main window. You can use the Save To File option on the Spy menu to write out the event list for future reference. As you can see in Figure 12-7 on the preceding page, each event includes a great deal of information. For example, when a method call returns, you get the CLSID, IID, offset into the interface vtable, and return code for the call. Using this information, you can figure out exactly what method was called.

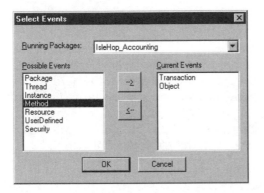

Figure 12-8. *Selecting the package to monitor using the MTS Spy utility.*

If MTS Spy doesn't provide the information you want, you can write your own event sink to monitor MTS events or you can modify the MTS Spy source code. See the MTS SDK for more information about writing your own event sink.

Visual Studio 6.0 Enterprise Edition includes a more powerful event-tracking application, called the Visual Studio Analyzer. The Visual Studio Analyzer uses a generic debugging event infrastructure that is supported by COM, MTS, ADO, and IIS. You can use this tool to collect diagnostic information about nearly every aspect of your distributed application. See the Visual Studio 6.0 documentation for more information about Visual Studio Analyzer.

The Windows NT Event Viewer

The Event Viewer is a Windows NT application that displays system-level, security-level, and application-level events that are written using the Windows NT event-logging API. Most of the system services you use in your application, such as COM,

MTS, the MS DTC, SQL Server, and so on, use the event log to record interesting information about the service. For example, DCOM writes events to the system event log whenever it cannot log on as a particular user account to run a server. MTS writes error message events to the application event log. You can also write to the event log from your own components and applications.

To run the Event Viewer, from the Windows NT Start menu choose Programs, Administrative Tools, and then the Event Viewer command, or double-click on EVENTVWR.EXE in your Windows NT system directory. The Event Viewer displays a list of events for one log at a time—system, security, or application—as shown in Figure 12-9. Double-click on an event to view a detailed description. The Event Viewer is particularly useful for detecting why system services don't seem to be running correctly or why components aren't created as expected.

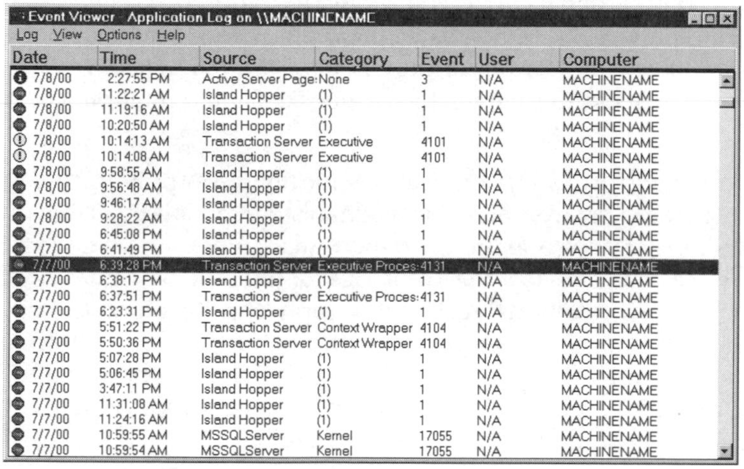

Date	Time	Source	Category	Event	User	Computer
7/8/00	2:27:55 PM	Active Server Page:	None	3	N/A	MACHINENAME
7/8/00	11:22:21 AM	Island Hopper	(1)	1	N/A	MACHINENAME
7/8/00	11:19:16 AM	Island Hopper	(1)	1	N/A	MACHINENAME
7/8/00	10:20:50 AM	Island Hopper	(1)	1	N/A	MACHINENAME
7/8/00	10:14:13 AM	Transaction Server	Executive	4101	N/A	MACHINENAME
7/8/00	10:14:08 AM	Transaction Server	Executive	4101	N/A	MACHINENAME
7/8/00	9:58:55 AM	Island Hopper	(1)	1	N/A	MACHINENAME
7/8/00	9:56:48 AM	Island Hopper	(1)	1	N/A	MACHINENAME
7/8/00	9:46:17 AM	Island Hopper	(1)	1	N/A	MACHINENAME
7/8/00	9:28:22 AM	Island Hopper	(1)	1	N/A	MACHINENAME
7/7/00	6:45:08 PM	Island Hopper	(1)	1	N/A	MACHINENAME
7/7/00	6:41:49 PM	Island Hopper	(1)	1	N/A	MACHINENAME
7/7/00	6:39:28 PM	Transaction Server	Executive Proces:	4131	N/A	MACHINENAME
7/7/00	6:38:17 PM	Island Hopper	(1)	1	N/A	MACHINENAME
7/7/00	6:37:51 PM	Transaction Server	Executive Proces:	4131	N/A	MACHINENAME
7/7/00	6:23:31 PM	Island Hopper	(1)	1	N/A	MACHINENAME
7/7/00	5:51:22 PM	Transaction Server	Context Wrapper	4104	N/A	MACHINENAME
7/7/00	5:50:36 PM	Transaction Server	Context Wrapper	4104	N/A	MACHINENAME
7/7/00	5:07:28 PM	Island Hopper	(1)	1	N/A	MACHINENAME
7/7/00	5:06:45 PM	Island Hopper	(1)	1	N/A	MACHINENAME
7/7/00	3:47:11 PM	Island Hopper	(1)	1	N/A	MACHINENAME
7/7/00	11:31:08 AM	Island Hopper	(1)	1	N/A	MACHINENAME
7/7/00	11:24:16 AM	Island Hopper	(1)	1	N/A	MACHINENAME
7/7/00	10:59:55 AM	MSSQLServer	Kernel	17055	N/A	MACHINENAME
7/7/00	10:59:54 AM	MSSQLServer	Kernel	17055	N/A	MACHINENAME

Figure 12-9. *The Windows NT Event Viewer.*

Tips for Mental Health

During local testing, it's important to maintain a disciplined approach to setting package, component, and interface attributes. An unexpected security or transaction setting can turn mild-mannered developers into raving lunatics. ("The code *looks* right, so why doesn't it work?!") You should also develop a consistent routine for shutting down applications, rebuilding components, and refreshing MTS packages. Observing the existing behavior in a component after fixing a bug is even more frustrating than forgetting to set transaction attributes correctly!

Testing the Distributed Application

After you have your application working on one machine, you should test it in a distributed environment before you turn it over to a system administrator for deployment. Your test environment should resemble the target environment as much as possible—in particular, it should reproduce any multiple-network protocols, COM transports, domains, or firewalls to restrict access to particular machines. In general, MTS applications should not require any special coding to work in these scenarios, but setting up your own test environment is a great way to test package settings and deployment instructions before you hand over your applications to the system administrator. Start with a simple deployment and build up to more complex deployments. For example, verify that your application works without a firewall in place before you test it with the firewall.

In addition to testing with a single client, you should test your application with multiple concurrent clients. You can do this with multiple client machines or by using a test harness that simulates multiple clients. The MTS Performance Toolkit, which we will discuss in Chapter 13, includes a sample multiple-client test harness.

The techniques described for testing applications locally also apply to testing applications in a distributed environment. Most administrative tools available on Windows NT let administrators operate on remote machines as well as local machines. For example, you can view the event logs for multiple machines from a single workstation. A few additional techniques apply specifically to the distributed environment. If your application works locally but you are unable to create objects remotely, verify that you have network connectivity between the machines and that DCOM is enabled. Also, check the event log for security problems that might prevent object creation or access.

The exact mechanism you use to test network connectivity depends on the network protocols available between your machines. Usually, TCP/IP or UDP/IP is used for DCOM communication. In this case, you can use the Ping utility to determine whether you can reach a particular machine. Pinging successfully does not guarantee that you will be able to communicate via DCOM, but at least you know that the machine can be reached.

You can use the DCOM Configuration utility, DCOMCNFG.EXE, to determine whether DCOM is enabled on a particular machine. This test is particularly important on Microsoft Windows 95 and Windows 98 clients, where DCOM is not enabled by default. Launch DCOMCNFG, select the Default Properties tab, and verify that the Enable Distributed COM On This Computer check box is checked.

If you are having trouble with basic COM or MTS functionality in your application, consider using one of the sample applications to verify that your machines are in good working order. The DCOM Simple sample, included in the Platform SDK, is a good way to test basic DCOM functionality. You can use the MTS Sample Bank, which is installed with MTS, to verify that your MTS installation is working correctly.

Be sure to consider *all* the system services involved in your application if you have a particularly bizarre error. For example, if your machines are having trouble contacting the domain controller or if a trust relationship between two domains disappears, DCOM's authentication goes haywire.

SUMMARY

Debugging and troubleshooting a distributed application is a complex undertaking, due to the sheer number of parts in the application. A divide-and-conquer strategy is absolutely necessary. Start by testing your components individually, outside the MTS environment. When you have the basic application logic working correctly, begin testing components within MTS, gradually building up to the full application running on a single machine. Once the application works on one machine, test it in a distributed environment.

Many tools are available that you can use to debug and troubleshoot your application. In addition to the source-level debuggers provided by your development tools, you should also learn how to use the administrative and diagnostic tools provided by the system software your application uses. In particular, the MTS Explorer and MTS Spy can be used to troubleshoot components running in MTS. The Windows NT Event Viewer is an often overlooked source of information about errors encountered by system software. You can also write to the event log, private files, system debugger, or desktop display from your components and applications, to provide diagnostic information in situations in which you are unable to use a source-level debugger.

13

Performance Validation

Getting your components and applications to work correctly is only half the battle—you also need to ensure that the application performs acceptably. In this chapter, we'll look at the goals of performance validation, as well as the overall process. We'll also examine some of the ways you can tune the performance of your components and applications.

> **NOTE** This chapter does not provide a comprehensive discussion of techniques for tuning every aspect of a distributed application environment; for references to additional information, see the bibliography.

Why Validate?

Performance validation is the process of ensuring that your application meets performance requirements now and in the future. You test your application, determine whether it meets requirements, and, if it does not, look for ways to tune the performance. Performance requirements are rarely met without some tuning so you need to consider performance throughout the development life cycle. Considering performance does not mean micro-optimizing every component, however.

Realize that what's important to the users of your application is overall system performance, not the performance of each individual component. Distributed applications have a lot of variables that can influence performance—hardware, communications links, system software configuration, application topology, and so on—regardless of how your components and applications are coded. (See Chapter 14 for more information about choosing an application topology.) There will always be a trade-off between ease of development, deployment, maintenance, and performance. The key to performance tuning is to do the minimal amount of work required to identify and eliminate—or at least reduce—bottlenecks in the overall system so that your application meets its performance requirements.

During performance validation, you will rarely be able to exactly duplicate the conditions in which your application will be deployed, especially early in the development life cycle. Thus, validation is a matter of extrapolating expected performance from the results of a series of controlled tests in environments resembling the deployed environment. The more closely the test environment resembles the deployed environment, the more confidence you can have that your application will meet performance requirements. However, the effort involved in creating such a test environment can greatly outweigh the reduced risk that your test results might be incorrect. Again, the key is to do only as much work as necessary to meet your goals to an acceptable degree of confidence and then *stop*. Performance validation is all about reducing the risk that your application will not achieve a *necessary* level of performance, not about tuning the application to the *ultimate* level of performance.

The Validation Process

It should be clear by now that defining the necessary level of performance requirements is a critical first step in the validation process. Once you have defined the requirements, you can identify a set of tests that should be conducted to measure performance. These tests should be conducted at various points during the development process to ensure that you are within striking distance of your performance requirements. As the application approaches completion, you can begin validating performance in the context of a test environment resembling the environment in which the application will ultimately be deployed. If your tests indicate that your performance requirements are not being met, you should conduct a series of controlled experiments to locate performance bottlenecks. You then remove the bottlenecks until your goals are met, as illustrated in Figure 13-1.

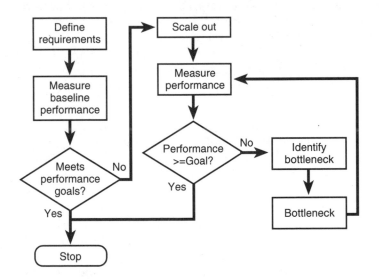

Figure 13-1. *The performance validation process.*

We will look at each of these steps in the sections that follow.

Defining Performance Requirements

We examined performance requirements briefly in Chapter 7. Here we'll get into the specifics of how to define a "good" performance requirement. Keep in mind that you should define your performance requirements up front, before you begin development and debugging. To define a good performance requirement, you must identify any project constraints, specify the services performed by the application, and specify the load on the application; you then use this information to select tangible metrics to measure and to determine the specific values that must be achieved for those metrics.

Identifying constraints

Some aspects of your project cannot be changed to improve performance. Some of these constraints were identified in Chapter 7 as deployment and security requirements. You might also have constraints on your schedule or your choice of development tools or technologies. For example, your application might need to be deployed by a certain date to meet certain contractual obligations. Your development team might have Microsoft Visual Basic expertise but no C++ expertise, making it impractical to develop components using C++. You might face some hardware constraints as well, particularly for user workstations. Whatever your constraints are, be sure to document them. These are factors that you will hold constant during performance tuning. If you cannot achieve satisfactory performance within these constraints, you might need to ask your management or your customers to revisit the constraints.

You should also start thinking about the aspects of your project that are not constrained. These are the factors you can modify during the tuning process to see whether performance can be improved. For example, can you implement your components in a different language? Can you use different data access technologies? Do you really need transactions? Can you add machines to your application topology? These questions can help you identify ways to remove bottlenecks in your system.

Specifying the services

Before you can measure performance, you need to determine what you are measuring the performance of. Applications typically provide one or more services to users. These services typically correspond to scenarios in the functional specification, as discussed in Chapter 7. Usually, each of these scenarios can be described as a set of transactions. Even if transactions are not involved, a sequence of interactions with the user takes place for each scenario. You should define the semantics of each performance-sensitive scenario—that is, define precisely what the user does and what the application service does in response, including how the service accesses databases and other system services. These definitions will drive the tests you use to measure performance.

In addition to defining which services should be measured, you should specify how often these services are used. For example, for the Island Hopper application, you might expect users browsing classified ads to account for 75 percent of system usage and users placing classified ads to account for 25 percent of system usage, with negligible usage of other services. Accurate estimates of the usage of various application services will help you create tests that closely mimic the expected usage of the system, improving the accuracy of your performance test results.

Specifying the load

You also need to estimate the load on the application. A common way to measure load is by identifying the number of clients that will use the application. A related measure is *think time*. Think time is the elapsed time between receiving a reply to one request and submitting the next request. For example, in the Island Hopper application, you might estimate that it takes about 60 seconds for a user to enter all the information required to place a classified ad. This would be the think time for the "Place a Classified Ad" scenario.

You should also consider how the load varies over time. For some applications, the load will remain fairly constant. Other applications will exhibit varying loads. For example, a payment processing application might have heavier usage during the week when payments are due. An insurance claims application would have a heavier load when a natural disaster such as a hurricane or tornado occurs. A help desk application might have a heavy load in the month following the release of a software upgrade. Using information about how the load varies over time, you can determine the peak and average loads on the system. Your performance requirements can be based on either or both of these measures.

Defining metrics and goals

Once you have identified constraints, services, and load, you need to define the specific performance goals, or requirements, for the application. First select the specific metrics you will measure. One common metric is total system throughput, in terms of transactions per second (TPS). This quantity is measured for a given mix of service requests (that is, transactions) and a given user load. Another common metric is *response time,* which is the elapsed time between submitting a request and receiving a reply. Response time metrics are often specified at a certain percentile—for example, you might specify that 95 percent of all requests must respond in less than one second.

After you select the appropriate metrics, you need to specify the required values for those metrics. These values should be realistic measures of the *necessary* performance of the application—"as fast as possible" is almost never the correct answer. A simple way to determine the TPS requirement is to divide the number of clients by the think time. For example, in the Island Hopper application we might determine that on average the application needs to support 1200 simultaneous clients with a 60-second think time. This gives us a value of 20 TPS for average load. Response time measures should take user expectations into account. In the Island Hopper application, once a user submits a classified ad, we might determine that the user will not wait longer than 5 seconds before deciding that the application is not working correctly. So we might specify the response time requirement as 95 percent response within 5 seconds over a 28.8 KB modem connection.

Measuring Performance

After you have identified the specific performance requirements, you can begin testing whether your application meets those requirements. It is important that you eliminate as many variables as possible from your tests. For example, bugs in your program can create the appearance of a performance problem. To compare test results from different performance test passes, you must be sure that your application is working correctly. It is especially important to retest application functionality if you have modified the implementation of a component or an application as part of the tuning process. Be sure that your application passes its functional tests before running performance tests. In addition to unexpected application changes, you should confirm that no unexpected changes have occurred in hardware, network traffic, software configuration, system services, and so on.

To tune performance, you need to keep accurate and complete records of each test pass. You must record the exact system configuration, especially any changes from previous test passes. You should record both the raw data and the calculated results from performance monitoring tools. These records not only help you determine whether you have met your goals, but can also help you identify the potential causes of performance problems down the road.

Defining performance tests

During each test pass, you should run exactly the same set of performance tests—otherwise you won't know whether any difference in results is due to the tests or to changes in your application. Try to automate as much of the performance test set as possible to eliminate operator differences.

During performance testing, you will measure and record values for the metrics specified in your performance goals. You should also ensure that the conditions defined in your goals for think time, transaction mix (mix of service requests), and so on are met. Within these constraints, you should make the testing as realistic as possible. For example, you'll want to test how the application performs when many clients are accessing it simultaneously. Usually, you will not be able to run a reproduceable test with multiple clients. However, you can simulate multiple clients in a reproduceable manner using a multithreaded test application, in which each thread represents one client. If your application accesses a database, you'll want to ensure that the database contains a realistic number of records and that your tests use random (but valid) values for data entry. If you use a small test database, the effects of caching in the database server will give you unrealistic test results. You might also obtain unrealistic results if data is entered or accessed in unrealistic ways. For example, it's unlikely that new data would be created in alphabetical order on the primary key.

The MTS Performance Toolkit provides sample test harnesses you can use as models for building automated test harnesses for your own applications. These sample test harnesses demonstrate how to collect TPS and response-time metrics, as well as how to simulate multiple clients using multiple threads. You'll usually want to build a test harness that lets you specify the transaction mix, think time, number of clients, and so on as input parameters. However, the rules for creating realistic random data will probably be encoded within the test harness itself.

NOTE   In addition to sample test harnesses, the MTS Performance Toolkit provides a great deal of information about the process of validating performance of MTS applications. You should read the MTS Performance Toolkit documentation as a supplement to this chapter. A beta version of the toolkit is contained in the MTSPERF.EXE file, which is located in the \Performance directory on the companion CD. Check the COM home page, *http://www.microsoft.com/com/*, or the Microsoft Platform SDK for updates.

Once you have created a test harness for driving your application, you should document all the invariant conditions for running the tests. At a minimum, these conditions should include the input parameters required to run the test harness. You should also document how to set up a "clean" database for running the test—that is, a database that does not contain changes made by a previous test pass—and the machine configurations used for the test. Usually, you will want to run the test harness on a separate machine from the MTS application, as this more closely approximates a production environment.

Determining baseline performance

After you have defined your performance goals and developed your performance tests, you should run the tests once to establish a baseline. The more closely your test environment resembles the production environment, the more confidence you can have that the application will perform acceptably after deployment. Remember, you should try to create a realistic test environment right from the beginning.

If you're lucky, the baseline performance will meet your goals and you won't need to do any tuning. More likely, the baseline performance will not be satisfactory.

However, by documenting the initial test environment and the baseline results, you have a solid foundation for your tuning efforts.

Scaling out to improve performance

If the baseline performance is not acceptable, you can often improve performance by *scaling out* your application. Scaling out means adding MTS server machines to your application topology to distribute the client load. You can also scale out by adding database servers and partitioning data access.

To add MTS server machines to your application topology, you install the same MTS packages on all the machines. You then generate a client install program for each machine. You statically allocate users to specific MTS servers by distributing the client install program from each machine to a specific set of users—this distributes the client load statically over multiple machines, which will usually substantially improve overall performance.

When multiple MTS servers or database servers are used in a transactional application, writing the Microsoft Distributed Transaction Coordinator (MS DTC) logs can add significant overhead, decreasing your application's performance. As we'll see in the section "Transaction Bottlenecks" later in this chapter, you can improve performance by using a single MS DTC for all machines.

Scaling out is often an attractive solution to meeting performance goals because it improves performance without requiring any code changes in your application. The cost of adding hardware to the application topology is usually much less than the development and testing costs associated with changing application code, especially relative to the performance gains. Scaling out might increase administrative overhead, but again the performance benefits typically outweigh the administrative costs.

Identifying and Eliminating Bottlenecks

If your performance requirements are not met after you scale out, or if scaling out is not an option, you should use the data from your test results to identify bottlenecks in the system and form a hypothesis about their cause. Sometimes the test data is not sufficient to form a hypothesis and you will need to run additional tests using other performance monitoring tools to isolate the cause of the bottleneck. Some commonly used tools for monitoring the performance of MTS-based applications are Microsoft Windows Task Manager, the Transaction Statistics pane in the MTS Explorer, Microsoft Windows Performance Monitor (PerfMon), and the Microsoft Visual Studio Analyzer.

The Performance tab in Task Manager, shown in Figure 13-2 on the following page, provides information about CPU and memory usage on a particular machine. The Processes tab provides information about CPU and memory usage by all the processes on that machine. You can use this information to determine at a high level where bottlenecks might be located.

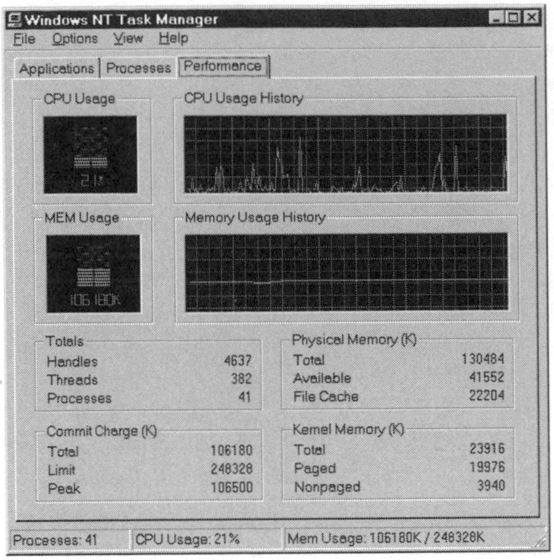

Figure 13-2. *The Performance tab in Task Manager.*

The Transaction Statistics pane in MTS Explorer, shown in Figure 13-3, can also be used to collect high-level information about your application's performance—that is, if the application uses transactions. You can determine how many transactions commit or abort during a test pass, as well as the minimum, maximum, and average response times. Note that these response times are for transactions only, not for the entire end-to-end scenario you probably want to measure. Also, these statistics do not distinguish between different types of applications in your system. However, you can use this information to get a rough idea of how distributed transactions impact your application's overall performance.

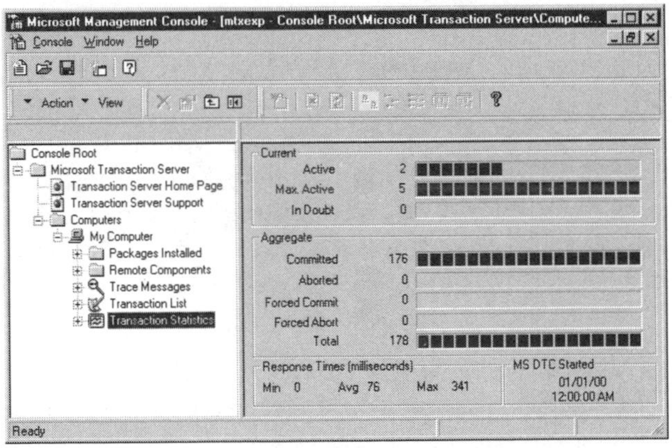

Figure 13-3. *The Transaction Statistics pane in MTS Explorer.*

PerfMon, shown in Figure 13-4, is a useful tool for identifying bottlenecks and suggesting possible causes. PerfMon is a GUI application that lets you observe various *performance counters* on a Microsoft Windows NT system. Performance counters measure the throughput, queue lengths, congestion, and other metrics associated with devices and applications. Although MTS itself does not currently provide any performance counters, you can use performance counters for devices such as memory, disks, and the CPU to identify many bottlenecks. System applications such as Microsoft SQL Server also provide performance counters that can help identify bottlenecks.

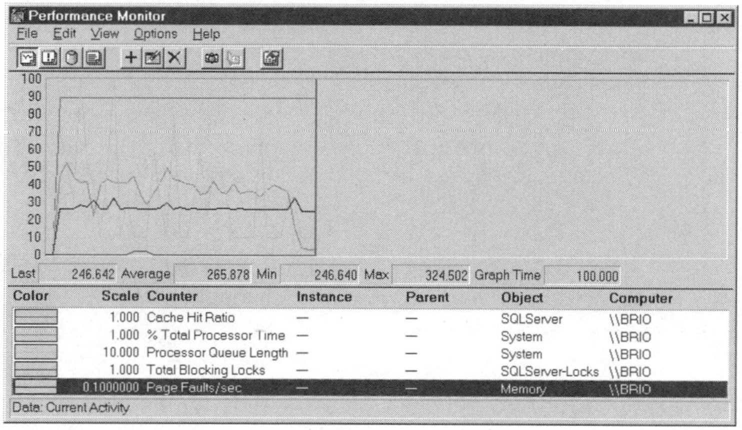

Figure 13-4. *The Windows Performance Monitor.*

You will probably want to chart a standard set of performance counters for every performance test. The most common performance problems in MTS applications are due to insufficient RAM, insufficient processor capacity, disk access bottlenecks, and database hot spots. Table 13-1 describes a set of performance counters you can use to identify these common bottlenecks.

Counter	Description	Bottleneck Symptom
Memory: Page Faults/Sec	Number of page faults in the processor	Sustained page fault rates over *5/sec* indicate that the system has insufficient RAM.
Physical Disk: % Disk Time	Percentage of elapsed time that selected disk drive is busy servicing read or write requests	Percentages over 85%, in conjunction with Avg. Disk Queue Length over *2*, might indicate disk bottlenecks, if insufficient RAM is not causing the disk activity.

Table 13-1. *Performance counters for identifying common bottlenecks.* *(continued)*

343

Table 13-1. *continued*

Counter	Description	Bottleneck Symptom
Physical Disk: Avg. Disk Queue Length	Average number of read and write requests queued up during the sampling interval	Queue lengths over *2*, in conjunction with % Disk Time over *85%*, might indicate disk bottlenecks, if insufficient RAM is not causing the disk activity.
System: % Total Processor Time	Percentage of time processors are busy doing useful work	Percentages consistently over *80%* indicate CPU bottlenecks.
System: Processor Queue Length	Instantaneous count of the number of threads queued up waiting for processor cycles	Queue lengths greater than *2* generally indicate processor congestion.
SQL Server: Cache Hit Ratio	Percentage of time that SQL Server finds data in its cache	Percentages less than *80%* indicate that insufficient RAM has been allocated to SQL Server.
SQL Server–Locks: Total Blocking Locks	Number of locks blocking other processes	High counts can indicate database hot spots.

NOTE Many other performance counters are available—you can find information about the counters, using PerfMon, tuning your system in the Platform SDK, the Windows NT Resource Kit, and other Microsoft resource kits.

The Visual Studio Analyzer, included with Microsoft Visual Studio 6.0, can also be used to monitor performance counters. In addition, it can be used to monitor events related to your application's components and communication between components. Both COM and MTS fire events that the Visual Studio Analyzer can capture, thus helping you to identify performance bottlenecks related to your component implementations. For example, you can identify method calls that are consistently slow.

NOTE Visual Studio 6.0 provides extensive documentation on using the Visual Studio Analyzer.

After you have collected data using the performance monitoring tools, you should know whether a bottleneck exists and what is causing it. Based on your hypothesis about the cause of a bottleneck, you need to devise and implement a solution to the problem. Sometimes this process is easy, but often the performance data does not give a clear indication of how the problem might be fixed. In this case, you might need to conduct a number of experiments, changing one aspect of the application or test environment at a time and observing how those changes impact performance. As you gain more experience with performance tuning, you'll begin to see common problems and solutions. Some of the common problems the Microsoft COM team has identified in its performance work are listed in the following section, "Common Bottlenecks." After you change the application or test environment to eliminate the bottleneck, you should retest the application to verify that the bottleneck has indeed been eliminated. If the change has no impact or makes performance worse, you should undo the change and try something else.

Common Bottlenecks

The performance group in the COM team has identified several common bottlenecks seen in MTS-based applications. These bottlenecks and some of the experiments done to identify them are described in the MTS Performance Toolkit. In this section, we will look at some of the more common bottlenecks and how to work around them.

SQL Server Bottlenecks

Both the communication protocol and the login credentials used for SQL Server connections can be tuned to provide better performance.

Client protocols

The named pipe communication protocol is the default client protocol for SQL Server. However, you can achieve better performance and higher scalability using TCP/IP as the client protocol. To use TCP/IP, first enable TCP/IP Sockets in SQL Server using the SQL Server Setup program. Then for each system that runs components that access SQL Server, use the SQL Client Configuration Utility to specify TCP/IP Sockets as the default network on the Net Library tab. You must stop and restart SQL Server in order to make the changes take effect.

Using the system administrator login

When you use the system administrator login to access SQL Server, the master database will be written to in every transaction. However, your application probably does not use the master database. To avoid the overhead of accessing the master database, create a specific login for the application, make the default database for the new login the database the application accesses, and use this login for all data source names (DSNs) or connection strings in the application.

Data Access Bottlenecks

Accessing data is an expensive process—you can almost always find ways of improving data access performance. This section describes a few of the data access gotchas to look out for.

File DSNs

As we saw in Chapter 8, File DSNs provide an easy way for developers to define the database they need to access. However, File DSNs have very poor performance because the system must continually open and read the .DSN file to determine the database connection parameters. You can achieve substantially better performance using User DSNs, System DSNs, or inline connection strings. You can create a User DSN or a System DSN using the ODBC Data Source Administrator. These types of DSNs might make system administration a little more complex, since you can no longer simply copy a .DSN file from one place to another. However, the performance gains typically outweigh the increased administration costs. You might also choose to modify your components to directly specify the connection string rather than using a DSN when opening ADO *Connection* or *Recordset* objects. This technique reduces the administrative impact, but you might need to rebuild your components if there are any changes to the database configuration.

ADO and OLE DB performance

Early versions of ADO and OLE DB scale poorly in multithreaded clients that use connection pooling, particularly on multiple-processor machines. This shortcoming can greatly affect the performance of MTS components and ASP pages. Microsoft Data Access Components (MDAC) 2.0 and later contain fixes for this problem—if you have the option to use MDAC 2.0 or later, you should do so. Otherwise, you can work around this problem by scaling out the application, hosting your MTS components on multiple server machines. Another work-around is to modify components that are bottlenecks to use ODBC directly.

Late-binding to data access components

As we've seen in earlier chapters, late-binding to COM components is inherently slower than vtable-binding or early-binding because late-binding must make multiple calls through the *IDispatch* interface for each method call in the client. In addition, there is the cost of packaging method call parameters into the data structures required by the *IDispatch Invoke* method. If your development tool provides support, using early-binding or vtable-binding will improve your application's performance.

Transaction Bottlenecks

Transactions can also be a source of bottlenecks. In this section, we'll look at two methods for tuning the MS DTC to enhance the performance of your application.

MS DTC log device

The MS DTC writes log records for every transaction. If the log is stored on a slow hard drive, it can create a bottleneck. You can easily improve the performance of an application that uses transactions by configuring the MS DTC to store its log on a dedicated, fast drive with a high-speed controller.

Multiple MS DTCs

By default, each machine running SQL Server and MTS will use a local MS DTC. The overhead of communicating between all the MS DTCs can impact your application's performance. You can reduce this bottleneck by configuring your system to use a single MS DTC. You can set up a remote MS DTC by stopping the MS DTC service, removing the MS DTC service from the local machine, and then using the MS DTC Control Panel applet to point to the machine on which the MS DTC is running.

Other Bottlenecks

The MTS Performance Toolkit provides a more complete list of potential bottlenecks. In this section, we'll look at just two more examples: accessing the system registry and dynamic memory allocation.

Accessing the system registry

Reading the system registry is an expensive process. If you are using the registry to store configuration information for your application, try to design your components and applications to read the information only once. Applications can then store the relevant information in local variables. Components can store the information in the Shared Property Manager (SPM) so that it is readily accessible to all objects in the process.

Dynamic memory allocation

Dynamic memory allocation is another expensive process that should be eliminated if possible. Allocation is especially expensive when heaps are created and destroyed. Microsoft Visual Basic 5.0 is particularly troublesome—it releases and re-creates project heap space on your behalf even when the heap space can be reused. To work around this problem, create a *Main* function in each project that takes out a reference to itself, as shown in the following code snippet:

```
Dim MyServerLock as ServerLock
Sub Main()
if MyServerLock is Nothing then Set MyServerLock = New ServerLock
End Sub
```

SUMMARY

Once you have created a working application, you need to ensure that it meets your performance requirements today and can scale to meet performance requirements in the future. Performance validation is a process for determining, to an acceptable degree of uncertainty and with an acceptable amount of effort, whether requirements are met. The goal is to minimize the risk that the application will not perform acceptably once it is deployed.

In order to validate performance, you must know what your performance requirements are. To define a good performance requirement, you must identify project constraints, specify services provided by the application, specify application load, and select tangible metrics with specific values that must be achieved. During validation, you test your application to see whether the requirements are met. If not, you tune the portions of the system that are bottlenecks and retest the application. This process is repeated until performance requirements are met. Some of the common bottlenecks in MTS-based applications are using the default system administrator login for SQL Server database access, using the named pipe communication protocol with SQL Server, using File DSNs to access databases, using early versions of ADO and OLE DB, using transactions when they aren't necessary, and using multiple instances of the MS DTC.

Ideally, performance would be tested in the environment in which the application will be deployed, but this is generally unrealistic. Usually, you will want to test performance throughout the development life cycle, to reduce the risk that you will find major bottlenecks within your components after development and testing are complete. In addition, the environment used for performance validation might differ from the deployment environment—the network load might be different, large numbers of clients might be simulated by a test harness, and so on. These differences introduce some uncertainty into the validation results, but this uncertainty is usually acceptable because of the high costs of exactly duplicating the deployed environment during testing.

A number of tools and documents are available to help you locate and reduce bottlenecks in your application. The MTS Performance Toolkit provides a wealth of information about the tuning process and common bottlenecks, as well as a sample test harness that you can modify to tune your own applications. Information about tuning Windows NT, SQL Server, IIS, ASP, and so on can be found on the Microsoft Web site. Several performance-tuning white papers available on the Web site are also referenced in the bibliography.

14

Deploying Your
Distributed Application

Now that your application has been tested, debugged, and tuned, it's time to deploy the application to its final destination. Usually, system administrators are responsible for deploying the application. However, understanding deployment issues can help designers and developers make better decisions about the application's physical design and implementation. And anyway, you're going to need to deploy the application to your development or test environment in order to test, debug, and tune it. In this chapter, we look at some of the considerations that go into defining an application distribution *topology* as well as the techniques used to deploy MTS application packages.

Choosing a Topology

An application distribution topology defines the type, number, and configuration of server machines your application will run on. Usually, MTS-based application packages are developed in such a way that they can be deployed on any server machine. This *location transparency* is key to building scalable, reliable applications. Location-transparent packages can run on multiple server machines to handle additional load with no loss in performance. Packages can also be replicated across a *cluster,* to provide better reliability if a server machine fails. A cluster is a group of physical machines that acts as a single logical machine.

A topology is selected based on the existing corporate computing infrastructure and policies, results of performance tuning, and any implementation-specific constraints on location transparency. When choosing a topology, you need to consider the placement of system servers such as Microsoft SQL Server, Microsoft Message Queue Server (MSMQ), and Microsoft Internet Information Server (IIS), in addition to the placement of your application packages.

Integrating into the Existing Enterprise

Most distributed applications will be deployed into an existing computing infrastructure, so certain aspects of the topology might be predetermined. For example, an application might use an existing database running on a dedicated database server machine. Corporate policy might dictate that applications cannot be installed on the database server machine. Therefore, you will need to deploy the application to another machine—and ensure that the appropriate communications protocols are in place, that connectivity exists between the machines, that the application can access the remote database with appropriate security credentials, and so on.

Corporate computing policies can also have a big impact when you are deploying applications that will be accessible to external users over the Internet. Typically, most server machines will run behind a firewall to prevent random external users from accessing confidential information. There might be multiple levels of firewalls, each with different restrictions on who can penetrate the firewall and what type of communication is permitted. You might be required to deploy Web servers, applications, and database servers behind different firewalls. And again, you'll need to ensure that appropriate communications protocols, physical connectivity, and security credentials are available between the machines.

If you are deploying an application that was developed in-house, integration issues like these should be documented in the application requirements, as discussed in Chapter 7, since these issues can have a substantial impact on the application's design. The application's physical design documentation might also contain suggestions for deploying the application based on known integration issues. If there are any implementation-specific constraints on how the application is deployed, these should also be documented in the physical design documentation, as discussed in Chapter 10.

Meeting Performance Needs

Although the existing computing infrastructure and policies might impose some constraints on how you deploy your application, you will probably still have some leeway in defining the application distribution topology. The results of performance testing and tuning, as discussed in Chapter 13, can help you further refine your topology. For example, you might be able to meet your performance goals with a single server, as long as the server machine meets minimum processor speed, memory, and disk access speed requirements, or if the DBMS is configured in a particular way. Alternatively, during performance testing you might have found that you could meet your performance goals by scaling out— that is, running the application and database on separate machines, running the application on multiple machines, or even partitioning the database across multiple machines.

Common Deployment Configurations

In this section, we'll look at some of the most common deployment configurations for MTS applications that use IIS and SQL Server. Most of the considerations mentioned here also apply to applications that do not use IIS.

Configuration 1: Using a single node

In the first configuration, shown in Figure 14-1, IIS, SQL Server, and the MTS application are all installed on a single server machine, or node. All clients communicate with that server machine. This configuration is the most straightforward to deploy and administer. You have no special security issues or firewalls to worry about since the entire server application runs on the same machine.

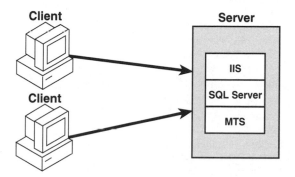

Figure 14-1. *Deploying the application to a single node.*

Because there are no cross-machine calls between IIS, MTS, and SQL Server, performance will be good for individual clients. If the MTS application is configured to run in-process, performance will be even better. The trade-off is that in-process MTS applications do not participate in role-based security.

An additional trade-off is that this configuration can support only a limited number of users. Adding memory, high-performance storage devices, or processors to the machine will let you support more users, but at some point you will reach the limit of available hardware. Once this limit is reached, you will need to deploy the application on multiple machines in order to support additional users. Thus, the single-node configuration is most useful for applications with a small user load.

Configuration 2: Placing IIS on a separate node

In the second configuration, IIS runs on one server machine and SQL Server and the MTS application run on a second server machine. Web clients communicate with the IIS server machine. This has the advantage of providing faster response for static pages and simple ASPs, since more machine resources can be dedicated to IIS. With two machines, the application can scale to larger numbers of users than in the single-machine case. And since MTS and SQL Server are running on the same machine, performance of data objects and business objects that use data objects should also be good.

This approach has some drawbacks, however. Calls from ASPs to MTS components are cross-machine calls, which are inherently slower than local calls and can cause performance bottlenecks. You might also run into difficulties if your server machines are on opposite sides of a firewall. Depending on the type of firewall separating the machines and on corporate policies regarding traffic through the firewall, configuring DCOM to work through the firewall can range from simple to impossible. You will have the most success with packet-filtering firewalls that permit you to specify which TCP ports should be opened.

Configuration 2 is useful for applications that consist primarily of static Web pages and simple ASPs, with limited use of MTS components and SQL Server databases. If the IIS server machine is not able to support the user load, the IIS site can be replicated to multiple machines and Domain Name Service (DNS) round-robin load balancing can be used to distribute client requests across the replicated server machines, as shown in Figure 14-2.

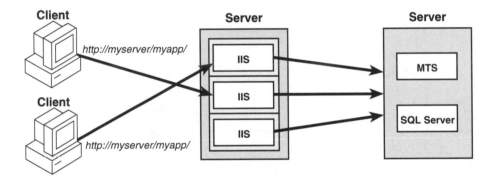

Figure 14-2. *Using DNS round-robin load balancing to determine which IIS machine receives each client request.*

DNS round-robin load balancing is an Internet standard that lets you use a single server name to refer to multiple physical machines. When a server name is referenced, the name is sent to a DNS name server for resolution into an IP address for one of the physical machines. The name server cycles through the list of physical machine IP addresses as resolution requests are received, thus balancing requests over all the machines.

A problem with this configuration is that all the IIS machines will be communicating with a single MTS/SQL Server machine, which will become a performance bottleneck as user load increases. Also, applications that store per-client state in ASP session variables will not work with DNS round-robin load balancing, since requests from one client machine are not guaranteed to be handled by the same server machine.

Configuration 3: Placing SQL Server on a separate node

In the third configuration, IIS and the MTS application run on one server machine and SQL Server runs on a second server machine. Clients communicate with the IIS/MTS machine. Since there are no cross-machine calls between IIS and MTS, response time for Web pages and the components they use will be good. If security and process isolation are not required and the MTS application is configured to run in process, performance will be even better. The application can scale to support more clients than in the single-node configuration.

The drawback, of course, is that all calls to SQL Server are cross-machine calls. Since database calls typically involve a lot of disk I/O and data processing on the SQL Server machine, these calls will be fairly slow anyway (compared to a component method call), so the extra cost of making the call cross-machine might not cause any problems. You should verify that the cross-machine calls do not cause a bottleneck that prevents your application from achieving its performance requirements. You might also need to adjust the ODBC connection pool time-out to account for the longer connection setup time over the network.

As with configuration 2, you might run into difficulties if your server machines are on opposite sides of a firewall. As discussed in Chapter 13, you will see better performance by using TCP as the communications protocol for SQL Server. Here too, depending on the type of firewall separating the machines and on corporate policies regarding traffic through the firewall, configuring access to SQL Server through the firewall over TCP can range from simple to impossible. You will have the most success with packet-filtering firewalls that permit you to specify which TCP ports should be opened.

Configuration 3 is useful for applications with low to moderate user load that access existing databases running on dedicated servers or databases that must be isolated from the Internet. Applications that need to support higher user load might be able to use a variation of this configuration in which the IIS/MTS server is replicated on multiple server machines and DNS round-robin load balancing is used to distribute client requests across the replicated machines. Applications that maintain per-client state in ASP session variables or the MTS Shared Property Manager (SPM) will not work with DNS round-robin load balancing. In addition, since all database requests are directed to a single SQL Server machine, you will eventually reach a limit on the user load that can be supported.

Another variation of this configuration uses static load balancing. In this variation, the IIS/MTS server is replicated to multiple server machines, but instead of using DNS round-robin load balancing to select an arbitrary machine to handle each client request, each server machine has a unique name. Each client machine is configured to use a specific server machine for all its requests, as shown in Figure 14-3. This variation can become difficult to administer as the number of users increases because the system administrator must determine which server machine each client machine should use. However, it will work with applications that maintain per-client state in ASP session variables or the SPM.

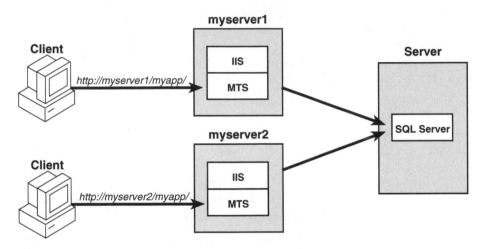

Figure 14-3. *Using static load balancing with SQL Server on a separate node.*

Configuration 4: Placing each database on a separate node

At some point, any configuration that places your application or the databases it uses on a single server machine will not be able to handle all user requests with acceptable performance. To support higher user load, the application and databases might need to be partitioned.

You can use several techniques to partition your application and databases. In configuration 4, multiple server machines host the SQL Server databases used by your application, as shown in Figure 14-4. Each server machine hosts one or more of the databases, with each database hosted on exactly one machine. MTS application packages are installed on the server machines closest to the data they use. This partitioning complicates deployment a little, since each machine that makes calls to components needs to know where the MTS components it uses are deployed. This configuration is compatible with replicating the IIS server and using DNS round-robin load balancing to handle client requests; it should be most useful for applications with moderate user loads that access multiple databases.

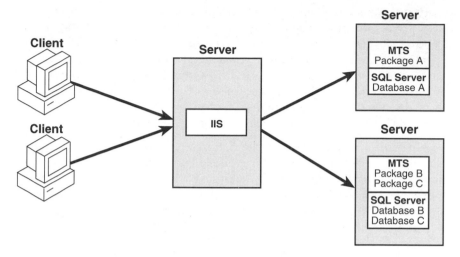

Figure 14-4. *Placing SQL Server databases on separate nodes.*

If you are using transactions and your transactions access multiple databases, a high percentage of the transactions might be distributed in this configuration. Distributed transactions are slower than transactions on a single machine, since the Microsoft Distributed Transaction Coordinator (MS DTC) must communicate with all the machines to coordinate the transaction. However, the increase in the time to complete one transaction is usually an acceptable trade-off, as the average time per transaction for large user loads is likely to decrease.

Similarly, since IIS and MTS/SQL Server are running on separate machines, you will encounter the performance and firewall issues mentioned earlier for configuration 2. Again, the increase in the time to complete a single method call or the administrative complexities of passing through a firewall are usually acceptable, since larger user loads can be supported. You should carefully test potential topologies to ensure that the application's performance requirements will be met.

Configuration 5: Partitioning the database

If your application uses a single database and you cannot restructure its tables into multiple databases or the application uses multiple databases but can't meet performance goals with each database on a separate server machine, the situation is a little more complicated. In these instances, you might need to create multiple copies of a single logical database, with each copy installed on a separate server machine. You can use SQL Server replication to propagate changes from one copy to another.

Configuration 5 is useful when a clear mapping exists between application users and subsets of the data values stored in the database. For example, all the users at a particular geographical location might update a local copy of the database. Periodically, these updates can be replicated to a master database at company headquarters so that users who perform operations across geographical locations have access to all the data they need. A portion of the database *key value* (the value used to identify a specific record) would depend on the geographical location to prevent collisions between updates from different sites.

In one variation of this configuration, the database is partitioned but the application is not. The MTS application packages are installed on a single machine. The components must contain code to determine which database server to use for any particular operation. This variation isn't particularly useful for most situations since any changes to the database configuration are likely to require changes to the components too.

In another variation, the MTS application is replicated to each database server machine. The components might use configuration information about the server machine to determine what data values are valid inputs for the machine. (Otherwise, you would need to code customized versions of the components for each machine.) Client machines or IIS servers are configured to point to particular database server machines. For example, all client machines at a particular site might point to a local IIS server that in turn points to a specific server machine with the MTS application and SQL Server database installed, as shown in Figure 14-5. This variation can be quite useful for geographically distributed deployments.

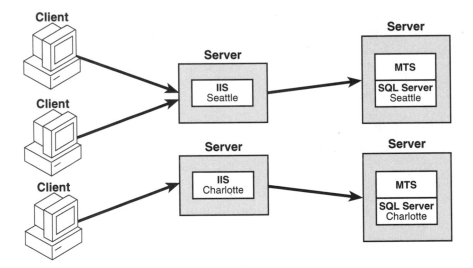

Figure 14-5. *Using a specific IIS server to access a geographically partitioned database.*

Configuration 6: Partitioning the application

In addition to partitioning the database, you might need to partition your application. Each MTS package in the application might be deployed to a different database. The most common way to partition applications is by functionality. For example, as shown in Figure 14-6, the business objects might be installed on the IIS machine while the data objects are installed near the data they access. Performance with this configuration should be quite good, as the calls from ASPs to business objects and the calls from data objects to SQL Server databases are local calls. Only the calls between business objects and data objects are cross-machine calls.

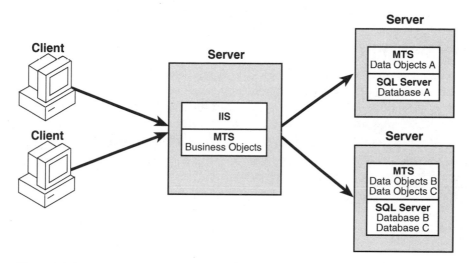

Figure 14-6. *Partitioning your application.*

Of course, this configuration has many possible variations, combining many of the features of our earlier configurations. As you add database partitioning, replication, load balancing, and so on to the configuration, deployment and administration become increasingly complex. The benefit is that your application should be able to support a very large user load. When you elect to use complex configurations, you should use the performance testing methods from Chapter 13 to verify that your application's performance requirements are met.

Fault Tolerance

If your application has stringent reliability or availability requirements, you might choose to deploy the application packages on a cluster. Recall that a cluster is a group of physical machines that acts as a single logical machine. At any given time, one physical machine is on line, providing services to clients. If that machine fails, another machine automatically takes over. Microsoft Cluster Server (MSCS) provides the services for coordinating actions within a cluster. Currently, MSCS supports clusters consisting of two machines.

MTS can be configured to work with MSCS (as can IIS and SQL Server). The physical machines in the cluster must have exactly the same MTS packages installed. The MTS Replication utility, MTXREPL.EXE, is used to replicate MTS catalog information across the cluster machines.

> **NOTE** The topic "Using MTS Replication" in the MTS Administrator's Guide explains how to configure a cluster with one or more MTS applications.

The Deployment Process

Once you have decided on a topology, you need to install components and packages on the server machines. Usually, developers will provide packages with partially configured security and transaction settings, rather than providing stand-alone components. You finalize the package settings during deployment. You can move components from one package to another, if necessary.

You also need to install the information required to connect to the server machines, along with any presentation layer applications, on each client machine. Developers will usually provide a setup program to install presentation layer applications; however, you will need to create a client install program for each package once you have decided where the packages will be installed.

You can use either the MTS Explorer or the scriptable MTS administrative objects to deploy your application packages. The MTS Explorer is most useful for one-time deployments. The administrative objects are useful when you need to install the same package to multiple servers or you need to install the package from a setup program. As mentioned in Chapter 10, the administrative objects are documented in the MTS 2.0 Programmer's Reference. In this chapter, we will focus on using the MTS Explorer to manually deploy application packages.

As we saw in Chapter 10, you might want to export two separate versions of a package in order to minimize the size of the client install program and eliminate unnecessary registry entries from client machines, as described here:

- The *full package*, which includes all the components that need to be installed on the server machine

- The *client package*, which includes only those components that are accessed directly by client applications

If you have both a client package and the full package, the procedure you follow to deploy the package is slightly different than if you have just the full package. If you have both a client package and the full package, you would follow these steps:

1. Install the prebuilt client package on the server machine.

2. Create the client install program.

3. Install the prebuilt full package on the server machine.

These steps are discussed in detail in the sections that follow. If you have only the full package, you would follow these steps:

1. Install the prebuilt full package on the server machine.

2. Create the client install program.

Once you have the full package installed on the server machine and have created the client install program, you finalize the package settings and then execute the client install programs on each client machine.

> **NOTE** If you do not have prebuilt packages, follow the procedures outlined in Chapter 10 to create them.

Installing a Prebuilt Package

To install a prebuilt package, start the MTS Explorer. In the left-hand pane, highlight the computer on which you want to install the package, and then select its Packages Installed folder. From the Action menu, choose the New Package command to start the Package Wizard, and then click the Install Prebuilt Packages button to display the Select Package Files screen, shown in Figure 14-7. After you have selected the packages you want to install, click the Next button to display the Set Package Identity screen, which lets you specify the user account the package will run under.

By default, the package identity is set to the interactive user. Although this setting is usually acceptable during application development, you will normally want to change it during deployment. (You do not need do this while you are installing the client package.) You should run your application packages under a specific user account that has the appropriate permissions to access any resources used by the package. Most server machines will not have an interactive user at all times, nor can you generally rely on a particular user being logged on. Running the package under a specific user account helps reduce odd run-time errors. You might also want to specify a user account with a password that does not expire because MTS caches the password to use while impersonating the user account.

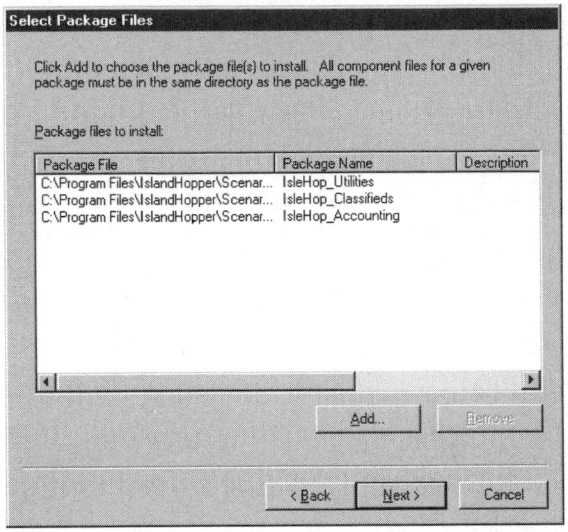

Figure 14-7. *Selecting prebuilt packages using the MTS Package Wizard.*

After setting the package identity, click the Next button again to move to the Installation Options screen. This dialog box lets you specify the directory in which your packages should be installed. By default, packages are placed in the \Program Files\MTS\Packages directory. If Microsoft Windows NT user accounts mapped to roles were saved with the package, you also have the option to add those during installation. Once you have set your installation options, click the Finish button to exit the Package Wizard. Your packages should now appear in the Packages Installed folder.

Creating a Client Install Program

After you have installed a package that contains the components client machines will access directly, you can create a client install program, using the procedure described in Chapter 10. When you export a package, the export utility creates a client install program in the Clients subdirectory of your package location.

By default, the client install program will point clients to the machine from which the package was exported. If you are exporting the package from the server machine, this is exactly what you want. If you are exporting the package from a different machine, you can change the destination machine name by highlighting My Computer in the left-hand pane of the MTS Explorer. From the Action menu, choose the Properties command to display the My Computer Properties window. Select the Options tab, and enter the desired server machine name in the Remote Server Name edit box, as shown in Figure 14-8. All client install programs you generate will point clients to this server machine until you change the remote server name again. This procedure comes in handy when you want to install an MTS package on multiple servers and have each client machine connect to a particular server. You export the package once for each server machine name and then distribute the machine-specific client install programs as appropriate.

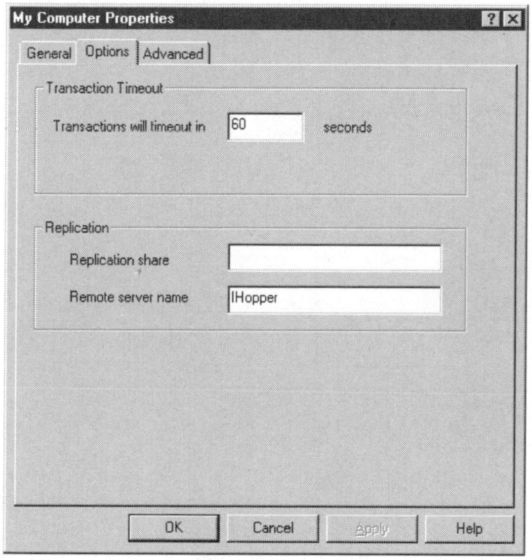

Figure 14-8. *Changing the remote server name in the MTS Explorer.*

Finalizing Package Settings

Once you have installed the full package on your server, you will probably need to make some changes to the package settings. Application developers will normally take care of setting activation properties, setting transaction properties, and configuring some security settings. Procedures for configuring these settings are described in Chapter 10. During deployment you populate roles and lock the package to prevent accidental changes.

Populating roles

All the appropriate security settings might not be known at development time. In particular, it is unlikely that roles in the package will be populated with user accounts. Populating roles is normally done during deployment.

To populate a role, highlight the name of your package in the left-hand pane of the MTS Explorer, and then select the package's Roles folder. Highlight the role you want to populate, and then select its Users folder. From the Action menu, choose the New User command to display the Add Users And Groups To Role dialog box, as shown in Figure 14-9. This is the standard Windows dialog box for selecting Windows NT user accounts. Select the user accounts or groups you want to add to the role, and then click the OK button to close the dialog box. The user accounts and groups will appear in the Users folder.

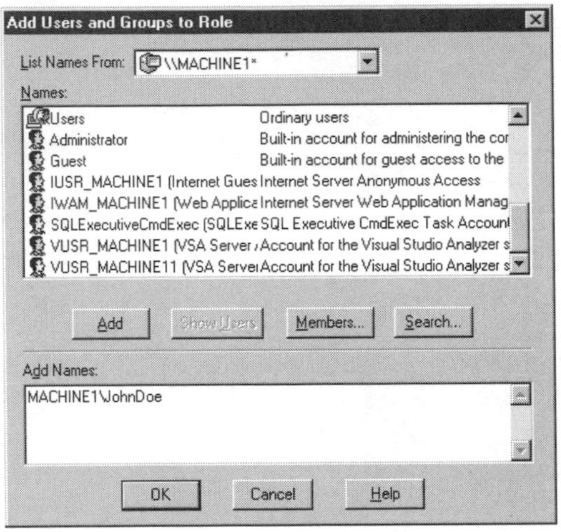

Figure 14-9. *Populating a role in the MTS Explorer.*

A convenient way to manage roles for MTS is to define a Windows NT group corresponding to each role in your application packages. Populate the role by adding the Windows NT group. Add the specific users who belong to the role to the Windows NT group. This technique is particularly useful if the same group of users must also be granted permissions to other resources, such as network shares or databases.

Locking the package

After you have finalized the settings, you should lock the package against changes, to prevent accidental changes to the package settings. To lock the package, select the name of the package in the left-hand pane of the MTS Explorer, and then choose the Properties command from the Action menu to display the package's Properties window. Select the Advanced tab, and then check the Disable Changes check box to prevent any changes to the package settings, as shown in Figure 14-10. You might also want to check the Disable Deletion check box to prevent the package from being deleted from the machine. If at some later time you need to make changes to the package settings, you can unlock the package by clearing the check boxes.

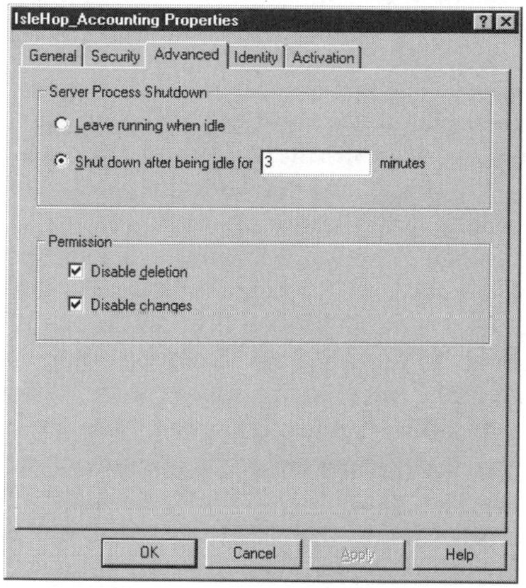

Figure 14-10. *Locking a package against changes in the MTS Explorer.*

Installing Client Programs

After your servers have been deployed, you need to distribute the client install programs, along with any presentation layer programs, to the client machines. For applications developed in-house, this process might be as simple as placing the programs on a network share and sending users an e-mail message telling them to click on the embedded link(s) to install the application. You might also want to create a single setup program that installs all the presentation layer programs and client install programs at once. (We'll leave that as an exercise for the reader.)

The most difficult part of installing client programs today is ensuring that users get the correct client install programs. If you have MTS packages installed on multiple server machines, you need to create a client install program that points to each machine and ensure that the program for each machine is distributed only to the users who should be using that machine.

SUMMARY

Once an application has been tested, debugged, and tuned, it must be deployed to its final destination. As a rule, system administrators are responsible for deploying the application. Since MTS application packages are usually location transparent, the system administrator has a great deal of flexibility in deciding how to deploy the application.

An application distribution topology is determined based on existing computing infrastructure and corporate policy, results of performance tuning, and any implementation-specific constraints. The topology must consider the placement of system servers such as SQL Server, MSMQ, and IIS in addition to the placement of your application packages. Topologies can range from a single server node to complex configurations of multiple servers. If you have high reliability or availability requirements, you might need to install the application on one or more clusters. As you add server machines to the topology, administration of the application becomes more difficult but you are able to support greater user load. There are trade-offs between the scalability achieved by distributing the application over more machines, the network traffic generated by cross-machine calls, cross-machine security considerations, and administrative complexity. It is important to find a balance that satisfies your application's performance requirements and provides room for future growth without being overly complex.

During deployment, the system administrator will install packages on server machines, export client install programs to be installed on individual client machines, and finalize the package settings. While activation properties, transaction properties, and some security settings can be set during development, the final security settings probably won't be known until deployment time. In particular, system administrators are usually responsible for populating roles with user accounts. Once the application packages have been installed, they should be locked to prevent accidental changes to their settings.

THREE

Beyond MTS

In Part Three, we'll look at some other technologies you can use today in your distributed applications. We'll examine how the COM Transaction Integrator (COMTI) can be used to connect MTS applications with IBM mainframe applications using the Customer Information Control System (CICS) or Information Management Systems (IMS). We'll also look at how to use Microsoft Message Queue Server (MSMQ) to build time-independent three-tier applications. And we'll take a look into the future, examining the features planned for the initial release of COM+.

15

Extending the Application

The techniques discussed in Part Two meet the needs of many distributed applications. However, some applications might need to use technologies other than COM, MTS, ADO, and ASP. Two of these alternative technologies were introduced in Chapter 6: the Microsoft COM Transaction Integrator (COMTI) and Microsoft Message Queue Server (MSMQ). In this chapter, we will look at how to develop components and applications that use these two technologies.

Developing Components with COMTI

COMTI, included with Microsoft Systems Network Architecture (SNA) Server 4.0 and later, is used to integrate Microsoft Windows DNA applications with transaction programs running under the Customer Information Control System (CICS) or Information Management Systems (IMS) on IBM Multiple Virtual Storage (MVS) mainframe computers. COMTI contains a Microsoft Management Console (MMC) snap-in for administering COMTI, the Component Builder for creating COMTI components, and the COMTI run-time proxy. These are installed when you select the COM Transaction Integrator option in the SNA Server setup program. SNA Server is used to provide LU 6.2 communications with the mainframe computer.

As we saw in Chapter 6, COMTI encapsulates CICS and IMS applications in Automation objects that can be accessed from PC-based client applications. The Automation objects are generated by the COMTI run-time proxy that runs within MTS. The run-time proxy uses a type library produced by the Component Builder to generate the Automation objects on-the-fly. The combination of the run-time proxy and the type library is called a *COMTI component*.

NOTE If you are not interested in interoperating with CICS or IMS, you can skip to the section "Developing Applications with MSMQ" later in this chapter.

Using the Component Builder

The COMTI Component Builder is a stand-alone GUI application that lets you automatically create a type library from the COBOL declarations of an existing CICS or IMS application, or vice versa. In this section, you will learn how to use the Component Builder to create COMTI components from existing CICS or IMS applications.

To create a component, run the Component Builder by selecting Programs, then Microsoft SNA Server, then COM Transaction Integrator, and finally Component Builder from the Start menu. Choose the New command from the Component Builder File menu to display the New Component Library dialog box, shown in Figure 15-1. In this dialog box, you enter the name of the type library you want to create, the name of the interface to define, a version number, and an optional description. You also specify whether the component is communicating with a CICS LINK, a CICS (the nonlinked model using straight LU 6.2 communication), or an IMS environment. In addition, you specify the transactional requirements for the component. Once these values have been specified, click the OK button to close the dialog box and continue creating your component.

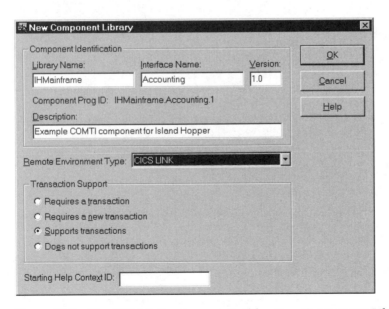

Figure 15-1. *The COMTI Component Builder New Component Library dialog box.*

Now you can use the COBOL wizard to import the COBOL data declarations from a transaction program and define methods on the interface exposed by your component. In the left-hand pane of the Component Builder, right-click your component, select Import, and then choose COBOL wizard from the pop-up menu. The COBOL wizard walks you through the process of importing data declarations, one method at a time. First you must specify a COBOL file to import, and then you can choose to create a method or a *Recordset* object. (If you run the wizard on an existing component, you can also update method or *Recordset* definitions.) *Recordset* objects are used to access arrays of COBOL tables, and can be accessed by clients as ADO *Recordset* objects. If you create a method from a COBOL program that includes a fixed-length or variable-length table in the data declarations, a *Recordset* type will be implicitly defined. If you create a *Recordset* object explicitly, you can specify the name of the *Recordset* type that will be defined.

Usually, you will choose to create a method. Choosing this option displays a wizard screen, on which you can specify the name of the method your COM clients will use as well as the information required to connect to the host program running on the mainframe. The wizard will provide reasonable default values for all these settings. After you have entered your own values, click Next to move to the next screen of the wizard, on which you specify the data declarations to use as parameters in the method call. Click Next to display a screen that lets you specify whether each parameter should be input only, output only, input and output, or a return value. As shown in Figure 15-2, the parameters *NAME* and *ACCNUM* have been specified as input only parameters and the parameter *ACCBAL* has been specified as a return value. When you click the Next button on this screen, the wizard indicates whether any errors have occurred while your selections were being processed. You can then click Finish to finalize the method definition.

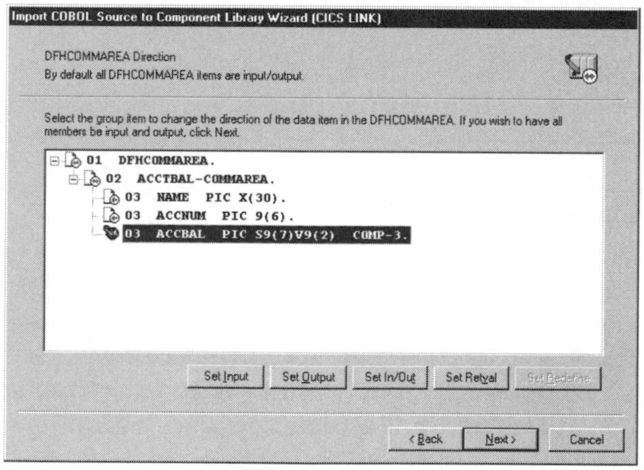

Figure 15-2. *Specifying parameters for a new COMTI component method.*

Once you have added all the methods you want in your component, choose the Save command from the File menu to generate the type library for your component.

Transaction programs supported by COMTI

Not every CICS or IMS program can be used "as is" by COMTI. Three types of transaction programs are supported by COMTI: CICS LINK, CICS (nonlinked model), and IMS. COMTI normally expects that each transaction program contains a single request/reply sequence. (The one exception is a transaction program that returns tables of data.)

CICS programs with embedded terminal logic must be restructured to separate terminal logic from business logic. If a CICS transaction program has already been structured to use a distributed program link (DPL), it will probably work as is. COMTI supports CICS LINK model programs with fixed-size *Recordset* objects but not with unbounded *Recordset* objects.

CICS nonlink model programs can use both fixed-size and unbounded *Recordset* objects. However, nonlink model programs are more complicated than LINK model programs. The transaction program must issue Advanced Program-to-Program Communication (APPC) or Common Programming Interface for Communications (CPIC) verbs to send and receive parameters. Transaction programs that want to participate in distributed transactions must also issue the appropriate verbs to implement Sync Level 2 and two-phase commit protocols.

Most IMS applications will probably work as is. When COMTI invokes a method, a message is sent to the IMS message queue. The transaction program runs in a message processing region and must issue Get commands to retrieve the input parameters. After processing the inputs, the transaction program must issue Insert commands to place the output parameters and return values into the message queue to be returned to COMTI.

Data types in COMTI

The Component Builder automatically maps COBOL types to Automation data types when COBOL data declarations are imported. COMTI provides default mappings for all the standard Automation data types. As mentioned, COMTI also supports mapping COBOL data tables to ADO *Recordset* objects. The developer can either accept the default mapping or override it with a compatible mapping. (The valid mappings are documented in the COMTI help file.) The mappings used are stored in the type library and are used by the run-time proxy to determine how to pass data to and from the mainframe transaction program. The run-time proxy also takes care of translating between Unicode and EBCDIC character sets.

Using COMTI components in distributed transactions

COMTI can include only CICS transaction programs in MS DTC coordinated distributed transactions. IMS transaction programs can't be included in distributed transactions until IBM provides Sync Level 2 support for IMS. If you mark a COMTI component as "requires a transaction" or "requires a new transaction," the mainframe transaction program must support Sync Level 2. If you mark a COMTI component as "supports transactions," the transaction program must support both Sync Level 0 and Sync Level 2 requests. If the transaction program supports only Sync Level 0, you must mark the COMTI component as "does not support transactions."

You will normally use a COMTI component from another component that provides the root transaction. The COMTI run-time proxy will call *SetComplete* for interface methods that complete successfully. It calls *SetAbort* for methods that fail or when the transaction program indicates the transaction should not commit. However, the run-time proxy cannot detect application-specific conditions that might cause the transaction to abort. In this case, the client component must detect the abort condition and call *SetAbort* itself.

Configuring a COMTI Component

After you create a component, you use the COMTI Management Console to configure the component. The COMTI Management Console is an MMC application that includes both the COMTI and MTS snap-ins.

Packaging for MTS

The first step in configuration is to add the component to an MTS package, following the procedures outlined in Chapter 10. The only file you need to insert into the package is the type library generated by the Component Builder; a COMTI snap-in extension ensures that the type library is recognized as a complete component. If you need to move the MTS package, the normal MTS package export facilities can be used.

Defining a Remote Environment

You will also need to define a COMTI Remote Environment to specify what connection to use to communicate with the mainframe transaction program. From the COMTI Management Console, select the Remote Environment folder, choose New from the Action menu, and then choose Remote Environment. The Add Remote Environment dialog box lets you specify the type of environment to create: CICS, CICS LINK, IMS, Diagnostic Capture, or Diagnostic Playback. The diagnostic environments are used for testing your component without a real mainframe connection.

Before you define a Remote Environment as CICS or IMS, you must use the SNA Server Manager to configure Local and Remote APPC LU aliases and APPC modes. Once these settings are configured, you can continue with the Remote Environment definition. After you click OK in the Add Remote Environment dialog box, the Remote Environment wizard displays a screen that asks you for the SNA attributes for this environment, as shown in Figure 15-3. Select the Local LU alias, the Remote LU alias, and the APPC mode from the drop-down lists on this screen, and then click Next to continue. On the next screen of the wizard, you can enter a name for the new Remote Environment and, optionally, a comment describing the environment in more detail. Clicking Next takes you to the final screen of the wizard, on which you can click Finish to create the Remote Environment.

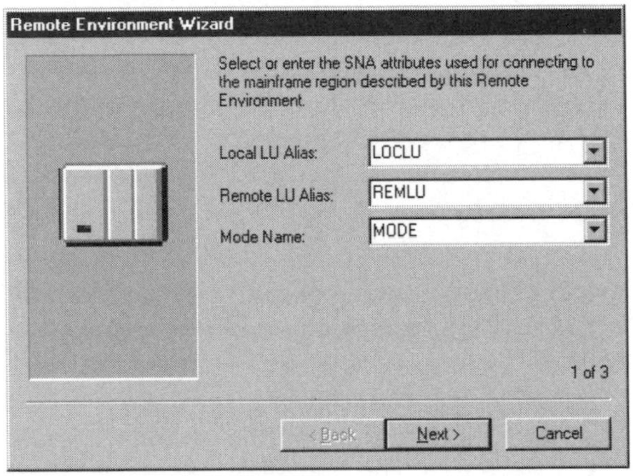

Figure 15-3. *Specifying the SNA attributes using the Remote Environment wizard.*

Every COMTI component must be assigned to a Remote Environment. When you install a component into MTS, the component will automatically be assigned to the default Remote Environment of the correct type (if one exists). If the component is not assigned to the correct Remote Environment, you can move the component from the COMTI Management Console. To do so, select the component you want to move, and then choose the Move command from the Action menu. In the Move Component dialog box, select the name of the destination Remote Environment from the drop-down list, and then click OK to close the dialog box.

Configuring security

Finally, you might need to configure the security settings for your COMTI component. COMTI components can be assigned security attributes just like any other MTS component. However, COMTI also needs to deal with security issues on the mainframe computer.

COMTI provides two security options: *package-level* and *user-level*. With the package-level security option, the Microsoft Windows NT identity of the MTS package is used to derive the correct mainframe security credentials, using the single sign-on support in SNA Server. With the user-level security option, the Windows NT identity of the client that invoked the COMTI component is used to derive the correct mainframe security credentials, again using the single sign-on support in SNA Server. An override can be used for either option to explicitly specify security credentials. In this case, no mapping is done; the specified security credentials are used directly.

To set package-level or user-level security on the Remote Environment, select Remote Environment in the COMTI Management Console and then choose the Properties command from the Action menu. Select the Securities tab, and then specify the security level. If you want to use explicit security, check the Allow Application Override check box.

> **NOTE** If you use explicit security, your application must provide a callback object that can be used to retrieve security credentials. The requirements for this callback object are described in detail in the COMTI Online Guide.

Once security is configured, your component is ready for use.

> **NOTE** See Angela Mills' excellent white paper "Using Microsoft Transaction Server 2.0 with COM Transaction Integrator 1.0" for further information about how COMTI works. This white paper is available from the COM home page at *http://www.microsoft.com /com/*.

Developing Applications with MSMQ

Let's shift gears now and look at another interoperability technology, MSMQ. MSMQ provides services that let you manage queues of messages and route messages between queues. While the messages have a standard format, the body of each message is application-specific. MSMQ can be used to build applications that interoperate with other messaging applications running on mainframe computers or with other time-independent applications.

The MSMQ Application Model

The basic application model for messaging applications is straightforward. An application creates a message and sends it to a queue. Another application—or another part of the same application—reads the message from the queue and processes it. If necessary, the receiver can respond by sending its own message. The sending application is not required to wait for a response from the reader. In fact, the sending and receiving applications don't even need to be running at the same time. Sent messages are stored in the queue until they are retrieved by a receiver. The persistent storage of unread messages makes message queuing extremely useful for scenarios in which the applications are time-independent, in which machines might be disconnected from the network, or in which receivers might not be able to process requests as quickly as they are generated.

MSMQ supports three types of machine configurations: *server, independent client,* and *dependent client*. Servers can use all the features of MSMQ. Independent clients can create and modify local queues and can send and receive messages just like MSMQ servers. Local queues and messages can be created even when an MSMQ server is unavailable. However, independent clients do not have the intermediate store-and-forward capability of MSMQ servers, nor do they store information from the distributed MSMQ database. Dependent clients require synchronous access to a MSMQ server and cannot be used in disconnected scenarios.

MSMQ queues can be transactional, meaning that sending a message to or receiving a message from a queue is an atomic operation that participates in a transaction. These actions can be combined with the work required to create or process the message to ensure that the entire operation of creating and sending or of receiving and processing a message succeeds or fails as a whole. Because the acts of sending and receiving messages can occur over a long period of time, these operations are part of two different transactions. If a transaction on the receiver fails, it might be necessary to provide a compensating transaction on the sender to undo the effect of the already completed send transaction. In addition, the act of waiting for a message to be received can be a lengthy operation and is typically nontransactional. Thus, the receiving action is usually divided into two parts. A long-lived object, application, or server running outside MTS, known as the *listener,* is used to wait for messages coming into the queue. When a message arrives, the listener calls a method on a transactional receiver component that retrieves the message from the queue and processes it.

MSMQ supports both public and private message queues. Public queues are registered in the MSMQ Information Store (MQIS) so that they can be located by any MSMQ application. Public queues are persistent, and their registration information can be backed up; thus, these queues are good for long-term use. Private queues are registered on a local computer and usually cannot be seen by other applications. Information about private queues is stored in the local queue storage (LQS) directory on the local computer. The advantage of private queues is that they have no MQIS overhead, which means they are faster to create, have no latency, and do not need to be replicated. In addition, they can be used when MQIS is not available. Private queues can be exposed to another application by sending the queue's location to the other application.

Queue properties are defined when the queue is created. The properties can be set by MSMQ or by the application. Properties include ways to identify the queue and ways to specify who has access to the queue, whether the queue is transactional, whether a journal of queue operations should be maintained, and more. You can also use the queue properties as filters to locate public queues that have particular characteristics.

Although the properties of the queue and the default properties of messages are defined at queue creation time, some properties can be specified for individual messages. Most of these properties have to do with "level of service." For example, you can set the type of acknowledgement messages MSMQ should send when messages are received at their final destination, security properties, whether the message should be transacted or recoverable, whether the message should be stored in the journal, and the priority of the message. Another property helps you correlate response messages with the original message that was sent.

Programming MSMQ Applications

MSMQ provides two ways to access MSMQ functionality. First, it provides a set of API functions. These functions are most easily used from C or C++ programs. The MSMQ API includes functions for creating, opening, and deleting queues; functions for locating existing queues and messages in queues; functions for sending messages and reading them in queues; and functions for setting and retrieving properties.

Second, MSMQ provides a set of Automation components that can be used from any language that supports Automation, including scripting languages. These components do not support all the functionality of the MSMQ API, but they do support the functions most often needed by applications: queue lookup, queue management, queue administration, message management, and transaction support. We will focus here on these Automation components.

The basic design pattern we will discuss for building MSMQ applications is shown in Figure 15-4. A *send component* is defined that exposes a COM interface, *IMyInterface*, in which each method has only input parameters and causes an MSMQ message to be sent. This send component is usually run within MTS, using MTS automatic transactions. It is much like any other business or data object we've discussed, except that each method opens a queue, builds a message, sends the message, and closes the queue. A *listener application* is created to watch for new messages in the queue. When a message is detected, the listener calls a *receiver component*. The receiver component exposes the same *IMyInterface* interface as the send component as well as an interface for triggering message reads, *IReadQueue*, which has one method, *MessageArrived*. The listener component calls *MessageArrived*, which receives the message from the queue, decodes the message, and calls the appropriate method of *IMyInterface*. The implementation of each *IMyInterface* method does the actual processing of the method. The receiver component is also usually a transaction component running within MTS.

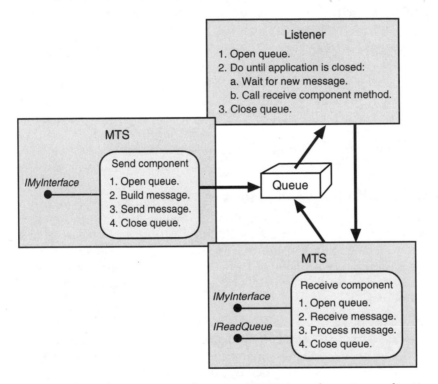

Figure 15-4. *A design pattern for using MSMQ in a three-tier application.*

<table>
<tr><td>NOTE</td><td>*IMyInterface* and *IReadQueue* are representative interface names used to describe this design pattern. You should define equivalent interfaces in your component, with unique IIDs, to implement this pattern.</td></tr>
</table>

The MSMQ object model

The Automation components provided by MSMQ are listed in the following table.

Component	Description
MSMQQueueInfo	Provides queue management
MSMQQueue	Represents an instance of an open queue
MSMQMessage	Represents a single message
MSMQQuery	Provides the ability to search for public queues
MSMQQueueInfos	Represents a collection of *MSMQ-QueueInfo* objects returned by *MSMQQuery*
MSMQEvent	Provides asynchronous notifications of message arrival
MSMQApplication	Provides a way to retrieve the machine identifier of a computer
MSMQTransaction	Provides a way to commit and abort transactions
MSMQTransactionDispenser	Creates a transaction object for internal transactions
MSMQCoordinatedTransactionDispenser	Creates a transaction object for external transactions coordinated by the MS DTC

The *MSMQQueueInfo* component can be used to create a new queue, open an existing queue, change a queue's properties, or delete a queue. There is one *MSMQQueueInfo* object for each queue. *MSMQQueueInfo* objects can be created directly or returned by a query.

An *MSMQQueue* object represents an open instance of a queue. This object is created when you open a queue using an *MSMQQueueInfo* object, and there can be multiple *MSMQQueue* objects per queue. The *MSMQQueue* component provides cursorlike behavior for moving through the messages in a queue. At any given time, the object is positioned at a single message.

An *MSMQMessage* object represents an individual message. You can use this component to create and send messages. The body of a message can be a string, an array of bytes, or any persistent COM object that supports *IDispatch* and

IPersistStream or *IPersistStorage*. Each *MSMQQueue* object contains an implicit set of *MSMQMessage* objects that are accessed via the *MSMQQueue Peek* and *Receive* methods.

The *MSMQQuery* component can be used to retrieve a set of public queues that meet particular criteria. The set of queues is returned as an *MSMQQueueInfos* collection of *MSMQQueueInfo* objects.

The *MSMQEvent* component is used to implement an event handler that receives notifications when messages are received at a queue or when certain error conditions occur. Each queue can be associated with one *MSMQEvent* object and the object can be associated with multiple queues, which lets you write a single generic event handler to perform common tasks. A reference to an *MSMQQueue* object is passed to the event handler, so it can perform application-specific processing as necessary.

The remaining components provide utility functions for MSMQ applications. The *MSMQApplication* component simply provides a method to retrieve a machine identifier. *MSMQTransaction* objects are created by either *MSMQTransaction-Dispenser* or *MSMQCoordinatedTransactionDispenser* objects when MSMQ applications want to programmatically control transaction boundaries, either using internal transactions or using the MS DTC, rather than using MTS automatic transactions.

Managing queues

Every component or application that needs to send or receive messages will need to create or open a queue and then close the queue when it has finished its work. All queues are created by calling the *MSMQQueueInfo Create* method—you create an *MSMQQueueInfo* object, set the queue properties you want, and then call *Create*.

The only required property for creating a queue is *PathName*. The *PathName* property has the format *<machine name>\<local queue name>* for public queues or *<machine name>\Private$\<local queue name>* for private queues, where *<machine name>* indicates where the queue's messages should be stored and *<local queue name>* specifies the queue name. For example, the following code snippet creates a private queue named *MyQueue* on the local computer and returns a reference to the *MSMQQueueInfo* object:

```
Function CreatePrivateQueue() As MSMQQueueInfo
    Dim qinfo as New MSMQQueueInfo
    qinfo.PathName = ".\Private$\MyQueue"
    qinfo.Label = "My Private Queue"
    qinfo.Create
    Set CreatePrivateQueue = qinfo
End Function
```

Once the queue is created, the *MSMQQueueInfo* object's *FormatName* property can be used to open the queue. Queues are opened by calling the *MSMQ-QueueInfo Open* method. You can get the *MSMQQueueInfo* object by creating the queue or by using an *MSMQQuery* object to locate an existing queue. When you open a queue, you specify the type of access you want and the type of sharing you want. You can obtain access to send messages, receive messages, or peek at messages in the queue. If you have receive access, you can also peek at messages. However, if you have peek access, you cannot receive messages. If you want receive access to the queue, you should also indicate whether anyone else can receive messages from the queue at the same time. For example, the following code snippet opens a queue once for sending messages and once for receiving messages with no sharing:

```
Dim qinfo as MSMQQueueInfo
Dim qSend as New MSMQQueue
Dim qReceive as New MSMQQueue
Set qinfo = CreatePrivateQueue()
Set qSend = qinfo.Open(MQ_SEND_ACCESS, MQ_DENY_NONE)
If qSend.IsOpen then
    ' The queue was successfully opened for sending messages.
    Set qReceive = qinfo.Open(MQ_RECEIVE_ACCESS, _
                              MQ_DENY_RECEIVE_SHARE)
    If qReceive.IsOpen then
      ' The queue was successfully opened for receiving messages.
    End If
End If
```

When you have finished using a queue, you simply call the *MSMQQueue Close* method to close the queue.

Sending and receiving messages

Sending messages is a straightforward process. After opening a queue for sending, you create an *MSMQMessage* object, set its properties, and call the *Send* method. If you have created a transactional queue, the message will participate in MTS automatic transactions by default. The *Body* property of the object is used to specify the contents of the message. This property can be set to any intrinsic Variant type, array of bytes, or a persistent object. The *MSMQMessage* object figures out what type of data is provided by inspecting the Variant data assigned to the *Body* property. Be aware that when you assign an object to the *Body* property, you should not use the Microsoft Visual Basic Set operator because the actual contents of the Variant data are copied into the message. The code snippet on the following page demonstrates how to send a string in a message using the default message properties.

```
Dim mSend as MSMQMessage
mSend.body = "This is the message body."
mSend.Send qSend
```

If your applications send multiple types of messages to the same queue, you will need to include some identifying information in the message body so that your receiving application can properly decode the message. You will also need to document the format of each type of message body so that receiving applications know how to process it.

Receiving messages is slightly more complicated. You can read messages synchronously or asynchronously. When a message is received synchronously, execution of the receiver is blocked until the message is available or a time-out period expires. When a message is received asynchronously, execution of the receiver continues until *Arrived* or *ArrivedError* events are received by an *MSMQEvent* object registered with the queue. However, even with asynchronous reads, the act of receiving a message might occur over a long period of time. Thus, it is usually impossible to wait for messages to be received within a transactional component.

To work around this issue, you can use a long-lived listener object, application, or server that opens the queue with peek access and waits for messages to be received. When a message is received, the listener calls a method on a transactional receiver object, which then reads the message from the queue and processes it. The following code fragment demonstrates how a simple listener might be coded, using the design pattern described above and assuming that the *MSMQQueueInfo* object has already been initialized:

```
Dim qPeek As MSMQQueue
Dim msgPeek As New MSMQMessage
Dim myReceiveObj As IReadQueue
Set qPeek = qinfo.Open(MQ_PEEK_ACCESS, MQ_DENY_NONE)
Set myReceiveObj = CreateObject("MyReceiveObject")
On Error Resume Next
do while (TRUE)
   Set msgPeek = qPeek.Peek(60000)
   If (Err = MQ_ERROR_IO_TIMEOUT) Then
      Loop
   ElseIf (Err <> 0) Then
      ' Handle error. For now, just exit.
      Exit Do
   Else
      ' Let receiver know there's a message.
      myReceiveObj.MessageArrived
   End If
Loop
⋮
```

The receiver component's implementation of *IReadQueue MessageArrived* could use synchronous reads to retrieve messages from the queue, which it opens for receive access, as shown in the following code fragment:

```
Dim qRead as MSMQQueue
Dim msgRead as New MSMQMessage
Set qRead = qinfo.Open(MQ_RECEIVE_ACCESS, MQ_DENY_RECEIVE_SHARE)
Set msgRead = qRead.Receive
If msgRead is Nothing Then
   ' Process error.
   GetObjectContext.SetAbort
Else
   DecodeMessage msgRead
   ' Assume no errors (would call SetAbort on error).
   GetObjectContext.SetComplete
End If
```

The *DecodeMessage* method would contain the code to parse the message and call the appropriate method of *IMyInterface*.

Configuring MSMQ Application Components

Once you have created send and receive components and a listener application, you will need to deploy these as part of your distributed application. If you want message sends and receives to participate in transactions, you should install the send and receive components in MTS packages, as described in Chapter 10. Since the send and receive components are likely to be used on separate machines, you should put them in separate components. The components should be marked as "requires a transaction" to ensure correct transactional behavior. The listener application should not be installed in MTS.

SUMMARY

Many applications need to interoperate with other applications. Three common scenarios are interoperating with existing transaction programs running on mainframe computers, interoperating with existing messaging applications running on mainframe computers, and interoperating between time-independent applications.

COMTI can be used to build wrapper components for existing transaction programs running under CICS or IMS on IBM mainframe computers. The COMTI Component Builder is used to create wrapper components from data declarations representing the mainframe application's interface. The developer does not need to write any code for these wrapper components; COMTI provides generic components that read type libraries generated by the Component Builder to determine how to communicate with the mainframe application.

MSMQ can be used to build components and applications that interoperate with existing messaging applications running on mainframe computers or interoperate with other time-independent applications. MSMQ provides both an API and a set of Automation components that developers can use to write components and applications to send and receive messages via message queues. One effective way to architect an application using MSMQ is to encapsulate sending messages within a component that exposes an interface with only input parameters for each method, using one method for each type of message sent. For time-independent applications running on Windows NT, a second receiver component is written implementing the same interface but performing the actual work for each method. A listener application waits for messages to be received at the message queue and calls methods on the receiver component to retrieve and process the messages.

16

COM+

In the preceding chapters, we have looked at the Microsoft technologies you can use today to build component-based three-tier distributed applications. Central to the Microsoft strategy is a programming model based on COM and, on the server, MTS. In September 1997, Microsoft announced that in the future COM and MTS would be unified. The name given to this unified set of component services is *COM+*. The initial release of COM+ is likely to appear in Microsoft Windows NT 5. In this chapter, we'll look at the features that are expected to appear in COM+ 1.0 and at how COM+ will affect distributed application development.

> **NOTE** At the time this chapter was written, COM+ 1.0 had just entered its initial beta; some details might change prior to release.

Moving Forward with COM and MTS

A key theme common to all the technologies we've discussed in this book is "making it easier"—that is, making it easier for the typical corporate developer to create distributed applications in a timely and cost-effective manner. COM+ builds on and extends COM and MTS to provide an even more powerful and easy-to-use architecture for developing, deploying, and administering highly scalable distributed component-based solutions. At the same time, Microsoft realizes that many companies have already made substantial investments in COM and MTS. Thus, a second key theme for COM+ is leveraging current investments. COM+ is an evolutionary technology that provides a solid foundation for future innovative component services.

A Unified Architecture

One way COM+ makes writing applications easier is by eliminating the distinction between COM and MTS. This distinction arose because MTS was implemented as a service on top of COM rather than as an integral part of COM. As we saw in Chapter 4, MTS provides a surrogate process for hosting MTS components and an executive that provides services to those components. When an object is created, the MTS Surrogate is launched and if necessary the MTS Executive is loaded; the executive then intercepts the creation request and generates a context wrapper for the object that will let MTS intercept calls to the object. MTS also associates an object context with the object during creation. This process is very different from the way COM objects are created.

In COM+, all objects are created the same way. COM+ is built on a general-purpose *activation and interception architecture* that lets COM+ associate an object context with every object as it's created and intercept calls to the object. During activation, COM+ will use attributes stored with the component or in application configuration information to determine which services, if any, the object uses. These services are built on the activation and interception architecture. COM+ keeps track of which services are in use and determines whether a call to the object requires work on the part of any of the services. If so, the services are automatically invoked at the appropriate point in the call. Instead of using a separate context wrapper to intercept calls, as MTS does, COM+ merges interception into the normal proxy/stub architecture already used to detect calls across apartment, process, or machine boundaries.

Although the architecture is general and all objects have an associated context, only classes implemented in DLL servers can be configured to use the COM+ services. Classes that are configured to use the COM+ services are known as *configured classes*; all other classes are known as *unconfigured classes*. Configured classes are hosted by the new COM+ Surrogate, which merges the features of the COM and MTS Surrogates and uses the standard COM Surrogate architecture.

A Unified Programming Model

What the unified architecture means for you as a programmer is that you can use all objects the same way, regardless of whether they use COM+ services. In MTS, to ensure that context information flows from one object to another, you must use the object context *CreateInstance* method. In COM+, you can just use the normal object creation API functions, such as *CoCreateInstanceEx* or Microsoft Visual Basic's *CreateObject*. Thus, instead of writing code that looks like this:

```
Dim ctxObject As ObjectContext
Dim subObject As IMyInterface
Set ctxObject = GetObjectContext()
Set subObject = ctxObject.CreateInstance("MyComponentProgID")
```

you would write code that looks like this:

```
Dim subObject As IMyInterface
Set subObject = CreateObject("MyComponentProgID")
```

In addition, COM+ supports a more general *moniker*-based creation mechanism. We haven't yet discussed monikers; basically, they are COM objects that provide a way to name objects. You provide a string name; the moniker finds the object for you. While monikers have always been part of COM, COM+ adds a standard moniker that understands how to create new objects called, appropriately, the *new moniker*. The moniker-based method is useful because it can be extended at any time to support new features by simply installing a new moniker component and telling developers about the string names the new moniker understands. Extending a system function like *CoCreateInstanceEx* to support new features, on the other hand, is very difficult. With the new moniker, you can write code such as this to create new objects:

```
Dim subObject As IMyInterface
Set subObject = GetObject("new:MyComponentProgID")
```

Other than these changes to object creation, developers of MTS-based three-tier applications won't see any major changes in writing COM+ applications. COM+ 1.0 is geared toward writing three-tier applications; the programming model it promotes is essentially the MTS programming model. Components that want to use COM+ services must meet the same requirements as they would for running in MTS. All existing MTS components will work without change in COM+.

As in MTS, COM+ emphasizes a declarative, attribute-based model for accessing services. You can set attributes using the COM+ administrative services discussed in the following section, "A Unified Administration Model." Attributes and other meta data about each class are stored in a *component library,* which supplements the information available in the component's type library. When a component is registered with COM+, information from the component library is cached in a registration database that COM+ uses during activation to determine how to create an object.

The goal of the component library is to make components completely self-describing, including all information needed to register the components. The information in the component library can be used by the COM+ registration service to register your components, eliminating the need for you to write registration code that directly manipulates registry entries under HKEY_CLASSES_ROOT. Because most developer tools generate this code for you, however, this feature probably won't affect you until your developer tools are updated to support COM+. For compatibility with existing components, COM+ will support components that register themselves under HKEY_CLASSES_ROOT as well as components that use the new COM+ registration mechanisms.

As mentioned, every COM+ object has an associated object context, which is associated with the object at creation time; it contains a set of attribute-value pairs that describe the object's execution environment. The exact set of attributes maintained in the object context depends on how the object's class is configured.

COM+ uses the object context to determine when specific services must be invoked. The object context is maintained by COM+ itself, based on the service attributes specified for components, classes, and interfaces, as well as the context of the object's caller. You cannot control the object context attribute values at run time. You may query the object context and call the methods it provides, however, in order to access COM+ services programmatically.

A Unified Administration Model

In addition to unifying the programming model, COM+ unites the COM and MTS administration models. A single tool, the COM Explorer, combines the functionality of the DCOM Configuration tool (DCOMCNFG) and the MTS Explorer. The administration model viewed through the COM Explorer is also available programmatically, using a set of scriptable administration objects. (These objects are extensions of the MTS 2.0 administration objects.) Although COM+ 1.0 does not offer a lot of new administrative functionality, the underlying unified administrative architecture has been designed so that future releases of COM+ can provide more flexible and powerful tools for administration and deployment, without requiring massive changes to the model exposed to developers and administrators.

The unified administration model will look very familiar to developers using MTS today, since the model is geared toward three-tier applications. The primary difference is that the terminology has been generalized. Instead of combining components into packages, you combine them into *applications*. You can create library applications and server applications, just as you create library packages and server packages in MTS. The model has also been enhanced to support the new COM+ services discussed in the following section, "New Services for Enterprise Applications."

You will also see some differences in the way applications are exported. COM+ can export server applications or client applications. Exporting a server application is much like exporting an MTS package, except that an application library (.APL) file is generated instead of a package (.PAK) file. Exporting a client application, on the other hand, takes advantage of new Zero Administration Windows (ZAW) deployment features. When you export a client application, a Microsoft Installer (MSI) application is generated that contains all the "client glue" needed for client machines to connect to your application. The MSI application can be assigned to a group of clients using the ZAW group policy editor and distributed through the Windows NT 5 Class Store. The Class Store is essentially a database that enables centralized deployment and management of applications, components, and services. This technique greatly simplifies the deployment of client applications.

New Services for Enterprise Applications

As you might expect, COM+ provides all the services provided by MTS 2.0. Most of these services have been enhanced in some way for COM+. Of particular interest to developers are object pooling, object constructors, compensating resource managers, and security enhancements. COM+ also adds several new services to help you write large-scale, enterprise-wide applications. These services are generally exposed via attributes and can be composed—in other words, you can pick and choose the combination of services you want to use. (In some cases, using one service will require the use of other services.) In the following sections, we'll take a brief look at the major features of COM+ that are not available in COM or MTS today.

Object Pooling

As we saw in Chapter 8, although MTS 2.0 appears to support object pooling via the *IObjectControl* interface, it doesn't actually pool objects. Whenever an object is deactivated, the object is destroyed. In COM+, objects can be pooled. When an object is activated, it is pulled from the pool. When the object is deactivated, it is placed back into the pool. However, there are some restrictions on which classes can be pooled.

The primary restriction is that a COM+ class that wants to support object pooling must not have thread affinity—that is, it cannot expect to run on the same thread for its entire lifetime. COM+ introduces the *thread-neutral apartment model* to help developers create classes without thread affinity. (In fact, this is the preferred threading model for COM+ classes.) In this model, an object is always called on the caller's thread, regardless of whether the thread is an STA thread or an MTA thread. To support the thread-neutral apartment model, a COM+ class must not use *thread local storage* (a mechanism to allocate storage for thread-specific data) or other thread-specific techniques. COM+ synchronization services can be used to protect component-wide and per-object data from concurrent access, or the class can implement its own concurrency control.

COM+ classes that want to support object pooling must use the thread-neutral apartment model or the free-threaded model; they cannot use the apartment threading model. In addition, the class must implement *IObjectControl* and must be aggregatable. Because not all COM+ classes can be pooled, simply returning *TRUE* from *IObjectControl CanBePooled* is not sufficient to enable object pooling. You must also add the class in a COM+ application and set its pooling-related attributes. First you must enable object pooling for the class, and then you can specify the minimum and maximum pool sizes as well as the length of time a client will wait before an object request times out. Once you have set the pooling-related attributes, COM+ will call *IObjectControl CanBePooled* to determine whether individual object instances can be pooled at run time.

COM Aggregation is a technique for reusing COM class implementations. In aggregation, one object (called the *outer object*) creates another object (called the *inner object*) and exposes the inner object's interfaces as if they were implemented by the outer object itself. An aggregatable object can be used as the inner object during aggregation. A COM class that is aggregatable must implement *IUnknown* in a specific way, as described in the Platform SDK documentation topic "Aggregation."

Clients do not require any modifications in order to use object pooling. As far as the client knows, it receives a pointer to a newly created object with every creation request. However, if pooled objects hold onto limited resources or the pool size is limited, clients should release pointers to pooled objects as soon as possible so that the pool is not depleted.

Object pooling is particularly useful for classes in which creating an object is expensive. If the cost of creating an object is more than the cost of maintaining the pool, object pooling can improve performance. Object pooling can help you gain the same kind of scalability benefits you get today from ODBC connection pooling for your own expensive resources.

Object Constructors

Object pools are maintained on a per-CLSID basis. In some situations, it might be handy to have several pools for the same basic type of object, but with different initialization information. For example, it might be useful to have several pools of objects that maintain database connections, in which each pool's objects use a pool-specific data source name (DSN) to establish the connection. A single COM+ class implementation could handle this scenario, if there was a way to specify the DSN at object creation time.

Specifying external initialization information is the purpose of COM+ object constructors. A generic COM+ class implementation supports object construction by implementing the *IObjectConstructor* interface. The construction string to be passed to objects of a particular CLSID that uses the class implementation is specified as a class attribute using the COM+ administrative tools. The *IObjectConstructor* implementation can retrieve the construction string during object creation and initialize the object appropriately.

Object constructors in conjunction with pooled objects provide an easy-to-implement alternative to full resource dispensers, which were discussed in Chapter 4. For example, ODBC connection pooling could be implemented using object pooling and object constructors. You could also use object constructors without using pooled objects. This technique is useful for situations in which you don't want to hard-code configuration information in objects. For example, in our discussion of building data objects in Chapter 8, we used a file DSN to hold information about the database to connect to. This way, administrators could adjust the DSN at deployment time without modifying the data objects. In Chapter 13, however, we saw that using a file DSN is relatively slow. If our data object supported *IObjectConstructor*, we could get the performance benefits of using either a system DSN or a connection string, with the flexibility of specifying the DSN information outside the data object implementation.

Compensating Resource Managers

Object pooling and object constructors help you write scalable applications that use transient resources but do not directly participate in transactions. *Compensating Resource Managers* (CRMs) are a mechanism whereby nontransactional resources can participate in transactions managed by the Microsoft Distributed Transaction Coordinator (MS DTC). CRMs are implemented as a pair of COM+ components, the CRM Worker and CRM Compensator, that perform the normal work of the resource and a compensating action. A compensating action undoes the effect of normal action. If the transaction aborts, the compensating action can correct for the normal action performed by the CRM as part of the transaction. CRMs do not provide the isolation capabilities of full resource managers, but they do provide transactional *Atomicity* (all or nothing) and *Durability* via the recovery log.

The CRM Worker performs the normal action for updating the resource as part of the transaction. This action is specific to the particular type of CRM and is accessed by application components that want to use the resource via a CRM-specific interface. The CRM infrastructure defines an interface the CRM Worker can use to write records to a durable log so that recovery can be performed in case of failure. All actions performed by a CRM must be *idempotent*—in other words, performing the action more than once will lead to the same state. For example, setting a field in a database record to a specific value is an idempotent action. Incrementing the field by a specific amount is not.

As mentioned, the CRM Compensator is responsible for providing the compensating action. The CRM Compensator implements an interface defined by the CRM infrastructure, which calls the CRM Compensator to notify it about prepare, commit, and abort phases of each transaction. During the prepare notification, the CRM Compensator can vote no to force an abort of the transaction. The commit notification is used to clean up after the normal action performed by the CRM Worker, and the abort notification is used to perform the compensating action. The CRM Compensator can also write records to the recovery log to indicate which actions have already been compensated for. During recovery after a failure, the CRM infrastructure reads the recovery log and calls the CRM Compensator to finish processing as if no failure had occurred.

To create a CRM, you write a CRM Worker and CRM Compensator component pair. These components are typically installed in a COM+ library application, so they are available to multiple server applications. A server application that wants to use a CRM must be configured to enable CRMs, using the COM Explorer. The application components that want to use the CRM simply create instances of the CRM Worker class and call methods of its CRM-specific interface to access the resource managed by the CRM.

CRMs are useful for managing private resources that you want to participate in transactions without writing a complete resource dispenser and resource manager. Developers of general-purpose resources will probably want to provide full resource dispensers.

Security Enhancements

In addition to features that help you use resources more efficiently, COM+ offers enhancements to the security model introduced in MTS. COM+ server applications can choose between role-based security, process access permissions (as used by COM applications today), or no security at all. COM+ library applications can be secured as well, unlike MTS library packages. However, because library applications run within another process, you cannot use process access permissions to secure a library application—you can only use role-based security.

Applications that use process access permissions can take advantage of additional security providers on Windows NT 5 and can use *delegate-level impersonation* and *cloaking* to affect the security credentials used during method calls.

> **NOTE**   In particular, the Kerberos security provider is supported; this provider supports remote mutual authentication between client and server machines. A Secure Sockets Layer (SSL) provider might be supported as well, but it was not supported in Windows NT 5 beta 2.

Delegate-level impersonation is established by the client process and allows a server to impersonate the client and to pass the client's credentials to remote machines. Previously, servers could only impersonate the client to access local resources. Cloaking is used to hide an intermediate server's identity from a destination server. For example, if ClientA calls ServerB, which then calls ServerC on ClientA's behalf, and ServerB has cloaking enabled, ClientA's identity will be used for calls to ServerC.

COM+ role-based security builds on top of the process access permissions security model, just as MTS role-based security is built on top of COM security. For applications using role-based security, COM+ performs security checks for all calls across an application boundary. Thus, if a library application is used by a server application and the library application is enabled for security checks, calls from server application components to library application components will be checked. In addition to application-level, component-level, and interface-level checks, COM+ permits roles to be assigned to individual methods of an interface.

COM+ also provides more extensive information about the security properties in effect for a particular call through the *ISecurityCallContext* interface. This interface supercedes the *ISecurityProperty* interface used in MTS. *ISecurityCallContext* lets you retrieve information about the identities of every caller along a particular chain of calls within an activity. You can also determine the security provider used to authenticate each call, the authentication level used, and the impersonation level used. This information can give you a very accurate picture of the events leading up to a particular method call, which is quite useful for creating audit trails, for example.

Queued Components

To date, COM and MTS have been used primarily for time-dependent applications. As we saw in Chapter 6, a time-dependent application is one in which the caller and callee must coexist at the time a method is called. This is the familiar synchronous method call model used by programming languages and COM. Time-dependent applications are easy to write, but they fail if the callee is unavailable. Many distributed applications do not really need to be time dependent. There might not be any requirement that the callee process calls immediately—as long as the calls are processed eventually. These applications are called *time-independent applications*.

Message queuing middleware can be used to implement time-independent applications. Communication occurs using one-way messages, which are sent to a queue by the caller for later retrieval by the receiving application. As we saw in Chapter 15, message queuing software such as MSMQ has its own set of API functions to master, with a unique programming model. This makes it difficult for developers to use message queuing in their applications. In COM+, developers can easily take advantage of MSMQ, without using the MSMQ API functions directly, using a subset of the standard COM+ programming model. The COM+ Queued Component system services handle all the details of queuing internally.

Figure 16-1 on the following page illustrates how queued components work. When a client application requests an object, the queued components *Recorder* is created for the object's class. The *Recorder* collects calls until a client-side transaction is ready to commit and then places one message in an MSMQ queue. This message contains information about all the calls made on the object. If the message is not added to the queue successfully, the transaction will abort.

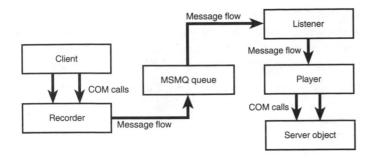

Figure 16-1. *COM+ queued components.*

On the server machine, when the application containing the queued component is running, COM+ creates a Queued Component *Listener* to retrieve messages from the queue. The *Listener* will pass the message on to a *Player* object, which translates the message back into COM method calls. These calls are passed on to the component like any other call. As on the client, removing a message from the queue is a transacted activity. If the message cannot be removed from the queue, the application server transaction will abort. If a queue contains a message that causes repeated rollbacks, the message is moved to a dead-letter queue so that the system administrator can examine the message and take corrective action as needed.

To use the Queued Component service, you simply create a COM class as usual. There are a few restrictions on the interfaces the class exposes for time-independent use. Most important, the interface methods can have only *[in]* parameters. The methods cannot pass information back to the caller using a method parameter or the method return code because the act of calling the method and the act of actually making the method call can happen at completely different times. The caller might not even exist when the actual method call is made.

Developers or administrators configure the class interfaces and their containing applications to use the Queued Component service by using the COM Explorer. The same component can be used either as a queued component or as a regular component with direct method calls. Each interface may be marked as a queueable interface using the COM Explorer. A class that exposes one or more interfaces marked as queueable is considered a queueable class. Likewise, a component containing one or more queueable classes is a queueable component. The containing application must be marked as a queued application in order for the Queued Component service to be invoked. You can also specify whether to automatically start the *Listener* using the COM Explorer. When a client application is exported, the relevant queue information will be included in the application.

Like the component developer, the client developer uses normal COM programming techniques and tools to access queued components. Objects are created using the moniker-based creation mechanism described earlier. A queue moniker is used to indicate that the client wants to create a queued component, as shown here:

```
Dim queuedObject as IMyQueuedInterface
Set queuedObject = GetObject("queue:/new:MyQueuedComponentProgID")
```

Once an object has been created, you can make method calls and set properties, just as for any other COM+ object. When you have finished with the object, you simply release it.

The main difference, for developers, between using queued components and regular COM components is in passing information back from the component to the caller. Queued components have a one-way communication path. One technique for dealing with this limitation is to create a second queued notification component that runs on the client application machine. The original component calls back to the client machine through this notification component. Another approach is to have the client application query an application-provided data store maintained by the queued component to obtain information about the results of a method call.

Another issue for application developers is recovering from transactions that fail on the server side after committing on the client. In this case, the client must be notified that an error has occurred and the client must then perform a *compensating transaction* to recover.

Queued components offer many of the benefits of message-based applications using the standard COM+ programming model. Because queued components are regular COM+ components (with certain restrictions on their interfaces), client applications can choose whether to call components deployed with queuing enabled using queued calls or regular calls.

Events

COM+ Events offer another new model to the application designer: the publish-and-subscribe model. Today in COM and MTS, there is a *tight binding* between the caller and the callee—that is, the caller must create a new object or be given an interface pointer to an existing object before it can make a call. Both the caller and the callee must exist at the same time with a communication path between them. If a caller wants to broadcast information to multiple callees, it must maintain the list of callees and make a synchronous call to each member of the list. (You might recognize this as the connection point model for events.) However, in many circumstances this tight binding is inappropriate.

In the publish-and-subscribe model, callers (or *publishers*) publish information via COM method calls, without worrying about who wants the information. The publisher informs the COM+ Event service that it has information to publish. *Subscribers* let the Event service know that they want to receive new information from the publisher as it becomes available. The Event service keeps track of subscriptions and forwards information from publishers to subscribers. The publisher does not need to know anything about the subscribers, and the subscribers don't need to know anything about the publisher other than the interface used to provide information.

Figure 16-2 shows how the COM+ Event service works. An application that wants to publish events (Publisher) creates and initializes an *EventClass* object to describe a COM class, known as an *event class,* that Publisher will use to fire events. The Publisher application does not actually implement the event class; it simply defines the class GUID, ProgID, and event interface and provides a type library. Once the *EventClass* object is initialized, Publisher tells the *EventSystem* to store information about the event class. Publisher's events are now available to subscribers.

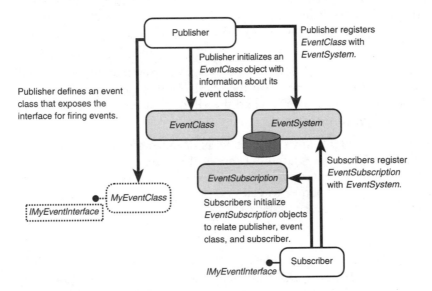

Figure 16-2. *The COM+ Event service architecture.*

Components that want to subscribe to events simply implement the event interface exposed by Publisher's event class. They do not need to contain any code to create the subscriptions; this can be done outside the components themselves. The subscription is defined by creating and initializing an *EventSubscription* object, which defines the relationship between Publisher, event class, and subscriber.

Once the *EventSubscription* object is initialized, the *EventSystem* object is told to store information about the subscription. The subscription can be persisted so that it remains available until it is removed from *EventSystem*.

To fire an event, Publisher creates an instance of its event class and calls methods on the event interface. The COM+ Event service will provide an implementation of the event class, based on information provided by Publisher. The method call implementations take care of passing the calls along to the event interface exposed by each subscriber. The COM+ Event service will create subscriber objects, if necessary.

In addition to this basic broadcast of events between a publisher and all subscribers, both publishers and subscribers can restrict how events are delivered. Publishers can write *publisher filters,* which are used to limit which subscribers receive a particular event. Subscribers can implement a special interface, *ISubscriberControl*, that is invoked just before an event is fired to the subscriber. The subscriber can use this mechanism to filter out particular events that aren't interesting to the subscriber or to transform the event into a call to a different interface method.

By adding a level of indirection between publishers of information and subscribers, the COM+ Event service offers a powerful way to connect independently developed applications. Since publishing events is no more complicated than making a few COM method calls and subscribers are simply COM components that implement a particular COM interface, it's easy for developers using any programming language to use the COM+ Event service.

In-Memory Database

Another new feature in COM+ is the *In-Memory Database* (IMDB). IMDB is exactly what it sounds like: a database that maintains its tables in memory. There are several reasons why having such a database might be useful.

Many applications need to retrieve fairly static data from persistent tables. For example, an application might use a table of valid zip codes and the corresponding city, state, and area code to automatically fill in the city and state fields of a data entry form when the user enters a zip code. A business object might use the table to validate the phone number for a given address. This table will be very large, and retrieving it from a persistent database over and over again will lead to performance problems. By using IMDB as a cache for the persistent database, the table can be loaded once from the persistent database into an IMDB database. Data objects would be configured to retrieve information from the IMDB database rather than the persistent database. Because memory is relatively cheap, this approach can be an inexpensive way to improve the performance of your applications.

While caching is primarily useful for read-only data, it can also be used for read/write scenarios. This technique can be useful when an application's data objects reside on a different machine than the database server. To reduce the network traffic involved in reading and writing the database, an IMDB cache can be configured on the data object server machine. Data objects can read and write to the IMDB. Updated records are propagated back to the persistent store when transactions commit. This approach works particularly well when the database can be partitioned such that only one machine is updating a particular subset of records through the cache.

IMDB also offers a powerful alternative to the Shared Property Manager (SPM) for managing shared transient state. Unlike the SPM, IMDB can be used to share information across server processes. Because IMDB is an OLE DB provider, ADO can be used to access information stored in an IMDB database. Developers are more likely to be familiar with the ADO interfaces than the SPM interfaces, making it easier to implement shared transient state.

Figure 16-3 shows how IMDB works. The COM Explorer is used to configure the IMDB server process to run on a particular machine. This process runs as a Windows NT service. The IMDB server process is responsible for managing IMDB tables and interacting with any underlying persistent databases. The database tables are kept in shared memory; the COM Explorer can be used to configure how much memory is set aside for these tables. IMDB also provides a proxy, which is an OLE DB provider that runs in each client process. The proxy can interact directly with the IMDB tables for read-only scenarios, but it must go through the server process for read/write scenarios or to request locks on the data.

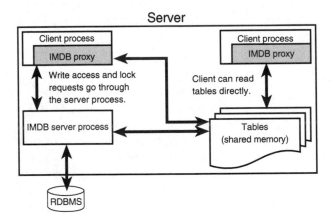

Figure 16-3. *Accessing the COM+ IMDB.*

In COM+ 1.0, IMDB is limited to a single machine. If information is cached from a persistent database to an IMDB database running on multiple machines, there is no coordination across machines. Likewise, transient state managed by an IMDB database is local to a machine. However, future versions of IMDB are expected to include a distributed cache coordinator and a lock manager, to enable coordination across machines.

IMDB imposes some restrictions on the types of database tables it supports. In particular, the tables must have primary keys, and all changes to the tables must be performed by the IMDB. This means that some database features such as auto-increment fields, time-stamp fields, and triggers cannot be used in an IMDB database. In addition, IMDB does not provide a query processor and does not permit tables to be partially loaded from a persistent store; instead, the entire table must be loaded. The table can be sorted and filtered using ADO *Recordset* objects.

Despite these restrictions, using IMDB from your components is straightforward. You can use either OLE DB or ADO to access IMDB tables. To do so, you provide a DSN to establish the database connection and then use normal OLE DB or ADO methods. The DSN is configured using the COM Explorer. You also use the COM Explorer to map the IMDB data source to a persistent data source and to define which tables, if any, are loaded from the persistent data source when the IMDB server process starts.

There are a few restrictions on which features of OLE DB or ADO you can use when IMDB is the data provider; these are documented in the Component Services section of the Platform SDK.

Dynamic Load Balancing

The preceding services are primarily developer oriented—to use these services, applications or components must be coded in a particular way. COM+ also offers a new service that does not require any special coding: *dynamic load balancing*.

As user demand on their systems grows, businesses need to be able to scale their applications to meet demand. A good way to scale is to replicate application servers across multiple machines. This technique also helps improve application availability—if one machine fails, clients can be redirected to a replica. Load balancing can be used to determine which replica each client connects to. The simplest approach to load balancing is static load balancing. With this approach, clients are assigned to a server machine by an administrator and always use that server machine. This method quickly breaks down when there are large numbers of clients who might not be known to the administrator. In addition, it cannot easily adapt to changing server load or server failures.

PART 3 BEYOND MTS

A better approach is dynamic load balancing. Dynamic load balancing is easier to administer, but it requires additional support from the system infrastructure. With this approach, applications are assigned to server groups and automatically replicated to all machines in the group. Clients are configured to use a load balancing router that will transparently direct client requests to a suitable machine based on dynamic run-time information collected by the load balancing analyzer. In COM+, server groups are called *application clusters*.

Figure 16-4 illustrates how COM+ load balancing works. First a COM+ server application is defined. Each component in the application that should be load balanced is configured to use load balancing by setting an attribute in its component library. The application is deployed on multiple machines, which are then defined as an application cluster using the COM Explorer. One of the machines in the cluster is selected as the load balancing router. Client machines are configured to create objects on the load balancing router. COM+ intercepts object creation requests on this machine and uses information collected from the other machines in the application cluster to determine where the object should be created. Once the object is created, the client communicates directly with the object; the router is not invoked on every method call.

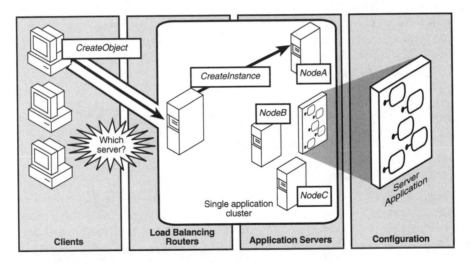

Figure 16-4. *COM+ dynamic load balancing.*

The load balancing service runs on all the machines in the application cluster. The router machine runs a load balancing analyzer to collect information from the other machines in the application cluster.

NOTE In its first release, COM+ will provide a simple response-time load balancing analyzer; however, the underlying architecture is completely general. In future releases, you might be allowed to add custom analyzers to the system.

The COM+ load balancing service gives administrators a straightforward way to scale applications to support increasing numbers of users without degrading application performance. Since it does not require any coding changes to applications or components, administrators can use this service with any application that has been installed into COM+ using the COM+ administrative tools.

SUMMARY

COM+ is the next stage in the evolution of Microsoft's component middleware. It integrates and extends the features of COM and MTS to make it easier to develop, deploy, and administer component-based applications.

COM+ makes development easier by unifying the COM and MTS programming models. It emphasizes a declarative model for accessing services, reducing the number of APIs developers must understand. Deployment and administration are simplified by uniting the COM and MTS administrative model and tools. In COM+, the distinction between COM and MTS disappears.

COM+ also simplifies development by providing a default implementation of the infrastructure services most distributed applications need, so developers do not have to implement and maintain infrastructure code themselves. Developers focus on writing their business logic and let COM+ handle the infrastructure. COM+ services are accessed by setting a few attributes on components, classes, or interfaces. COM+ improves on all the services found in MTS 2.0 and adds queued components, the Event service, IMDB, and dynamic load balancing via application clusters.

Customer investments in COM and MTS will be fully preserved by COM+. All existing COM and MTS components and applications should continue to work without modification, with no loss in performance. In most cases, modifying components or applications to use COM+ features is simply a matter of deploying components using the COM+ administrative services and setting attributes. The techniques for developing distributed, component-based applications discussed in this book will continue to work for COM+, with some minor changes in terminology and tools.

Appendix

About the 3-2-1 Program

Microsoft believes that the best way to get started building distributed applications is to tackle a simple application first. In a 3-2-1 project, a working prototype of a *three*-tier distributed application is built, using *two* developers, in *one* month. By working on a simple application, you can discover the ease-of-use and productivity benefits of Microsoft Windows DNA without worrying about all the nontechnical issues that can complicate larger-scale projects. 3-2-1 projects are also a great way to evaluate competitive technologies—you can build the same application using each technology and compare the results of the projects. Once you've determined whether Windows DNA meets your needs, you'll have the experience you need to start moving on to more complex applications.

A 3-2-1 project should involve a well-defined, real-world application from your business. For example, you might choose to build a Web front end to an existing application, migrate an existing two-tier application to three-tier, or prototype a subset of a larger, existing application's functionality. It's important to choose a portion of the business that the project team already understands so that the team does not need to learn the business *and* learn how to build three-tier applications in the one-month project period.

3-2-1 projects normally involve Microsoft Windows NT Server, COM, and MTS. You might also choose to use MSMQ, IIS, or COMTI in your application. The application is usually built using a development tool and language the project team is already familiar with. Likewise, 3-2-1 projects usually access existing data sources, using either data access technology the development team is familiar with or ADO. The goal is to minimize the number of new things the project team needs to learn.

You can try a 3-2-1 project either on your own or in conjunction with a consultant who is already familiar with Windows DNA and the 3-2-1 process. When you work with a consultant, you will usually spend one week learning about Windows DNA technologies and planning the scope of your project. The second week is spent on the conceptual, logical, and physical design of the application. The final two weeks of the project are spent implementing the components. At the end of the project, you have a working prototype as well as documentation about the vision, scope, and design of the project. If you are interested in working with a Microsoft consultant on your 3-2-1 project, contact your local Microsoft sales office.

You can use this book as a guide to learn about the Windows DNA technologies and how to implement an application. You should plan on spending one week reading the book and selecting a project, one week on design, and two weeks on coding. You'll have the greatest success if the developers selected for the project team are already familiar with the development tool and language used to implement the application. Be sure to limit the scope of your project to something that you feel could reasonably be developed over a two-week period using technologies the developers are already familiar with.

BIBLIOGRAPHY

This bibliography is by no means a comprehensive record of written material on the topics covered in this book, but every reference listed here is one I have read or one that has been recommended to me by someone I respect. In addition to the white papers that were mentioned in the text or that I used as references while writing this book, I have included the Web pages on the Microsoft Web site that provide access to the latest white papers for specific topics.

Analysis and Design

Booch, Grady. *Object-Oriented Analysis and Design with Applications*. 2nd ed. Redwood City, Calif.: Benjamin/Cummings, 1994. ISBN 0805353402.

Fowler, Martin, with Kendall Scott. *UML Distilled: Applying the Standard Object Modeling Language*. Reading, Mass.: Addison Wesley Longman, 1997. ISBN 0201325632.

Gamma, Erich, et al. *Design Patterns: Elements of Reusable Object-Oriented Software*. Reading, Mass.: Addison-Wesley, 1995. ISBN 0201633612.

Larman, Craig. *Applying UML and Patterns: An Introduction to Object-Oriented Analysis and Design*. Upper Saddle River, N.J.: Prentice Hall PTR, 1998. ISBN 0137488807.

Meyer, Bertrand. *Object-Oriented Software Construction*. 2nd ed. Upper Saddle River, N.J.: Prentice Hall PTR, 1997. ISBN 0136291554.

Shan, Yen-Ping, and Ralph H. Earle. *Enterprise Computing with Objects: From Client/Server Environments to the Internet*. Reading, Mass.: Addison-Wesley, 1998. ISBN 0201325667.

Unified Modeling Language home page: *http://www.rational.com/uml/index.html*.

General Distributed Computing Technologies

Components

Szyperski, Clemens. *Component Software: Beyond Object-Oriented Programming*. New York: ACM Press, 1998. ISBN 0201178885.

Databases and Data Modeling

Date, C. J. *An Introduction to Database Systems*. 6th ed. Reading, Mass.: Addison-Wesley, 1995. ISBN 020154329X.

Melton, Jim, and Alan R. Simon. *Understanding the New SQL: A Complete Guide*. San Mateo, Calif.: Morgan Kaufmann, 1993. ISBN 1558602453.

Rozenshtein, David. *The Essence of SQL: A Guide to Learning Most of SQL in the Least Amount of Time*. Fremont, Calif.: SQL Forum Press, 1996. ISBN 0964981211.

Silberschatz, Abraham, Henry F. Korth, and S. Sudershan. *Database System Concepts*. 3rd ed. Boston, Mass.: McGraw-Hill, 1998. ISBN 0070310866.

Messaging and Queuing

Blakeley, Burnie, Harry Harris, and Rhys Lewis. *Messaging and Queuing Using the MQI: Concepts & Analysis, Design & Development*. New York: McGraw-Hill, 1995. ISBN 0070057303.

Transaction Processing

Bernstein, Philip A., and Eric Newcomer. *Principles of Transaction Processing*. San Francisco: Morgan Kaufmann, 1997. ISBN 1558604154.

Gray, Jim, and Andreas Reuter. *Transaction Processing: Concepts and Techniques*. San Mateo, Calif.: Morgan Kaufmann, 1993. ISBN 1558601902.

Microsoft Technologies

Microsoft Corporation. "Windows DNA: Building Windows Applications for the Internet Age." White paper, October 1998: *http://www.microsoft.com/dna/overview/dnawp.asp*.

Microsoft Developer Network Online: *http://msdn.microsoft.com/developer/default.htm*.

Microsoft SiteBuilder Network: *http://www.microsoft.com/sitebuilder/*.

Microsoft SiteBuilder Network Workshop: *http://www.microsoft.com/workshop/default.asp*.

Microsoft Windows DNA home page: *http://www.microsoft.com/dna/default.asp*.

Microsoft Windows NT Server home page: *http://www.microsoft.com/ntserver/default.asp*.

Components

Box, Don. *Essential COM*. Reading, Mass.: Addison-Wesley, 1998. ISBN 0201634465.

Box, Don, et al. *Effective COM Programming: 50 Ways to Improve Your COM and MTS-Based Applications*. Reading, Mass.: Addison-Wesley, 1999. ISBN 0201379686.

Brockschmidt, Kraig. *Inside OLE*. 2nd ed. Redmond, Wash.: Microsoft Press, 1995. ISBN 1556158432.

Chappell, David. *Understanding ActiveX and OLE*. Redmond, Wash.: Microsoft Press, 1996. ISBN 1572312165.

Eddon, Guy, and Henry Eddon. *Inside Distributed COM*. Redmond, Wash.: Microsoft Press, 1998. ISBN 157231849X.

Egremont, Carlton. *Mr. Bunny's Guide to ActiveX*. Reading, Mass.: Addison-Wesley, 1998. ISBN 0201485362.

Grimes, Richard. *Professional ATL COM Programming*. Olton, Birmingham, U.K.: Wrox Press, 1998. ISBN 1861001401.

Grimes, Richard T., et al. *Beginning ATL COM Programming*. Wrox Press, 1998. ISBN 1861000111.

Grimes, Richard T. *Professional DCOM Programming*. Wrox Press, 1997. ISBN 186100060X.

Lhotka, Rockford. *Professional Visual Basic 5.0 Business Objects*. Olton, Birmingham, U.K.: Wrox Press, 1997. ISBN 186100043X.

Microsoft COM home page: *http://www.microsoft.com/com/default.asp*.

Pinnock, Jonathan. *Professional DCOM Application Development*. Olton, Birmingham, U.K.: Wrox Press, 1998. ISBN 1861001312.

Rector, Brent, and Chris Sells. *ATL Internals*. Reading, Mass.: Addison-Wesley, 1999. ISBN 0201695898.

Redmond, Frank E., III. *DCOM: Microsoft Distributed Component Object Model*. Foster City, Calif.: IDG Books Worldwide, 1997. ISBN 0764580442.

Rogerson, Dale. *Inside COM*. Redmond, Wash.: Microsoft Press, 1997. ISBN 1572313498.

Sessions, Roger. *COM and DCOM: Microsoft's Vision for Distributed Objects*. New York: Wiley Computer Press, 1998. ISBN 047119381X.

Stafford, Paul. "Writing Microsoft Transaction Server Components in Java." White paper, May 1997. MSDN: *http://msdn.microsoft.com/developer/news /feature/010598/mts/mtssummary2.htm*.

Database Technologies

Bath, Kamaljit. "Remote Data Service in MDAC 2.0." White paper, July 1998: *http:/ /msdn.microsoft.com/developer/news/feature/datajul98/remdata.htm*.

Hussey, Peter. "Designing Efficient Applications for Microsoft SQL Server." MSDN, PDC 1997 conference paper: *http://www.microsoft.com/data/reference /wp2/designingappssql_4jzm.htm*.

Lazar, David. "Microsoft Strategy for Universal Data Access." White paper, October 1997: *http://www.microsoft.com/data/udastra.htm*.

Microsoft Data Access home page: *http://www.microsoft.com/data*.

Microsoft SQL Server home page: *http://www.microsoft.com/sql*.

Scott, Tony. "Microsoft SQL Server Optimization and Tuning." MSDN.

Soukup, Ron. *Inside Microsoft SQL Server 6.5*. Redmond, Wash.: Microsoft Press, 1997. ISBN 1572313315.

Vaughn, William R. *Hitchhiker's Guide to Visual Basic and SQL Server*. 6th ed. Redmond, Wash.: Microsoft Press, 1998. ISBN 1572318481.

Internet Technologies

Cluts, Nancy Winnick. "Maximizing the Performance of Your Active Server Pages." White paper, March 1998: *http://www.microsoft.com/workshop/server/asp /maxperf.asp*.

Fleet, Dina, et al. *Teach Yourself Active Web Database Programming in 21 Days*. Indianapolis, Ind.: Sams, 1997. ISBN 1575211394.

Francis, Brian, et al. *Beginning Active Server Pages 2.0*. Olton, Birmingham, U.K.: Wrox Press. ISBN 1861001347.

Francis, Brian, et al. *Professional Active Server Pages 2.0*. Olton, Birmingham, U.K.: Wrox Press, 1998. ISBN 1861001266.

Isaacs, Scott. *Inside Dynamic HTML*. Redmond, Wash.: Microsoft Press, 1997. ISBN 1572316861.

Microsoft Scripting Technologies home page: *http://msdn.microsoft.com/scripting*.

Microsoft SiteBuilder Network DHTML, HTML, and CSS home page: *http://www.microsoft.com/workshop/c-frame.htm#/workshop/author/default.asp*.

Microsoft SiteBuilder Network Server Technologies home page: *http://www.microsoft.com/workshop/c-frame.htm#/workshop/server/default.asp*.

Moore, Mike. "Tuning Internet Information Server Performance." White paper, October 1997: *http://www.microsoft.com/isn/techcenter/tuningIIS.asp*.

Stephenson, Michael, et al. "IIS 4.0 Tuning Parameters for High-Volume Sites." White paper, March 1998: *http://www.microsoft.com/workshop/server/feature/tune.asp*.

Middleware Technologies (MTS, MSMQ, COMTI)

Dickman, Alan. *Designing Applications with MSMQ: Message Queuing for Developers*. Reading, Mass.: Addison-Wesley, 1998. ISBN 0201325810.

Gray, Steven D., and Rick A. Lievano. *Microsoft Transaction Server 2.0*. Indianapolis, Ind.: Sams, 1997. ISBN 0672311305.

Homer, Alex, and David Sussman. *Professional MTS and MSMQ Programming with VB and ASP*. Olton, Birmingham, U.K.: Wrox Press, 1998. ISBN 1861001460.

Houston, Peter. "Building Distributed Applications with Message Queuing Middleware." White paper, 1998.

Houston, Peter. "Integrating Applications with Message Queuing Middleware." White paper, 1998.

Mills, Angela. "Using Microsoft Transaction Server 2.0 with COM Transaction Integrator 1.0." White paper, January 1998: *http://www.microsoft.com/com/wpaper/com_mtscomti.asp*.

Microsoft MSMQ home page: *http://www.microsoft.com/ntserver/nts/appservice/exe/overview/MSMQ_overview.asp*.

Microsoft SNA Server home page: *http://www.microsoft.com/sna/*.

Microsoft Windows NT Server white papers page: *http://www.microsoft.com/NTServer/Basics/TechPapers/default.asp*.

Windows and Presentation Layer Programming

Armstrong, Tom. *Designing and Using ActiveX Controls*. New York: M&T Books, 1997. ISBN 1558515038.

Blaszczak, Mike. *Professional MFC with Visual C++ 5*. Olton, Birmingham, U.K.: Wrox Press, 1997. ISBN 1861000146.

Denning, Adam. *ActiveX Controls: Inside Out*. 2nd ed. Redmond, Wash.: Microsoft Press, 1997. ISBN 1572313501.

McKinney, Bruce. *Hardcore Visual Basic*. 2nd ed. Redmond, Wash.: Microsoft Press, 1997. ISBN 1572314222.

Petzold, Charles. *Programming Windows 95*. 5th ed. Redmond, Wash.: Microsoft Press, 1998. ISBN 157231995X.

Rector, Brent E., and Joseph M. Newcomer. *Win32 Programming*. Reading, Mass.: Addison-Wesley, 1997. ISBN 0201634929.

Richter, Jeffrey. *Advanced Windows*. 3rd ed. Redmond, Wash.: Microsoft Press, 1997. ISBN 1572315482.

Shepherd, George, and Scot Wingo. *MFC Internals: Inside the Microsoft Foundation Class Architecture*. Reading, Mass.: Addison-Wesley, 1996. ISBN 0201407213.

INDEX

Mary Kirtland is the program manager of the Microsoft COM team. Since joining the COM team in January 1997, she has harassed the developers and testers of technologies including Structured Storage, DCOM for Microsoft Windows 95, and COM Internet Services. In addition, she has written white papers and magazine articles about the COM team's technologies and has delivered presentations at developer conferences around the world. Now that she has finished this book, she is hard at work on *Inside COM+*, also for Microsoft Press.

Before joining the COM team, Mary spent three years in Microsoft Developer Support, helping customers resolve problems with MFC, COM, and other technologies. In case you're starting to wonder whether Mary has ever done any real development work, rest assured that in the eight years between giving up on a Ph.D. in chemistry and joining Microsoft, Mary developed numerous data acquisition and analysis applications for MS-DOS, Windows, and embedded systems.

When she's not thinking about COM, Mary tries to keep her house from becoming a public eyesore or health hazard, reads every historical mystery she can get her hands on, listens to classic jazz, and collects animation art. You can reach Mary at *marykir@microsoft.com*.

The manuscript for this book was submitted to Microsoft Press in electronic form. Galleys were prepared using Microsoft Word 97. Pages were composed by Microsoft Press using Adobe PageMaker 6.52 for Windows, with text type in Garamond and display type in Futura Medium. Composed pages were delivered to the printer as electronic prepress files.

Cover Graphic Designer
Tim Girvin Design

Cover Illustrator
Glenn Mitsui

Interior Graphic Artists
Joel Panchot, Travis Beaven

Principal Compositor
Paula Gorelick

Principal Proofreader
Mary Rose Sliwoski

Indexer
Julie Kawabata

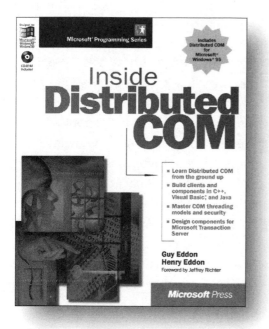

MICROSOFT LICENSE AGREEMENT
(Book Companion CD)

IMPORTANT—READ CAREFULLY: This Microsoft End-User License Agreement ("EULA") is a legal agreement between you (either an individual or an entity) and Microsoft Corporation for the Microsoft product identified above, which includes computer software and may include associated media, printed materials, and "on-line" or electronic documentation ("SOFTWARE PRODUCT"). Any component included within the SOFTWARE PRODUCT that is accompanied by a separate End-User License Agreement shall be governed by such agreement and not the terms set forth below. By installing, copying, or otherwise using the SOFTWARE PRODUCT, you agree to be bound by the terms of this EULA. If you do not agree to the terms of this EULA, you are not authorized to install, copy, or otherwise use the SOFTWARE PRODUCT; you may, however, return the SOFTWARE PRODUCT, along with all printed materials and other items that form a part of the Microsoft product that includes the SOFTWARE PRODUCT, to the place you obtained them for a full refund.

SOFTWARE PRODUCT LICENSE

The SOFTWARE PRODUCT is protected by United States copyright laws and international copyright treaties, as well as other intellectual property laws and treaties. The SOFTWARE PRODUCT is licensed, not sold.

1. **GRANT OF LICENSE.** This EULA grants you the following rights:

    a. **Software Product.** You may install and use one copy of the SOFTWARE PRODUCT on a single computer. The primary user of the computer on which the SOFTWARE PRODUCT is installed may make a second copy for his or her exclusive use on a portable computer.

    b. **Storage/Network Use.** You may also store or install a copy of the SOFTWARE PRODUCT on a storage device, such as a network server, used only to install or run the SOFTWARE PRODUCT on your other computers over an internal network; however, you must acquire and dedicate a license for each separate computer on which the SOFTWARE PRODUCT is installed or run from the storage device. A license for the SOFTWARE PRODUCT may not be shared or used concurrently on different computers.

    c. **License Pak.** If you have acquired this EULA in a Microsoft License Pak, you may make the number of additional copies of the computer software portion of the SOFTWARE PRODUCT authorized on the printed copy of this EULA, and you may use each copy in the manner specified above. You are also entitled to make a corresponding number of secondary copies for portable computer use as specified above.

    d. **Sample Code.** Solely with respect to portions, if any, of the SOFTWARE PRODUCT that are identified within the SOFTWARE PRODUCT as sample code (the "SAMPLE CODE"):

    i. **Use and Modification.** Microsoft grants you the right to use and modify the source code version of the SAMPLE CODE, *provided* you comply with subsection (d)(iii) below. You may not distribute the SAMPLE CODE, or any modified version of the SAMPLE CODE, in source code form.

    ii. **Redistributable Files.** Provided you comply with subsection (d)(iii) below, Microsoft grants you a nonexclusive, royalty-free right to reproduce and distribute the object code version of the SAMPLE CODE and of any modified SAMPLE CODE, other than SAMPLE CODE (or any modified version thereof) designated as not redistributable in the Readme file that forms a part of the SOFTWARE PRODUCT (the "Non-Redistributable Sample Code"). All SAMPLE CODE other than the Non-Redistributable Sample Code is collectively referred to as the "REDISTRIBUTABLES."

    iii. **Redistribution Requirements.** If you redistribute the REDISTRIBUTABLES, you agree to: (i) distribute the REDISTRIBUTABLES in object code form only in conjunction with and as a part of your software application product; (ii) not use Microsoft's name, logo, or trademarks to market your software application product; (iii) include a valid copyright notice on your software application product; (iv) indemnify, hold harmless, and defend Microsoft from and against any claims or lawsuits, including attorney's fees, that arise or result from the use or distribution of your software application product; and (v) not permit further distribution of the REDISTRIBUTABLES by your end user. Contact Microsoft for the applicable royalties due and other licensing terms for all other uses and/or distribution of the REDISTRIBUTABLES.

2. **DESCRIPTION OF OTHER RIGHTS AND LIMITATIONS.**

    - **Limitations on Reverse Engineering, Decompilation, and Disassembly.** You may not reverse engineer, decompile, or disassemble the SOFTWARE PRODUCT, except and only to the extent that such activity is expressly permitted by applicable law notwithstanding this limitation.

    - **Separation of Components.** The SOFTWARE PRODUCT is licensed as a single product. Its component parts may not be separated for use on more than one computer.

    - **Rental.** You may not rent, lease, or lend the SOFTWARE PRODUCT.

    - **Support Services.** Microsoft may, but is not obligated to, provide you with support services related to the SOFTWARE PRODUCT ("Support Services"). Use of Support Services is governed by the Microsoft policies and programs described in the user manual, in "on-line" documentation, and/or in other Microsoft-provided materials. Any supplemental software code provided to you as part of the Support Services shall be considered part of the SOFTWARE PRODUCT and subject to the terms and conditions of this EULA. With respect to technical information you provide to Microsoft as part of the Support Services, Microsoft may use such information for its business purposes, including for product support and development. Microsoft will not utilize such technical information in a form that personally identifies you.

- **Software Transfer.** You may permanently transfer all of your rights under this EULA, provided you retain no copies, you transfer all of the SOFTWARE PRODUCT (including all component parts, the media and printed materials, any upgrades, this EULA, and, if applicable, the Certificate of Authenticity), **and** the recipient agrees to the terms of this EULA.

- **Termination.** Without prejudice to any other rights, Microsoft may terminate this EULA if you fail to comply with the terms and conditions of this EULA. In such event, you must destroy all copies of the SOFTWARE PRODUCT and all of its component parts.

3. **COPYRIGHT.** All title and copyrights in and to the SOFTWARE PRODUCT (including but not limited to any images, photographs, animations, video, audio, music, text, SAMPLE CODE, REDISTRIBUTABLES, and "applets" incorporated into the SOFTWARE PRODUCT) and any copies of the SOFTWARE PRODUCT are owned by Microsoft or its suppliers. The SOFTWARE PRODUCT is protected by copyright laws and international treaty provisions. Therefore, you must treat the SOFTWARE PRODUCT like any other copyrighted material **except** that you may install the SOFTWARE PRODUCT on a single computer provided you keep the original solely for backup or archival purposes. You may not copy the printed materials accompanying the SOFTWARE PRODUCT.

4. **U.S. GOVERNMENT RESTRICTED RIGHTS.** The SOFTWARE PRODUCT and documentation are provided with RESTRICTED RIGHTS. Use, duplication, or disclosure by the Government is subject to restrictions as set forth in subparagraph (c)(1)(ii) of the Rights in Technical Data and Computer Software clause at DFARS 252.227-7013 or subparagraphs (c)(1) and (2) of the Commercial Computer Software—Restricted Rights at 48 CFR 52.227-19, as applicable. Manufacturer is Microsoft Corporation/One Microsoft Way/Redmond, WA 98052-6399.

5. **EXPORT RESTRICTIONS.** You agree that you will not export or re-export the SOFTWARE PRODUCT, any part thereof, or any process or service that is the direct product of the SOFTWARE PRODUCT (the foregoing collectively referred to as the "Restricted Components"), to any country, person, entity, or end user subject to U.S. export restrictions. You specifically agree not to export or re-export any of the Restricted Components (i) to any country to which the U.S. has embargoed or restricted the export of goods or services, which currently include, but are not necessarily limited to, Cuba, Iran, Iraq, Libya, North Korea, Sudan, and Syria, or to any national of any such country, wherever located, who intends to transmit or transport the Restricted Components back to such country; (ii) to any end user who you know or have reason to know will utilize the Restricted Components in the design, development, or production of nuclear, chemical, or biological weapons; or (iii) to any end user who has been prohibited from participating in U.S. export transactions by any federal agency of the U.S. government. You warrant and represent that neither the BXA nor any other U.S. federal agency has suspended, revoked, or denied your export privileges.

DISCLAIMER OF WARRANTY

NO WARRANTIES OR CONDITIONS. MICROSOFT EXPRESSLY DISCLAIMS ANY WARRANTY OR CONDITION FOR THE SOFTWARE PRODUCT. THE SOFTWARE PRODUCT AND ANY RELATED DOCUMENTATION IS PROVIDED "AS IS" WITHOUT WARRANTY OR CONDITION OF ANY KIND, EITHER EXPRESS OR IMPLIED, INCLUDING, WITHOUT LIMITATION, THE IMPLIED WARRANTIES OF MERCHANTABILITY, FITNESS FOR A PARTICULAR PURPOSE, OR NONINFRINGEMENT. THE ENTIRE RISK ARISING OUT OF USE OR PERFORMANCE OF THE SOFTWARE PRODUCT REMAINS WITH YOU.

LIMITATION OF LIABILITY. TO THE MAXIMUM EXTENT PERMITTED BY APPLICABLE LAW, IN NO EVENT SHALL MICROSOFT OR ITS SUPPLIERS BE LIABLE FOR ANY SPECIAL, INCIDENTAL, INDIRECT, OR CONSEQUENTIAL DAMAGES WHATSOEVER (INCLUDING, WITHOUT LIMITATION, DAMAGES FOR LOSS OF BUSINESS PROFITS, BUSINESS INTERRUP-TION, LOSS OF BUSINESS INFORMATION, OR ANY OTHER PECUNIARY LOSS) ARISING OUT OF THE USE OF OR INABIL-ITY TO USE THE SOFTWARE PRODUCT OR THE PROVISION OF OR FAILURE TO PROVIDE SUPPORT SERVICES, EVEN IF MICROSOFT HAS BEEN ADVISED OF THE POSSIBILITY OF SUCH DAMAGES. IN ANY CASE, MICROSOFT'S ENTIRE LIABILITY UNDER ANY PROVISION OF THIS EULA SHALL BE LIMITED TO THE GREATER OF THE AMOUNT ACTUALLY PAID BY YOU FOR THE SOFTWARE PRODUCT OR US$5.00; PROVIDED, HOWEVER, IF YOU HAVE ENTERED INTO A MICROSOFT SUPPORT SERVICES AGREEMENT, MICROSOFT'S ENTIRE LIABILITY REGARDING SUPPORT SERVICES SHALL BE GOVERNED BY THE TERMS OF THAT AGREEMENT. BECAUSE SOME STATES AND JURISDICTIONS DO NOT ALLOW THE EXCLUSION OR LIMITATION OF LIABILITY, THE ABOVE LIMITATION MAY NOT APPLY TO YOU.

MISCELLANEOUS

This EULA is governed by the laws of the State of Washington USA, except and only to the extent that applicable law mandates governing law of a different jurisdiction.

Should you have any questions concerning this EULA, or if you desire to contact Microsoft for any reason, please contact the Microsoft subsidiary serving your country, or write: Microsoft Sales Information Center/One Microsoft Way/Redmond, WA 98052-6399.